CONTEMPORARY HOTEL SALES

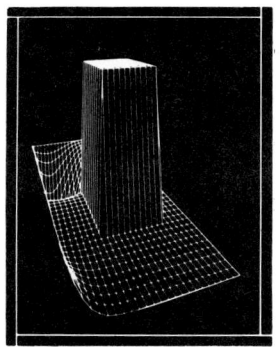

CONTEMPORARY HOTEL SALES

A Study of Current Hotel Business Promotion Procedures and Practices

ANDREW SCHWARZ
Professor, Hospitality Division
Sullivan County Community College

DAVID C. DORF, CHSE
Dave Dorf Associates

Prentice Hall, Englewood Cliffs, New Jersey 07632

Library of Congress Cataloging-in-Publication Data

Schwarz, Andrew.
    Contemporary hotel sales : a study of current hotel business
promotion procedures and practices / Andrew Schwarz, David C. Dorf.
        p. cm.
    Includes index.
    ISBN 0-13-174038-5
    1. Hotels, taverns, etc.—Marketing.   I. Dorf, David C.
II. Title.
TX911.3.M3S33   1992
647.94'068'8—dc20
                                                    912-16643
                                                       CIP

Acquisitions editor: Robin Baliszewski
Editorial/production supervision
    and interior design: Ed Jones
Cover design: Ben Santora
Cover art: Melvin L. Prueitt, *Computer Graphics:*
    118 Computer-Generated Designs, Dover Publications, Inc.
Prepress buyer: Mary McCartney and Ilene Levy
Manufacturing buyer: Ed O'Dougherty
Page layout: Marty Behan
Editorial assistant: Rose Mary Florio

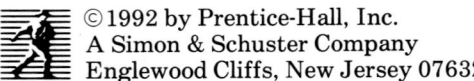

© 1992 by Prentice-Hall, Inc.
A Simon & Schuster Company
Englewood Cliffs, New Jersey 07632

Printed in the United States of America

10 9 8 7 6 5 4 3 2

ISBN 0-13-174038-5

Prentice-Hall International (UK) Limited, *London*
Prentice-Hall of Australia Pty. Limited, *Sydney*
Prentice-Hall Canada Inc., *Toronto*
Prentice-Hall Hispanoamericana, S.A., *Mexico*
Prentice-Hall of India Private Limited, *New Delhi*
Prentice-Hall of Japan, Inc., *Tokyo*
Simon & Schuster Asia Pte. Ltd., *Singapore*
Editora Prentice-Hall do Brasil, Ltda., *Rio de Janeiro*

This publication is dedicated to the memory of
Adrian W. Phillips, CHSE
Executive Vice President of the Hotel Sales
and Marketing Association International, 1952–1965
The "Dean" of Hotel Sales Executives

CONTENTS

PREFACE

This is an unusual book on hotel promotion in that the title does not contain the word *marketing!* This does not mean that the marketing concept is not considered in this book; indeed, it is the overall guiding philosophy in each and every chapter.

But this publication is designed primarily as a basic and introductory text on hotel sales promotion. Thus some of the more esoteric "high-tech" concepts of marketing have been downplayed (but certainly not ignored!). Emphasis is placed on illustrating the more direct, daily sales and merchandising activities that are undertaken by the majority of those responsible for business promotion within the lodging sector of the hospitality industry. You can look upon this book as a "back to basics" text. Those basics have, of course, been upgraded. You might even call them *sophisticated fundamentals.*

Emphasis is also placed on the viewpoints and influences of the ever-changing and increasingly experienced users of hotel accommodations and facilities. Recognition of consumer needs and wants is the modern method of successful selling in today's contemporary marketplace. The product—the hotel—has also undergone significant changes compared with its original concept of a "home away from home." So this book will combine both buyer and seller viewpoints. It will draw upon both the personal observations and experiences of prominent industry executives who represent a wide variety of different properties, as well as key customers who reflect a wide spectrum of major potentials.

We have included numerous photographs, examples, "editorial" observations, "commentaries," and illustrations. In some instances, pictures are laid out in "story-board" format, and the text includes numerous situations presented in "running dialogue" style. This may make you think of TV or the movies—and that is our intention. Not only may the information be easier to absorb, but it is in line with our personal philosophy that much of the hospitality industry is in reality "show biz." Those who specialize in hotel sales (as well as those responsible for servicing) are, for the most part, actors and actresses (or as they like to call the employees in the Walt Disney theme parks, "cast members").

In the world of entertainment (of which much of the hospitality industry is an integral part), one of the key factors is the concept of *visibility*. Be seen and be recognized—*who knows you* can be more important in the long run than who you know. This is especially important in the field of hotel sales.

As a student of hotel, restaurant, and travel management, you will have many unique opportunities to meet industry leaders as well as prominent, influential buyers of hotel facilities and services. You will find them readily at hospitality and customer trade shows; seminars, workshops, and conventions; during student sales blitz programs, summer internships, and other practical work experiences; and at various occasions when industry executives visit your school. Make your contacts early. Even such preliminary networking can prove valuable later in your career. One of the key points to consider now is that when you get out into the industry, you will be entering a highly competitive business climate.

A successful and rewarding career, whether in the sales and marketing department, the rooms division, the food and beverage department, or in other key administrative and operational areas, will depend largely on a combination of the positive promotion of your property or company—and the positive promotion of yourself.

Andrew Schwarz
David C. Dorf

ACKNOWLEDGMENTS

The authors would like to thank the following professors of hospitality management programs for their review of the initial draft manuscript and for their many constructive critiques, observations, and suggestions:

- Neil Cornthwaite, Canadore College, North Bay, Ontario, Canada
- George J. "Jack" Neumann, New York University, New York, NY
- Daniel O'Brien, Rochester Institute of Technology, Rochester, NY
- Howard Reichbart, Northern Virginia Community College, Annandale, VA

Our appreciation to the contributors of materials, samples, and quotes, who are appropriately credited within the text, and also to Neil Ostergren, CHSE, vice president of Robinson, Yesawich & Pepperdine, New York; Al Bard, vice president of Bill Bard Associates, Monticello, NY; and Fernand Girard, executive director of the Association Hoteliere Internationale Des Directeurs Des Ventes, Montreal, Quebec, Canada, for their encouragement and special review.

Thanks also to Ali Dorf and Linda Marshall for their assistance in "modeling" many of the pictorial illustrations on sales office setups and sales calls procedures, and to Suzanne McGoldrick and Elizabeth McGoldrick for their assistance in the manuscript preparation.

ABOUT THE AUTHORS

The co-authors of this book come from what on the surface seems to be completely opposite backgrounds.

PROFESSOR ANDREW SCHWARZ joined the Hotel Technology Division of Sullivan County Community College, Loch Sheldrake, New York, in 1968, and was named the division's academic coodinator in 1976.

Schwarz has more than 25 years of teaching experience in such areas as food preparation, purchasing, control, service, and management, including instructorships in the Hotel Technology Department of New York City Community College and at Pratt Institute.

He is a highly active member of the Council on Hotel, Restaurant, and Institutional Education (CHRIE); has chaired the Academic Activities Committee of the Hotel Sales and Marketing Association International (HSMAI) for the past 15 years; and is on the Education Committee of the New York State Hospitality & Tourism Association.

DAVID C. DORF, CHSE, is a graduate of the School of Hotel Administration at Cornell University. He was on staff at the Hotel Sales and Marketing Association International for 35 years, serving as director of education and training, before retiring at the end of 1989 to teach and write. He also served HSMAI as staff administrator of their Certified Hotel Sales Executive (CHSE) program.

He is president of his own company, Dave Dorf Associates, specializing in "Hospitality Education for Profit-Minded Marketing" and "Hospitality Training for Sales-Minded Servicing."

He has authored such books as *Marketing for the Hospitality Industry*, prepared for the Canadian Department of Manpower, several courses in hotel sales promotion for the Educational Institute of the American Hotel & Motel Association, and more recently, co-authored the EI publication, *Managing Conventions and Group Business*.

Dorf is a member of the Cornell Society of Hotelmen (serving twice as class director), the Council of Hotel and Restaurant Trainers (CHART), the American Society for Training and Development (ASTD), and CHRIE.

As was stated earlier, their backgrounds seem to be totally different (Schwarz comes from the "back of the house" and Dorf from the "from of the house"). Yet Dorf worked his way through four years of college by cooking 40 hours a week, and Professor Schwarz teaches courses in sales promotion and advertising at his college. They have worked together during the past 15 years jointly presenting seminars and workshops throughout the United States and Canada, Austria, Iceland, Ireland, Norway, and Sweden.

This "diversified team approach" has direct application to the hotel sales and marketing function. In any hotel, the best "management team" is the one headed by a sales-minded general manager and an operationally oriented director of sales (or marketing)—a key concept stressed throughout this book.

TO THE STUDENT

For many of you, this will be your introductory text in hotel sales. It is assumed, however, that you already have a basic knowledge of the hospitality industry, especially the fundamental concepts of hotel organization.

The so-called "classic" method of organizationally "dividing the house" is to group the various departments into two main classifications. The *back of the house* includes the food and beverage department, housekeeping, security, maintenance, and engineering. The *front of the house* consists of the administrative offices, the front office, reservations, accounting and auditing, and sales and marketing.

With the acceptance and growth of the sales and marketing function as an integral and essential part of hotel operations, the modern management function within a property is often split into two separate areas: *operations* and *marketing*. An oversimplified distinction still sometimes used in the industry is directly related to a basic business equation:

$$\text{profit} = \text{revenue} - \text{expenses}$$

The difference between the two elements of management is sometimes casually explained as follows: Marketing is responsible for generating revenue; operations is responsible for controlling and decreasing expenses. In reality, operations and marketing have joint and mutually supportive responsibilities in both areas. This philosophy will be explained later, but for introductory purposes, the following groupings of key hotel departments under either "operations" or "marketing" offers a generalized overview of hotel management organization.

Operations

Executive and administrative offices

Rooms division (front office and reservations)

Food and beverage

Purchasing

Accounting and auditing

Housekeeping

Security

Repairs and maintenance

Recreation and entertainment

Human resources management (personnel)

Human resources development (training)

Marketing

Sales

Advertising

Public relations and publicity

Convention servicing

Banquets and catering

Market research and customer analyses

These breakdowns are by no means standard or "cast in concrete." In some hotels, where the majority of business is obtained from conventions, other group meetings, and contractual arrangements with companies for the individual business traveler, you may find the entire rooms division (front office and reservations) reporting directly to the marketing department. In some resort operations, recreation and entertainment may be considered part of the marketing function. In a few of the newer or re-positioned operations, the training function (formerly part of personnel administration) has become a major responsibility of the sales/marketing department.

More fully detailed sample organizational charts and sample job descriptions will be presented later in the book. But this initial organizational briefing should be helpful, especially while studying the first two chapters.

You may have noted that we have been bouncing back and forth among the terms *sales, marketing,* and *sales and marketing.* Others in the industry also tend to use the terms interchangeably. Some of the distinctions are covered in the opening chapters.

At the risk of a further oversimplification, a primary distinction we would like to introduce now is, in effect, a variation on the old question: Which came first, the chicken or the egg? Let's reword this as: Which comes first, the product or the market? Relating this specifically to the lodging industry, one could further rephrase this as: "Should we build a hotel first and then find markets for it?" or "should we first study the market and then build a property based on what the market desires or demands?" The first method (product first) is the traditional sales concept; the second consideration (market first) is the contemporary marketing approach. Depending on circumstance, it is often industry practice to do both.

CONTEMPORARY HOTEL SALES

one

START

A few years back, a story made the rounds of the hospitality industry about a hotel sales executive who was trying to book future group business from an executive of an automobile firm. In addition to being an administrative official, this executive was responsible for his division's sales and dealership meetings.

In the course of discussion and negotiation, the auto executive tried to pin down the hotel to committing *current* room rates and food and beverage prices for the next three years. The hotel sales executive stated that because of ever-increasing operating costs, he was not able to make this type of financial commitment.

"Why not?" asked the potential buyer.

"Well, let me in turn ask you this," replied the hotel sales executive. "Would you be able to lock me into today's prices for one or more of your fine cars should I wish to purchase the equivalent models three years from now?"

"Of course not," retorted the meeting planner.

"Why not?" queried the sales exec.

"Because I'm a businessman," replied the buyer.

"And so am I," responded the hotel sales executive, "so am I!"

For most of its history, the enterprise represented by hotels, inns, and resorts was not really thought of by the public as a business. Very often, it was portrayed rather negatively, especially in literature, television, and the movies. At best, hotels were viewed as rather informal, easy-going, family facilities—rather like an extension of the home. The concepts of financial management, personnel administration, budgeting and fiscal responsibility, operations, and especially sales and marketing, did not seem to fit into the public's perception of what we now call the hospitality industry.

CHANGING CONCEPTS

Within the last 30 or so years, the public's concept of the hospitality industry has changed dramatically. Hotels, food operations, destinations, travel, and other components of the overall hospitality industry are prominently featured on the financial pages of newspapers, magazines, and other media. Sometimes they even make front-page headlines, such as the opening of a new casino in Atlantic City or Las Vegas, or a new theme park complex in Florida, California, or in Paris or Tokyo. There is a heightened public awareness of the financial value of the hospitality industry as well as the contributions it makes to a wide variety of different sectors of the economy.

Of perhaps even greater significance is the change of image among those working in the industry as well as those who are considering entering it as a professional career. For far too long, especially in the United States, hotels were not necessarily high on the lists of most people seeking an occupation or career. In addition, the term "businessman" or "businesswoman" was not generally applied to a person employed in the industry, regardless of title or responsibility.

However, the dramatic changes in the nature of the industry during the past 30 to 40 years have resulted in a corresponding change in the qualifications, capabilities, and abilities of those who are now a part of it. For example, today's contemporary lodging industry faces the following key challenges:

- Worldwide competition, particularly in some of the newer destination areas, such as central and eastern Europe
- Modernization, renovation, and expansion
- Modern technology and computerization

- Constant growth in a business climate where new construction and the total worldwide inventory of rooms still substantially outpaces overall increased demand
- Increased customer sophistication and changing lifestyles, where an increasingly experienced public seeks "more, bigger, better, and different"
- Maintenance of "brand-name loyalty" among a more knowledgeable public that has an ever-expanding line of hotel products from which to choose
- The growth of nontraditional hotel alternatives. These include all-suite properties, extended-stay facilities, sophisticated bed and breakfast operations, and self-contained conference centers

These challenges are comparable to those faced by virtually any other major industry or field.

BIG BUSINESS

The hospitality industry, which once was largely thought of as a small-unit business—or more properly a collection of small units (often with the not necessarily complimentary tag of "Ma and Pa operation")—is now big business. For example, a number of individual properties have a market value of over $1 billion *each*. A cost of $100,000 per room is not unusual for new hotel construction, and that cost can jump to $750,000 or more for a new casino hotel. Some older properties are being renovated at costs that are more than double or triple their initial construction cost. So the traditional nineteenth–early twentieth century concepts of keeping the lobby doors open and setting a good table are hardly a contemporary recipe for financial success.

TODAY'S CHALLENGES

Having set the stage, let's introduce some basic questions as they relate to the business challenges within today's highly active and intensely competitive industry:

1. How does one obtain a profitable level of business, especially in today's highly competitive climate?
2. How does one recoup the costs of initial financial investments, upkeep, modernization, and expansion?
3. How does one build and maintain guest loyalty, resulting in repeat and referral business?
4. How does one end up (as every business should) making a profit and delivering a justified return on investment (ROI)?

The logical follow-up query to this initial set of questions is: How and where does one start?

THE STARTING POINTS

The starting points, reduced to their basic elements, would include:

- Researching the marketplace to determine the types of customers available and their respective needs, wants, hopes, and desires with respect to the lodging industry

- Researching your own property to develop features and benefits that would satisfy the needs, wants, and so on, of those market segments that you believe you can best accommodate and satisfy
- Specifically identifying the types of business that would have the greatest potential for developing the highest volume of profitable business
- Contacting, directly, or indirectly, those who influence or make travel plans or who make decisions related to travel plans
- Persuading such persons to visit and use your facilities
- Keeping them on your property for as long as possible
- Getting them to spend as much as possible while with you
- Convincing them to return as well as to recommend your facility to friends and business associates

This perhaps overly simplified process goes by a variety of names:

- Business promotion
- Sales promotion
- Selling
- Sales and servicing
- Marketing

Although each of the terms above has basic distinctions (later, these will be compared), they are all linked by a common concept—that like any operating-for-profit business, a hotel must:

1. Go out into the marketplace (rather than waiting for the marketplace to come to it).
2. Persuade potential users that it can offer a set of products or services that will satisfy their personal and professional needs and wants.
3. Convince potential users to try the products or services.
4. Deliver the product to the users' fullest satisfaction.
5. Maximize repeat and referral usage (i.e., make your customers your best salespeople).

For the time being, let's use the term *sales* (or *selling*) or *business promotion*. The essential point is that in the modern business world, no hotel can afford to be passive ("Let's sit back and wait for the people"), but instead, must be active and competitive ("Let's go out and get our proper and profitable share of the public").

This philosophy, too, is a fairly contemporary development. With few exceptions, sales promotion activities have been refined only within the past 50 years. The *marketing concept*, which includes the sales function among numerous other promotional activities, has become a common discipline only within the last 25 years.

One of the present authors remembers a conversation in 1959 with a prominent European hotel director. The hotelier related the fact that he was almost asked to resign from an influential professional organization because of a rumor that he was actually going to companies and associations and asking them for business. He was told in no uncertain terms that a true hotelier does not "beg for business . . . that's not polite!" He must develop the right reputation and business will then come to him. However, the rapid expansion of international hotel chains, generally American-based, quickly changed that outdated philosophy.

This point is illustrated dramatically by the change in membership composition of what is now known as the Hotel Sales and Marketing Association International. Founded in 1927, HSMAI is an organization of sales-minded hospitality industry executives. During 1959 (the year of the European hotelier's story), HSMAI had 1329 members. Of this total, 169 represented 12 countries outside the United States. Just 10 years later, total membership had grown to 4020—a 216 percent increase. During the same period, the membership outside the United States had grown to 732 executives (from 73 countries), a 333 percent increase. Quite a change in the acceptance of sales promotion, not just domestically but throughout the world.

In this book we take a close look at the sales function and how it relates to hotel operation, as well as how it is integrated to the other components of the overall promotional umbrella known as marketing. Emphasis is also placed on the follow-up disciplines that occur after the sale is made, particularly service and satisfaction. To set the stage for Chapter 2, it is appropriate now to introduce a number of basic, yet essential concepts relating to the hotel product.

THE HOTEL PRODUCT

In general, the lodging industry offers the general public four distinct types of physical products:

1. Sleeping accommodations (rooms and suites)
2. Food and beverage facilities (for individual dining as well as group social functions)
3. Function space (for conventions, meetings, exhibits, and social events)
4. Activities facilities (for health, fitness, recreation, and entertainment)

Nearly all properties offer all of these in varying styles, sizes, quantities, qualities, and costs. But for the majority of the industry, an individual hotel cannot be "all things to all people." Instead, a specific property should have:

1. Specific facilities and services . . . directed at
2. Specific groups of people (market segments) . . . directed at
3. Specific times . . . with a
4. Specific range of rates

So how does a particular operation position itself to attract a profitable volume of business when the competition offers basically the same product lines and services? The answer to that question will be discussed throughout the remaining pages.

HOTEL RESPONSIBILITIES

In the process of operating as a business, a hotel has an obligation as well as a responsibility to conduct a *profitable* enterprise. Recognizing this is the first step in answering the question just posed.

FIGURE 1–1 Profit triangle.

There must be an intertwined, threefold commitment (see Figure 1-1) on the part of hotel management to satisfy the needs and wants of:

1. Those who invest time, money, and personal efforts in developing and expanding the property's potential
2. Those who work in the hotel and deserve a fair return for their efforts
3. The customers who look to the property to satisfy a wide variety of personal and professional objectives and goals

To fulfill this "business trilogy" commitment properly and profitably requires the development of a feasible program of business promotion. A quick look at some key industry changes in the immediate past (the preceding three decades) can offer a perspective on the growth of promotional activities and the reasons behind them.

Analyses of product, market, and competitive changes and trends (and the *reasons* for the changes) are essential before even considering a specific business promotion program. Otherwise, you could end up with the "wrong people using the wrong ammunition at the wrong time against the wrong target audience." The result would be an extremely ineffective, inefficient, and costly exercise in futility.

THE TRANSITION OF THE 1950s

To offer a bit of historical background, we can start with the 1950s, for these were largely traumatic years for most of the hospitality industry. The euphoria of the immediate postwar travel boom in the last half of the 1940s offered the hospitality industry a boom era of high 90 percent occupancies. But this soon gave way to the realities of extensive building, changing consumer interests and spending priorities, global competition, and the emerging attractiveness of the hotel industry as a business investment and career potential.

This attractiveness had its down side, however. The industry was being invaded by people who in many cases really had no business being in it to begin with. The four scenarios shown in Figure 1-2 offer some not-too-positive industry profiles, which unfortunately were far too prevalent during this period. But it was this very transition stage that set the foundation for the "scientific" approach to sales and marketing.

FIGURE 1–2 Four scenarios from the transition "stage" of the 1950s, featuring "actors" who should have never been in the "play."

Scene 1: The Happy Family Summer Hotel

The Happy Family has run its 120-room summer hotel for the past 18 years.

While some employees were hired for specific tasks, everyone pitched in to operate the property. Many local people were employed and the operation seemed to thrive.

It offered family-style accommodations and had a high amount of return business, though the property did little or no advertising. New business was usually generated to the Happy Family Summer Hotel by present or past guests.

It was still early in the spring of the current year, but it appeared that both inquiries and reservations were extremely slow in coming in. The Happy Family was aware that the surrounding area had started to develop industrially and they thought that this would indeed help bring in additional guests. They noticed that there were more people in the area and they were basically younger. Most of them had families and the Happys naturally assumed that this would increase their business.

Yet, all indicators were that their business for the coming summer would decline dramatically.

Scene 2: The Midcareer Couple

Sally and Bert have been married for 30 years. They were in their mid 50s, had raised a family, and were looking for something new in their lives. Both had worked from the beginning, except when Sally had taken a few years off to be with their children.

Bert was able to retire with a fairly good pension. He had spent the last 25 years as head custodian at Central School, where Sally had been teaching. Sally had a retirement plan which allowed her to retire with a flexible payout.

They had saved money over the years for a "rainy day" and fortunately never needed it. The neighborhood they lived in had grown and their home had more then tripled in value over the years. The two children were finished with college and both had good career positions.

What they thought they would like to do was to retire—but not stop living. They saw an advertisement from a franchise motel chain. They could be owner/operators; the chain would teach them everything they would need to know—and training was definitely needed. They would have a place to live, income, the opportunity of meeting people, and be able to relocate to an area they both liked. They could sell the house, take early retirement, and use their savings to get started.

Three years later they were both ready to look for other work. They had their franchise but were barely making ends meet. They were using their retirement money to cover costs.

Scene 3: The Professional Partnership

Mike, Jerry, Bill, and Jim were all professionals. They lived in the same neighborhood and had known each other for years. In fact, they had formed a partnership and pooled their funds to build the professional building that housed their offices. They saw that the area around their community was growing in many directions. A large shopping mall was being constructed, and plans for a small industrial park were also being discussed.

One evening when they were all out with their wives, there was a little bragging among them about how well things were going—and the conversation turned toward the future. It seemed like out of nowhere there sprang the idea and then the concept of opening a medium-sized hotel complex. They laughed, but it kept coming up again and again. They called it a night but agreed to meet over lunch later that week.

Over lunch it came apparent that each had been giving the idea a lot of thought. Why not? They were making good money, they already had a partnership, they knew the area, and they knew that the area was going to grow.

True, they didn't know anything about the hotel business, but it sounded like it would be a great concept. They could buy some land, build a hotel complex incorporating several different types of properties, and hire someone to run it for them.

After a number of years, they could sell it to an up-and-coming hotel chain and they could all retire. A hotel, restaurant, some recreational facilities, convention and meeting space, catering services to the new industrial park: they would have all bases covered.

Four years later, the partnership was on the verge of bankruptcy. The only income they had was from their respective practices.

Scene 4: A Part of the Dream

Pierre Schmidt and his family arrived in this country several years ago from Europe. They brought with them very little in the way of possessions, although they had some money. Most important, they wanted to be part of "the dream." They were willing to work hard and long if need be, and were looking for a business that would give them income, housing, and growth potential.

In Europe, they had been employed in the service industry and felt that this would be a good place to start here. They lived with friends for the first year and went to work for a hotel and restaurant on the outskirts of a major city, on a connecting road to the airport.

There was no question that they were learning the business from the bottom up. The 85-room operation was independently owned and the present owners wanted to retire, sell, and move south. This was the chance that Pierre and family were waiting for. They knew the operation and it provided them with room and board. The location was great and they felt sure that future growth would come. They studied the books from the previous years of operation, raised the monies for the down payment, and were ready to reap the benefits of being at the right place at the right time.

Three months later the expansion they expected came—but not in the manner they wished. A new major limited-access road was being planned to connect the airport directly with the city. An industrial park was being planned as well—but it would be located on the new roadway.

Pierre Schmidt and his family started to worry.

In today's competitive environment, promotion must be done in a structured, businesslike manner. "Let's go out and make some sales calls." "Let's write some letters to some business executives." "Maybe we should do some advertising this year." These and other "flying by the seat of your pants" approaches were common in the 1950s and even into the 1960s.

There was, however, increasing pressure by owners and operators (who are responsible for bottom-line profits) to have their sales executives sell more:

1. Intelligently
2. Effectively
3. Efficiently
4. Profitably

For the salesperson, the "report-back" emphasis, which had been on how many contacts or calls you made today, shifted to how much *profitable* business you booked today.

Booking business on a cost-effective, profit-producing basis meant that sales executives had to learn something about the following:

- The property—and its pluses and minuses
- Potential markets—and what they are looking for
- Decision-making processes—and the specific decision makers
- The best means of reaching each key decision maker, including not only the types of selling tools but the appropriate ways and times to use them
- Techniques of effective sales presentations
- Methods of follow-up and evaluation of efforts

These activities created a new definition for the term *sales,* which previously had been more-or-less characterized as the "process of soliciting business through direct contact with a potential user or prospect." During the 1960s, to be effective and productive, sales executives had to extend this basic definition, primarily by learning to do their "homework" on both the product and the potential purchaser.

THE MARKETING CONCEPT MODEL

There then evolved in the early 1970s a *model* for organizing these various activities and correlating them with other promotional methods, such as advertising, direct mail, public relations, and publicity. Introduction of the marketing concept in its structural sense* eventually became popularized as the *marketing cycle* (see Figure 1–3). The cycle usually operates on an annual basis, with "research and analysis" as the starting point. In its practical applications, that term readily translates into the key word: *study.*

---

*We emphasize "structural" because there are scores of marketing definitions, including a philosophical distinction that marketing is primarily customer oriented whereas selling is basically product oriented.

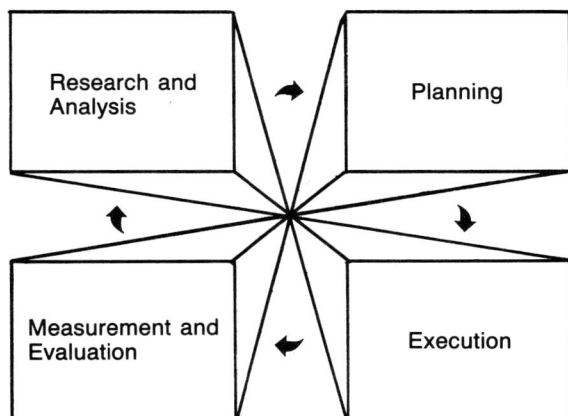

FIGURE 1-3 The basic components of the marketing cycle. The *execution stage* is composed primarily of what is commonly termed "sales," for example, the methods of customer contact.

So next, on to Chapter 2, where we specifically concentrate on a study of:

- *The product:* the basic hotel and its many variations
- *The market:* the customer: the user of the product
- *The competition:* from both within and outside the hospitality industry
- *The methods:* the means of selling and servicing—in essence, of bringing the product and the market together

two

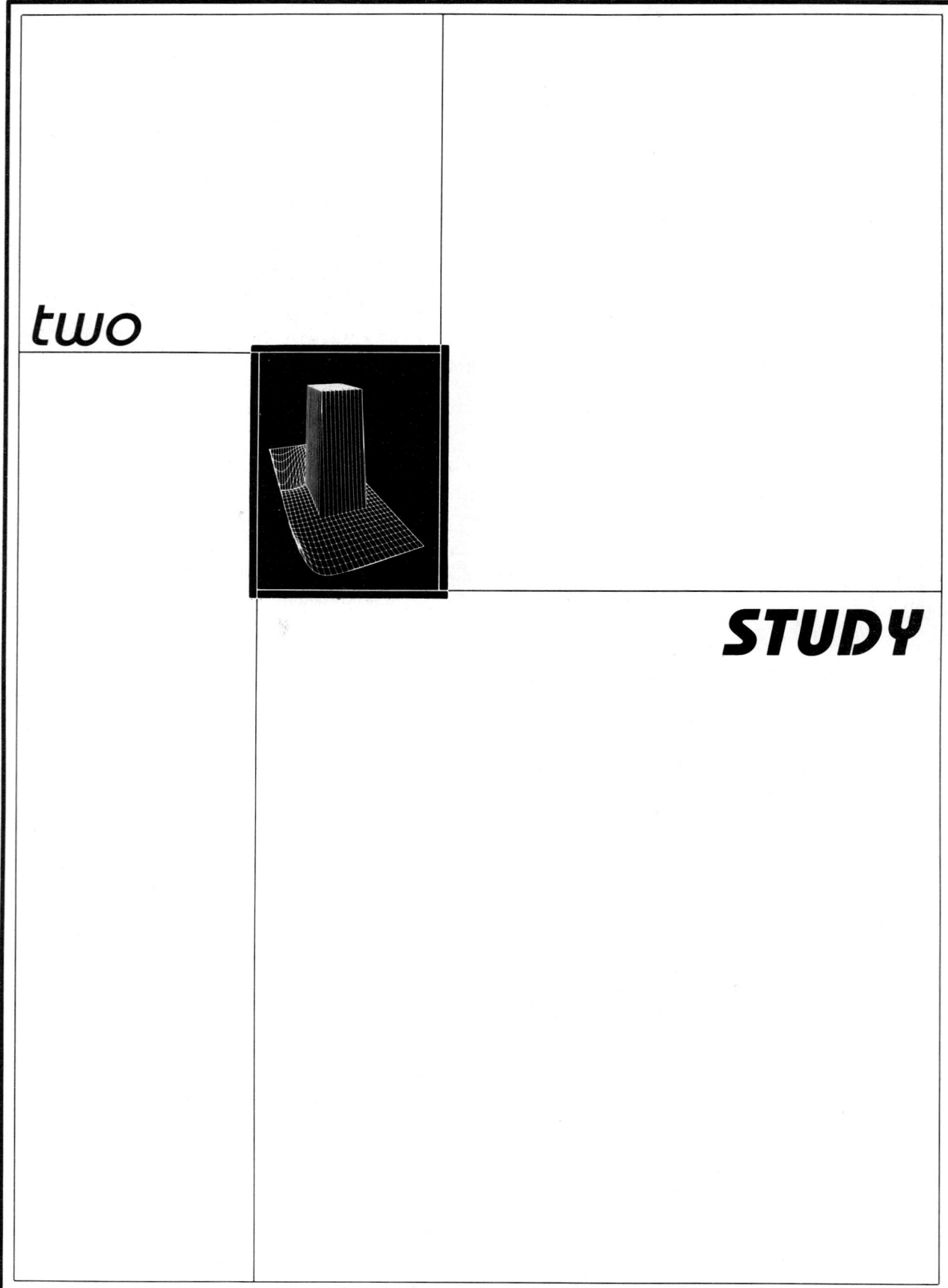

STUDY

A LOOK AT THE CONSTANTS

In Chapter 1 we offered an overview of the history of the sales function within the hospitality industry. This was done not only to acquaint you with what "was" but also to support the later premise that "what was" is not that much different from "what is" and "what will be."

Hotel sales and marketing—particularly packaging, merchandising, and promotion—are largely based on the concept of "variations on the constants." Because of this, sales and marketing are highly *creative* disciplines.

Initially, these constants are related directly to the *product.* Virtually every lodging establishment throughout the world offers the same fundamental physical product constants:

- Sleeping accommodations
- Eating and drinking facilities
- Space for social gatherings, business meetings, and exhibits
- Recreational, entertainment, and health and fitness facilities
- Personal and business services and amenities

These, in turn, are promoted to the public (or more properly, specific segments of the public) through a combination of sales and promotional methods. But here again, there is a fixed amount of constants that can be employed to attract guests to a property, such as:

- Personal (face-to-face) selling
- Telephone selling ("telemarketing")
- Direct-mail advertising (including such collateral materials as folders and brochures)
- Print advertising (newspaper and magazine)
- Broadcast advertising (radio and TV)
- Outdoor and transportation advertising (billboards, signs, and posters)
- Internal promotion, such as lobby displays, elevator cards, folders, brochures, and electronic signs

The following may sound like an oversimplification, but in the hospitality industry, we are really concerned with just three major components:

1. *The product:* our property, its surroundings, its facilities, services, amenities, and staff
2. *The market:* our present customers, past guests, possible new customers, and also those who do not and never did business with us
3. *The competition:* their products and their markets—what we have that they do not, and what they have which we do not

The primary responsibility of the sales and marketing function, stripped of all fancy words, is *to bring a profitable share of the market to a particular property or organization, despite its competition.*

PURPOSE AND GOAL

It might be helpful at this stage to establish the distinction between the purpose of a hotel and the goal of a hotel. The *purpose* is *customer oriented*. It is a philosophical as well as a functional reason for the hospitality industry's existence (as well as justifying an individual property's "reason for being"). This basic purpose is to take care of the needs of people who require housing, dining, meeting, and recreational facilities outside their own business or personal environments.

Another way of looking at this is to recognize that hotels are really part of the *communications business*. Part of their purpose is to offer people a place to come together, meet, discuss, learn, network, and otherwise communicate with each other for a wide variety of both personal and professional reasons. Some of these could include:

Personal

- Family outings, vacations, gatherings, and reunions
- Individual social functions: weddings, honeymoons, and anniversaries
- Created social functions: "second honeymoons" and "escape" packages
- Group social functions: civic and social club meetings
- Other receptions and banquets (cultural and charity)
- Reunions: high school, college, fraternal, military
- Testimonial dinners, office parties, and other company social events
- Meetings: hobby groups, sports clubs, and other "common interest" avocational organizations

Professional

- Association and professional society conventions
- Corporate sales and management meetings
- Union conventions
- Training and other self-improvement workshops
- Stockholder meetings
- Trade shows, exhibitions, and product launchings
- Incentive "vacations"

The *goal* of a hotel, on the other hand, is *product oriented*. In pure and simple terms, it is *to make money* . . . to make a profit for those who invest their money, time, and effort in the property or company. Another term for this function is *profit production*, a concept that in practice is the ultimate responsibility of the sales and marketing department.

Tying this all together, the specific goal of any hotel must be to maximize profit production but to do so in a way that maximizes its purpose as it relates to solving the needs and wants of the customers it attracts (see Figure 2–1). This balance is necessary because the hospitality industry is (and has been for most of its existence) in a buyer's market. It is a user-driven industry simply because the supply of rooms around the world (and in most individual countries, states, and cities) significantly exceeds the overall demand.

General occupancy levels in most areas of North America have, for the past decade, averaged between 65% and 75%. The inventory of rooms (supply)

Purpose   Goal

FIGURE 2–1 Balance between purpose and goal.

generally increased by 3 to 4% each year during the 1980s, but the same-period increase in annual demand generally averaged around 2%. This does not imply that demand is specifically limited. In fact, the double-barreled challenge of the hospitality industry is to get *more people* to use hotels, to use them *more often,* and to use them for *different purposes.* For all practical purposes, the market-place is virtually unlimited. Thus, to be successful, an individual property must be able to sell and service more efficiently and effectively than its competitors.

It also means that an individual property has the added responsibility of working cooperatively with *area* sales and promotional agencies (such as the local convention and visitors bureau), with suppliers (such as airline, bus, and other transportation companies), and at times jointly with other properties—to stimulate overall local and area demand for the existing facilities. These concepts suggest that sales and promotion is not a "hit or miss" proposition but rather, one that requires constant study, planning, implementation, evaluation, and restudy.

WHAT TO STUDY—AND WHY

Because of the complex scope of today's hospitality industry, it is essential that a hotel executive be a student of the business long after the completion of formal academic education. Constant *research and analysis* are essential before undertaking any sales and promotional activity.

The broad area of research and analysis involves the study of:

- The tangible *products* and their many forms and uses
- The intangible *services* and their relationships to these products
- The *marketplace*—the various groups of potential customers, their characteristics, and their purchasing habits
- The *competition*—their differences as well as their similarities with respect to products, services, customers, and both marketing and operational methods
- *Outside forces,* such as global economics, politics, and governmental regulations (customs procedures, visas, and duty-free shopping) and their impact on travel and tourism*
- *Trends and projections,* both short-term and long-range, as they relate to each of the above

TYPES OF INFORMATION

There are three general types of information that relate to urgency of use:

1. *"Nice to know" information:* offers a perspective on the industry and is helpful in providing background information and an overall view of changes, trends, innovations, and challenges. (Much of the material in this section and the preceding one falls within this classification.)

---

*An increasingly significant outside force relates to the impact of *taxes* on pricing and competitive positioning. This includes value-added taxes (VATs), city and state occupancy or room taxes, food and beverage taxes, and sales taxes, among others.

2. *"Need to know" information:* facts, details, and data that are essential to the proper fulfillment of responsibilities, objectives, and goals. (Profiles of the hotel and its facilities and of its key market areas, which will be illustrated later in this section, are examples of "need to know" information essential to making effective marketing decisions and specific sales presentations.)

3. *"Combination" information:* nearly any time you have two factors, you can always come up with a third, a combination of the two.

As an example, let's say that you are making 50 or 60 sales calls in a given area. You begin to notice that many of the decision makers' names that you have on your contact list are being replaced by new executives. This qualifies as "need to know" information, to be recorded immediately and sent to the sales office to update records and mailing lists.

At the same time, you note that many of your contacts (who were middle-aged men) are being replaced in travel and meeting planning positions by younger women. At the time that you note this, this is not essential information for you in making a sales presentation. It is nice to know, and it can possibly help you to vary your presentation to fit the persons with whom you are talking. But when you mention this later to the sales or marketing director of your hotel, the information could become essential to the planning of advertising programs for the coming year.

Information can also be categorized as primary or secondary. *Primary information* is from direct sources: You collect it as a result of personal observation, conversation, surveying, and so on. Or you obtain it directly from a source with which you are associated, such as information on where your guests come from, how they make their reservations, how long they stay, and how they pay, which can be obtained from the registration cards kept in the front office. *Secondary information* comes from other people or outside sources. Newspaper and magazine articles, published survey reports made by accounting firms, and statistical data from the Census Bureau fall within this category.

It is easy to generalize the results of broad-based industry research. It should, for example, provide overviews on the general state of the industry, signal changes and innovations, and forecast similar overall changes in the characteristics of the marketplace. However, it is more meaningful to the daily activities of the hotel sales department if specific *objectives* are predetermined, which relate to the immediate operating needs of the property. These can then guide research and study efforts toward obtaining practical, useful, and usable data and information.

RESEARCH OBJECTIVES

Initially, research and analysis should be able to provide a unit operation or a group of properties (chains, franchises, referral groups), with detailed information and direction relating to:

1. Where you are at the present time, in terms of positioning, business volume, and competitive advantages

2. Where you should be at the end of a given time period, in terms of fulfilling objectives and goals

3. Why you aren't where you should be (if you have not reached current goals)

4. Where your competition is now

5. What your competition is doing now that you are not doing, and to whom and why it might be consequential

6. What the various market segments are looking for today

7. How and why it differed from yesterday

8. What these same market segments are likely to look for tomorrow

9. How this relates to your current product, and what changes may be needed to keep up with both the market and the competition

This type of research is both directional and functional. The information gained will prove valuable to those executives who determine and guide policy, as well as to those responsible for the planning and execution of both current and future operations and sales efforts.

FUNCTIONAL STUDY

It is the functional study that is of concern to most people who enter the lodging industry, usually in either a starting sales position or in an entry-level operating area such as in the front office. So to get a feeling for the practical applications of study as they relate to the sales function, let's set up a scenario where you have accepted your first sales position at a medium-sized hotel. You will be an *account executive* (a more modern term for what was commonly called a *sales representative*). Your primary duties will be "out in the field," calling on people who are responsible for making accommodations and travel arrangements for members of their companies or organizations. We will call your property the Center City Hotel, your community is Center City, and the two main "feeder cities" are Caboose City and State City.

It is the first day on the job. Orientation and training vary widely within the industry. In some cases you might be given a fairly comprehensive orientation regarding the property, its surroundings, the competition, feeder cities, and so on. In other cases, it might be just a brief overview; in still other situations you might have to shift for yourself.

For this exercise, though, we will assume that you have already had some practical experience making sales calls in the key market areas through student sales blitz programs and "in the field" internships. Whatever the situation, you realize that you personally must study, research, fact-find, and analyze a considerable amount of information, facts, and data before going out to sell.

Sometimes working backwards can prove productive, especially for illustrative purposes. So what follows now will be one style or format for recording and tabulating the results of such an initial study. In effect, these would become "working documents," which would provide you with the information needed to make productive sales calls and to sell intelligently, effectively, efficiently, and profitably.*

The first items of information you would probably want to know would be, in simple terms, *where are we* (Figure 2–2), followed by *what are we*. Then might come an evaluation of *who else is there*.

This competition analysis would normally be done on a market segment basis. We indicated at the start of this little exercise that you would be responsible for securing business from the segment known as the *individual business*

*The methods of obtaining and recording such information are discussed and illustrated in Chapters 5 and 6.

Sample Location Overview

The 300-room Center City Hotel is located just off the north–south four-lane interstate highway on a main business route 2 miles from Center City (population 185,000). Center City is a rapidly growing industrial community with a large and expanding industrial park, a 250-bed hospital and clinic, and a medium-sized airport that can handle all types of aircraft except jumbo jets.

Other communities and points of interest within a 200-mile radius include:

1. **Communities:**
   - *Caboose City:* 140 miles, 50,000 population
   - *State City:* 177 miles, 600,000 population
2. **Attractions:**
   - *Majestic Canyon National Park:* 64 miles
   - *Frontier Village:* 75 miles
   - *Wandering Gardens Historic Restoration:* 105 miles
   - *Stoned Forest State Park:* 105 miles

FIGURE 2-2 Overview of a property location, with emphasis on community and nearby attractions.

travel market (also called the *individual corporate travel market*). These are the people who travel for business-related reasons on behalf of their companies or business firms. This will be the segment we will use for illustrative purposes. We'll finish with a detailed analysis of the market areas in which you will be making sales calls (call that the "where" of *where you should be*—and *what you should know*).

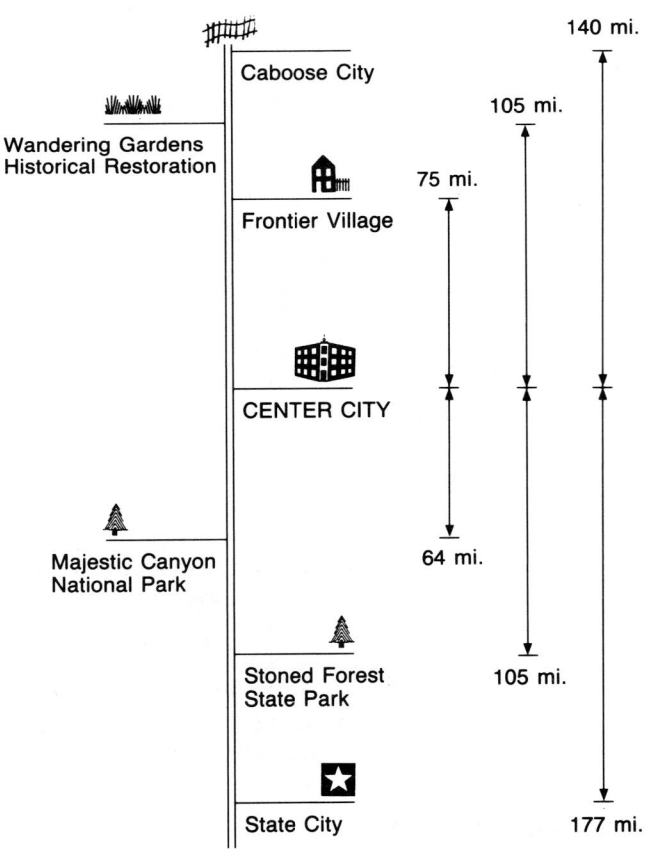

FIGURE 2-3 "Working" mileage map of Center City, its feeder cities, and surrounding attractions. One might extend this by adding "drive time" figures, based on normal traffic conditions and applicable state speed limits.

These basic data should then be supplemented with a simplified mileage map (one you might even prepare yourself). This should indicate not only distances between your community and the nearest key feeder cities but also main points of interest. (For illustrative purposes we are focusing on individual business travelers.) But such guests will often mix business with leisure and may even extend a day to take in the sights or just "wind down" and relax. Such a guest then shifts into another market segment, and becomes an individual leisure traveler. If business travelers are impressed with your leisure-time facilities and attractions, both on property and off the premises, they may return at a later date with the family for a more lengthy vacation.

Figure 2–3 illustrates one style for a "working" mileage map based on the preceding information. You should prepare a similar chart of the city and surroundings. This would include a general view of the immediate area, your location relative to transportation facilities and primary points of interest, and the location of your main competitors. It might take the form (with or without mileage) shown in Figure 2–4. Detailed street maps of both your community and the cities where you will be making sales calls are also "musts," especially from a time-management point (remember the phrase "selling efficiently"?).

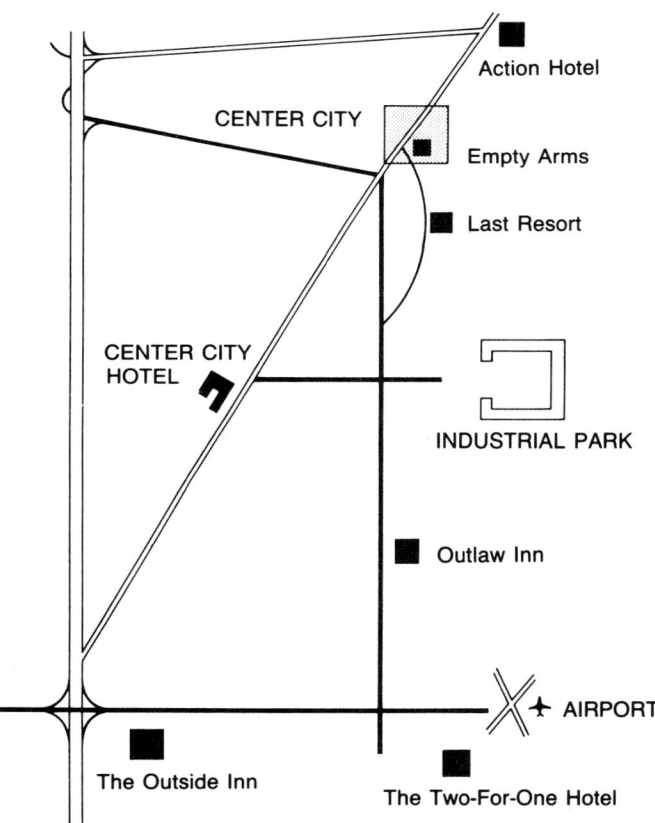

FIGURE 2–4 Center City Hotel, its competitors, and the immediate surroundings.

PROPERTY FACILITIES AND SERVICES

One of the very first actions that you would take upon being hired is to study your hotel thoroughly—in other words, to research and analyze your product. Figure 2–5 outlines the minimum information you should readily have at the

```
┌─────────────────────────────────────────────────────────────────────────┐
│                                                                           │
│   Basic Property Profile: Center City Hotel                               │
│                                                                           │
│      1. General Features                                                  │
│         a. 300 rooms (including 12 suites), within a 10-story, full-service, medium-rise │
│            property                                                       │
│         b. All rooms air-conditioned, cable TV, direct-dial phone         │
│         c. Unlimited free parking                                         │
│      2. Dining and Entertainment                                          │
│         a. Dining room, seating 125, open for lunch and dinner, offering both Ameri- │
│            can and Continental cuisine                                     │
│         b. 24-hour coffee shop, seating 65                                │
│         c. Lobby lounge for drinks and light snacks                       │
│         d. 24-hour room service                                           │
│      3. Special Facilities and Features                                   │
│         a. Top-floor concierge club                                       │
│         b. Outdoor year-round swimming pool and jacuzzi                   │
│         c. Snack and beverage service available in pool area              │
│      4. Meeting and Banquet Facilities                                    │
│         a. 11,000-square foot function space for groups of 10 to 650      │
│         b. Main ballroom, 7000 square feet, can be subdivided into four meeting │
│            rooms of 1750 square feet each                                 │
│         c. Four additional breakout rooms of 1200, 1100, 900, and 800 square feet, │
│            respectively                                                   │
│         d. Promenade foyer between two main meeting areas for registration, coffee │
│            breaks, tabletop exhibits                                       │
│                                                                           │
└─────────────────────────────────────────────────────────────────────────┘
```

FIGURE 2-5 *Basic property profile or product analysis.*

"tip of your tongue," using the Center City Hotel for illustrative purposes. This general outline should be backed up on paper with more detailed specifics. For example, of the 300 guest rooms (first item under general features):

- How many are single-bedded, double-bedded, twin-bedded; with king-size or queen-size beds; and so on?
- How many connecting rooms are there?
- How many corner-room accommodations are there?
- How many of the suites are one-bedroom/with parlor, two-bedroom, and so on?
- Are any suites bi- or trilevel?

When it comes to convention and meeting space, greater detailed information must be readily available. General floor plans such as illustrated by Figure 2–6 are essential. Backing up the floor plans should be detailed capacity break-downs of each room, generally in chart form, as shown in Figure 2–7. It is important, incidentally, to include ceiling heights (for audiovisual setups) as well as metric dimensions if your meeting market includes international groups.

Again, although for this walk-through example we are concentrating on the individual business traveler, you should always recognize the dual roles that most customers play. The commercial traveler in your hotel may also be responsible for planning sales meetings, product demonstrations, departmental training programs, company social events, and so on. So you need to have group business information with you at all times.

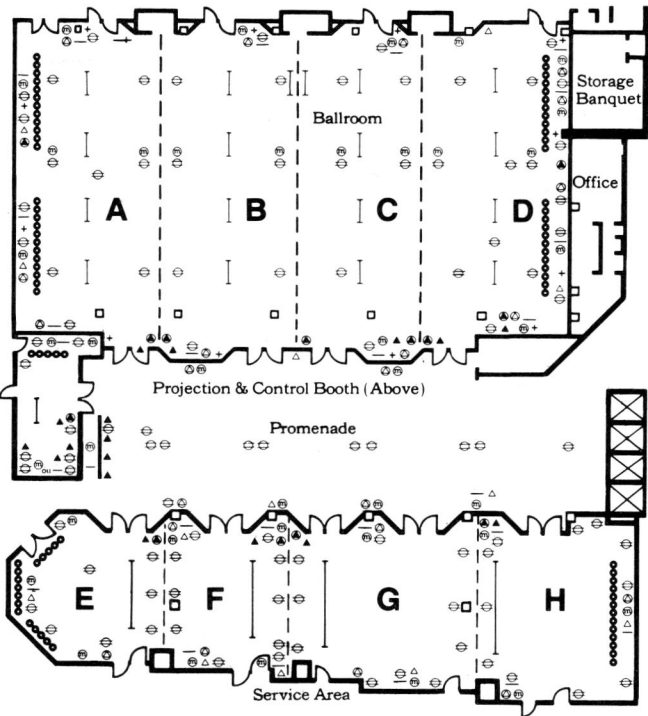

FIGURE 2–6 Center City Hotel's function space floor plan.

ROOM	DIMENSIONS (FT)	HEIGHT (FT)	FT²	CAPACITY			
				THEATER	SCHOOLROOM	RECEPTION	ROUNDS
Ballroom	100 × 70	25	7000	850	450	950	650
A, B, C, D	25 × 70 each	25	1750	125	85	150	140
E	30 × 27	15	810	80	50	95	80
F	31 × 29	15	890	85	50	95	80
G	40 × 30	15	1200	120	65	125	90
H	40 × 27.5	15	1100	100	60	120	85

FIGURE 2–7 Room capacity chart for the Center City Hotel's function room area.

COMPETITION ANALYSIS

Studying what you have to sell is only half of the preliminary product research you must undertake before going out to sell. The other half relates to a similar study of your competition. *Shopping the competition* is the common industry term for this type of research.

For the sake of illustration, let's assume that you have determined your competition, bearing in mind that in many instances, different properties will be competitive in varying degrees for different market segments. Your initial research on them would involve gathering objective, factual data, particularly in relation to rates and pricing structures.* Specifically, the types of rate information that you would be seeking on each competitor would include:

---

*Bear in mind the legal ramifications of discussing rates with competitors, which varies among countries but is a very strong issue in the United States.

- Size (number of rooms)
- Average occupancy for specific periods
- Overall average daily rate (ADR) for all segments
- Average daily rate for a specific market segment
- Special rates that might apply to a particular market (e.g., corporate rate, convention rate, government rate, etc.)
- Breakfast (if complimentary, is it continental or full buffet?)

Figure 2-8 shows a rate comparison chart for the individual business travel market; similar comparisons would be prepared for other major market segments and might include other criteria (such as public space rentals and food and beverage function charges for the meetings market). After this has been charted out for each major market segment (i.e., individual business traveler, leisure traveler, conventions and meetings, etc.), a more interpretive analysis, often in a narrative style, can be prepared. Figure 2-9 is an abbreviated working sample. Other criteria can also be comparatively examined, such as the advertising, printed literature, and other promotional tools used by each of your competitors.

The factors just presented are observable, tangible, measurable criteria that can be fairly easy to compare among properties. But there are additional, *nontangible* means of comparing what on the surface may seem to be similar properties, such as:

- Reputation (especially for dependability)
- Knowledge (by sales staff of property, markets, and competitors)
- Sensitivity (to client's needs)
- Creativity
- Quality (of product, service, and staff)
- Staff training (particularly in the area of servicing)
- Dedication and commitment (of all personnel)
- Perceived operating philosophy

FIGURE 2-8 Competitive rate analysis chart.

Competitive Rate Analysis
Target Market: Individual Business Traveler

Property	Rooms	Average Occupancy (%)	ADR Overall	ADR IBT	Rack Rates Single	Rack Rates Double	Corporate Rates Single	Corporate Rates Double	Complimentary Breakfast Continental	Complimentary Breakfast Full
Outlaw Inn	149	71	$60	$60	$65	$65	$50	$50		×
Last Resort	326	63	77	65	70–115	95–175	60	85		×
Action Hotel	198	72	28	26	30–45	45–65	25	40	×	
Empty Arms	317	59	37	41	45–75	65–100	40	55		
Center City Hotel	300	68	58	60	60–95	85–145	55	75		
Average	258	67	52	50	54–79	71–110	46	61		
Median	300	68	58	60	60–75	65–100	50	55		

Competitive Rate Analysis

TARGET MARKET: Individual Business Traveler

1. Outlaw Inn has one rate single, one rate double—for everyone at all times. Offers full complimentary breakfast buffet; packs rooms with amenities and extras. Appeals to midmarket business traveler.
2. Last Resort located on city perimeter; goes after upscale business executive. Emphasizes recreational outlets; offers full breakfast around poolside in good weather.
3. Action Hotel appeals to budget-conscious business travelers, especially manufacturers' reps, government employees, and families for the weekends.
4. Empty Arms is the oldest hotel in the area, built in 1937. Relies more on convention and meeting business than other properties, which sometimes conflicts with the individual business market. However, when there are no conventions or meetings, will offer special corporate rates—same price for single or double.
5. The Center City Hotel at the present time seems to be positioned toward the middle of the market, with a "median" product line and rates. Other than minor repairs and replacements, the property has not been renovated since it opened 10 years ago.

FIGURE 2-9 Narrative style competition analysis.

This type of checklist or similar guide is also used by the customer, who also "shops the competition."

COMPETITIVE EVALUATION

When determining the competition, one must be careful to evaluate realistically who the *real* competition might be. Too many hotels, for instance, claim that their competitors are properties that are in fact several notches above them. They may do this to upgrade the image they think they have (or should have) with potential customers.

One "second-party" method that hotels can employ is to check with selected guests and clients. Ask them who they would consider to be your competitors for a particular market, and why. You may, for example, think that hotel X is competing against you for the business traveler chiefly on the basis of price, when actually the business travelers coming into your area prefer property Y because of its more accessible location. Or if hotel X is indeed your major competitor, it may not necessarily be because their rates may be lower, but that their service and dependability are perceived to be higher than yours.

MARKET AREA PROFILES

So far in this illustrative example, you have studied what you have to sell and who will be selling against you (your counterparts in competitive properties). You will also need to be thoroughly familiar with *where* you will be selling. Such market area profiles are essential for determining the total business potentials within a given area or community. Sample basic outlines for three different types of communities, offering three distinctive and different profiles, are shown in Figures 2-10 to 2-12.

Center City (185,000 population)

1. Basic population consists of both blue- and white-collar workers, the majority of whom are directly affiliated with businesses in the industrial park area
2. One morning newspaper
3. Three local radio stations: 24-hour FM "easy listening," 24-hour FM "hits of the '50's and '60's," and 24-hour AM "contemporary"
4. Civic and service clubs include the Chamber of Commerce, Jaycees, Kiwanis, Lions, Toastmasters, and a "lead exchange" morning breakfast club
5. Airport serviced by four national airlines, one international carrier, and two commuter lines
6. 250-bed hospital and clinic
7. Two-year community college with programs in arts and sciences, humanities, and hotel management
8. Three travel agencies and one local bus company
9. 92 companies located in the industrial park:
   a. 57 light industry and small manufacturing
   b. 11 pharmaceutical
   c. 10 food processing
   d. 8 computer
   e. 6 electronic assembly

FIGURE 2-10   Profile of Center City, the local market base for the Center City Hotel.

FIGURE 2-11   Profile of State City, the Center City Hotel's primary feeder city.

State City (600,000 population)

1. State City is the state capital and its key population groupings consist of both professional and political executives and administrative/secretarial support staff personnel.
2. Three daily newspapers: a morning paper aimed at the 24- to 45-year-old, middle-income, midmanagement-level worker, with emphasis on sports, entertainment, special features, and real estate listings; an evening paper targeted to the middle-aged, high-income executive, with emphasis on financial and political news and features; and a "satellite" paper that appeals to younger, entry-level government staff workers, housewives, and students.
3. Five local radio stations (all 24-hour): FM "classical," FM "easy listening," FM "rock," AM "news, weather, and talk," and AM "contemporary country."
4. Five area TV stations: three major network affiliates, an independent locally owned station featuring popular reruns, and one educational (public service) station.
5. 194 national associations, 31 regional groups, and 76 state associations headquarter in State City, representing manufacturing, agricultural, and forestry interests primarily.
6. Civic and service organizations include the Chamber of Commerce, Jaycees, Rotary, Kiwanis, Elks, Lions, Zonta, Toastmasters, Toastmistresses, and two businessmen's breakfast clubs.
7. Airport served by eight national airlines and two commuter lines, each having at least two daily flights. Daily service is also provided by each of two international carriers, with flights to and from Canada and Europe.
8. Eleven travel agencies and three bus companies are located in the city.
9. A four-year state university is located in the central downtown area. Enrollment is 8500 full-time students within seven different degree areas, including a bachelor of science degree program in hotel, restaurant, and travel management, with an enrollment between 400 and 450 students.

Caboose City (50,000 population)

1. Located on a transcontinental rail line in a largely agricultural/forestry area.
2. Some small localized industries, including feed-processing plants, canneries, and lumber mills.
3. One afternoon newspaper with "something for everyone," especially heavy on local news.
4. Two local radio stations: AM sunup-to-sundown "local news and easy listening" and 24-hour FM "country."
5. Civic and service clubs include the Chamber of Commerce, Grange, 4-H, and local historical society.
6. One local bus company serving the community and schools.

FIGURE 2-12 Profile of Caboose City, the Center City Hotel's secondary feeder city.

SITUATION OVERVIEW

What we have done so far is to illustrate the type of basic information one should gather in order to get a "feel" for the property and its markets. As you do this type of study and begin analyzing the various types of information, some patterns should emerge as far as certain business challenges.

You undoubtedly would have been given some specific indications from whoever hired you as to some of the challenges and quite possibly your specific role in helping meet them. It is quite possible that you might have been hired specifically to overcome one or more of these challenges: for example, "we need you to concentrate on retaining existing commercial business as well as further developing government business coming from State City." This challenge becomes even more critical because in your study you come across several newspaper feature stories indicating that two new competitive properties were planning openings within the next 12 months:

1. *The "Two-for-One" Hotel:* 160 all-suite units especially designed for the business traveler
2. *The "Outside Inn":* 200 rooms; featuring pitch-n-putt, two jogging paths, and indoor/outdoor health and spa facilities—also aimed primarily at the business traveler

So the data, facts, and general information gained from your various studies of the situation leads to a situation overview, outlined briefly as follows:

1. The Center City Hotel opened on January 1, 1979, at the beginning of the industrial park development. For the first five years it enjoyed an average occupancy between 83 and 85%.
2. The property currently relies on the individual business travel market for 40% of its room nights and 52% of its "in-house" revenue.
3. Average occupancy has been declining from its opening year of 85% to the current 68%, due partly to dependency on one primary market and the increased competition from other properties for that same segment.
4. Other potentials should be looked into, especially since the property does enjoy a central location with respect to the surrounding leisure-market attractions.

5. The property has excellent function space as to size, layouts, flexibility, and customer "control," yet these facilities have been underutilized throughout the property's history.

6. Group business potentials need more attention, especially in light of the industrial park growth and the general increase in the number of small meetings.

PROPERTY INFORMATION

The sources of information on the property are perhaps the most readily available of all. Brochures, folders, floor plans, meeting room diagrams and audio-visual equipment lists, internal literature in lobbies and guest rooms, and samples of advertising and publicity items can readily provide details on the operation necessary for you to "learn the product," so as to be able to talk intelligently and convincingly to customers and prospects.

Many hotels, especially those in resort areas, now prepare videocassettes highlighting the property and its surroundings. Although intended to be used primarily in conjunction with sales calls (or mailed to key business prospects, such as meeting planners, travel agents, and tour operators), they can also offer a new sales executive an excellent overview of the facilities and attractions of both the property and the community or area.

WALKING THE PROPERTY

A basic, yet highly essential product analysis technique is to walk through the property, to familiarize yourself firsthand with such features as:

- *Guest rooms:* number, types, general decor, furnishings
- *Food and beverage outlets:* location, capacities, menus, style of service, hours of operation, entertainment
- *Meeting and function space:* location, dimensions and capacities, functional and audio/visual equipment
- *Recreation facilities:* pool, golf and tennis, health and fitness center

Work forms similar to those shown at the end of Chapter 6 can be used to record the information gained through a property walk-through. But these forms record mainly the *features* of the property as they would be seen through your eyes—that of the seller. It is an old but true cliché that people do not buy features; they purchase *benefits*. A property and area analysis as seen through your customers' eyes is developed in Chapter 3.

three

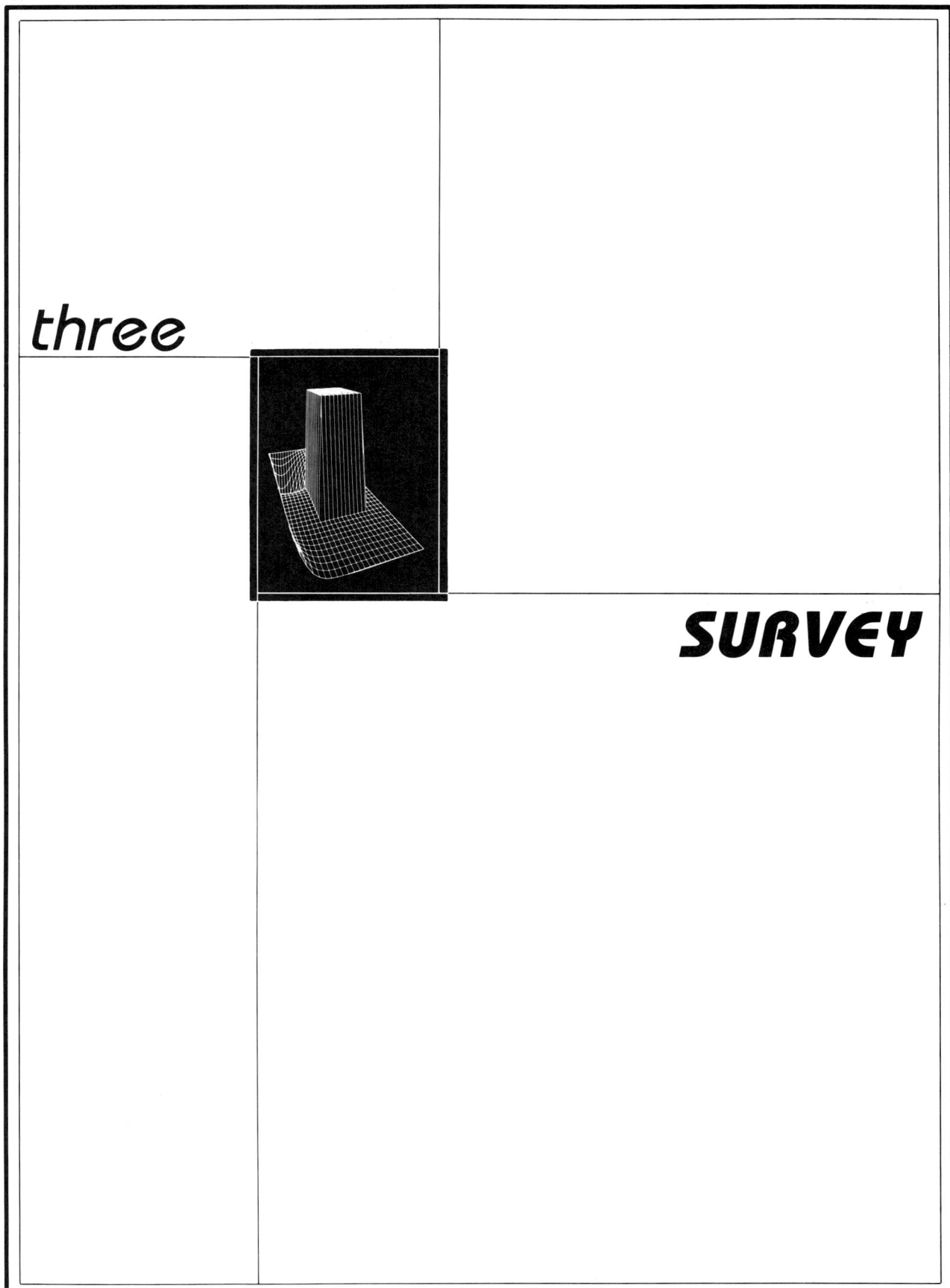

SURVEY

So far we have walked you through a property from the point of the sales executive, the person who will be selling the facilities of the hotel to a prospective client or group of customers. As we mentioned at the end of the preceding chapter, this type of study concentrates on the *features* of a property. However, such features would be relatively meaningless to the user unless transformed into *benefits*.

In the old days of "strictly selling," the basic practice was for sales executives to concentrate on selling the features of the property, using all of their personality and persuasion skills (and sometimes "tricks") to make the sale. Under the *marketing concept*, the selling approach takes on an entirely different direction. The main thrust in the marketing philosophy is for the sales executive to *motivate the customer to purchase benefits*. To do this effectively, those responsible for selling must understand and use what amounts to a "second language."

We have seen that the hotel property has a set of tangible product features and a similar set of intangible features. In the same manner, various groups of hotel customers have varying sets of tangible needs and intangible wants and desires.

CUSTOMER NEEDS AND WANTS

For this chapter, let's use a running illustration of a meeting planner for a state association of bankers that holds an annual convention for three days. The meeting is the type sometimes characterized as a "work and play" convention, because there is a fairly equal mix of educational programming and social and recreational activities.

Spouses and families are encouraged to attend, and the meeting planner will rely on the cooperation and assistance of the hosting property to aid in promoting such attendance.* A variety of indoor and outdoor recreational programs are customarily scheduled separately for the spouses and children. There will also be numerous opportunities for them to get together with the regular attendees for free-time activities when no educational sessions are scheduled.

Initially, a number of fundamental key questions must be answered since they affect the basic decision-making process. The hotel sales executive must be totally prepared to respond to them in a positive and satisfactory way:

1. What type of tangible and intangible needs would the meeting planner need to have fulfilled in order to have a successful meeting and meet the personal and professional goals of the majority of participants (including delegates, spouses, and other family members)?

2. How does the meeting planner determine which property would fulfill the needs and desires of the majority of the attendees? Another way of looking at this question: Since attendance at this type of convention is purely voluntary, what type of facility would appeal to the majority of the membership of the organization and therefore be most likely to attract the greatest number of participants?

3. What are the budgetary concerns of the group, and what are their effects on the selection process?

*Both parties benefit from greater attendance: the hotel in increased room, food, and beverage revenues; and the meeting planner's organization in increased revenues from registration fees and "breakage" on food and beverage functions.

TANGIBLES AND INTANGIBLES

We will shortly take a ride with our meeting planner as he or she surveys a property as a potential site for our illustrative meeting. But first, a quick look at the two main types of needs with which the typical planner is usually most concerned.

1. *Tangible needs:* those that are quantifiable and can be stated in terms of numerical units, linear dimensions, or specific time frames
2. *Intangible needs:* those that cannot be put into units but which are perceived through the senses

The following are some examples of each as they relate to conventions and meetings:

Tangible Needs	Intangible Needs
• Specific dates	• Change
• Length of stay	• Escape
• Sleeping-room mix	• Adventure
• Special suites	• Romance
• Staff accommodations	• Relaxation
• Ground transportation	• Silence
• Registration and storage	• Space
• Receptions and meals	• Solitude
• Meeting rooms	• Safety
• Exhibit space	• Security
• Audiovisual equipment	• Control
• Recreation and entertainment	• Recognition
	• Activity
	• Education
	• Fulfillment
	• Self-improvement

REQUIREMENTS SURVEY

Using these starter checklists (there are other items which could be added to each), the meeting planner would then survey the specific requirements that must be fulfilled to conduct a particular meeting properly. The result might look similar to the sample requirements guide illustrated in Figure 3-1. That list, incidentally, is primarily intended to be a preliminary guide to determine whether a particular property would make a "fit" as far as being capable of handling the overall needs of the group.

This is not the more fully detailed *event sheet* that is used by both the meeting planner and the hotel for the servicing of the convention. That form (see Chapter 6) sets forth the setup details in chronological order, function by function. But the requirements checklist illustrated certainly forms the base for the event sheet.

Basic Requirements Checklist

1. Name of Event:	State Bankers Annual Convention
2. Dates:	Friday–Sunday, August 3–5, 19—
3. Expected Attendance:	350 delegates + 150 spouses
4. Rooms Mix:	150 king doubles
	100 double-doubles
	5 VIP (one bedroom and parlor) suites
5. Food and Beverage:	Two receptions, three luncheons, one dinner
6. Meeting Rooms:	One general session meeting room to seat 450 auditorium style, six breakout rooms seating up to 65 each classroom style
7. Audiovisual:	35-mm slide projector, overhead projector, videocassette playback plus four TV monitors, screen, blackboards, and flipcharts
8. Recreational:	Golf, tennis, and a variety of other outdoor and indoor sports and fitness facilities
9. Location:	Not necessarily restricted to the state; suburban or resort generally preferred
10. Atmosphere and Ambience:	Casual, informal, and relaxed

FIGURE 3–1 Checklist of a client's basic requirements.

SITE INSPECTION CHECKLIST

Other organizations, such as training groups, may use a very detailed checklist because of their greater needs for multiple-meeting-room setups and more sophisticated audiovisuals. Figure 3–2 is the site inspection checklist developed by the Council of Hotel & Restaurant Trainers (CHART).

FIGURE 3–2 Detailed inspection checklist used by the Council of Hotel and Restaurant Trainers to survey sites for its semiannual convention. (Courtesy of CHART.)

CHART Site Inspection Checklist

Name of facility: _____

Address: _____ City: _____ ZIP: _____

Telephone: _____ Salesperson: _____

Inspection date: Month: _____ Date: _____ Year: _____

Sleeping Rooms	Total	Rack Rate	Convention Rate
Singles	_____	_____	_____
Doubles	_____	_____	_____
Twins	_____	_____	_____
Parlors	_____	_____	_____
One-Bedroom suites	_____	_____	_____
Two-Bedroom suites	_____	_____	_____
VIP suites	_____	_____	_____

Will the facility establish a "run-of-the-house" rate for the meeting?

Single occupancy $_____

Double occupancy $_____

Amount of room tax added to the rates above: _____%

FIGURE 3-2 *(cont.)*

Is there a telephone charge for local calls? $_____
Absolute room block cutoff date: _____
If the hotel is not sold out one week prior to the meeting, will additional sleeping rooms be committed to the organization if they are needed?

Yes _____ No ____

Complimentary Accommodations Policy
One regular sleeping room for each _____ room nights paid
One one-bedroom suite for each _____ room nights paid
One two-bedroom suite for each _____ room nights paid
One VIP suite for each _____ room nights paid

Front Office Policies
Hotel prefers (insists) that reservations be received:
_____ Through the organization.
_____ By the hotel directly.
The organization's VIP rooming list is required by the hotel _____ days prior to the meeting.
Check-in time: _____   Check-out time: _____
Is early check-in permitted and possible?   Yes _____ No _____
Is late check-out permitted and possible?   Yes _____ No _____
Will guests be preregistered?   Yes _____ No _____
Is baggage check provided?   Yes _____ No _____
What is the price per bag? $_____
Is VIP check-out provided for:
   All guests?   Yes _____ No _____
   Organization VIPs?   Yes _____ No _____
Will the hotel direct bill guests?   Yes _____ No _____
Will the hotel cash checks for guests?   Yes _____ No _____
What is the daily limit? $_____
List all credit cards honored by the hotel:

_____   _____
_____   _____
_____   _____

Deposit Policies
Amount of deposit required: $_____ per room (single)
                                     $_____ per room (double)
                                     $_____ per room (suite)
Can a standard deposit be set for all rooms? If so: $_____
What is the hotel's overbooking policy? _____
_____
_____

Will the hotel agree to pay, *in cash*, double the deposit to any organization member who holds a confirmed reservation and is not housed in the hotel on the dates specified on the confirmed reservation form sent by the hotel to the organization member?

Yes _____ No _____

If no, why not? _____
_____
_____

Accounting
Will the hotel establish a master account for the organization?

Yes _____ No _____

The final bill will be mailed _____ (#) days following the meeting.
Must any or all of the master account be paid to the hotel prior to departure?

Yes ____ No ____ If so, how much? $_____

_____ % discount off total bill may be deducted if total bill is paid by the organization within _____ (#) days of receipt.

General Information
Are all guests rooms INDIVIDUALLY air-conditioned?   Yes _____ No _____
Are there remodeling plans being contemplated?   Yes _____ No _____
   Anticipated starting date: _____
   Anticipated completion date: _____

FIGURE 3-2 (cont.)

Hotel guest parking:	Inside	_____	(Cost) $_____
	Outside	_____	(Cost) $_____
	Self-park	_____	(Cost) $_____
	Valet	_____	(Cost) $_____

Complimentary parking for organization cars: _____ (#) cars
_____ (#) days

Is there an auto rental agency in the facility?   Yes _____ No _____
If yes: Name of agency: _____
          Name of manager: _____
          Telephone number: _____
Is laundry service available?   One-day _____   Other _____
Is it valet service?   Yes _____ No _____
Is baby-sitting service available?   Yes _____ No _____
                                                    Cost per hour: $_____
Is room service available?   Yes _____ No _____
          Normal hours: _____ a.m. to _____ p.m.
          Are these hours adjustable to fit the format of the meeting?
                                                            Yes _____ No _____

Promotional Assistance

Are promotional brochures supplied?   Yes _____ No _____
                                                    Cost: $_____
Are postcards supplied?   Yes _____ No _____
                                                    Cost: $_____
Other promotional aids or assistance available through the facility:

_____
_____
_____
_____

Liquor Policies

Is there a bottle shop in the facility?   Yes _____ No _____
If no, is there a bottle shop nearby?   Yes _____ No _____
What is the price from room service?   Per drink: $_____ Per bottle: $_____
Note here the corkage policy of the facility. How much per bottle, if any, if liquor
is purchased elsewhere and brought into the facility for hospitality purposes?

_____
_____

Food and Beverage Services

Obtain a complete set of menus for general food and beverage services within the
facility.
_____ Restaurant _____ Room service _____ Wine lists _____ Others

Additional Rules, Regulations, and Policies

List here all established rules, regulations, and policies governing the use of decorations, signs, public exhibits, etc.

_____
_____
_____

Shipping and Receiving Department

Note: Visually inspect this department before leaving the property!
Is it clean and orderly?   Yes _____ No _____
Name of manager: Day _____
                          Night _____
Can an area be set aside during the meeting for the sole use of the organization?
                                                            Yes _____ No _____
Will the organization person in charge have access to the storage area 24 hours a
day?
                                                            Yes _____ No _____
Normal hours this department is open: From _____ to _____.

FIGURE 3-2 *(cont.)*

What is the best method for delivery of goods to the facility?

Air _____

Train _____

Truck _____

In the opinion of the facility, which is the best carrier to use?

Name: _____

Address: _____

City: _____   Zip: _____

Telephone: _____

What is the proper manner in which to address shipments to the facility?

_____

_____

_____

_____

General Surroundings

Be aware of the general neighborhood around the property.

Is it clean? Yes _____ No _____

Is it well lighted? Yes _____ No _____

Are there sidewalks? Yes _____ No _____

Can meeting attendees walk to nearby restaurant
and other facilities in relative safety? Yes _____ No _____

Do you see frequent police patrols? Yes _____ No _____

General Comments: _____

_____

_____

_____

Public Transportation

How far is it to the closest major airport? Miles _____

Minutes _____

Taxi fare to this airport: $_____

Bus fare to this airport: $_____

Does the facility provide free shuttle service
to and from this airport? Yes _____ No _____

Will the facility increase its normal "runs" to this
airport during peak arrival and departure times
for meeting attendees? Yes _____ No _____

Is there public transportation to major shopping
areas nearby? Yes _____ No _____

What is the approximate fare to nearby shopping? Bus $_____

Taxi $_____

How far is it to nearby shopping areas? Miles _____

Minutes _____

Special Features

Are shopping tours available? Yes _____ No _____

Are sightseeing tours available? Yes _____ No _____

Is a golf course available? Yes _____ No _____

Are tennis courts available? Yes _____ No _____

Is there a swimming pool for guests of the facility? Yes _____ No _____

Indoor: _____

Outdoor: _____

What specialities does the facility have to offer, e.g., private parties in entertainment lounges, supplying entertainment, welcome reception for organization guests, theme party decorations, etc.?

_____

_____

_____

_____

Churches

Indicate the distance from the facility to the closest in each denomination.

Baptist _____   Congregational _____

Catholic _____   Episcopal _____

FIGURE 3–2 *(cont.)*

Jewish	_____	Mormon	_____
Lutheran	_____	Presbyterian	_____
Methodist	_____	Others	_____
			_____
			_____

Gratuities

Does the facility provide blanket gratuities to all
employees who work on a meeting?   Yes _____ No _____

Preferred Suppliers

Ask the facility for a list of those suppliers they prefer to use *for their own functions.*
The list should contain (in each instance) the name of the company, address, tele-
phone number, and the name of the person to contact.
   Audiovisual firm
   Florist
   Photographer
   Other

General Impressions of the Property

Is the lobby area clean and neat?   Yes _____ No _____
Are elevators clean (carpets and ashtrays)?   Yes _____ No _____
Are room service trays visible in hallways around
10:00 a.m. and 2:00 p.m.?   Yes _____ No _____
Are there long lines outside restaurants during
peak food service periods?   Yes _____ No _____
Is food service in the restaurants fast or slow?   _____
When you ate a hotel entree in the facility's res-
taurant, was the food hot?   Yes _____ No _____
Was the food in the facility's restaurants (hot or
cold) good?   Yes _____ No _____
Considering the city in which the facility is lo-
cated, were food prices in the restaurants: Average _____
                                                         High _____
                                                         Low _____

What is the "average" price on the menu for:
Coffee shop: Breakfast $ _____   Lunch $ _____   Dinner $ _____
Dining room: Breakfast $ _____   Lunch $ _____   Dinner $ _____
Note: Obtain a copy of the menu from each of the restaurants in the facility, the
            capacity of each restaurant, and the hours of operation for each.
Are front desk personnel friendly and helpful?   Yes _____ No _____
Are bellmen friendly and helpful?   Yes _____ No _____
Are hosts and hostesses in restaurants cordial
and helpful?   Yes _____ No _____
What is the attitude of personnel in the shops
within the facility?   _____
Are directional signs within the facility accurate
and easy to follow?   Yes _____ No _____
Are meeting rooms easy to locate and reach?   Yes _____ No _____
Is it necessary for meeting attendees to use eleva-
tors to get from one meeting room to another?   Yes _____ No _____
Is there easy stairway access from one floor to an-
other in the meeting room areas?   Yes _____ No _____
Are there formal seating areas in the public space
for those attending the meeting to have informal
discussion groups?   Yes _____ No _____
Sit or stand in the lobby and listen to the com-
ments of people who are obviously guests in the
facility.
   Do they generally seem pleased?   Yes _____ No _____

Public Meeting Space Inspection

Obtain a complete floor plan of all public meeting space in the facility.
   Floor plans should show capacities of each room for various styles of room
   setups, e.g., theater style, banquet style, schoolroom or classroom style, etc.

FIGURE 3-2 *(cont.)*

Are all meeting rooms soundproof?   Yes _____ No _____
Do all meeting rooms have built-in sound systems?   Yes _____ No _____
Are sound systems in the various rooms good
enough to use for your meeting?   Yes _____ No _____
Does the facility have portable sound systems
available for use in those rooms with no built-in
system?   Yes _____ No _____
What is the availability of rest rooms in the general meeting room area?
    How many for men? _____(#)
    How many for women? _____(#)
    Are they clean?   Yes _____ No _____
    Are they well supplied?   Yes _____ No _____
What is the availability of public telephones in the general area of the meeting
rooms?
    How many? _____(#)

General Condition of the Meeting Rooms
Are they clean?   Yes _____ No _____
Is the carpeting in good condition?   Yes _____ No _____
Are the acoustics good?   Yes _____ No _____

Major Meeting Room
Is it well lighted?   Yes _____ No _____
Can "mood lighting" be accomplished without
extra expense? (cocktail parties, banquets, etc.)   Yes _____ No _____
Is there a staging area for a head table and/or pro-
gram participants?   Yes _____ No _____
Does it have a permanent stage?   Yes _____ No _____
    If yes, note exact dimensions: ____ in. wide,   ____ " deep,   ____ " high
Is there an area for a reception?   Yes _____ No _____
Are the acoustics of the room good?   Yes _____ No _____
Is the public address system good?   Yes _____ No _____
Where are light controls located?

_____
_____
_____

Meeting Room Equipment
While you are on-site, personally inspect as much of this equipment as possible and
make notes on any that may be in need of repair or that do not suit your specific
needs.

You may want to prepare a separate list of the items contained in this list and leave it
with the facility representative for completion and mailing to you after your inspection.

	Number	*Cost per Day*
Lavalier microphones	_____	_____
Wireless microphones	_____	_____
Floor/podium microphones	_____	_____
Floor microphone stands	_____	_____
Table microphone stands	_____	_____
Overhead projectors	_____	_____
Opaque projectors	_____	_____
16-mm projectors	_____	_____
Filmstrip projectors	_____	_____
Flipcharts	_____	_____
Easels	_____	_____
Blackboards	_____	_____
8' × 8' Projection screens	_____	_____
10' × 10' Projection screens	_____	_____
12' × 12' Projection screens	_____	_____
Table lecterns	_____	_____
Floor lecterns	_____	_____

FIGURE 3–2 *(cont.)*

	Number	Cost per Day
Projection stands	_____	_____
Table linen	_____	_____
Colors available: _____	_____	_____
Other equipment available:	_____	_____
_____	_____	_____
_____	_____	_____
_____	_____	_____
_____	_____	_____

General comments and observations about equipment:

_____

_____

Note: In many facilities, a private audiovisual firm has a contract to supply audiovisual equipment within the facility. This firm should be contacted during the inspection and the equipment should be inspected and a price list obtained.

Name of firm: _____

Address: _____ City: _____ ZIP: _____

Telephone: _____ Name of contact: _____

Other Available Services   Cost per Hour / Day / Copy / Etc.
Secretarial   _____
Copying   _____
Security guards (unarmed)   _____
Others:

_____   _____
_____   _____
_____   _____
_____   _____

Next, let's go back to the example of our state banker's group. Let's assume that their meeting planner (or site selection committee) will be surveying various properties for consideration as possible sites for the group's next annual convention.

A PROPERTY WALK-THROUGH

One of the ways (though not the only method) is for the planner or the committee to physically walk through each property or area under consideration, correlating the group's tangible and intangible needs with the features of each property and its surroundings. This would be similar to the way you, as the new sales executive, would have walked through the property to acquaint yourself with its accommodations, facilities, and services. But there would be a key difference from the buyer's point of view. Remember the beginning of this section when we talked about features versus benefits and the fact that the seller must be able to understand a "second language," that of the buyer?

Here is where the meeting planner also does a translation from one language to another: the language of features (the property) must be translated into the language of benefits. This language must focus on what the buyer needs or wants from the property to fulfill the objectives and goals of the meeting. (An example: *Location* is a feature; *accessibility* and *privacy* are potential benefits that can be derived from that feature.)

Let's follow our meeting planner through a site inspection of an actual property (Figure 3–3). This could be considered a walk-through survey of the tangible aspects of the property from the buyer's viewpoint.

Surveying the Tangibles

Feature: Directional signs
Benefit: Accessibility

Feature: Large free parking area
Benefit: Convenience and cost savings

Feature: Main hotel housing plus separate deluxe facilities
Benefit: Accommodation upgrades for VIPs, speakers, and key staff

Feature: Large spacious lobby
Benefit: Gathering points for social and business interaction (helps promote membership "bonding")

Feature: Detached convention hall
Benefit: Control, security, and minimizing of distractions

FIGURE 3–3 A property survey from the customer's viewpoint, translating the key observable features into benefits that will satisfy the needs and wants of both the planner and the convention attendees. (Photos courtesy of Earle Tunick, Resort Photo Service, and the Villa Roma Resort Hotel, Callicoon, New York.)

FIGURE 3–3 *(cont.)*

Feature: Lounges, dining rooms,
            and clubhouse
Benefit: Free-time on-property
            options for social gatherings

Feature: Golf, tennis, handball
Benefit: Choice of leisure-time
            activities for the more
            athletic attendees

FIGURE 3–3 *(cont.)*

Feature: Miniature golf, bocce,
and horse and carriage
Benefit: Free-time options for
the more leisurely oriented

FIGURE 3–3 *(cont.)*

Feature: Indoor racquetball, tennis, pool, miniature golf, bocce, shuffleboard, game room

Benefit: Flexibility (i.e., ''rainy-day'' activities options)

FIGURE 3–3 *(cont.)*
Feature: Winter sports programs
Benefit: Flexibility in selecting meeting dates due to availability of year-round activities

FIGURE 3–3 *(cont.)*

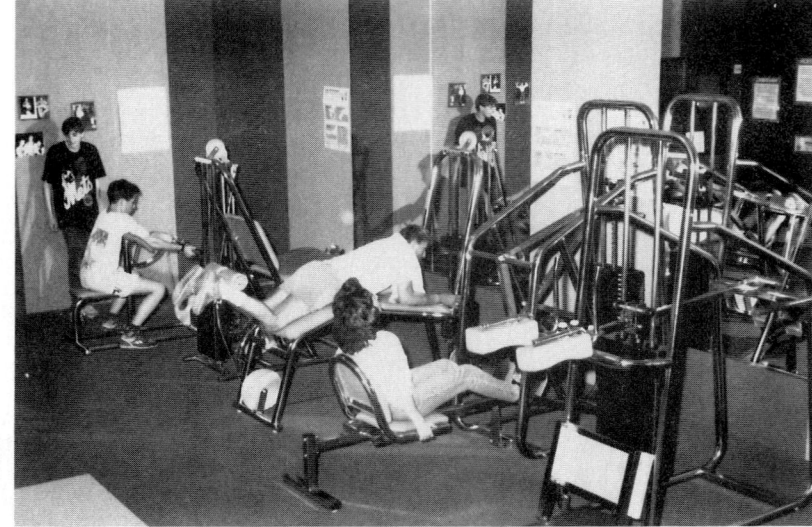

Feature: Fitness center
Benefit: Appeal to health and
            fitness

Feature: Night club
Benefit: Evening entertainment
            for desirable mix of
            work and play; also,
            flexibility of meeting
            space as the room can
            be used for general
            sessions during the day

Feature: Off-premise points of
            interest
Benefit: Change of pace and
            setting

A variation of property surveying occurs when meeting planners visit properties during times when other groups are holding meetings very similar in size, composition, and program needs as theirs. In that way, they can not only observe a "physical fit" but also note the quality of service as well as many other intangibles (Figure 3–4).

FIGURE 3–4   Meeting planners often like to inspect properties when groups similar to theirs are in session. They can observe such intangibles as atmosphere and ambience, and the effect they have on the activity levels of both speakers and their audiences. These illustrations would indicate that the overall setting lends itself well to stimulating attentiveness, participation, and both formal and informal discussions. (Authors' photos of the 1986 CHRIE Convention, used with the permission of the Council on Hotel, Restaurant, and Institutional Education.)

Surveying the Intangibles

A JOINT BUYER AND SELLER FUNCTION

Some of you are perhaps wondering why we have suddenly switched to the buyer's side. After all, isn't this book about the techniques of selling? That is exactly the point—to sell properly, sales executives must be able to survey their products from the users' viewpoints. Sales executives should follow the same procedures their customers use when evaluating a property. They must be able to view the facility as it relates to providing benefits that will solve the tangible and intangible "needs, wants, and desires" mix of each of its main forms of business.

Initially, "walking the house" is intended to acquaint, and later to refresh, the sales executive regarding what is *available for sale*. It is also necessary to acquaint and refresh the sales executive with what is available for the customer to *purchase*.

This may seem like a minor philosophical point. But it becomes highly essential when making sales calls and preparing advertising and other printed promotional literature that we do indeed talk the "language of the buyer."

Doing your own analysis of your property, and relating its features to the main requirements of various types of customers, is only the beginning of the research and analysis process. Many additional sources of details, facts, and data on the marketplace, your competition, and industry trends will be discussed in the next chapter.

four

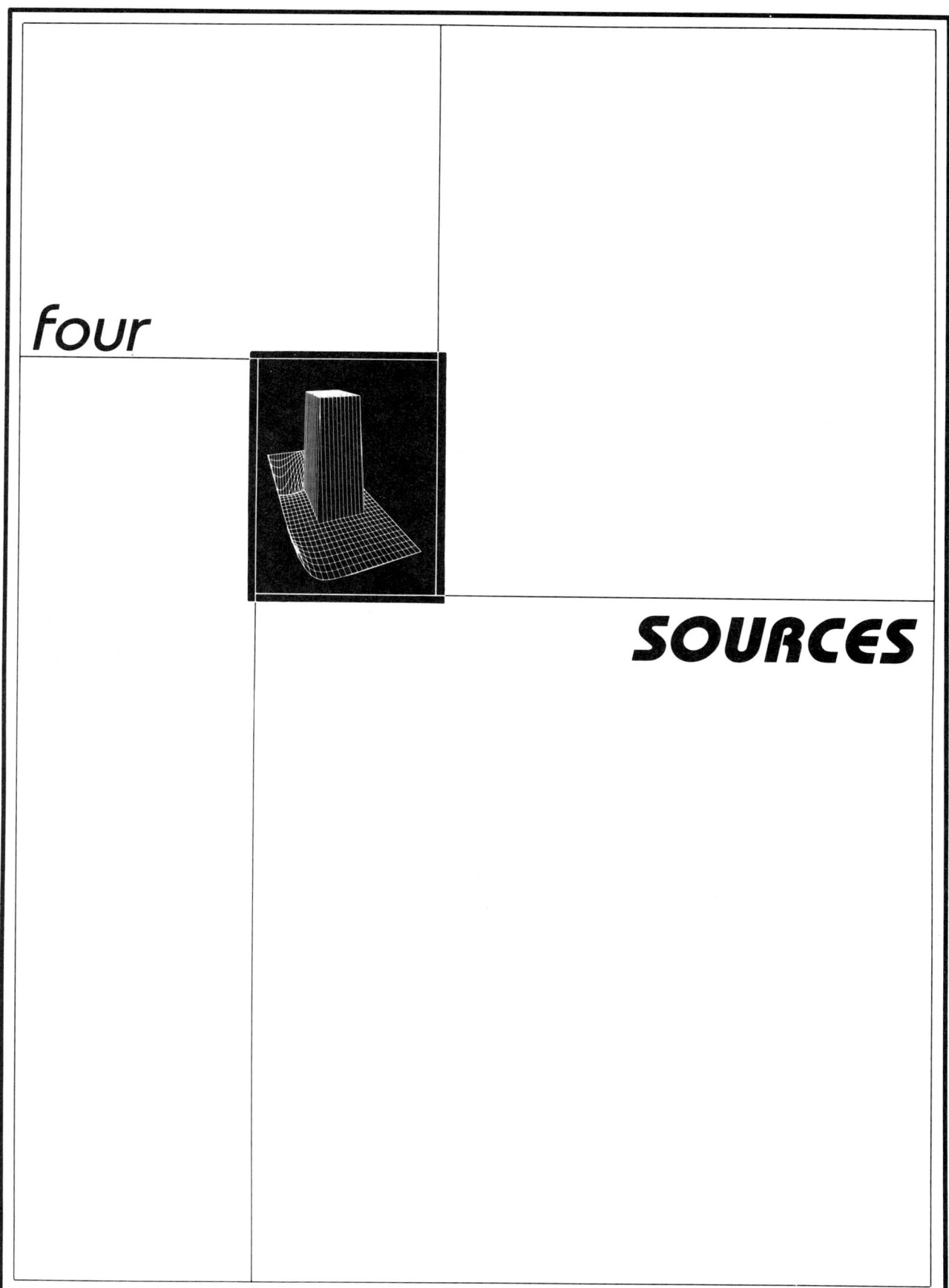

SOURCES

A classic story of the early 1960s concerns a young college graduate hired as the sales manager of a medium-sized property. In those days there was a distinct shortage of salespeople, and hotels were hiring virtually anyone who could smile to "go out and sell."

"What are my functions; what exactly am I supposed to do?" he asked the manager.

"Go out and get us some business," came the rather terse reply.

"Well, how do I do that, where do I go, what do I say?" asked the newly hired and eager sales executive.

"If I knew the answers to all those questions, do you think I'd have hired you?" responded the not-too-sympathetic manager. "Just go out and make some calls."

The story concludes with our young and intrepid sales executive reporting back to the manager after a full day of calling on companies located in a nearby industrial park.

"How did you do?" asked the manager.

"OK, I guess," replied the eager young sales executive. "I made 30 calls, and I'm sure I could have made another dozen, but several people asked me what I was selling and I had to waste some valuable time explaining it to them!"

As we have seen in Chapter 3, there is a substantial amount of basic knowledge about product, market, and competition that even the beginning sales executive must acquire before going out and making sales calls. Much of this can be obtained through the property's orientation and training program (where there is one). A great deal more is available through individual study, exchange of information with other executives, attendance at area workshops and seminars, and other general educational opportunities, such as college summer courses for industry.

INFORMATION DETERMINATION

Before seeking out sources of information, one should ask:

1. What types of information do I need to perform my job best?
2. Why would I need it; of what practical use will it play in my sales responsibilities and in reaching both my own and the property's objectives and goals?
3. Who can supply this information?
4. How do I obtain it most effectively?

Such information generally will sort itself into:

1. Data and statistics relating to the various markets on which one is concentrating
2. Similar information on the competition and its business mix
3. Forecasts of trends that will affect the way one does business and their potential impact on the current products and services being offered

MARKET NEEDS INFORMATION SOURCES

A key area where information would be most critical for a sales executive relates to the needs of those customer groups that form the primary markets for the property. In many larger operations, sales executives have become specialists. Each may be responsible solely for securing business from a specific segment of the market, as shown by the titles in a portion of a large property's sales and marketing department organization chart (see Figure 4–1).

Each executive would be responsible for obtaining general information on his or her designated segment, as well as specific information on the individual accounts that each has been assigned. An analysis of the market's general *needs* would be critical to an understanding of the segment, especially what it looks for in the way of facilities and services. Also of consequence would be an analysis of trends relating to any changes in its overall composition (i.e., changes relating to the group's average age, predominant sex, income and educational levels, lifestyles, etc.).

FIGURE 4–1 Sales manager's organizational chart.

Regardless of whether you are talking about the individual vacation traveler or the association meetings market, the following checklist can serve as a starter guide to the basic sources of information.

Information Sources for Analyzing Customer Needs

- Observations (you and your staff)
- Guest complaints (verbally or through letters and questionnaires)
- Direct research ("pulse" surveying)
- Industry association studies (AH&MA and HSMAI)
- Market surveys from trade associations, publishing companies, and independent consulting firms
- Reports from hospitality accounting firms
- Government reports (especially from the Census Bureau)
- Real estate and relocation trend reports
- Allied membership in customer organizations
- Attendance at customer organization meetings and trade shows
- Articles in customer, travel, and hotel industry trade papers and magazines (see the Appendix for selected listings)
- Articles in consumer magazines and newspapers, especially those containing special business and travel sections
- College and university hospitality trade journals (which often contain current studies and research project reports by faculty and graduate students)
- College libraries (especially those that prepare quarterly or annual indexes of trade press articles)
- Trade and professional association libraries (many of which have a "service of information")
- Your chain or franchise headquarters

There are many other means and sources for collecting information. One that is often overlooked is the *HWH technique*—calling on your contacts in associations and organizations (usually by phone) and simply asking "Hey, what's happening?" (or words to that effect).

COMMUNITY SOURCES

The hotel business differs from most other industries in that the flow consumption is generally from the user (the guest) to the producer or supplier (the property) rather than the other way around. It could be diagrammed as shown in Figure 4–2.

Using a "hub and spoke" analogy, the hotel and the community in which it is located serves as the hub, with the spokes serving as the transportation means from the rim where the feeder cities (points of origin) are located (see Figure 4–3).

Depending on economic conditions, there can be considerable movement of people back and forth between the community where a hotel is located and its feeder cities. The greater the two-way flow between communities, the greater the potential for business. Thus the local community itself can be a key source of information.

Here are some community *economic* indicators that can offer information on marketplace activity:

- New office building construction, expansion, and renovation
- Housing demands (building permits)
- Highway department traffic surveys
- Highway building and expansion
- Population shifts
- Retail sales volume
- Sales tax receipts
- Food and beverage tax receipts
- Occupancy tax receipts
- Airline traffic reports
- Airport departure tax receipts

FIGURE 4–2 Consumption flow charts.

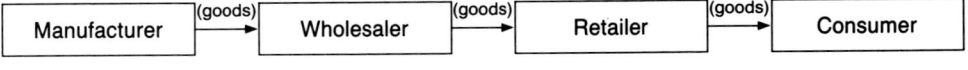

- Most Industries:

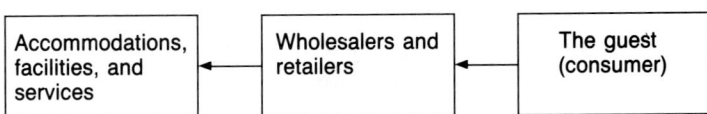

- Hotel Industry:

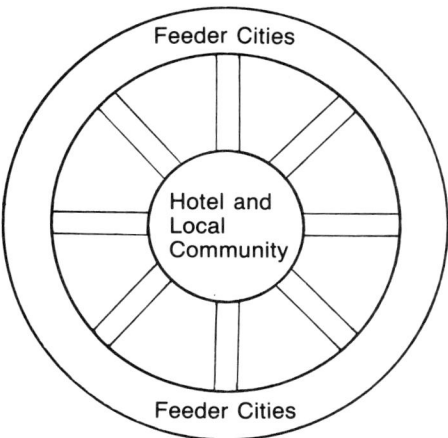

FIGURE 4-3 "Hub and spoke" analogy.

- Special business and real estate sections in local newspapers
- Classified ads in local newspapers and on radio
- Competitive advertising in key feeder cities

ADDITIONAL LOCAL SOURCES

Active involvement in the community can be especially helpful. It offers a direct means of obtaining the latest up-to-date information as to what is (and what may be) happening in the area that may affect lodging demand in general and specific business opportunities for an individual property. Two examples of outlets for community involvement are discussed next.

Lead Exchange Clubs

An interesting source of current community information found in many cities is the *breakfast club* or *lead exchange club*. Members meet informally, usually once a week at breakfast, and network with each other. The group is generally composed of one representative from each major type of business or profession, and in the larger cities, there may be a number of different lead exchange organizations.

Civic and Service Clubs

Membership in local civic and service clubs is also another excellent source of information, as well as offering opportunities for visibility and contacts for direct business possibilities. In many hotels, memberships in various organizations will be allocated among the staff so that there is representation in all local groups.

SOURCES FOR COMPETITION EVALUATION

A number of years ago, one of the present authors was having lunch with the new manager of a local hotel, who mentioned that she wanted to know the origin of the business of her competitor across the street. Both hotels were similar in size and features, and the majority of people staying at both arrived by car.

"Ask him," I suggested; "give him a call or go over and chat with him."

"Already did," said the new manager, "and he said I'd have a better chance of flying to the moon than to get that type of 'confidential' information out of him."

"Boy," I replied, "does he have a lot to learn about cooperating with neighbors for the benefit of all. I tell you what, invite me back for dinner, give me one of your front desk staff, and we'll go across to his parking lot and count license plates. And I'll bet you one other thing; your 'friendly guy' across the street doesn't have the slightest idea where his business is coming from."

The end of the story: We counted plates by state, recorded the plate numbers, checked with a motor vehicle bureau to get the city or county from each state plate, and made a nice little chart. And yes we did; we mailed a copy of this informal "point of origin" survey to the manager across the street!

The point of the story: Information on the competition is readily available, and it is rather futile to try to hide it. When it is not so apparent, one of the great attributes of the hospitality industry is the general willingness to share appropriate information with each other, for mutual benefit.

Here are some of the main sources and methods of obtaining information on your competition:

- Snoop! (That is an obvious method, with both advantages and drawbacks.)
- Look at their reader boards (a "dignified" form of snooping, which virtually every sales executive has done one time or another).
- Study their advertising.
- Eat and sleep at competitive properties (and also have friends and relatives do the same after staying at yours for comparison purposes). In other words, "shop" your competition.
- Keep your eyes and ears open at hotel industry conventions and meetings. Listen especially during group discussions and idea exchanges.
- Be a "joiner," especially local civic and service organizations which are made up of area business executives who may have occasion to talk about your competition.
- Read the trade press, both the news items, which can tell you about expansion plans and the like, and the case study feature articles, which may contain information on a competitor's current and future plans.
- Phone your competition and ask.
- Honestly exchange information, but be aware of possible legal ramifications. In the United States, do not discuss rates and food/beverage pricing, standardization of practices, or anything that could be construed as a violation of antitrust or restraint of trade.
- Study the reports of hotel accounting firms, especially those concentrating on the local hotel/restaurant industry. It can give you information on how your property compares with your local competition.
- Study financial information, which can give you additional facts and figures. For example, local newspapers in some communities publish the occupancy or "bed" tax collections from each hotel because they are forwarded to the state treasury and are often a matter of public record. If you know what was collected during a particular month, you can readily

calculate the total room revenue, which divided by the number of days of the month gives you the average daily room revenue. The number of rooms is readily available, and the monthly percentage of occupancy is also very often a matter of published record. All these figures in turn will allow you to calculate each competitor's average daily rate (ADR).

- Keep your ears open for what your customers, prospective guests, and key decision makers say about the competition, especially during sales calls. (But be careful not to say anything negative about your competition and not to agree with a customer who "knocks your competition.")

- Attend customer conventions and meetings, especially those from groups composed of meeting planners, travel agents, tour operators, and transportation company officials.

- Gather information informally during your property's "happy hour," "manager's breakfast," or similar in-house gatherings. Listen actively to complaints and compliments on both your property and on the competition.

In addition to offering useful information on the community, the local newspapers can be an excellent source of information on your competitors. For example, let's set up a situation where a hotel is thinking of opening a restaurant that would be aimed specifically at the local community. Who's the competition; what does each do in terms of annual sales; what's the average dinner check; and how many employees does each have?

Confidential information—very probably! Certainly, one requiring a lot of expert research, probably through an outside consulting firm. But not necessarily—it can depend on how much detailed information your local newspaper will publish, which in turn will depend on the operating and editorial policies of the paper.

How much information on your competition can a newspaper offer? It all depends on where you are and on the editorial policy of the paper. The epitome of public information on hotel operation must surely occur in Atlantic City, New Jersey, where in addition to the casino stats (such as the monthly "take" of each casino and the amount per slot machine), hotel statistics such as the average room rate, percentage of occupancy, and room, food, and beverage revenue are printed regularly in the local newspaper.

PRIMARY AND SECONDARY SOURCE INFORMATION

Most of the information we have been discussing is basically *secondary source information.* It is not obtained directly by the person using it but comes through an intermediary or a chain of information gatherers. The data may originate, for example, through the figures obtained by questionnaires and then "crunched out" by the U.S. Census Bureau, passed along through a magazine such as *American Demographics,* reprinted in a national newspaper such as *USA Today,* and then picked up by local newspapers.

Primary information is that picked up directly at the source, such as that gained by personally interviewing guests in your hotel. Other examples of primary information include data obtained from your own property records. These often originate in the accounting department, reservations office, and the front office, in addition to the data maintained and updated in the sales office. These would include information on registration cards, guest folios, guest history cards, billing records, and so on. Data and facts from these sources can then be extracted and recorded appropriately in usable form in the sales office for a variety of purposes.

One such use, for example, is a *guest evaluation profile,* illustrated in Figure 4-4. This information, especially when compared with the same period for previous years, can indicate not only the comparative value of a certain type of business but also various trends regarding growth, decline, and changes. With today's computers, this type of information can be readily "tracked" and comparisons can easily be charted or graphed.

Other key *primary information* sources for determining how best to reach the various markets would include the researching of company and association

FIGURE 4-4 Guest evaluation profile, derived from readily available primary information recorded on other departmental records. Similar profiles can be developed for other categories of business, such as the individual leisure traveler, as well as for specific segments such as honeymooners or senior citizens.

GUEST EVALUATION PROFILE:
Individual Business Traveler (IBT)
Month Ending January 199__

Operational Data
1. Number of guest nights..2,211
2. Percentage of total occupied rooms..38%
3. Percentage of double occupancy 11%
4. Average daily rate (IBT)..$60.00
5. Average daily rate (all segments).......................................$78.00
6. Average daily folio charge (IBT) $69.00
7. Average daily folio charge (all segments) $93.00
8. Contribution to total gross revenue...22%

Marketing Information
1. Average length of stay...1.8 days
2. Point of origin (%):

New York City 44	New England 11
Philadelphia 21	Europe 3
Northern New Jersey 20	Other 1

3. Transportation (%):

Plane (full trip) 31	Train 16
Fly/drive....................... 22	Bus................................14
Car (full trip) 17	

4. Key Demographics:
   Sex (%):

Men.............................. 53	Women...........................47

   Occupation (%):

CEO/COO...................... 2	Staff...............................10
VP/dir 11	Self-employed.................20
Dept. head/mgr 30	Other 4
Supervisor...................... 23	

5. Reservation method (%):

Corp. contract 41	Airport phone 7
Secretary/self................. 29	Walk-in 6
Travel agent 17	

Service Usage

	% IBT	% All Others
1. "Preferred Points" club enrollees	31	27
2. Concierge floor users	17	11

FIGURE 4-4 (cont.)

3. Services and facilities usage:		
Sauna	24	17
Pool	27	33
Fitness center	47	23
Jogging track	16	33
Racquetball	8	19
Room service	22	17
Coffee shop	53	39
Dining room	14	22
Cocktail lounge	41	33
Business center	47	18
FAX	39	9
Laundry/valet	8	11
4. Guest questionnaire:		
Returns	13	11
Responses (Overall ratings):		
Excellent	21	14
Very good	27	12
Good	33	27
Fair	12	34
Poor	7	13

membership directories and direct personal contact with hotel and travel arrangement decision makers within the community and feeder cities.

The following checklist pinpoints some of the main sources (both primary and secondary) that are used by most hotels for most types of business:

- Current guests
- Previous guests
- Inquiries and cancellations
- Friends and business acquaintances of current guests
- Credit-card holders
- Telephone directories
- Special phone directories (business and governmental agency listings)
- Professional directories
- Club, organization, and association membership lists
- Travel agents, hotel representatives, tour operators, and transportation companies
- Local business firms
- Local clubs and organizations
- Corporate directories (some of which are grouped according to annual company earnings)

PROFIT CENTER SOURCES

Most hotels have four main *profit centers* for which sources of business need to be researched:

1. Rooms
2. Food
3. Beverage

4. Other departmental (laundry and valet, telephone, recreation and entertainment, store rentals)

Within these revenue-producing areas are numerous subdivisions. Food sales, for instance, could involve revenue potentials from:

- Coffee shops
- Regular (family-style) restaurants
- Specialty or theme dining rooms
- Formal dining rooms
- Room service
- Food functions from local civic and service clubs
- Takeout (retail) sales
- Takeout box-lunch sales for guests (especially in resorts)
- Off-premise catering (offices, industrial plants, and homes)
- On-premise food store (minimart) sales
- Lobby and floor corridor vending machine sales
- In-room minibar sales

One procedure to pinpoint both markets and sources would be to prepare a simple chart to be used initially as a guide for each of the preceding subdivisions. An example for *food functions* is shown in Figure 4–5. This procedure could then be followed for each of the other food outlets listed above and then continued for each of the other profit centers: rooms, beverage, and other departmental income.

To further expand the initial guide, names, addresses, and phone and fax numbers could be added for the key contacts for each line item. Sounds like a lot of work, perhaps. But this is one of the procedures that must be followed in setting up and maintaining sales office records and files, especially when starting up a system for a new or expanded property.

FIGURE 4–5 Market and source checklist guide for food function business. A separate chart could be prepared for each of the key profit centers, with the markets listed in the left-hand column and the applicable sources for each selected from the "menu" in the right-hand column. This could then be further extended by including specific contact names, addresses, and so on, for each source.

Markets	Sources
• Conventions and other group meetings • Local clubs and organizations • Business firms • Local receptions, parties, and dances • Political meetings • Testimonial dinners • Reunions • Receptions and weddings • Confirmations and bar mitzvahs	• Previous function holders • Civic and service club officers • Local business executives • Officers of hobby groups, stamp clubs, bridge and chess clubs • Local political heads • School, university, and alumni officials • Priests, ministers, and rabbis • Bridal secretaries and bridal store owners

MARKET SEGMENT SOURCES

The hotel profit center analysis is by no means the only method of researching sources in an organized manner. Another approach is to look at the major market classifications and determine the sources of business for each of those that will be actively solicited.

Sales office records are often maintained according to the major market classifications, especially where the account executives are specialists, as described earlier in this section. The sources for business would be grouped according to the segment. In Chapter 5 we provide examples of general profiles and business sources for the individual business traveler, the individual leisure traveler, and the group leisure market. But a variation on the individual business traveler source profile is illustrated in Figure 4-6, to offer an example at this time.

SOURCES FOR PERSONAL AND PROFESSIONAL IMPROVEMENT

In addition to researching sources of profitable business, today's hotel sales executive must actively be a "student of the business" in order to be successful both professionally and personally. The industry keeps changing virtually overnight:

- New products and services come on line constantly.
- Customer needs and wants seem to change daily.

FIGURE 4-6 General target market source checklist.

Sources of Business

TARGET MARKET: Individual Business Traveler

1. On the road "undecided" travelers
2. Corporate traffic managers (NPTA)
3. Travel agents
4. Chamber of commerce
5. Industrial firms listings
6. Office building locator boards
7. Convention attendees or convention overflow (delegates are also often individual business travelers)
8. Other overflow
9. Leisure market travelers (vacationers or people traveling to attend sports events, cultural attractions, and other area recreation are also business travelers at other times)
10. Group leisure travelers (those on tour buses might have an occasion to revisit your area on company business)
11. Sales calls on companies in the area to determine their housing needs (i.e., visiting executives from "home office," salespeople, buyers, etc.)
12. Real estate and relocation firms
13. Airlines and car rental companies
14. Advertising in newspapers, magazines, "in-flight" magazines, radio, and TV; also through PR and publicity
15. Tie-ins with reservations systems; 800 numbers
16. Hotel representation offices in key market cities
17. Recommendations and referrals ("radiation advertising")
18. Repeat customers (the best and most cost-efficient source of all!)

FIGURE 4–7 Hospitality trade associations generally hold an annual convention as well as regional and local seminars and workshops. These educational programs offer excellent opportunities for industry executives (and in many instances also student attendees) to gain information and exchange ideas relating to industry techniques, tools, and methods. In some meetings, discussion sessions are taped and reprinted in journals and other publications, to add to their educational value. (Courtesy of the Council on Hotel, Restaurant, and Institutional Education.)

- New technology may make today's procedures obsolete by tomorrow morning.
- New and sharper competition can spring up across the street virtually over a weekend (modular construction).
- The personnel entering the industry—both buyers and sellers—are better educated and trained than their immediate predecessors.*

So what can one do to "keep on top" of all these changes? Fortunately, there is plenty of resource material available to those in hotel sales and marketing to constantly update and increase their knowledge and professionalism.

Among the chief sources for developing one's personal and professional skills and abilities are:

- Trade association conventions, seminars, and workshops (see Figure 4–7). (Also see Appendix D for a list of key hospitality trade associations, most of whom hold annual meetings and many of whom hold additional buyer–seller meetings, such as the annual HSMAI-ICP conference of the Hotel Sales and Marketing Association International and the Insurance Conference Planners Association.)

---

*All of this seems to remind us of the old saying about three types of people: those who watch things happen; those who make things happen; and those who ask, "Hey, what happened?"

FIGURE 4-8 Cornell University's summer program at the School of Hotel Administration's Center for Professional Development is one of a growing number of institutions offering to those in the industry educational opportunities in an academic surrounding. Over 14 of the 80-week-long courses are on sales and marketing topics. (Courtesy of Cornell University's School of Hotel Administration.)

- Hotel school summer courses. The oldest and perhaps best known is the 7-week program at the Center for Professional Development at Cornell University (Figure 4-8). Selected CPD courses are also presented at other times "off campus" throughout the world.
- Graduate school programs specifically designed for those in industry. (Additional information is presented on the following pages under the heading "Executive Master's Programs.")
- Hotel-school-sponsored symposiums open to both students and industry.
- Hotel-school-sponsored educational meetings between industry executives and educators.
- Industry certification programs, such as the Certified Hotel Administrator (CHA) offered by the American Hotel and Motel Association and Certified Hotel Sales Executive (CHSE) administered by the Hotel Sales and Marketing Association International, as well as customer organizations that have programs such as Certified Meeting Professional (CMP) and Certified Travel Counselor (CTC).*
- Trade magazines from both the lodging industry and those representing customer groups. (See the list in the Appendix.)
- Sales and marketing textbooks and pamphlets, both general and those specifically oriented to the hospitality industry.
- Training programs available from chains and franchise organizations.

*This can additionally offer an excellent opportunity for *cross-training*. We know of at least one person who is a CHA, CHSE, and CMP; another who is a CHA, CHSE, and CTC.

EXECUTIVE MASTER'S PROGRAMS

A recent development relating to sources for educational opportunities is the introduction of master's degree programs tailored to those in industry. These are specifically directed at candidates who ordinarily would have difficulty taking the traditional year or two off from their full-time jobs to pursue an advanced degree.

A pioneer in this type of program is the School of Food, Hotel, and Tourism Management at the Rochester Institute of Technology, Rochester, New York (see Figure 4–9). RIT's "Executive Leader Master's Program Option" in Hospitality–Tourism Management requires a total of only eight weeks on-campus residency during a two-year period of concentrated study. Credit toward a Master of Science degree is also given for industry experience.

THE GUEST AS A SOURCE

To conclude this chapter properly, we should bring you back to the main subject: sources as they relate to the securing of business. It has been mentioned several times that hotel guests are themselves an excellent source for additional business. It is relatively easy to obtain full information on your *room guests,* since they must fill out registration cards. In some operations, particu-

FIGURE 4–9   The Rochester Institute of Technology offers an "accelerated graduate degree program option that has been specifically designed and tailored for Hospitality–Tourism professionals who want to gain the skills they need to excel without interrupting their careers to earn it." Applicants must have a minimum of three years of relevant business experience. (Courtesy of Rochester Institute of Technology, School of Food, Hotel, and Tourism Management.)

The premise which guides the executive leader instructional strategies is that: "Our executive leaders are colleagues in training rather than students who will someday be colleagues."

RIT Executive Leader Master's Program Option

Only eight weeks to completion. With all prerequisites in place, two intensive consecutive two-week summers in June and August will earn you the credit hours you need for your master's degree. The 1991 summer session will be held June 10–21 and August 5–17.

Additional courses that may be needed to satisfy degree requirements are offered through remote delivery as well as individual instructional modules. This long-distance learning approach significantly minimizes the interruptions and intrusions of attending traditional on-campus classes.

Credit for professional experience with approval from department chairperson.

Based on a "service quality" philosophy with financial and managerial applications relevant to service-oriented enterprises.

Theoretical and practical principles and skills that can be applied immediately as solutions and remedies in the workplace.

Dedicated exclusively to hospitality–tourism professionals.

larly resorts, additional detailed information is recorded on guest history forms, which readily lend themselves to computerization.

You can also directly ask guests to suggest other names: friends, relatives, neighbors, business associates, social contacts, and others. One way of doing this is by handing a questionnaire to guests as they are standing in line to register, especially when they are known to represent a specific market segment.

You could have different questionnaires for different types of guests. If, for example, the majority of those checking in on a Monday morning are primarily individual business travelers, the questionnaire might ask for the names of the company executives responsible for planning meetings, or those in charge of social activities or involved with corporate relocations.

On the other hand, if the guests are vacationers, the questionnaire might ask for the names and addresses of friends and relations who might similarly enjoy the property's recreational facilities and social activities.

The so-called "manager's cocktail party" (now often replaced by the "manager's breakfast" because of potential third-party liability considerations) is fairly common in certain sections of North America among certain types of operations. This, too, can be a particularly effective source for generating referral business, especially where the guests are primarily business travelers. In some U.S. and Canadian hotels, breakfast may be included within the room rate, similar to what is done in many European countries.

But what about hotels that do substantial food and beverage volume from the local business community? How can they get the names of prospects who are obviously familiar with part of the property's facilities but who may never have stayed overnight?

There are a number of ways of tracking this source. One of the oldest but still one of the most effective is the collection of business cards which are dropped into a "fishbowl" located either at the front desk or at the entrance to the coffee shop, dining room, or lounge. A periodic drawing for a complimentary lunch or dinner or a weekend stay, or a prize such as an attaché case, is often used as a response-generating incentive.

RECOMMENDATIONS AND REFERRALS

Recommendations and referrals can be substantial cost-effective business sources because they are "guest generated" (i.e., the customer is your salesperson) and require little direct expenditure.

These can include:

- Individual travelers referring their friends and neighbors to you
- A satisfied corporate meeting planner in charge of training sessions favorably mentioning you to other company training directors
- The same corporate executive recommending you to other officials within the company as a site to consider for meetings of their own departments
- A happy association convention planner recommending you to his or her counterpart in other associations
- Attendees at conventions recommending your property to the meeting and social activities planners of their own companies or firms
- Recommendations by convention speakers, panelists, entertainers, exhibitors, and so on.

- Local contacts within the community: everyone from civic and social club officers and members to restaurant owners, gas station operators, taxicab drivers, and many others in a position to recommend or steer business your way

THIRD-PARTY SOURCES

Another segment of sources consists of third-party (or intermediary) individuals, firms, and organizations, such as:

- Local convention and visitors bureau
- Chamber of commerce
- Travel agents (both retailers and wholesalers)
- Tour brokers
- Transportation company executives
- Multiple management company administrators
- Hotel representation firms

Since the potential business available from these sources is generated largely through direct selling approaches, they are covered in more detail in Chapter 7.

DIRECTORY AND LISTING SOURCES

To conclude this chapter, let's develop a little scenario where you have been appointed the sales director of a property which will open in a year.

One of your primary responsibilities will be to set up the files, records, and systems of soliciting, booking, servicing, and reselling the appropriate mix of business. The physical aspects of establishing a sales office will be covered in Chapter Six, "Set Up." But while this administrative organizing is being done, you will also start determining specific sources of business, contacting them, and setting up specific files and records for each.

It is essential that a hotel have an appropriate amount of business "on the books" prior to the day it physically opens. There are many organizations whose lead time for selecting sites for their conventions and meetings may be one or more years. For leisure travel, many vacationers make plans six months to a year or more in advance. Contracts with companies for corporate business travel are generally drawn up on an annual basis.

So, how would you, the newly hired sales director, in essence "start from scratch?"

If the hotel is part of a chain or franchise system, the regional and national sales office can be of considerable assistance to providing sources for leads and contacts. But affiliated or independent, one of your primary jobs will be to identify sources and actively solicit business from them.

Among the key sources for developing an initial set of prospect lists are:

1. Commercial mailing lists.
2. Directories of business decision-makers.
3. Advertising in trade and consumer publications.

Very specifically, the purposes and objectives of contacting the sources of business will be to:

1. Create awareness of the property before it opens.
2. Establish an image and gain recognition.
3. Directly contact, or stimulate inquiries from, the appropriate business sources.
4. Convert such contacts into bookings.

Commercial Mailing Lists

For many, one of the easier ways of starting out is to obtain mailing lists from commercial direct mail houses. Lists are generally two main types: (1) *rented*, which is a one-time use of the labels, and (2) *purchased*, where you in effect "own" the list and can use it as often as you desire. A third alternative, which involves a more substantial investment, is to ask the mail order house to compile a "custom-made" list for you, based on specific parameters: for example, 300 companies headquartering in the northeastern part of the United States who hold training meetings in the New England States, who prefer to meet in resorts during the week, and whose average size group is 50 or fewer persons.

Lists can be purchased by category (e.g., insurance company meeting planners, corporate training directors) and often can be subdivided by geographic area or by zip code groupings. While such a source may often initially seem easier as far as securing names, the list is basically composed of "suspects," not "prospects." It will then be up to you as sales director to do a mailing (usually a return postcard), asking key questions regarding the size of group, type of meetings, geographic and time preferences or constraints, and name/address of key decision-maker.

Another source of mailing lists would be the membership rosters of customer organizations. Many associations offer their membership list on labels for purchase; in other cases, one must join the organization to have access to the list. In addition, many groups print a directory of their membership, which may be (but not always) available for purchase.

A listing of trade organizations, including customer groups, appears in the Appendix.

Directories

There are a number of directories that list business sources for the major market classifications. A few representative examples in the group business category include:

1. *The Encyclopedia of Associations,* Gale Research Company, Detroit, Michigan, which lists and describes over 14,000 national trade and professional associations within 17 different categories.
2. *National Trade and Professional Associations,* Columbia Books, Inc., Washington, DC, lists 6,200 active trade and professional organizations and labor unions.
3. *The Salesman's Guide,* New York, publishes three separate directories listing corporate meeting planners, association meeting planners, and premium, incentive, and travel buyers (see Figure 4–10).

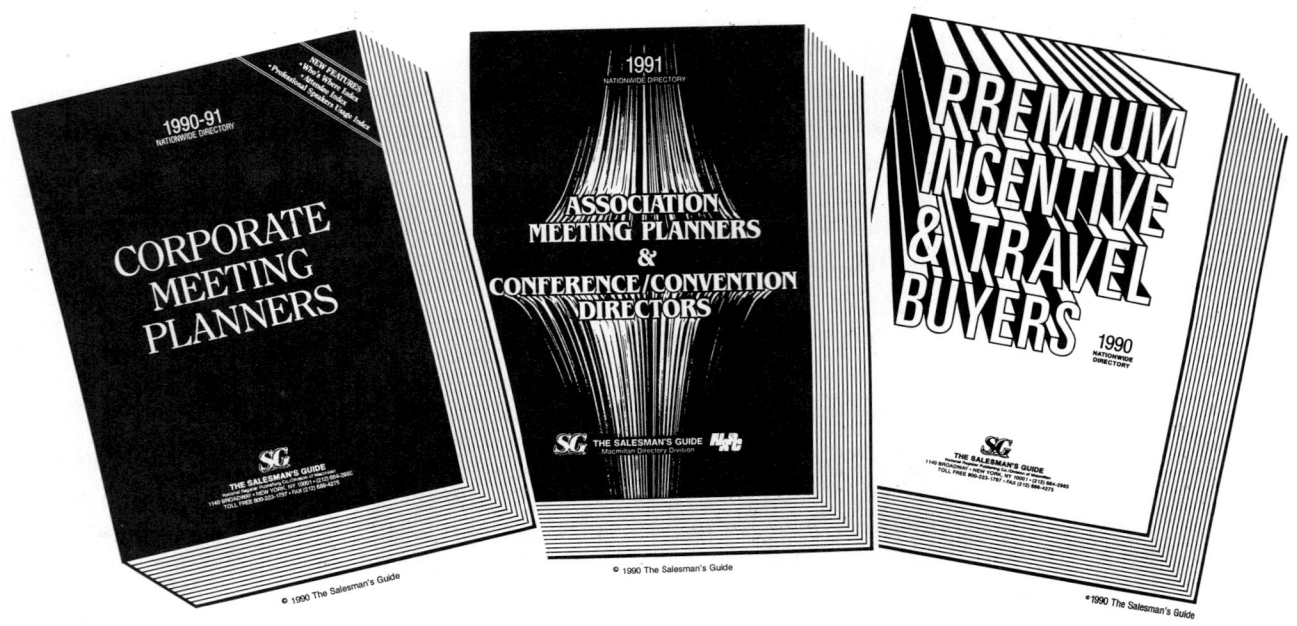

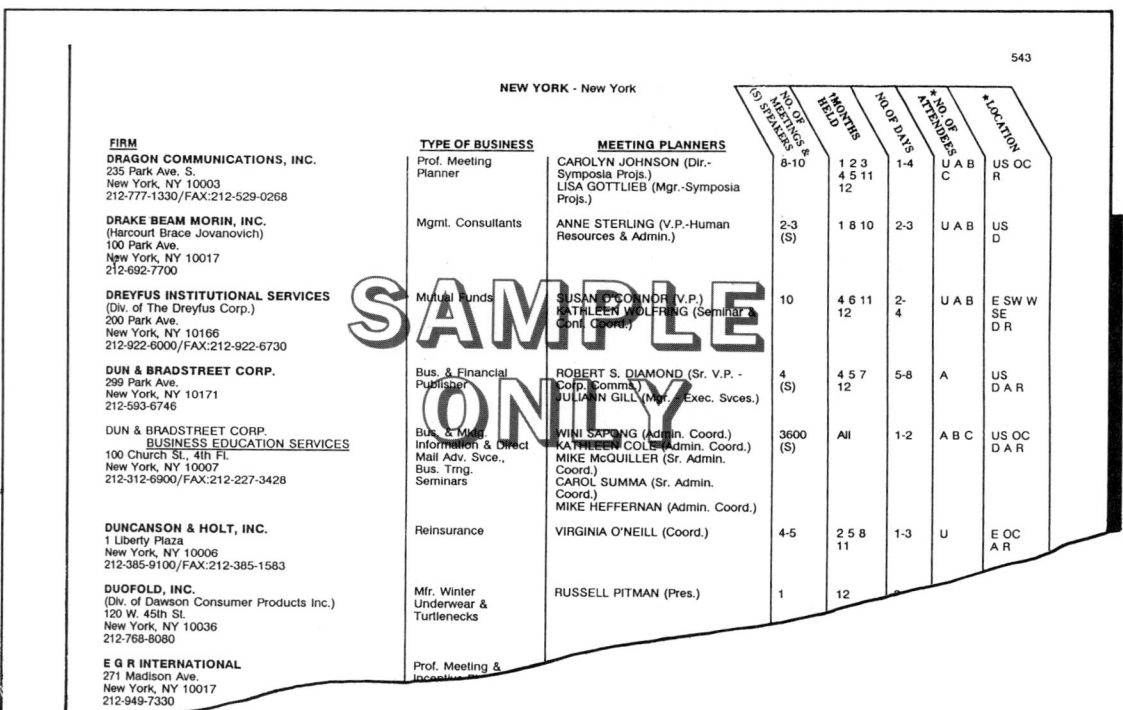

543

NEW YORK - New York

FIRM	TYPE OF BUSINESS	MEETING PLANNERS	NO. OF MEETINGS & (S) SPEAKERS	MONTHS HELD	NO. OF DAYS	* NO. OF ATTENDEES	* LOCATION
DRAGON COMMUNICATIONS, INC. 235 Park Ave. S. New York, NY 10003 212-777-1330/FAX:212-529-0268	Prof. Meeting Planner	CAROLYN JOHNSON (Dir.-Symposia Projs.) LISA GOTTLIEB (Mgr.-Symposia Projs.)	8-10	1 2 3 4 5 11 12	1-4	U A B C	US OC R
DRAKE BEAM MORIN, INC. (Harcourt Brace Jovanovich) 100 Park Ave. New York, NY 10017 212-692-7700	Mgml. Consultants	ANNE STERLING (V.P.-Human Resources & Admin.)	2-3 (S)	1 8 10	2-3	U A B	US D
DREYFUS INSTITUTIONAL SERVICES (Div. of The Dreyfus Corp.) 200 Park Ave. New York, NY 10166 212-922-6000/FAX:212-922-6730	Mutual Funds	SUSAN O'CONNOR (V.P.) KATHLEEN WOLFRING (Seminar & Conf. Coord.)	10	4 6 11 12	2- 4	U A B	E SW W SE D R
DUN & BRADSTREET CORP. 299 Park Ave. New York, NY 10171 212-593-6746	Bus. & Financial Publisher	ROBERT S. DIAMOND (Sr. V.P.-Corp. Comms.) JULIANN GILL (Mgr.-Exec. Svces.)	4 (S)	4 5 7 12	5-8	A	US D A R
DUN & BRADSTREET CORP. <u>BUSINESS EDUCATION SERVICES</u> 100 Church St., 4th Fl. New York, NY 10007 212-312-6900/FAX:212-227-3428	Bus. & Mktg. Information & Direct Mail Adv. Svce., Bus. Trng. Seminars	WINI SAPONG (Admin. Coord.) KATHLEEN COLE (Admin. Coord.) MIKE McQUILLER (Sr. Admin. Coord.) CAROL SUMMA (Sr. Admin. Coord.) MIKE HEFFERNAN (Admin. Coord.)	3600 (S)	All	1-2	A B C	US OC D A R
DUNCANSON & HOLT, INC. 1 Liberty Plaza New York, NY 10006 212-385-9100/FAX:212-385-1583	Reinsurance	VIRGINIA O'NEILL (Coord.)	4-5	2 5 8 11	1-3	U	E OC A R
DUOFOLD, INC. (Div. of Dawson Consumer Products Inc.) 120 W. 45th St. New York, NY 10036 212-768-8080	Mfr. Winter Underwear & Turtlenecks	RUSSELL PITMAN (Pres.)	1	12			
E G R INTERNATIONAL 271 Madison Ave. New York, NY 10017 212-949-7330	Prof. Meeting & Incentive						

FIGURE 4–10 These three publications are among the leading resources available to hospitality sales executives for the purpose of researching, qualifying, and prospecting the three main markets of group business. The Directory of Corporate Meeting Planners lists approximately 18,400 individuals responsible for planning off-site meetings for over 12,000 companies; The Directory of Association Meeting Planners provides information on over 8,200 national associations that hold conventions and smaller meetings on a regular basis; and The Directory of Premium, Incentive & Travel Buyers contains over 20,000 executives responsible for purchasing all categories of premium and incentive programs, including incentive travel, for 11,400 firms. (Courtesy of *The Salesman's Guide,* Macmillan Directory Division, New York, NY.)

While these reference sources provide more information on each group, you will still need to contact likely prospects for screening and qualifying.

Advertising

Although the subject of advertising, including direct mail, will be covered in Chapter 8 "Support," we'll take a quick look at it here as it relates to the topic of sources. It differs from the other two major source categories in that the responses generated from advertising initially flow from the potential business source to the hotel, rather than the other way around.

Here, too, you as the sales director at the new property will be involved in selecting publications and other media for placing "pre-opening campaign" advertising. These could be considered sources for conveying both "tell and sell" messages to specific audiences. Much of this type of advertising will include a coupon or "tip-in" reply card to stimulate responses.

The Appendix contains a listing of trade publications, grouped according to "hotel/restaurant," "customer," "travel," and "consumer." In addition to advertising, some of the customer publications, such as "Meetings and Conventions" and "Successful Meetings," publish annual directories of hotel listings, which offer an additional opportunity for exposure to likely business sources.

Another example of combined advertising/directory listing opportunities, especially for those seeking to contact travel agents and corporate travel directors, is the *Hotel & Travel Index* and the *Hotel & Travel Index ABC International Division*, published by the Reed Travel Group, Secaucus, New Jersey. The 1991 editions reach 300,000 North American travel agents and corporate travel planners and 250,000 worldwide agents and corporate planners respectively.

Once the property opens, the procedures just described do not cease. Your involvement with business sources will be one of constant searching, qualifying, updating, and reevaluating, as groups change in size and decision-making criteria, new organizations are created, others merge, and new decision-makers replace the ones with whom you previously worked.

PLAYING DETECTIVE

With all this positive prying and snooping, it sounds as if a hotel sales executive must also be a detective. Quite possibly, for one of the key terms used in developing business sources is "looking for leads." Once the leads have been uncovered, they are "suspects" until they have been screened for business potentials. Once screened or qualified, they are grouped into various "prospect" classifications and categories, a process called *segmentation*, the subject of the following chapter.

five

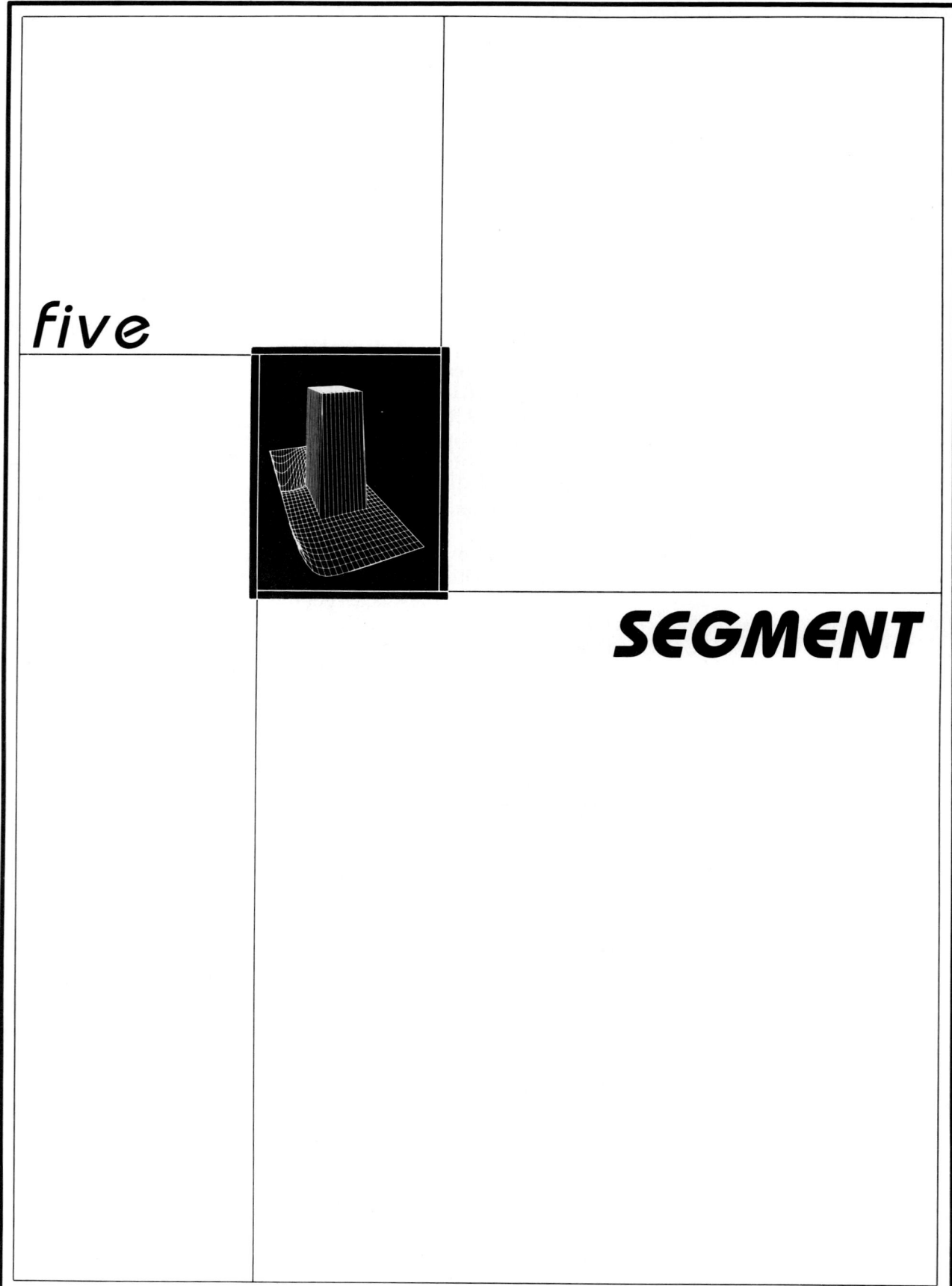

SEGMENT

While gathering facts and information on the property, its competition, and the marketplace, one cannot help noticing that such data usually seem to fall into a number of different groupings. There appear to be numerous types of hotel operations, many distinct multifaceted competitors, and seemingly endless types of market segments. Prior to the 1950s, such classifications were relatively simple:

1. Hotels were either *city* or *resort, deluxe* or *commercial.*
2. Their guests were either *transient* or *permanent, individual* or *group.*
3. Travel was either for business (*commercial*) or for leisure (*vacation*).

PRODUCT SEGMENTATION

The birth of diversified product segmentation can be traced to the development of the *motel* concept in the 1950s. Previously known (and in most cases, not too positively) as motor courts, new variations came about with the rapid increase in highway development and motor travel.

Motels, motor inns, motor lodges, motor hotels, and combinations such as "hotel and motor inn" attempted to focus on variations within a product segment. Sometimes the differences were not too clear. But conceptually, for example, the motor lodge was primarily rustic in nature, the motor inn emphasized food service, and a high-rise motor hotel was a standard hotel that provided generally free on-premise parking.

This concept has been further refined as it relates to other examples of other types of properties. The *budget hotel,* for example, has its subclassifications:

- Economy budget
- Limited-service economy
- Full-service economy
- Luxury budget (not to be confused with "deluxe economy"!)

Today, there are numerous ways of segmenting the basic lodging product, depending on the purposes behind such classification. Hotels can initially be grouped according to *location:*

- Center city
- Suburban
- Rural
- Airport

- Highway
- Mountain resort
- Seashore resort
- Offshore island resort

They can also be classified according to *service**:

- Economy (or budget)
- Standard
- Deluxe

---

*This is not to be confused with the *quality* of the product, since you can have a super, top-of-the-line, limited-service economy facility.

Pricing offers another means of product differentiation:

- Economy or budget
- Midprice range
- Deluxe
- Luxury

Style provides yet another method of classifying lodging accommodations, particularly some of the more nontraditional types of operations. On the international level, one may especially find chateaus, palaces and castles, private mansions, and seaside villas converted into hotel facilities. At the other end, one may also find hunting lodges and fishing camps (many of them "rustically deluxe") which offer housing, full food and beverage operations, and even meeting facilities.

In many areas of the world outside North America, there is a fairly standardized one-star to five-star grade classification system, generally based on the quantity and quality of services and amenities as well as physical aspects. In some countries, these ratings may be established by a government agency or other official evaluation body. These star classifications are often prominently featured in advertising, as illustrated in Figure 5–1. In the United States, there

FIGURE 5–1 This hotel chain magazine ad specifically indicates the three-, four-, and five-star classifications of its various properties. In many rating systems, the differences are based on the availability and the style of specific features (number and types of suites, type of dining cuisine) are not necessarily reflective of the quality of the available facilities and service. (Courtesy of Sokos Hotels, Helsinki, Finland.)

are a number of private rating and award systems: the American Automobile Association's Diamond ratings, the Mobil Travel Guide's Star ratings, *Meetings and Conventions* magazine's Gold Key awards, and *Successful Meetings* magazine's Pinnacle awards.

But we are not yet done with segmenting the product. You can then further divide the types of properties according to their predominant physical characteristics, such as *size* and *layout*. You could then come up with such distinctions as:

1. B & B (bed and breakfast)
2. Single-story low-rise
3. Single- or double-story courtyard
4. All-suite
5. Conference center
6. Country club
7. Casino hotel/resort
8. Multiuse facility

The multiuse property (also called mixed-use facility or multiple-use complex) is an increasingly popular adaptation of combined product packaging. In resorts, this is often a combination of transient, time-sharing (interval ownership), condominium, and single-family housing. In city operations, this can be a combination of hotel, restaurant, shopping center, recreation, and entertainment outlets, all under one roof.

An example of the evolution of a multiple product line on the chain/franchise level can be seen in the Quality International system (which in the summer of 1990 was renamed Choice Hotels International). It started out with one product line, named Quality Courts, dropped that name, and expanded into four main types of physical products (see Figure 5–2).

With further acquisitions of three additional systems, Choice Hotels International redesigned its corporate logo to reflect its new name and its seven major product lines, as shown in Figure 5–3. In addition, some of the segments, such as Clarion, have their own unique product lines, such as conference centers and the Clarion Carriage House Inns. On the global scene, Choice operates Calinda in Mexico and is affiliated with Quality Inns in Australia and New Zealand.

It is interesting to observe that a number of hotel systems that originally started out with the intent of offering one single product type nationwide, have now joined the product-segment "bandwagon." The Holiday Inn system now

FIGURE 5–2 Corporate logos. (Courtesy of Quality International.

Quality International

Inns · Hotels · Suites · Resorts

FIGURE 5-3   New corporate logo reflecting Quality International name change to Choice Hotels International.

includes Garden Court, Express, and Crowne Plaza. Days Inns similarly developed Days Hotels, Days Suites, and Daystops, in addition to the original Inns.

Another example of brand name segmentation (as well as illustrating the current practices of mergers, acquisitions, and sales) is Howard Johnson. Originally positioning itself within a wide-banded midpriced lodging tier, it developed into five main variations (see Figure 5-4).

FIGURE 5-4   Brand name segmentation.

ACQUISITIONS AND MERGERS

To further illustrate how extensive product-line acquisitioning can get, Howard Johnson was then acquired by Prime Motor Inns, which also prior to the summer of 1990, owned or operated the Ramada and Rodeway systems, as well as individual properties bearing Sheraton, Holiday, and other franchise system names. During the summer of 1990, Quality acquired Rodeway, and Howard Johnson and Ramada were purchased by Blackstone Capital.

In the meantime, Accor S.A., a European system based in Paris, bought the American budget chain Motel 6 to parallel its European Accor Formula 1 budget hotels. In addition to now having both American and European economy segments, Accor has such varied product lines as Sofitel (luxury), Ibis and Urbis (midpriced), and Novotel and Mercure (aimed at the business traveler).

COMPANY EVOLUTION

Some companies, such as Marriott, may have started out with a single product line (high-rise hotels in the Washington, D.C. area), but as market segments developed and grew in terms of purchasing power, additional product lines evolved. Currently, the Marriott system also includes "specialty brands" such as Courtyards by Marriott, Marriott Suites, Residence Inns, and Fairfield Inns. Each specifically appeals to certain types of facility users.

The key implication of such product segmentation is the current philosophy followed by most chain and franchise companies. In effect they are saying, "We can offer something for everyone. And as people move up the business or personal lifestyle ladder, we can meet their new and perhaps more upgraded requirements and wishes with a variety of distinctively different product lines."

PERCEPTION SEGMENTATION

Most of the preceding methods of segmenting properties were largely on the basis of physical or price differentials. Within these categories there is yet another system of subclassification, based on such intangible factors as ambience, atmosphere, operating philosophies, and perceptual distinctions. These can be important to the decision maker, particularly when faced with selecting one property from a number of possibilities, all of which could equally solve the buyer's specific physical needs (number of rooms, function space, meeting equipment, availability of dates, rates, etc.).

These perceptual factors also become important in personal selling as well as media advertising, since they can provide those descriptive adjectives and adverbs that can help "position" the property in the minds of the listener or reader. The following list (in alphabetical order) offers some of these descriptive "modifiers," compiled from various headlines in hotel newspaper and magazine ads:

- Accessible
- Affordable
- Airy
- Captivating
- Charming
- Classy
- Comfortable
- Cozy
- Distinguished
- Elegant

- "European"
- Fashionable
- Friendly
- Functional
- Historic
- Informal
- "International"
- Intimate
- Intriguing
- Prestigious

- Professional
- Quality-conscious
- Remarkable
- Renowned
- Rustic
- Spirited
- Sumptuous
- Unique
- Unspoiled
- Victorian

And we must include those two ubiquitous terms found in so many ads in convention and group business travel planner's magazines: "conventional" and "unconventional."*

By now, all these classifications and subclassifications must be mind-boggling. Indeed, there is much confusion since there are no standard systems of classification nomenclature. We recently saw a chart in a magazine comparing the number of "convention hotels" in a given area with the number of "resort hotels," "highway hotels," and "suburban properties."

But resorts, highway, and suburban properties can also function as convention hotels. So this seemed akin to the old cliché of "comparing apples with oranges," and thus the figures (for whatever purposes they were being collected) were relatively meaningless. The practical utilization of product segmentation for sales and marketing applications must be related to one of the dominant "buzzwords" of the 1980s: *market segmentation*.

GUEST PROFILING

The forerunner of what we call market segmentation was an internal process known as *guest profiling*. In the early days of hotel sales promotion, many people were hired as sales representatives or sales managers (very often with little, if any, hotel experience) and told to "go out and get us lots of business from the public." This "public" was composed of anybody and everybody presumed to have any need or desire for hotel facilities and services—in other words, just about anyone.

Starting in the 1950s, however, hotels began seriously to track the information gathered internally from guest registration cards (and in some of the larger resorts, from the more fully detailed guest history cards), as well as from other sources, such as:

- Reservation inquiries
- Rooming lists
- Guest folios
- Convention history reports
- Reservation department and accounting office reports

*Without making any comments pro or con, here are two samples: "For an Unconventional Convention" and "We Offer More Than Just a Conventional Location."

Basics of Guest Profiling

Who: an analysis of guests by type: individual business travelers, families, tour groups, meeting delegates, etc.

What: an analysis of each of the above in terms of age, sex, occupation, marital status, income, and prior travel experience

Where: a geographic breakdown of origin by city, state, and country

When: time of arrival and departure analyses for each type of guest, according to day of week, week of month, month or season of the year

Why: the reasons that drew each type of guest to both the area and the property

How: a means of transportation analysis: car, bus, train, plane, including names of specific carriers and points of origin

---

FIGURE 5–5 Main categories of guest profile data that can be readily obtained from a hotel's internal records.

- Sales office records and booking reports
- Observation (guest-contact employees can very often offer firsthand information on customer trends)*

When tracking, some sales-minded executives began noticing that certain patterns were forming. First, the general types of data could initially be sorted into six major groups using the key words "who, what, where, when, why, and how" (see Figure 5-5). From these data, general market profiles could be drawn up which pinpointed the main characteristics of (and highlighted the differences between) various segments of the public. This could then be supplemented with working sales information such as the general *sources* of business for each segment. Specific market profiles could then be developed for each major customer grouping, as illustrated in Figures 5-6 to 5-8.

FIGURE 5–6 General market profile of the individual business traveler.

INDIVIDUAL BUSINESS TRAVELER

General Profile

Traditionally, the primary market for a majority of properties, regardless of size or location, with the exception of total leisure resort destinations

In North America, generally travels by car or plane or may take a plane and rent a car at the destination ("fly–drive" combination). In other areas of the world, train travel may be more prevalent, combined with car rentals at stopover points

As a group, represents the most knowledgeable and sophisticated group of customers

The woman business traveler becoming increasingly important; may represent the majority of business travelers by the turn of the century

Travel patterns no longer restricted to the center of the city; may also utilize airport or suburban properties

---

*Some progressive hotels were doing this type of data collecting as early as the 1920s and 1930s, but it was not a prevalent industry practice until the 1950s.

Length of stay greatly reduced from what it was several decades ago; may stay only one or two nights rather than a full week in a given area, and may even travel to three or four cities in two days or less using commuter airlines

In a hurry; wants quick check-in and check-out without having to stand in line; looks for fast meal service, especially at breakfast

Desires quick and efficient valet and laundry service

Tends to dress in a more informal, casual manner (no ties in dining room, etc.)

Expects color TV and air-conditioning

Looks increasingly for special services and amenities relating to business activities, such as secretarial and translation services, availability of telex, cable, and FAX, rooms with special writing desks and proper lighting, phones with two separate lines, and knowledgeable concierge

Generally uses credit cards for payment; increasingly looks for "instant check-out" procedures

Business Sources

Cost of personal calls and telephone calls usually prevents direct solicitation of the business traveler on an individual basis. In larger organizations, contact is usually made with a company passenger traffic manager or corporate travel agent, who is responsible for volume purchases on a contract basis. In smaller companies, contact with key secretaries can prove productive.

Membership list of the National Passenger Traffic Association (NPTA)

Real estate and relocation agencies

Industrial firms listings

Office building and industrial park locator boards

Telephone directory "yellow pages"

Telephone directory "blue pages" (for government business travel)

Newspaper, magazine, radio, and TV advertising, to promote name and image to individual travelers, especially those making their own arrangements; also, advertising in in-flight magazines on airlines from key feeder cities

Airline and car rental company contacts

Tie-ins with reservations systems; 800 numbers

Hotel representation offices in key market cities

Contacts with local companies to determine housing needs of visiting executives from the "home office" as well as those of other corporate visitors, such as dealers, distributors, and buyers

Overflow business from nearby properties

Recommendations and referrals

Repeat customers (the best and most cost-efficient source of all)

FIGURE 5–6 (cont.)

FIGURE 5–7 General market profile of the individual leisure traveler.

INDIVIDUAL LEISURE TRAVELER

General Profile

An ever-increasingly important "growth" market due to longer vacations, long weekends (4-day workweeks in some industries and areas), extended holiday weekends, longer life expectancies, emphasis on health, fitness, and recreation, and increased disposable income.

Television, newspaper travel sections, consumer and travel magazines, and "peer pressure" from neighbors, friends, and associates ("keeping up with the Joneses") have whetted travel appetites. For many, travel has become a necessity rather than a luxury.

Mobility: Express highways (especially interstate systems), the rediscovery of train travel in the United States, charter buses (sometimes referred to as "land cruisers"), special discount fare programs for planes, and car rentals all help make travel easier.

Emphasis on health and physical fitness has stimulated business among spas, "country club"-style resorts, and other facilities offering a wide variety of indoor and outdoor activities.

New and remodeled city properties are built with a resort environment. Enclosed "skylight" recreational areas, exercise and fitness rooms, and other activities for the whole family on a year-round basis.

Leisure market increasingly moves "both ways." Suburban and rural residents can be attracted to city properties (particularly multiuse, "galleria-style" facilities), especially during weekends.

People increasingly want to do and participate. Creative promotions built around specific themes are increasingly popular. These can include packages relating to history, holidays, nationalities, sports, music, special events, etc.

Business Sources

The business traveler ("Come Back with the Family," "Stay Another Day," etc.)

The local market ("Run-Away" weekends, midweek "breakaways," "Run Away with Your Spouse," second honeymoons, and a wide variety of creative theme packages and promotions)

Specialized markets: families, senior citizens, student/faculty—especially through groups and organizations to which they belong

Convention attendees (extending the stay after the meeting is over)

Retail travel agents and wholesalers, especially those promoting individual packages for sporting, musical, and cultural events

Travel agent and travel writer familiarization trips (FAM trips), including those co-sponsored by airlines, tourist boards, and other destination sellers

Airlines, cruise ships, and other transportation companies

Virtually anyone—a tourist can be a banker or lawyer in sports clothes

FIGURE 5–7 *(cont.)*

FIGURE 5–8   General market profile of the group leisure traveler.

GROUP LEISURE MARKET

General Profile

The same reasons leading to increased individual leisure travel have also stimulated group leisure travel, especially among previously inexperienced travelers who may require "assurance and security" as motivators.

This market is very often "destination oriented": popular resort areas, historical sites, cultural centers, sporting events, fairs, and expositions.

Very often, members travel in groups to share common experiences, hobbies, and avocations. Fall foliage tours, bird-watching and other nature tours, cross-country hiking, and historical "pilgrimages" are some examples.

Particularly attractive to certain market segments: senior citizens, women's organizations, social and church groups, civic and service clubs.

Often thought of as composed primarily of the ''budget-conscious''; however, as indicated, group outings also appeal to those who like to share common interests, especially those of a specialized nature.

Business Sources

Retail travel agents and wholesalers

Tour operators and packagers

Airlines and charter bus companies

Organizations such as NTA (National Tour Association) and ABA (American Bus Association)

Church groups

Sports clubs (skiing, hiking, bowling, fishing, etc.)

Social and civic clubs

Ethnic organizations and nationality clubs

Political organizations

Senior citizen groups

Collectors' clubs

Hobby and avocational groups: camera clubs, amateur astronomy and geology clubs, etc.

High school and college class trips (both recreational and ''required'')

Association meeting planners (for both pre- and postconvention trips)

Corporate meeting planners, or others in a company, who may be responsible for social outings and other group leisure activities

Special creative programs originated by the property, incorporating rooms, meals, transfers, sightseeing, sports, and other recreational activities

FIGURE 5–8 *(cont.)*

VALUE PROFILING

Returning to the topic of guest profiles, these are specifically intended to identify the characteristics of a property's *current* market mix. The basic starting point is the determination of this market mix. In its simplest form, for a given time period, it is a percentage breakdown of business from the main types of

FIGURE 5–9 Market segment comparative value chart. This one is based on the number of room nights. Similar tracking can be made of the basis of room revenue, total expenditures, and so on.

1990 Center City Market Mix (by Percentage of Occupied Rooms)

	JAN.	FEB.	MAR.	APR.	MAY	JUNE	JULY	AUG.	SEPT.	OCT.	NOV.	DEC.
IBT	50	62	40	36	20	10	8	8	20	30	35	18
GBT	31	15	36	26	18	19	14	10	28	26	38	22
ILT	6	8	14	17	30	35	40	42	21	16	18	42
GLT	13	15	10	21	32	36	38	40	31	28	9	18

Key: IBT, Individual Business Traveler
         GBT, Group Business Traveler (Conventions and Meetings)
         ILT, Individual Leisure Traveler
         GLT, Group Leisure Traveler (Tour)

customer markets, the number of room nights, and total expenditures (including rooms, food and beverage, and other income).

But greater details could be produced from accounting and reservations offices records, which would offer the sales department information on where and when greater selling efforts should be directed. Figure 5-9 indicates the additional types of data that can be used practically in determining the value and the trends of each type of major customer group.

COMPARISON PROFILING

Guest profiles record primarily the characteristics of people currently utilizing the property. Sales and marketing people, however, need to know whether or not each segment is:

1. Making a positive contribution to the income of the property, especially in relation to the costs of securing and servicing that component.
2. Likely to expand in its potential value. In sales and marketing terminology, is a particular segment a "growth market"?

One method of determining this is to do an analysis of a given market segment for a specific period, comparing the information and data with the same period in previous years. This is usually done on a monthly basis, contrasting the current month with its counterparts five years ago, 10 years ago, or for each year within a given period. With computers, one cannot only readily plot this information but can easily generate graphs and charts that can visually pinpoint changes and trends.

Many of these changes can be especially meaningful when setting up the following year's marketing plans. Here are several examples, which might be derived from an analysis of a point-of-origin study:

1. *Print advertising:* An increase in the proportion of people using fly–drive packages, coupled with the increase in drop-in business from executives driving airport rentals, might suggest placing more advertising in in-flight magazines.
2. *Direct selling:* An increase in the number of business travelers coming from the New England area, and a corresponding decrease in arrivals from New York, might suggest a shifting of direct mail advertising and personal calls efforts into the New England industrial marketplace.

So when we discuss how to make sales calls in a later section, remember that the answer to *where* one makes calls, and *how often,* largely originates in the information obtained and analyzed from guest profile comparisons.

MARKET SEGMENTATION

During the formative 1950s and 1960s, sales-oriented hotel executives started to recognize the importance and practical use of the information gained by analyzing groups of people who shared common characteristics. As the general public became more educated and spent more time in leisure-time activities, it became evident that the sharing of interests, hobbies, and avocations also caused people to form common-interest organizations and associations. This in turn meant that it would be much easier and more cost-effective to reach this formerly unorganized leisure-oriented market since:

1. There were now easily identifiable decision makers who could decide on travel and hotel arrangements for large groups of individual leisure travelers.
2. Members of the leisure market attended conventions, educational seminars, and other forms of group meetings which related to their outside interests, and therefore offered additional group business opportunities.
3. Associations printed membership rosters, and direct-mail houses offered tailored lists according to interest areas. Hotels could thus utilize direct-mail advertising in a targeted manner and "talk the language of the reader."*
4. The emergence of many special-interest magazines, some of them for the general public, others published by various associations for their members, also allowed hotels to target advertising to those market segments it wished to develop for individual leisure travel.

SEGMENTATION MEASUREMENTS

As you can see from the preceding profiles, the basic segmentation process groups people primarily according to the primary reasons why they travel: leisure, business, health/fitness—and whether they are in groups or by themselves. But it soon became evident that there were other special characteristics of people within these broad groupings which were easily recognizable. More important, people having certain sets of characteristics viewed things differently than people with others.

Each subgrouping seemed to have different evaluation criteria when selecting destinations and accommodations. Additionally, they were either "turned on" or "turned off" by varying sales and servicing methods and seemed to "flock" together into specialized organizations, clubs, and societies. The subgroupings seemed to be based on either observable, tangible characteristics such as age, sex, and marital status (*demographics*) or on lifestyles (*psychographics*),† as shown in Figures 5–10 and 5–11.

Soon sales and marketing executives were talking about getting their fair share of the emerging growth market segments, such as the blue-collar worker, the youth market, the government business traveler, the international visitor, and the senior citizen, to name just a few. They were also seeking subgroupings within each segment that would be most attracted to, and compatible with, the profiles of their respective properties. This could be considered a practical variation of "The Matching Game."

The senior citizen market, for example, was largely ignored by most hotels until the late 1970s (with certain exceptions, such as St. Petersburg and Miami Beach, Florida). Today, it is one of the most studied, researched, and sought-after of all segments for both domestic and international travel.

*In Chapter 8 we describe how to prepare and use direct-mail advertising aimed at specific market segments.

†One of the key distinctions between "demographic" and "psychographic" characteristics is that demographics are generally more fixed and usually cannot be readily selected, changed, or altered according to one's personal desires. A person's psychographic profile, initially influenced by home, church, school, and other social settings and environments, can sometimes be dramatically changed. People can select and later adjust their lifestyles or can be influenced by outside forces. These influences can include peer pressure, the search for status, the persuasiveness of advertising, and changes in society in general.

KEY METHODS OF SEGMENTING THE MARKETING

- Demographics
- Psychographics
- Sensation-Seeking Scale

DEMOGRAPHICS

- Age
- Sex
- Marital Status
- Family Size
- Education
- Occupation or Profession
- Income
- Origin or Background
- Hotel or Travel Experience

PSYCHOGRAPHICS

- Extrovert or Introvert
- "Swinger" or Inhibited
- Futurist or Traditionalist
- Liberal or Conservative
- Trend Setter or "Keeper Up With The Joneses"
- Self-Confident or Non-Confident
- Active or Passive
- Participant or Spectator
- Impulsive or a Planner
- Allocentric or Psychocentric

SENSATION-SEEKING SCALE

- Thrill and Adventure Seeking
- Boredom Susceptibility
- Experience Seeking
- Disinhibition

FIGURE 5–10 Several methods of segmenting the market.

FIGURE 5–11 Psychographic matrix that is based on confidence and activity levels. The answers to specially prepared multiple-choice questions can be plotted within each of the four quadrants. The majority of responses falling within a specific quadrant indicate the general type of psychographic profile (i.e., active self-confident, passive non-confident, etc.)

Psychographic Profile

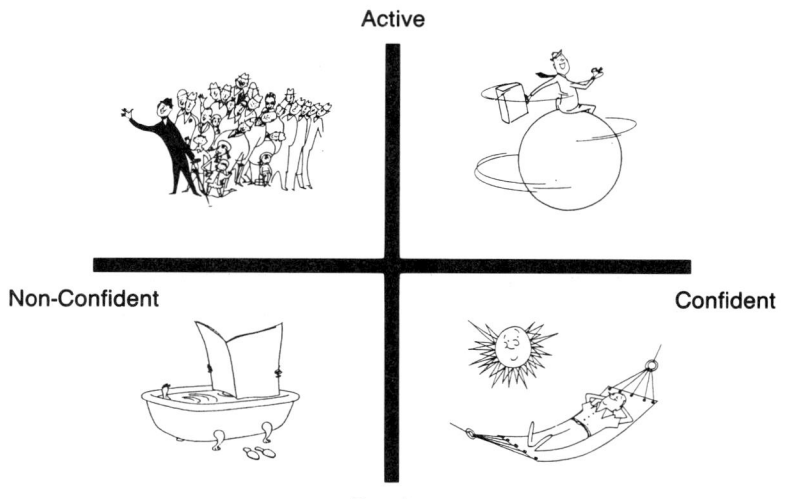

THE NEW LANGUAGE OF SEGMENTATION

Soon a whole new language emerged, popularized largely by the press, and marketeers talked endlessly about "lips," "dinks," "simps"—and particularly in the hospitality industry, "SMERFs."* Figure 5–12 defines some of the more common American *demographic* labels, and Figure 5–13 outlines a European system for naming and defining a combined demographic-psychographic set of profiles.

SMERFs: social, military, ethnic, religious, and fraternal

YMCAers: young, married, childless achievers

SIMPs: single income, money problems

POOSSLQ: people of opposite sex sharing living quarters

DINKs: double income, no kids

LIPS: low income, parents supporting

FIGURE 5–12 A few of the many American demographic designations that have become popular during the past few years.

Jack the Lad:
- Single
- Adventurous
- Stylish
- Image conscious
- Chauvinistic
- Unreliable

Know My Place:
- Low income
- Settled
- Moderate viewpoints
- Nonindividualistic

9 to 5'ers:
- Well paid
- Secure
- Highly educated
- Moderate social attitudes
- Satisfied at work
- Self-assured

Rebels:
- Highly educated
- Disillusioned
- Low aspirations
- Little concern for health or image

Family Man:
- Middle class
- Traditionalist
- Settled
- Lacks ambition

Reach for the Sky:
- Highly work oriented
- Dissatisfied at work
- Ambitious
- Aggressive
- "Troubled" home life
- Image conscious
- Relatively insecure

New Puritan:
- Teenagers
- Career oriented
- High earners
- Careful savers
- Health conscious
- Insecure
- Conformists

FIGURE 5–13 European classification system that combines both demographic and psychographic factors.

*Originally, "SMERF" was spelled "SMERFE" and stood for "social, military, ethnic, religious, fraternal, and educational" groups and organizations. Today, the last "e" has been dropped because modern educational organizations no longer share most of the characteristics of the other groups.

FIGURE 5–14 *(cont.)*   The Health and Fitness Market

(Courtesy of Robinson, Yesawich & Pepperdine, Maitland, Florida)

The Midscale Suburbanites

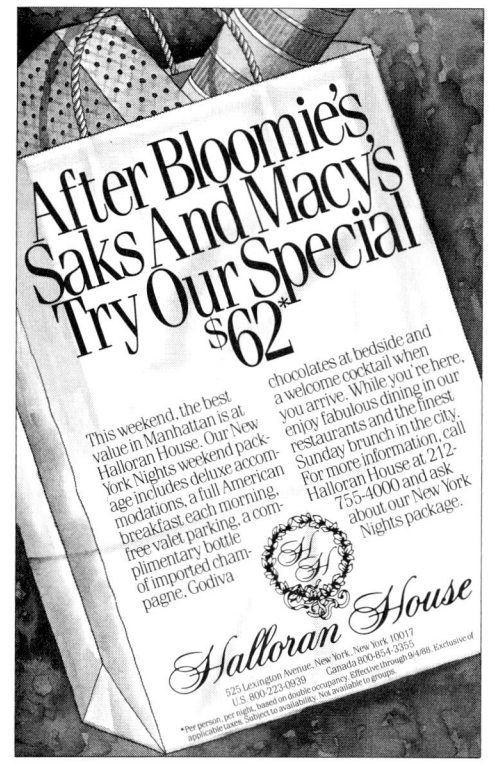

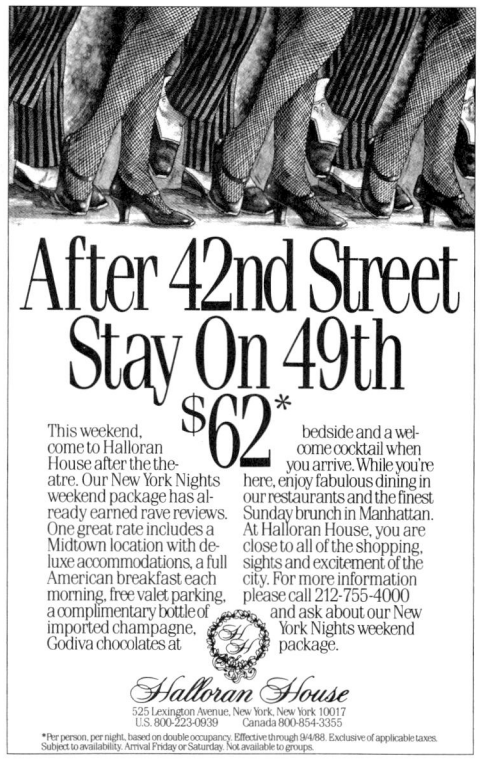

(Courtesy of Robinson, Yesawich & Pepperdine, Maitland, Florida)

The Serious Independent Outdoor Enthusiast   **The Affluent Active Escape-Seeker**

(Courtesy of Lithographics, Inc., Altamonte Springs, Florida)

FIGURE 5–14 *(cont.)*

SEGMENTATION DUALITY

Although it seems neat and easy to put people into nice and tight classifications, a very key point about human nature must be observed. Not everyone can fit into a specific role at all times. People tend to be "actors" and will often role-play according to the situation. An *active self-confident* person who may customarily vacation in "name" destination areas each year (such as Hawaii, the Riviera, or the Caribbean) may turn into a totally *passive non-self-confident* when taking a first-time business trip overseas to an area where there are substantial differences in language and social customs. A convention delegate may be categorized as a group business traveler from 9:00 A.M. to 3:00 P.M. when attending business sessions and working luncheons, and turn into an individual leisure traveler between 3:00 P.M. and midnight. This duality is well recognized in the advertisement shown in Figure 5–15.

SEGMENTING THE SEGMENTS

Where will it all end? No longer satisfied with just segments, we now find demographers looking for strata and substrata and all sorts of microsegments. Yet there is some justification for some types of properties to take a look at the *international, upscale, active-confident, senior citizen, woman, corporate business traveler,* especially during soft business periods when you may really be "scratching" for business.

FIGURE 5-15 The dual nature of a market segment is used as a selling point in this ad. [Courtesy of the Ventura (California) Visitors and Convention Bureau.]

The same "segmenting the segments" concept equally applies to the overall *leisure market.*

A major component of leisure travel involves people particularly interested in sports and recreational activities. They can be initially classified according to the specific activity (golf, tennis, fishing, boating, hiking, etc.). Their involvement can then be further classified as either vocational (professional) or avocational (amateur).

Using the segment "amateur golfers," one can further subsegment this according to the *degree* of interest and involvement:

1. *Golfing vacationers:* Those who include golf among many other recreational activities.
2. *Golfing business travelers:* Those on business trips who are at times "leisure travelers"—and plan on including golf as a key part of their free or spare time activities (and who additionally may use the links as a meeting point with business associates or clients).
3. *Social group golfers:* Attendees at conventions and other group meetings who are not avid golfers but who will play to establish and fortify friendships and other networking opportunities. Many organizations, especially

those known as "work and play groups," will specifically program golf tournaments on their agenda.

4. *Sports-minded golfers:* Those whose travel arrangements are predicated on the availability of a variety of recreational outlets including golf.

5. *Golf enthusiasts:* Those whose vacation plans are primarily built around and almost exclusively devoted to being "on the greens."

Through various research methods, one can identify individuals who fall into one of these subsegments—and then reach them through direct mail and targeted advertising messages. How did the industry get to such microfractionalization? Figure 5–16 offers one possible historical perspective.

FIGURE 5–16   Short history of market segmentation.

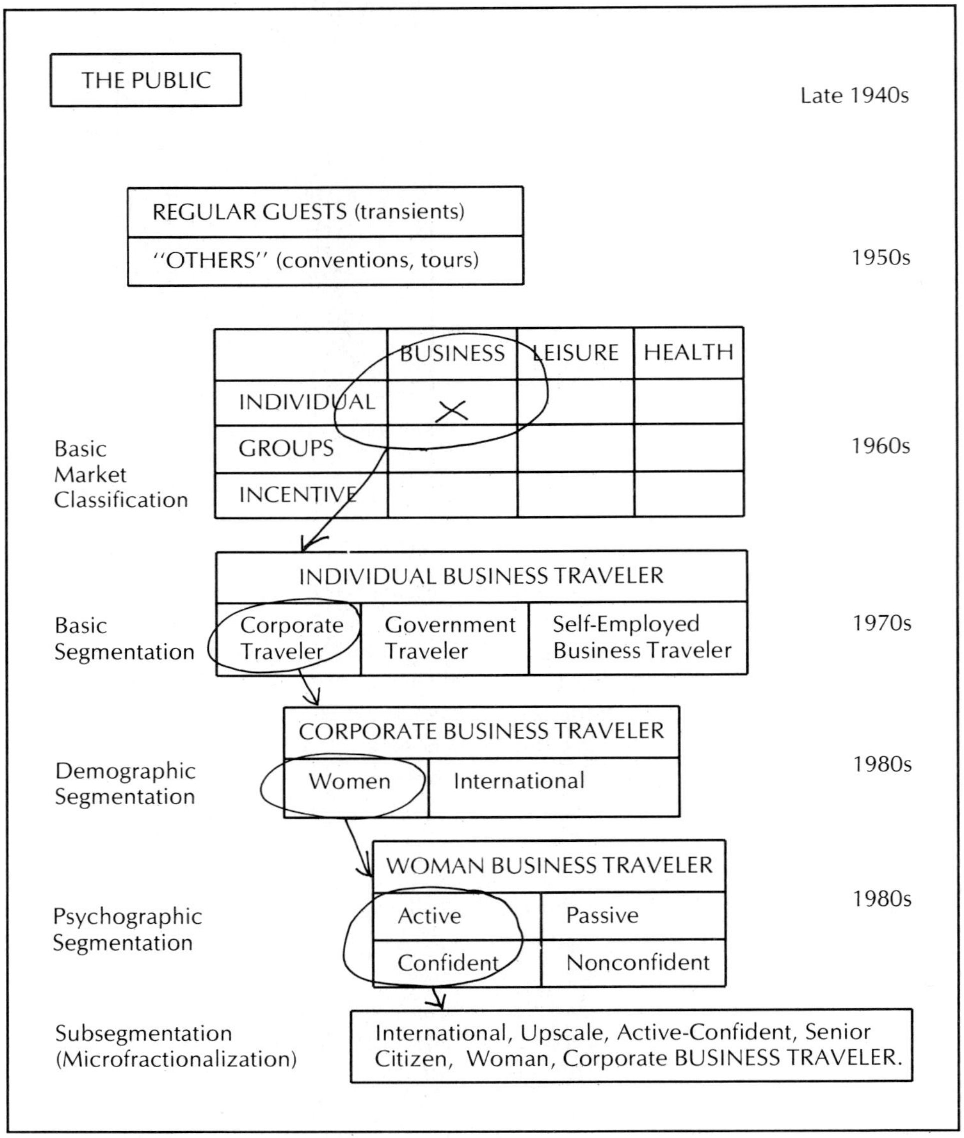

SORTING IT ALL OUT

An ever-increasing but necessary "flood" of statistical data is constantly being "crunched out" by such agencies as the U.S. Census Bureau, publications such as *American Demographics,* and companies such as National Demographics and Lifestyles Inc. (See the Appendix for samples of detailed demographic and lifestyle profiles.) It becomes a challenge to determine which information is essential to the sales executive, particularly in day-to-day selling activities.

One way of sorting it all out may be to group data, as we discussed briefly in Chapter 2 into the "nice to know" (informative) and the "need to know" (practical, useful, and usable). We might even term this process *information segmentation,* and Figures 5–17 and 5–18 illustrate a sample of each.

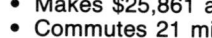

PROFILING THE "AVERAGE"

The Average American Male

- Makes $25,861 annually.
- Commutes 21 minutes to work.
- Average age is 31.
- Is 5'8" in height.
- Weighs 173 pounds.
- Has a 34-inch waist.
- Most common name is Robert.

The Average American Female

- Makes $16,030 annually.
- Average age is 33.
- Is 5'4" in height.
- Sleeps 9 minutes more than males (just over 8 hours).
- Most likely to be named Linda.

Based on 1987 figures

FIGURE 5–17 Example of "nice to know" information.

FIGURE 5–18 Example of what could turn out to be "need to know" information.

Travel Demographics

Reasons for Travel
1. Quest for new experiences.
2. To get away—physically and mentally.
3. To expand one's knowledge and horizons.
4. Curiosity.
5. Change of lifestyle (role-playing).
6. Business contacts.
7. Need and desire to share and exchange information and viewpoints.
8. Health, fitness, and therapy.

Impact of the "Baby Boomers": By 1990, the baby boomers will be in the 30–50 age category. In the United States there will be 76 million of them, and because of

their prior intensive lifestyles (hippie, yippie, yuppie, and ''me'' generations), they will tend to be:
    Highly educated
    Affluent
    Health, body, and nutrition conscious (fitness and diet)
    Adventure seeking

The 25–45 Age Category (in 1990)
    1. Will represent 45 percent of the U.S. population and 50 percent of all consumer expenditures.
    2. Are more comfortable with travel. Travel is exciting to them and has a high priority in their lifestyles.

65-and-Over Age Category (1990)
    1. Will be 13 percent of the U.S. public.
    2. Will be an organized force of 30 million people.
    3. In many cases will be the head of a retired household where one or more of the parents will be residing (super senior citizens).
    4. Has few travel restrictions relating to business commitments. Fairly significant amount of discretionary dollars (disposable income) due to minimal expense allocations for housing, home furnishing, or direct education.

Other Significant 1990 Projections
    1. 45 percent of the individual business travel market will be composed of women.
    2. 41 percent of the U.S. population in the 20-year-or-older category will be single.
    3. Nearly two-thirds of all couples will be two-income families (more minivacations).

FIGURE 5–18 *(cont.)*

Regardless of the type of information one collects in order to do an effective selling job, you can rest assured that it will be voluminous, detailed, and ever-changing. But the general, yet significant segmentation information, especially that relating to sales and servicing considerations, can readily be maintained in "digest" form. Figure 5–19 shows a format devised by the present authors for use as a market segment profile guide.

FIGURE 5–19 Some sample profile guides for various market segments, which record key information on the size, scope, needs, and other aspects on each. Such information can be easily maintained on a basic word processor or personal computer, and readily updated. This page relates to the overall meetings market; the following pages profile the maturity (senior citizen) market and the government travel market.

Market Segment Profile Guide: Meetings Market

Size:	Over 1.25 million meetings held in 1987
Value:	1974: $9 billion
	1984: $34 billion
	1986: $38 billion
	1987: $47 billion
Needs:	Great variety, according to the type and purpose of meeting. However, two key selection criteria for most meetings relate to:
	1. Quality of food service
	2. Size, layout, and quality of function space
Incentives:	• Knowledgeable, professional service staff
	• On-time reliability (wake-up calls, midday-break service, reception and meal service, guest room and meeting room availabilities)
	• Sharing of facts and figures (pre- and postconvention briefings)

FIGURE 5–19 (cont.)

> • Creativity (theme functions, staging, spouse programs, free-time activities)

Philosophy objective: Create the impression that the "person with the badge" is our most important guest.

Personal observations: _____

_____

_____

_____

Market Segment Profile Guide: Maturity Market

Size:	Americans age 50+
	1987: 63 million people
	1996: 76 million people
	2025: 113 million people
Value:	Americans age 50+ (1987)
	$860 billion total income
	$662 billion disposable income
	Americans age 55+ (1987)
	330 million room nights
	49 million trips
Needs:	• Good price/value considerations
	• Reliable, consistent rate discount program
	• First-floor accommodations
	• Nonsmoking rooms (majority do not smoke)
	• Staff sensitivity (patience and understanding)
Incentives:	• Empathic, well-trained staff (especially at the front desk)
	• Availability of bell or porter service
	• Manned elevator service
	• Tailored activities

Philosophy objective: The senior citizen market is an important growth segment with a great deal of variety within that specialized market.

Personal observations: _____

_____

_____

_____

Market Segment Profile Guide: Government Market

Size:	Well over 1,000,000 travelers (1988)
Value:	$5.8 billion in 1987
	$6.1 billion in 1988
	(about 30% of that is for lodging)
Needs:	Per-diem sensitivity (any overages for lodging and meals must come out of their own pockets)
	Attitude sensitivity (especially to the discounted rate)—Don't call it the "cheap" rate; call it an "adjusted" or "special" rate.
Incentives:	• Room upgrades
	• Complimentary breakfast
	• Free local phone calls
	• Complimentary coffee and newspaper
	• Economical room service

Philosophy objective: Eliminate the feeling of "second-class" citizen among government travelers

Personal observations: _____

_____

_____

_____

The old days of keeping everything in one's head (or perhaps in a 3- by 5-in. file card), and using one's car as the sales office have long passed. The wealth of detail and data needed to keep pace with both industry and market-place changes, as well as the many different working forms used to record transactional details between buyer and seller, requires a centralized and inte-grated system of filing and record keeping, as the next chapter will illustrate.

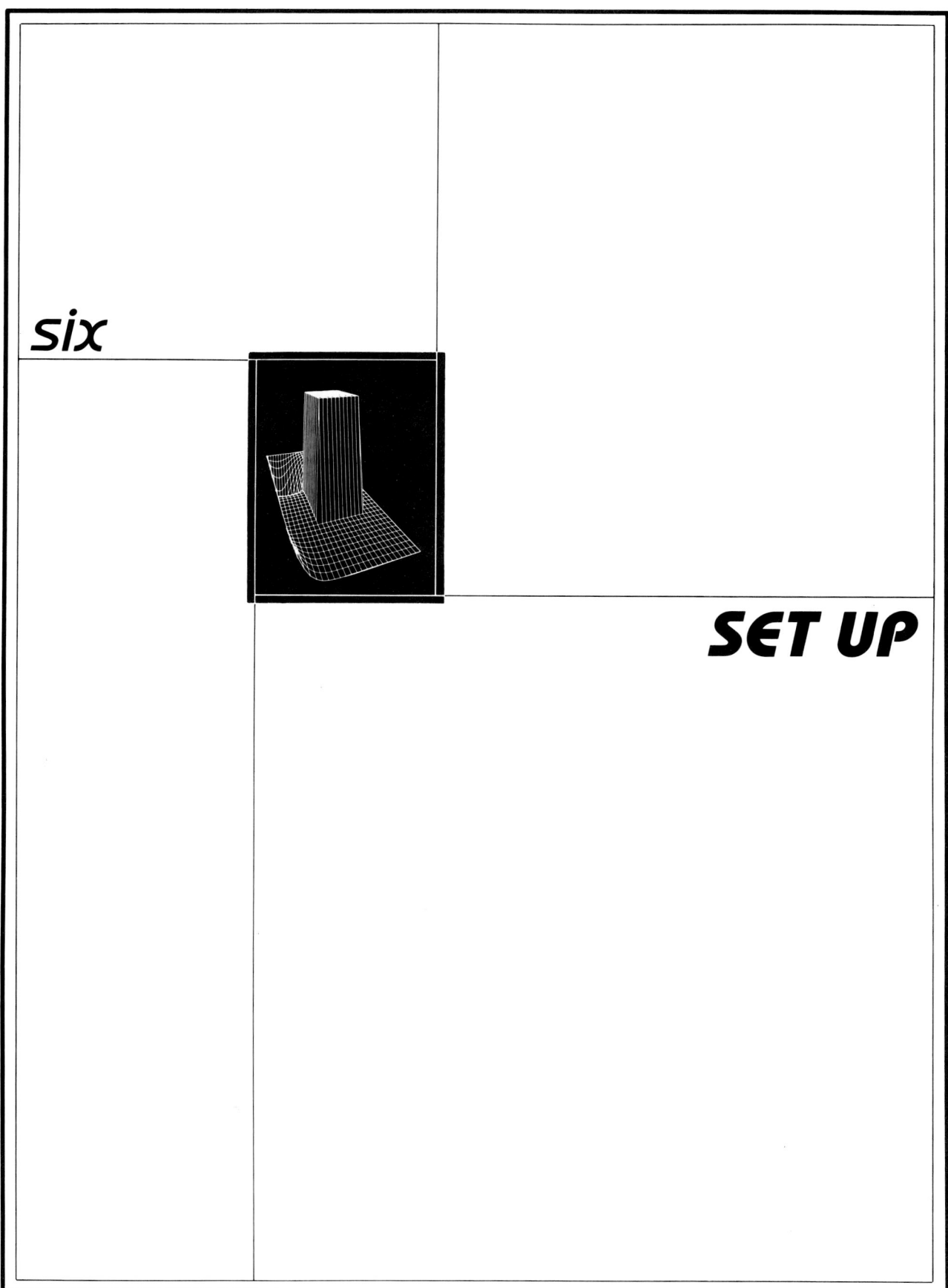

six

SET UP

Many executives who make a career in hotel sales tend to think of themselves as outgoing, gregarious, and extroverted (the basic "Type A" personality)—certainly not the type to be tied down to the regular, day-after-day routines of paperwork and pencil pushing. Although selling is primarily an active, external function, it is essential that every sales executive establish or be able to report to a home base. This can either be on property, or in the case of many regional and national sales managers, at a separate corporate sales office located in a major feeder city.

SALES OFFICE FUNCTIONS

Regardless of location, the primary functions of a hotel sales office would be to:

1. Properly record, store, and constantly update data and information on each sales account and on each key potential source of business.
2. Establish an information retrieval system so that necessary information can systematically be brought to the attention of the appropriate sales executive at the proper time for specific action.
3. Review "neutralized" or "dead" files* periodically to determine if and when they can be reactivated.
4. Operate an ongoing system of accounts management to coordinate staff efforts and time on the best possible cost-effective basis.
5. Provide a business setting for implementing the sales and marketing function, which includes research and analysis, planning, implementation, review, and interdepartmental coordination.

All of this may sound rather formidable, so let's look at it from another perspective. In simpler terms, how profitable would an operation be if the sales executives called only on those accounts they wanted to call on, at the times that suited them, with no information on whom they were calling, and no way of properly recording what transpired? The result would obviously be MBC: "management by chaos"! So as much as most salespeople tend to dislike "paper shuffling," it is vitally important to set up a physical office and a workable system of files, records, and procedures.

LOCATING THE SALES OFFICE

There's an old joke about a meeting planner walking up to the front desk of a hotel and asking directions to the property's sales office. The punchline usually has at least three alternative endings, depending on the reason for telling the story:

1. *Newly hired room clerk:* "Sales office? Hey, I've only been here one day and they're already selling the hotel!"
2. *Know-nothing room clerk:* "I don't know where they keep the sales office; all I know is what's on top of and behind this desk."
3. *Sarcastic room clerk:* "The sales office, ah, yes. Well, sir, you go to the very end of that corridor, take the service elevator to the basement, tiptoe

*These are files on former customers who no longer can do business with you, or no longer desire to.

through the employees' locker room and the men's showers, and you should find it somewhere behind the engineer's office.''

As much as we dislike admitting this, these responses are not on over-exaggeration of what can still be found in far too many instances.

GENERAL PHYSICAL CONSIDERATIONS

Let's first look at some of the *physical* considerations when establishing a functional sales office:

- Location
- Size
- Design and layout
- Decor, furnishings, and fixtures
- Materials and supplies

Location

Visibility and *accessibility* are the two key words in physically locating the sales office. In smaller properties, the sales office is very often combined with the offices of the key operating personnel. The administrative offices would include the general manager, accounting, reservations, banquets, and sales. In very small operations, the sales office might even be part of the general office area adjacent to or behind the front desk and shared with the front-office and reservations personnel.

On the other hand, larger properties must consider the feasibility of separating certain parts of the sales and marketing department into separate offices according to key functions. For example, the administrative part of the sales and marketing office (including all the files) might be located on the ground or lobby level, the convention services offices could conveniently be located on the main meeting floor near the ballroom or amphitheater, and the catering/banquet office could be adjacent or close to the area where most of the food functions would be held.

But irrespective of whether the office is a single unit or physically split up, the two primary considerations should be visibility and accessibility. In other words, is the sales office easy to find and be seen by potential customers who may be specifically visiting the property or who may be "dropping in" unexpectedly while on the property for other purposes (dinner, attending social functions, vacationing, etc.).

Figure 6-1 shows two location layouts that illustrate a high degree of visibility and accessibility by making the sales office a key focal point of the property (in short, "you can't miss it!"). The location pictured on the left is directly adjacent to the street entrance and right across the lobby from another high access point, the dining room. The second illustration shows an office right where "the action" is—a high-traffic area between two lounges and across from the front desk.

To these physical considerations must be added the factor of *employee awareness.* Does the staff of the hotel, especially the bell staff, maids, and other guest-contact employees, know where the sales office is and how to provide

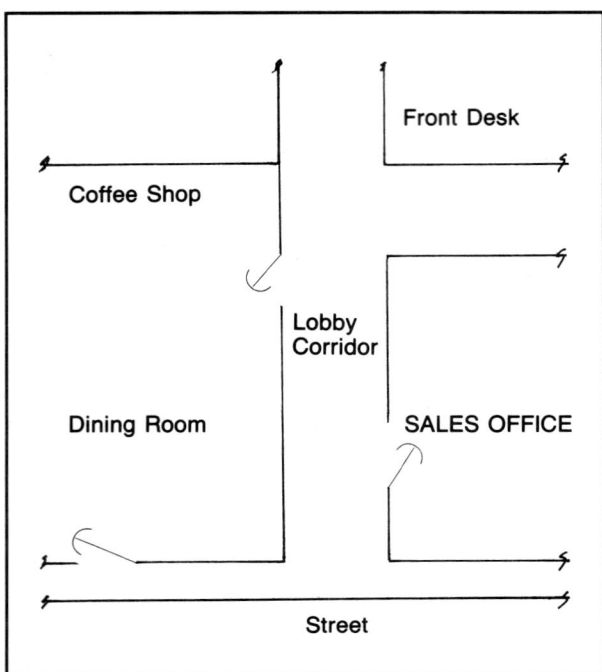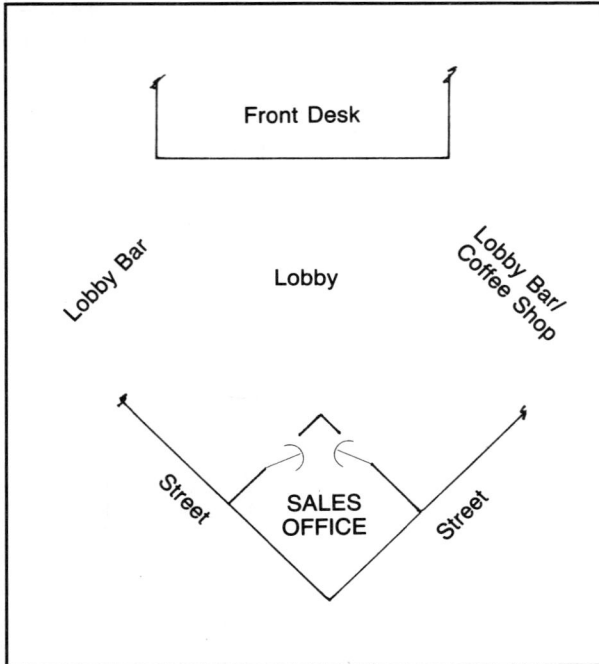

FIGURE 6–1 Highly visible sales office locations.

asy instructions on how to reach it? A good, ongoing training program can be helpful (and is actually essential) to this effort.

Size

There are no set formulas for relating the physical size of the sales office to the number of sales executives or the size of the hotel. A basic consideration, of course, would be the best utilization of available space. Other factors come into play, however, such as:

1. The amount of outside traffic (number of guests and prospects who visit the office) and its relation to the needed size of the reception area.
2. The need for "board room" space for pre- and postconvention briefings between meeting planners and hotel department heads.
3. The centralization of the sales and marketing department staff. Are the convention servicing, banquet and catering, and reservations departments "housed" together with sales and marketing, or do they each have their own offices in other locations?
4. Size, type, and number of communications and filing systems, especially the degree of computerization and the need for various types of separate computer workstations.
5. The comparative volume of group business. A hotel deriving the majority of its revenue from conventions and other groups, and whose market areas include national and international accounts, would need more filing and records-maintenance space than would the same-sized property which concentrates primarily on the individual traveler.

6. The need for separate areas for each sales executive for private discussions with clients or potential customers.

7. The overall working philosophy of the staff: Do they feel more comfortable and are they more productive in separate enclosures, or do they wish to function more in the open within a team approach?*

As can be seen from this checklist, the size of the sales office from property to property would have to vary depending on its dual use as a functional work station and a sales/servicing meeting point with customers and potential clients.

Design and Layout

The design and layout of sales offices are also directly tied into the previous considerations of location and size, and the same factors of size, scope of markets, and philosophy that were just discussed would also apply to office layout.

Some additional items to consider would relate to the location of the reception area (which should be up front close to the door) and the location of the central files (from the standpoint of work flow and office traffic patterns). Figure 6–2 illustrates two different layout designs for a hotel sales/marketing department. The top illustration is for a seven-person department, where the filing systems are primarily manual. The bottom sketch is for a 12-person department, which uses an "island" layout for its computerized systems.

There are some additional factors, especially in the larger properties, which can have a substantial impact on both size and design and layout:

1. Do corporate sales personnel, such as district or regional sales managers for the chain or franchise with which the property is affiliated, have or share space in the property?

2. Is there "satellite" office space for convention servicing and catering personnel, for use as functional operating offices adjacent to the main meeting/banquet areas?

The foregoing considerations also relate to the working philosophy of the hotel. In some properties, sales and marketing executives are expected to spend a good portion of their time in their offices—doing research, initiating contacts and following up leads by phone, and scheduling on-property appointments and site inspections with customers and potential prospects. In some properties, there is also the operating philosophy that the account executive who books a specific piece of business is also required to be on the scene to ensure that all servicing details are carried out.

In other hotels, salespeople spend most of their time on the road, and the accounts they book are turned over to the inside convention manager or convention service coordinators for follow-up and servicing. Since the major portion of their time is usually spent in the meeting and banquet areas, they generally must have office space as close to those facilities as possible, especially so that the meeting planners or their committee heads can readily locate them in case of last-minute changes or emergencies. All of this leads us into an area where personal preferences may play a part: that of decor and furnishings.

*This is often a cultural consideration. Japanese executives, for example, often have centralized workstations for groups of six or more, to spur the constant exchange of ideas and to promote team creativity.

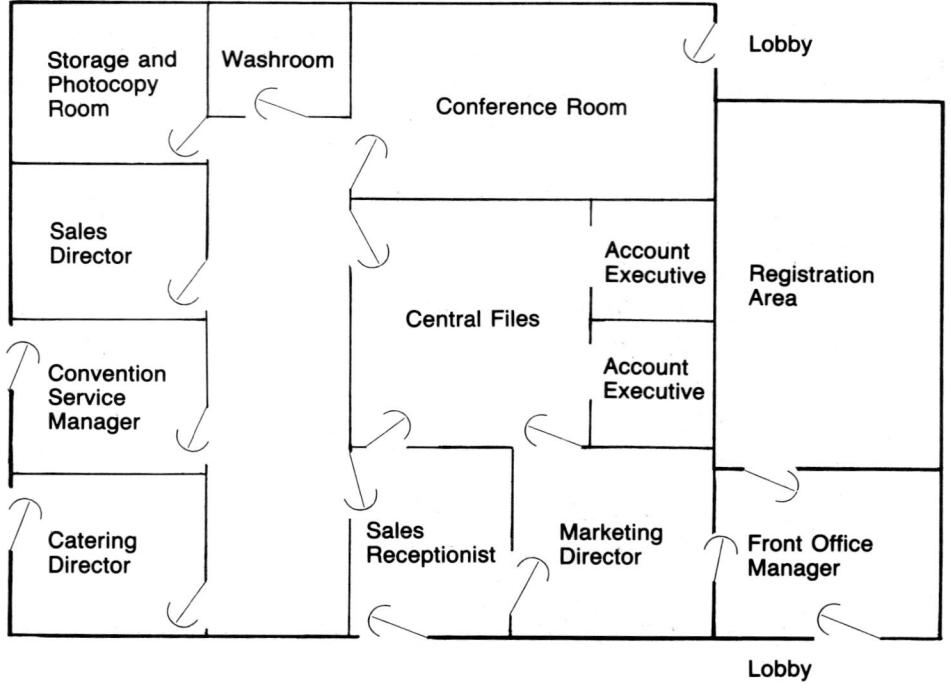

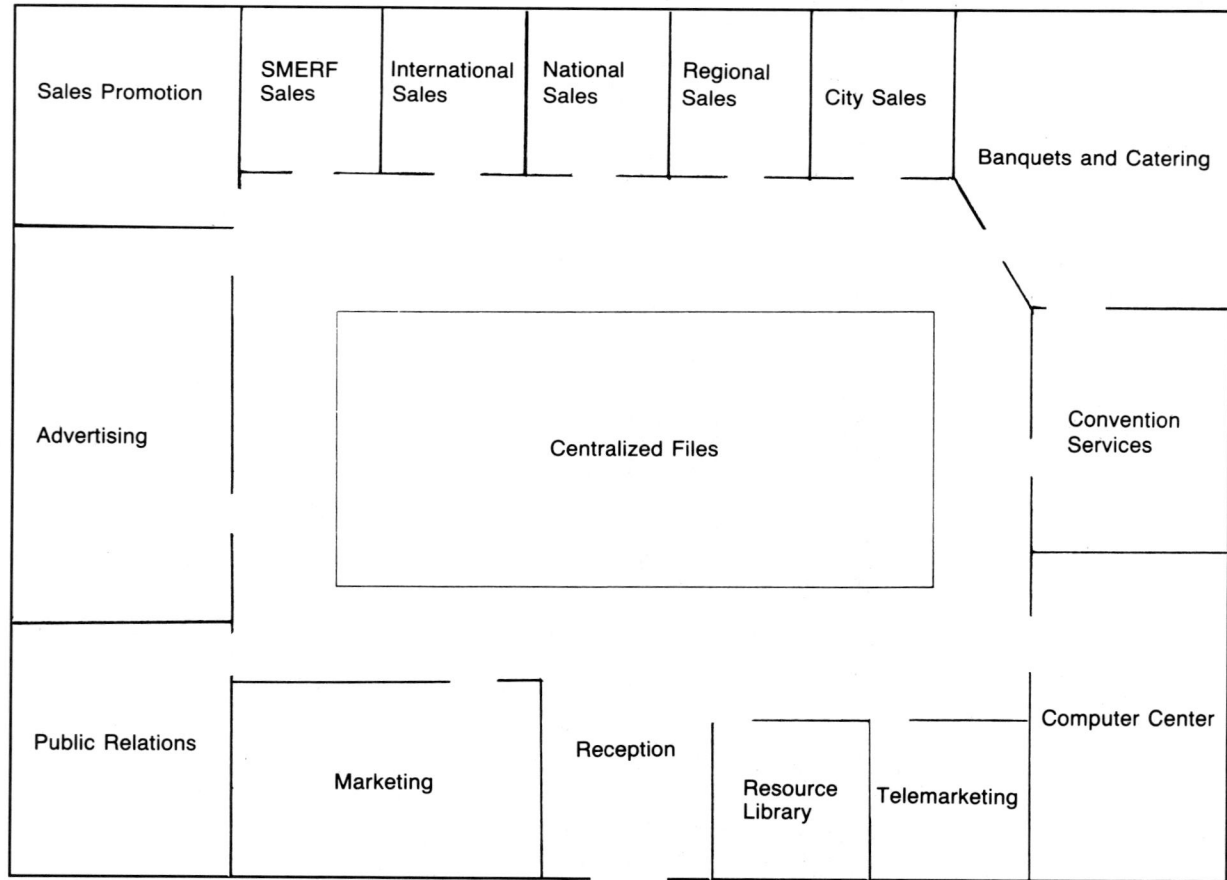

FIGURE 6–2 Sample layouts for a hotel sales/marketing department.

Decor, Fixtures, and Furnishings

It has been said to us by many a meeting planner that the hotel industry seems to be one of the leading purchasers of pictures and paintings of horses. Which may be fine for a dude ranch or western resort but somewhat out of place in a large center city east coast or New England hotel.

It would be more useful from a selling viewpoint to include pictures of the property "in action," such as

- Special meeting room setups
- Creative food displays and gourmet buffets
- Creative theme parties
- Special sports, recreational, and fitness facilities
- Framed reprints of notable feature stories on the property or key executives

As with so many other factors, there are no hard and fast rules, but some common-sense guidelines can be helpful in matching decor and related details to the image the property should present.

1. *Image* is the operative word. The decor and furnishings should ideally be a blend of a business-like atmosphere and a friendly ambience.
2. The decor and furnishings should similarly reflect the *positioning* of the property. Elegant, upscale furnishings are appropriate for a deluxe property; a more modest contemporary design concept would be suitable for the budget or economy hotel.
3. Decor style should also be related to the *tone* of the establishment. Does the hotel have a European flavor, or is it more reflective of an historical Early American style? Is the overall architectural theme of the property traditional, nostalgic, contemporary, or futuristic?

Although compromises may have to be made between the esthetic and the functional (do computers come in French Provincial?), it must also be remembered that the sales office should reflect the image of the entire operation, especially as seen from the eyes of the customer. Also, although it should not totally reflect the personal tastes of each member of the sales department, some individuality can be important, especially where the sales executives spend a good portion of their time in their offices. So more and more, one does see reflections of personal preferences in the selection of pictures, plants, carpeting, and other decorative furnishings, which can be important in establishing a comfortable, compatible, and hopefully a more productive working environment.

Other items, such as framed testimonial letters and awards (both personal and professional), are also part of the decor consideration. These can serve as sales tools and should be conspicuously placed in high customer traffic areas such as corridors or reception rooms.

A fairly new consideration which we mention here because it doesn't quite fit elsewhere—relates to the office walls themselves. Because of the changeover to computerized systems (which can be a bit noisy), it is becoming increasingly important to select materials that have the best possible soundproofing capabilities. This is especially true when considering nonsupporting, modular office wall units.

Materials and Supplies

In this chapter we will *not* discuss supplies as they would relate to secretarial needs, but specifically from the sales and marketing viewpoint. The sales office, especially the reception area, can be an excellent on-premise, point-of-purchase selling environment. The same supplies that the sales executive should readily have on hand (either on the road or in the office) should also be available for pickup by or distribution to potential customers who may drop by casually.

These supporting display materials could include:

- Rack folders and convention brochures
- Chain/franchise system directories
- Brochures from "sister properties"
- Floor plans and room capacity charts
- Banquet menus
- Audiovisual and other equipment listings
- Service directories
- City maps and brochures
- Area attractions brochures and maps
- Business cards

Many of these items, particularly in the reception area, should be available in quantity for "take-home" use. (Let the customers be your salespeople—give them the tools to help them make the sale.)

FUNCTIONAL CONSIDERATIONS

The preceding portions of this chapter dwelt primarily with the more cosmetic (how it *looks*) aspects of setting up the sales office. The remainder of the chapter will focus on the functional (how it *works*) considerations of sales office operations. Within this functional area, we cover such topics as:

1. Tables of organization (and organizational charts)
2. Job descriptions
3. Records and filing systems
4. Sales executive's work forms

TABLES OF ORGANIZATION

Before any system of files and records can be established, a consideration of the types of business and the market mix must be established for the property, as discussed in Chapters 4 and 5. The types of business and the relative value of each segment (i.e., that segment's contribution to both gross sales and profits) must be determined according to the property's general objectives and specific goals.

An operating decision must then be made as to whether the responsibilities of the sales managers and the account executives within a table of organization will be set up according to:

1. *A market segment basis:* individual business travel market, group business market, travel and tour
2. *Geographic territorial coverage:* northeastern sales manager, west coast sales manager
3. *A combination segment/territory:* New England travel and tour manager, midwest corporate sales manager

This decision would be more consequential in a larger property. In the smaller one-person sales office, the answer could be "all of the above—at the same time"! This consideration will be especially important in setting up the main filing system and for such administrative functions as time, territory, and records management.

Tables of organization will also depend on how many people there are in the sales and marketing department, whether functions will be combined (e.g., director of sales and catering), and as has been discussed before, whether the department also includes servicing personnel, catering staff, and reservation and front office employees.

Here again, there are no hard and fast rules as to the number of personnel to be included in the sales/marketing department. One so-called "rule of thumb" uses as its basis one full-time sales executive for each 100 rooms up to 500 rooms; after that, $1\frac{1}{2}$ persons for each additional 100 rooms. This should only be looked upon as a possible starting point. Other variables will affect this. For example, a higher ratio of sales personnel to rooms might be called for if:

*   The property's primary business mix comes from convention and group leisure business, rather than the individual business or leisure traveler.
*   The sales department is also wholly responsible for individual room, food and beverage, and other departmental income areas.
*   Sales executives are responsible for servicing the business they book rather than turning it over to the inside convention servicing department after booking.
*   The main competition is aggressively promoting business from the same sources as the hotel.

For illustrative purposes, Figure 6–3 shows several organizational charts, with the differences based primarily on the difference in property size.

JOB DESCRIPTIONS

Job descriptions, which detail the specific responsibilities and functions of each title on the organization chart, are another essential working tool in the sales office. One of the challenges of the hospitality industry is that there is no uniformity of titles. A sales manager in one hotel may be the top (and perhaps only) sales and marketing executive for that property. In another operation, the sales manager may report to an assistant director of sales, who reports to a sales director, who in turn reports to the vice president of marketing.* A number of detailed sales and marketing job descriptions are listed in the Appendix.

*On the other hand, to add to the confusion, one of the present authors met a vice president–marketing who was actually a one-person sales department in an 88-room inn. When asked why that particular title, the response was: "My daddy, who owns the inn, thinks it would be impressive when I meet people." This is not being said in a negative way: There are company presidents who have tens of thousands of employees, and there are company presidents with less than 10.

To help pinpoint the main responsibilities of key executives in sales and marketing positions, the following position description guide was prepared by the Hotel Sales and Marketing Association International for its pamphlet "Career Tips in Hotel Sales and Marketing":

Vice President–Marketing: establishes annual marketing programs aimed at developing maximum business volume and profits for rooms, food, beverage, and other department outlets; undertakes both product and market research, analysis, and planning; formulates fiscal goals and objectives; prepares sales forecasts, strategies, action plans, and promotional budgets; trains and develops sales and servicing personnel; and supervises and coordinates all related promotional activities such as direct selling, advertising, publicity, and public relations.

Director of Sales: administers, coordinates, and supervises the activities of sales department executives who are responsible for soliciting and servicing conventions, sales meetings, tours, and other groups requiring public space and room accommodations. Also helps create and implement programs aimed at developing room, food, and beverage business from the individual business and leisure traveler.

Director of Advertising: develops coordinated advertising programs and campaigns involving newspapers, magazines, radio and TV, outdoor advertising, and direct mail—and works closely with advertising agencies in the creation and production of advertising and promotional literature.

Director of Public Relations: responsible for developing positive programs directed at maximizing the property's "image" and its relations with the community, its employees, its guests, the industry, and the general public.

International Sales Manager: coordinates activities specifically aimed at stimulating and developing individual and group business from areas outside the country.

Regional Director of Sales: responsible for soliciting accounts within a specific

FIGURE 6–3 Sample sales/marketing department organizational charts: (a) for a smaller property of 100 to 150 rooms and less; (b) for a medium-sized property of between 500 and 750 rooms; (c) for a large hotel in the 1500 to 2000 + room category. In plan (c), some sales executives are assigned to specific market segments; others, to a combination of segments and territory. Note that this 27-person organization chart only includes staff, not the meeting room setup crew, banquet waiters, and other service personnel who would also be considered part of the sales and marketing department. Also, although convention service and catering are shown as part of this department, neither front office nor reservations are included, as they might be in some of the newer organizational concepts.

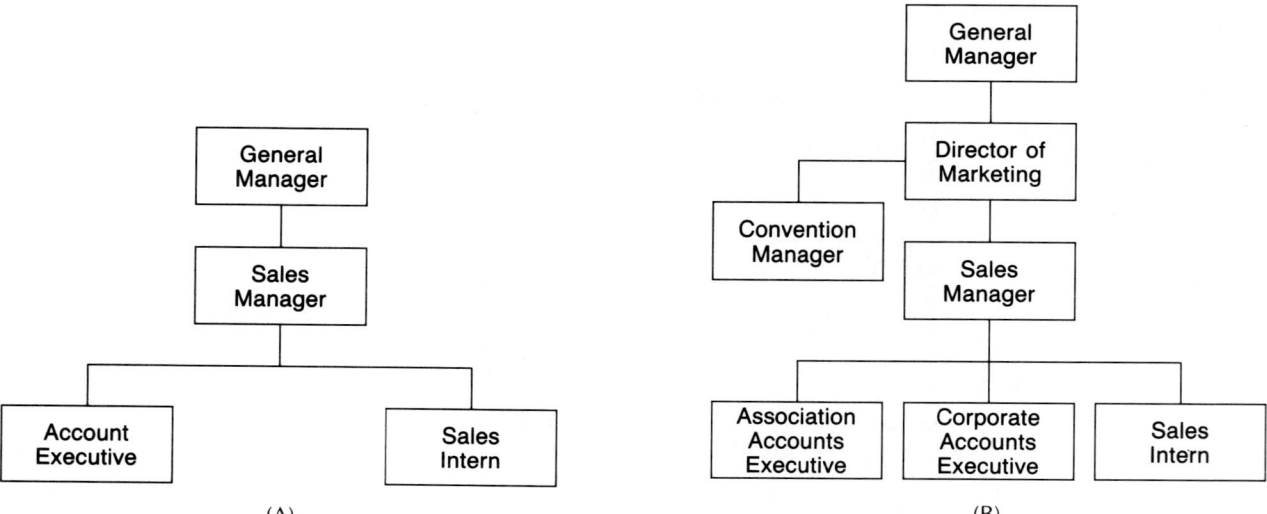

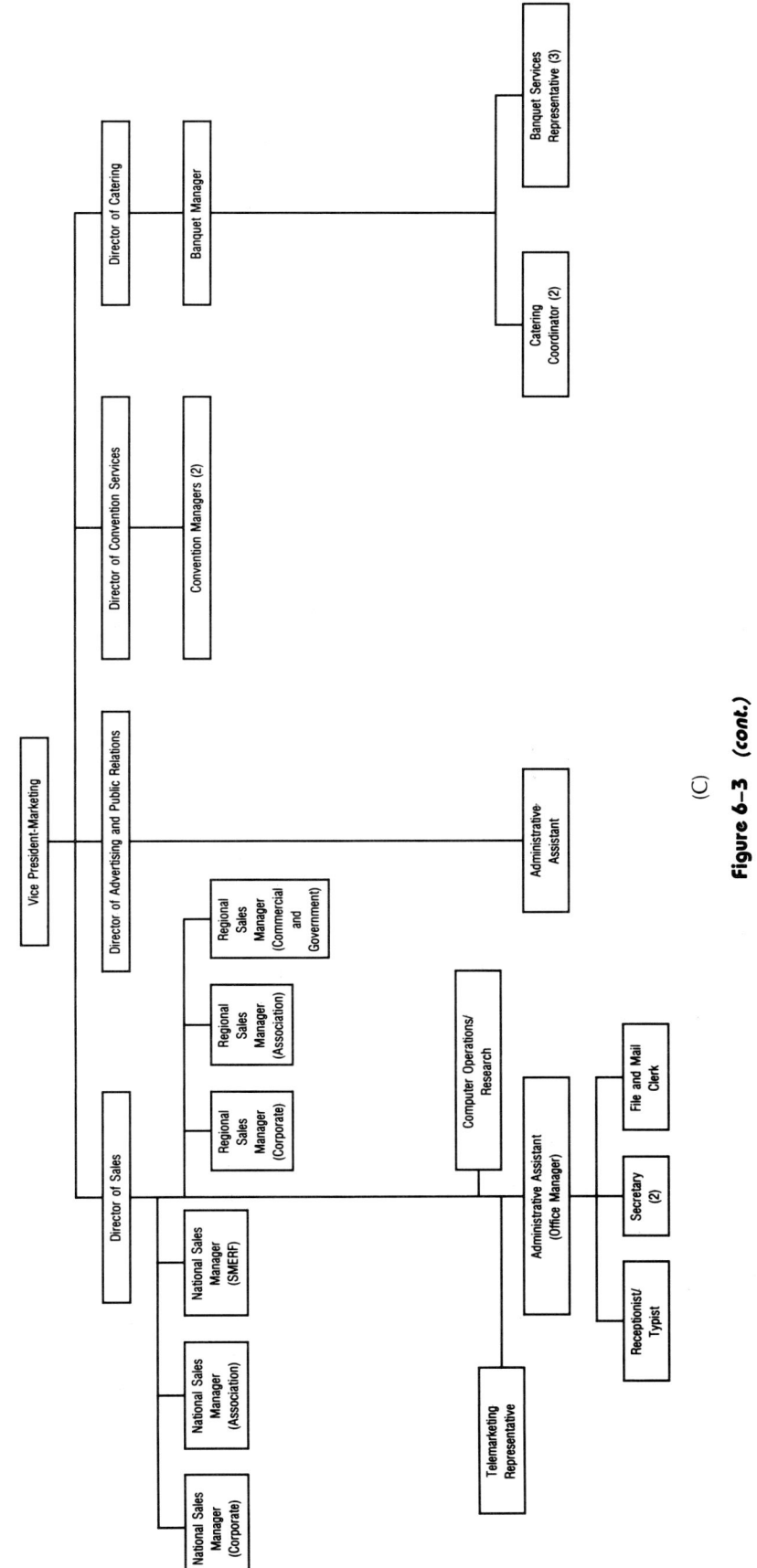

Figure 6-3 *(cont.)*

(C)

geographic region; generally (though not always) working within a chain or franchise system. Also may coordinate promotional activities for the properties within that region, and supplies input relating to advertising, sales promotion, and publicity.

Tour and Agency Manager: responsible for developing both group and individual business through personal contacts with travel wholesalers, travel agents, tour operators, transportation companies, and carrier representatives.

Convention Service Manager: coordinates the activities of all hotel departments to assure maximum service to conventions and other groups once they are in the hotel, and is responsible for supervising all "in house" activities of the groups which involve hotel services.

Account Executive or Sales Representative: directly contacts both repeat and new business prospects on a regularly established basis, through personal calls, telephone, and direct mail, for the specific purpose of booking a continuous flow of profitable business.

These thumbnail sketches would be expanded to provide more fully detailed job descriptions that would relate specifically to the objectives and goals of the property. They can also serve a variety of additional purposes, such as training new staff executives and as one of the means of evaluating sales performance. Organizational charts and job descriptions can serve as practical guides to establishing and maintaining records and files, which form the heart of the sales and marketing administrative function.

RECORDS AND FILING SYSTEMS

Sales administration could be the subject of an entire book in itself. Since this book is intended primarily as an introduction to the sales and selling functions, we just offer an overview of some of the basic sales office systems, with emphasis on how they relate to the daily activities of the sales executive.

Types of Files

The backbone of the sales office is its filing systems. Although size and market scope will cause some practical variations, most systems can initially be grouped within the following main classifications:

1. *Association files:* includes trade association and professional societies, avocational, hobby, and other common-interest groups of people who are "bound together" by a shared profession or interest and not by a common corporate affiliation.
2. *Corporate files:* maintained for each company that offers both group and contract (volume) individual business potentials.
3. *Travel and tour files:* includes tour brokers, wholesalers, travel agents, and incentive houses that are the contacts for group leisure travel.
4. *Banquet files:* contacts for social and civic club food and beverage functions, and other sources of volume food and beverage business, which customarily do not involve room sales.

These four main groupings are commonly maintained separately. For manual and computer back up systems, each individual organization, company, and agency has its own 9- by 12-in. manila file folder, usually kept in alphabetical order.* In larger hotels, the association files may be further segmented into national, regional, state, and local sections and may be color-coded on the tab to indicate educational organization, professional association, avocational group, labor union, and SMERF subclassifications.

In smaller properties, detailed file segmentation may not be necessary: The name labels on the manila folders can be color-coded to indicate type and geographic scope of each organization.

In addition to these main categories, there are often two additional sorting classifications: *hold* (or *pending*) files, whose business potentials are not yet fully established, and *neutralized* (or *dead*) files for groups that have been removed from the regular files because they currently cannot or will not conduct business with you.

In automated systems, computer programs can be written to follow all of these systems of file classifications.[†]

Records

Records generally refer to the work forms and supporting correspondence that are maintained within each file. They document what you know about each organization, what types of business you have previously done with each, the value of the group, and when and how each should next be contacted for future business. In addition, records serve as the means of updating information on the many changes in contact personnel, size, composition, and requirements of each business source.

Although there is a tremendous variety of working records that can be used in a sales office, the most common ones maintained inside the manila file folders include:

1. *Front sheet:* contains the basic and essential information about the account.

2. *Report of interview (or call report) forms:* detail each personal contact between the sales executive assigned the account and the account's representative.

3. *Letters of proposal:* outline the facilities and services the hotel can offer to fill a potential buyer's specific needs and wants as they relate to a specified event or function.

4. *Contracts (or letters of agreement):* legally binding documents prepared after the booking, detailing the obligations and responsibilities of both buyer and seller for fulfilling the specific requirements relating to rooms allotments, rates, food and beverage prices, equipment rentals, meeting room and exhibit area charges, and so on.

5. *Booking forms:* often color-coded for the three main booking categories: tentative, confirmed, or canceled. They contain the key setup and servicing details relating to each function and are often prepared in six or more copies for distribution to reservations, food and beverage, housekeeping, and other key departments.

---

*Some properties use a *key word* alphabetical sorting system. The challenge, however, is in deciding what the key word would be for an organization such as the "Galactic Federation for Interplanetary Petroleum and Gas Exploration."

[†]Despite the proliferation of computer programs and systems, the majority of hotels still rely either totally or in part on manual procedures for working and maintaining sales files.

As soon as a booking is made, the space necessary for the group's meetings, exhibits, receptions, and meal functions is "blocked off" in the function book (see Figure 6–4). There may be later adjustments, such as changing of rooms, should the group's preliminary attendance estimates significantly vary between the time of the booking and the arrival time for the meeting or function.

Therefore, periodic communications between the sales executive and the meeting planner or function representative is essential to the proper servicing of the account as well as the best utilization on the part of the hotel of its available public space. The function book thus serves as a control—as well as a booking record.

6. *Credit evaluation forms:* for credit-checking purposes, especially used with first-time groups.

FIGURE 6–4 Function room scheduling books are generally made specifically for a particular hotel to reflect that property's booking requirements. Each daily page is dated and has the names of the meeting or group dining facilities, the times segmented as you require, and space to enter key details about group requirements. It is customary practice that confirmed bookings are entered in pen while tentative bookings are written in pencil. Both Sales and Catering have access to the function book, but it is also customary that a property maintains only one function book, even when the Banquet or Catering departments operate independent of the Sales/Marketing function. Computerized programs are now available which may complement (but do not necessarily substitute for) the manual entry system. (Courtesy Hodges and Irvine; St. Clair, MI; 313–329–4787)

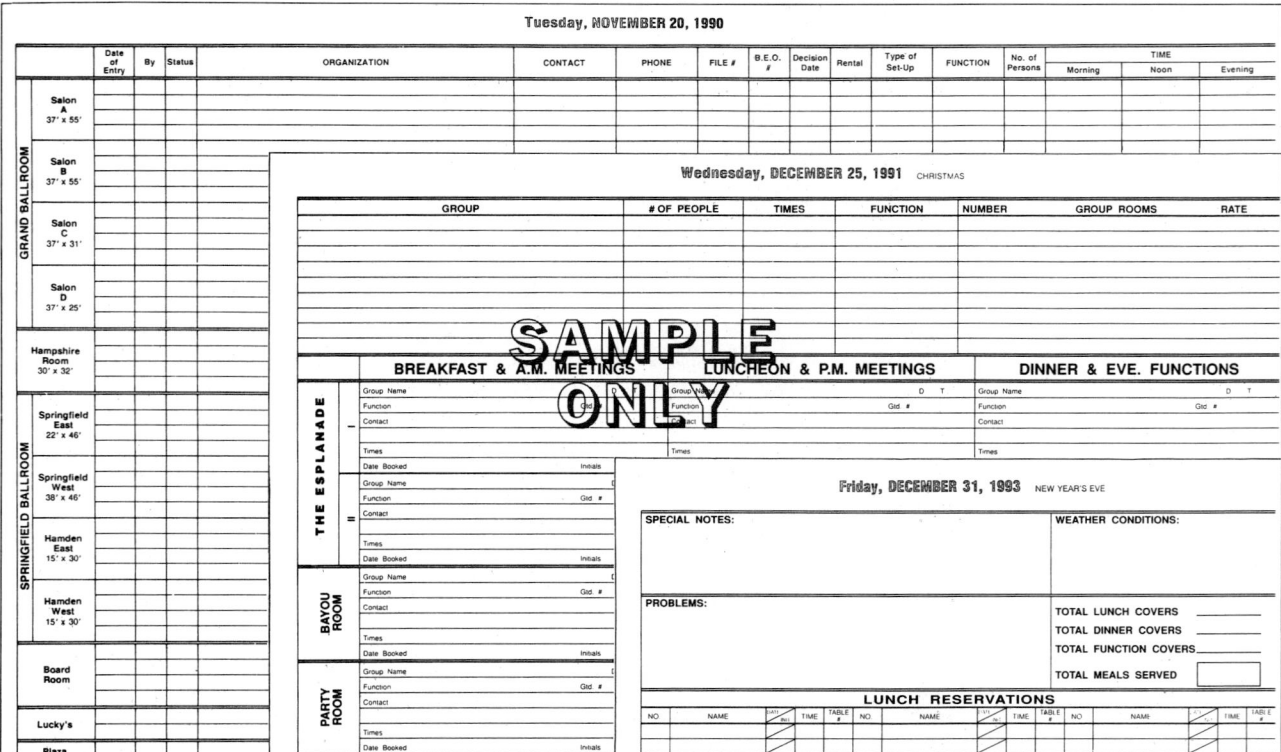

7. *Detailed department head memorandums:* used primarily for conventions and corporate sales or training meetings. They outline in great detail the accommodations required and the meeting room setups, audiovisual equipment, staging, food and beverage service, and other servicing details and instructions for each event, in chronological order.

8. *Banquet/food function sheets:* detailed servicing forms used for each food and beverage function.

9. *Post convention (or convention evaluation) reports:* basically a group "guest history" report, they record the value of a particular event in terms of room, food and beverage, and other departmental revenues. They also contain performance information, such as arrival and departure patterns, sleeping-room pickups, comparisons between meal guarantees and actual covers served, unusual requirements, compliments and complaints, and so on.

Sample illustrations of many of these forms and records are shown in Figure 6–5.

FIGURE 6–5 Typical call report form. (This and the following samples courtesy of Sands Hotel, Casino & Country Club, Atlantic City, New Jersey.)

Sales Call Report Form (Phone Call & Personal Call)

SALESMAN _____   DATE _____

ORGANIZATION _____
CONTACT _____
ADDRESS _____
PHONE _____
OTHER CONTACTS _____

BUSINESS POTENTIAL:
    TYPE OF FUNCTION _____

    MONTH _____   MEETING SPACE:
    ARRIVAL _____
    DEPARTURE _____
    # OF PEOPLE _____
    # OF ROOMS _____
    EXHIBITS _____

PAST/FUTURE HISTORY:
82 _____
83 _____
84 _____
85 _____
86 _____
87 _____
88 _____
89 _____

                        DECISION MAKER _____
                        WHEN _____

COMMENTS: _____

FOLLOW UP: _____

FIGURE 6–5 (cont.) Multipurpose booking report that can be used for a variety of purposes, as indicated in the upper left corner.

SALES BOOKING   **THE SANDS HOTEL & CASINO**

O DEFINITE   O TENTATIVE
O DEFINITE   O TENTATIVE
   CANCELLATION   CANCELLATION
O LOST   O DATE CHANGE
   BUSINESS

REPRESENTATIVE _____
TODAY'S DATE _____   TYPE OF CALL O Personal OVER FLOW
                                                    O Telephone Yes
FROM _____ TO _____   O Letter   No
                                                    O No Call

NAME OF GROUP _____   DIVISION OR MEETING _____
NAME OF CONTACT _____   TITLE _____
ADDRESS OF CONTACT _____
AREA CODE-TEL. NO. ____ CITY ____ STATE ____ ZIP ____ TOTAL RM. NIGHTS ____

Month → DATE / ROOM TYPES → DAY	SUN	MON	TUE	WED	THU	FRI	SAT	SUN	MON	TUE	WED	THUR	FRI	SAT
DOUBLE/ DOUBLE														
KINGS														
SUITES EUROPEAN														
SUITES DELUXE														
SUITES MINI														
TOTAL UNITS														

RATES	COMP. ROOMS	RESERVATIONS BY:	BILLING	CHG.	INDIV.	CANCELLATION AND LOST BUSINESS INFORMATION
SINGLE OCC.		O ROOMING LIST	ROOMS	O	O	
DOUBLE OCC.		O RESERVATION CARDS	INCIDENTALS	O	O	
TRIPLE OCC.		O INDIVIDUAL	OTHER	O	O	
QUAD. OCC.		O THEIR FORMS				
PARLOR		O HOUSING BUREAU	DEPOSIT REQUIREMENTS			
BRM SUITE MINI		O OTHER	O NONE O FULL PREPAY			
BRM SUITE DELUXE		O INNS ON THE PARK	O 1 nt. deposit			
BRM SUITE EUROPEAN		CUTOFF DATE:	O OTHER DATE REQUIRED and amount ($)			

MEETING ROOM RENTAL ____ PARKING ____ DECISION DATE ____

ADDITIONAL COMPS _____

BILLING INSTRUCTIONS _____

PROGRAM _____

ENTERED _____

FILE COPY   SL51-4-83

CREDIT REFERENCE REQUEST

Sands
Hotel & Casino · Atlantic City
Hotel Credit Department

P.O. Box 627
Indiana Avenue & Brighton Park
Atlantic City, New Jersey 08404
609-441-4110

Nº 3793

NAME: _____
Individual or Organization Responsible for Payment

BILLING ADDRESS: _____ Zip Code

CONTACT: _____ Telephone

NAME & TITLE OF INDIVIDUAL TO APPROVE PAYMENT _____ Telephone

BANK REFERENCES: _____

| Bank Name | Account No. | Location | Telephone |

| Bank Name | Account No. | Location | Telephone |

TRADE REFERENCE: _____

| Company Name | Address | Telephone |

PREVIOUS DIRECT BILLINGS:

| Hotel/Restaurant Name | Address | Telephone | Date Attended |

| Hotel/Restaurant Name | Address | Telephone | Date Attended |

| Hotel/Restaurant Name | Address | Telephone | Date Attended |

1. I (we) hereby authorize Sands Hotel & Casino to conduct a complete credit investigation on the above.
2. I (we) shall pay the amount or amounts due, upon receipt of Invoice.

Please return credit application by _____ Date _____ Authorized Signature

────── Office Use Only ──────

SALES REPRESENTATIVE: _____ DATE: _____

DATE OF EVENT: ___/___/___ to ___/___/___

SALES VALUE: ___ Rooms / ___ Food / ___ Beverage / ___ Total / ___ Number

DEPOSIT RECEIVED: $ _____ PREVIOUS BOOKINGS: _____ Dates

TYPE OF CHARGES TO BE BILLED TO MASTER ACCOUNT:
☐ ROOMS ☐ RESTAURANT CHARGES ☐ BEVERAGE CHARGES ☐ PARKING
☐ HOSPITALITY SUITES ☐ BANQUETS ☐ SHOW TICKETS ☐ MISCELLANEOUS

MASTER ACCOUNT CODE _____ Director of Sales' Signature

CREDIT OFFICE: APPROVED _____ DECLINED _____ RATING _____

RECOMMENDATIONS: _____
Hotel Credit Manager's Signature

| B1 | B2 | T1 | P/DB1 | P/DB2 | P/DB3 | LA | LD | CRT | A/R | RESERV. | S/B | ROLO |

HAC4-283

FIGURE 6–5 (cont.) This credit reference form is used to protect both buyer and seller by indicating who is authorized by the group to sign for various types of charges.

FIGURE 6–5 (cont.) Attachment to the preceding group confirmation form which lists various food and beverage functions, such as banquets, receptions, and other social gatherings.

GROUP FUNCTION RESERVATION

Sands
HOTEL, CASINO & COUNTRY CLUB / ATLANTIC CITY

( ) Definite ( ) Tentative ( ) Change ( ) Cancellation

The space listed below is being held for the following...

NAME OF GROUP: _____

DATES: _____

CONTACT: _____ PHONE NUMBER: _____

Date	Time	Function	Room	Set Up	# People

Salesperson: _____ Date: _____

47-1008-486

GROUP CONFIRMATION

Sands
HOTEL, CASINO & COUNTRY CLUB / ATLANTIC CITY

DATE: _____ SALESPERSON: _____ STATUS: _____

ORGANIZATION: _____

CONTACT: _____ TITLE: _____

ADDRESS: _____ CITY: _____

STATE: _____ ZIP: _____ TELEPHONE: _____

ARRIVAL (DAY/DATE) _____ DEPARTURE (DAY/DATE) _____

ROOM TYPES	DATE DAY	SUN	MON	TUE	WED	THU	FRI	SAT	SUN	MON	TUE	WED	THU	FRI	SAT
SINGLES															
DOUBLES															
SUITES: PARLOR + 1 BEDROOM															
SUITES: PARLOR + 2 BEDROOMS															
TOTAL UNITS															

METHOD OF RESERVATIONS: _____ (ROOMING LIST DUE DATE: _____)

RATES: $ _____ (SINGLE/DOUBLE); $ _____ (TRIPLE); $ _____ (QUAD) + _____% tax *(SUBJECT TO CHANGE)*

FINAL CUTOFF: _____ (With a cancellation policy of 48 hours prior to arrival for individual cancellations)

SUITES AND RATES: _____

PARKING RATE: _____ COMPLIMENTARY ROOM POLICY: _____

MEETING ROOM RENTAL: _____ AUDIO/VISUAL RENTAL: _____

COMPLIMENTARY CONSIDERATIONS: _____

DEPOSIT POLICY: _____

PREPAYMENT POLICY: _____

BILLING INSTRUCTIONS: _____

PROGRAM: See attachment "Group Function Reservation"

I understand that check-in time is 3:00 p.m. and check-out time is 12 Noon, unless other arrangements have been made. Check-in on Sundays is 6:00 p.m. I understand that any food and beverage to be consumed in conjunction with my program must be purchased through the Hotel. If my group is tax exempt, I will provide the SANDS with a valid certificate of exemption (ST-5) prior to arrival. My signature constitutes acknowledgement of the information herein.

SIGNED _____ TITLE _____ DATE _____

If applicable, please provide your ATC, IATA, ICC, or PUC #: _____

Group arrivals are subject to baggage handling charges: $ _____

WHITE - Sands   YELLOW - Client   PINK - File   47-3000-1285

FIGURE 6–5 (cont.) The basic working document of the booking, which additionally serves as a key source of information to be included in the client's 9- by 12-in. master file.

FIGURE 6–5 (cont.) Multipurpose rooming list form which can be used for VIP housing, corporate meetings, tour groups, and so on.

ROOMING LIST

Sands HOTEL, CASINO & COUNTRY CLUB / ATLANTIC CITY

NAME OF GROUP: _____

MAJOR ARRIVAL DATE: _____

MAJOR DEPARTURE DATE: _____

NAME OF CONTACT: _____

BILLING CODE:
#1. Pay own room, tax, & incidental charges.
#2. Room & tax only to Master Account.
#3. All charges to Master Account

INSTRUCTIONS: Please type or print neatly; place last name first, followed by title and first name (example: Doe, Mr. John). For double rooms, please note names of both occupants on one line. Note appropriate billing code number by each room or name.

ARRIVAL	DEPARTURE	NAME (Last name first)	ROOM NO. (Hotel use)	TYPE OF ROOM	BILLING INFO.

PLEASE COMPLETE AND RETURN TO SALES DEPARTMENT 30 DAYS PRIOR TO ARRIVAL.
Indiana Avenue and Brighton Park, Atlantic City, New Jersey 08401 (609) 441-4150 (Hotel Sales Office)

47-1007-1285

SALES TIME RECORD ANALYSIS

NAME _____

MONTH _____   DATE _____

	PHONE ACTIVITY SOLICITATION	SALES CALLS		CORRESPONDENCE	CONVENTION SERVICES	COMMENTS
		IN OFFICE	OUTSIDE			
MONDAY						
TUESDAY						
WEDNESDAY						
THURSDAY						
FRIDAY						
SATURDAY						
SUNDAY						
WEEKLY TOTALS						

POST CONVENTION REPORT

Sands.
HOTEL, CASINO & COUNTRY CLUB / ATLANTIC CITY

GROUP: _____

DATES OF MEETING: _____

RATES: _____ SINGLE/DOUBLE _____ SUITES

ROOM UNIT PICKUP

DAY	SUN.	MON.	TUES.	WED.	THURS.	FRI.	SAT.	TOTAL
DATES								
BLOCKED								
OCCUPIED								

TOTAL ROOM REVENUE _____

SUITES USAGE (ROOMNIGHTS)

BLOCKED						
OCCUPIED						

OTHER

SHOWS						
FIGHTS						
GOLF						

TOTAL REVENUE _____

FOOD & BEVERAGE

TYPE OF FUNCTION	DATE	GUARANTEE	COST PER	TOTAL

TOTAL F & B REVENUE _____

WEEKLY ACTIVITY REPORT

No. of Solicitation Phone Calls _____

Salesperson: _____ Week Ending: _____   No. Booked from Phone Solicitation _____

STATUS	DATES	GROUP & AVERAGE RATE	INCREASE	DECREASE	NET TOTAL
Definites & Def.Cancel.	Day & Date				
TOTAL DEF. TOTAL DEF. CAN.					
Tentatives & Ten.Cancel.					
TOTAL TENT. TOTAL TEN. CAN.					

NUMBER OF SALES CALLS _____ IN PERSON (Either on property or on the road).

FIGURE 6–5 *(cont.)* This postconvention report records the value of a particular meeting. It is a most important aid in future bookings and should become an integral part of the group's master file.

FIGURE 6–5 *(cont.)* Several administrative forms that relate to sales staff activities. The upper left shows a daily time analysis record; the lower right form is a weekly activity record.

SUPPORTING CARD FILE SYSTEMS

Many of the forms just described and illustrated are kept in individual manila file folders that form the central filing system (as well as entered on diskettes in a computerized sales office). There are also supporting systems for maintaining other types of records, often for ease of locating information and actually "working the files."

The three most common quick-reference card systems (usually maintained manually on 3- by 5-in. or 5- by 8-in. cards) are:

1. *Master file cards:* keyed to the file folders and kept in alphabetical order. They contain essential working data such as name of group, types of meetings, addresses and phone numbers of key contacts or decision makers, average attendance, and prior meeting history. In effect, they are a condensed version of the *front sheet*.

2. *Geographic file cards:* contain the same basic information as above, but often in abbreviated form. They are maintained in *geographic* order by state or region and city and are especially useful in hotels where the account executives work specific territories. They are also essential for conducting "sales blitzes."
3. *Trace (or "tickler") file cards:* indicate the name of the group, type of meeting, the permanent trace month, and the temporary trace date. They are kept in chronological order by day and month. This is the primary follow-up system used by account executives and indicates what actions are to be taken to follow up, book, or rebook the specific accounts to which each person has been assigned. The common procedure in larger hotels is to have a sales secretary "work" the tickler files each day and place the applicable file folders on the desks of the appropriate account executives on the trace dates for review and action. As soon as the necessary action on each account is completed, a new trace date is penciled in, the file folder returned to the central files, and the trace card refiled for the next tracing (see Figure 6–6).

FIGURE 6–6 Quick reference systems used to support the main file kept on each account.

MINI-CREEK GEOLOGICAL SOCIETY

FILE FOLDER TAB
(Maintained in alphabetical order, though the "Key Word" may be underscored for additional sorting purposes)

MINI-CREEK GEOLOGICAL SOCIETY — Annual Meeting
Dr. Rocco ("Rocky") Stone, Exec. Director
Baron Heinrich von Fledermaus, President
333 North Gladstone Avenue
Margate, New Jersey 08402
Phone: 609/823-2132
FAX: 609/823-0139
Attendance: 450 (no spouses)
88/Aug/Granite, NH, Stoney Inn
89/Aug/Boulder, CO, Rocky Lodge
90/Aug/Reykjavik, Iceland, Lava Hotel
91/Feb/Grey Rocks, Ont, Canada, Grande Majestic Hotel

MASTER CARD
(for quick reference)

MINI-CREEK GEOLOGICAL SOCIETY — Annual Meeting — January
Trace Date January 7, 1992

TRACE CARD
(with permanent trace month and "working" trace date)

MINI-CREEK GEOLOGICAL SOCIETY — Annual Meeting — New Jersey (Atlantic City)
Dr. Rocco ("Rocky") Stone, Exec. Director
Baron Heinrich von Fledermaus, President
333 North Gladstone Avenue
Margate, New Jersey 08402
Phone: 609/823-2132
FAX: 609/823-0139

GEOGRAPHIC CARD

There are other forms that we will not cover here, except for the following brief listing, since they relate to sales and marketing administration. These include business flowcharts, business forecasts, daily revenue reports, monthly booking reports, YTD (year to date) comparative bookings analysis reports, and an entire host of other forms and records which are tied into a property's annual marketing plan.

COMPUTERIZATION

By now, you must be somewhat overwhelmed by the paperwork and seemingly tedious pencil pushing which is all part of the administration and management of a sales and marketing office. Indeed, many a complaint is heard along the lines of, "I spend so much time recording what I'm doing that I don't have the time to do all I could be doing."

Fortunately, automation and computerization offer a great potential for easing the administrative burden, especially in the areas of recording and virtually instantaneous retrieval of information and data. Both the geographical file systems and the follow-up trace files are especially suited to computerization, as are guest history reports, function book (or "diary") entries, booking logs, and the like (see Figure 6–7). Despite the ever-increasing use of computers,

FIGURE 6–7 Work form used to enter information into a computerized client history system. (Courtesy of Marriott Hotels.)

```
HS0010R1  11/30/88          MARRIOTT HOTELS DIVISION - ARMS - MARKET RESEARCH CLIENT ACCOUNT HISTORY                    PAGE

NN008501 ROBERT MORRIS ASSOCIATES                                           MARKET    BANKING        LAST UPDATE  11/88
                                                                            KEYWORD   MORRIS         LAST CONTACT 11/88
 SLS/MKH  1616 PHILA NAT BANK BLDG        PHILADELPHIA      PA    19107      MULT/MGM N               QUALITY     FOCUS
 TRACE DATE  01/15/89                                                        ACT/TYPE                CREDIT      U
 (05) MS TINA SHAFFER                 MEETINGS MANAGER          215-851-9113 ALSO SCHEDULE SMALL REGIONAL MTGS AND A SMALL ANNUAL B
 (10) MS MIRIAM KELLY                 SECRETARY                 215-851-9100 OARD MTG. TINA'S ASST IS MIRIAM KELLY.
 (99) NATIONAL ACCOUNT NUMBER         N087210
*****************************************************      CALL REPORT   *********************************************************
11/16/88-BOSTON & SF UNDER CONSIDERATION FOR '92 & '93. FOLLOW UP IN MIDDLE JANUARY.

 NN00850101   FALL CONFERENCE                   TOP DOLLAR MTG, OPEN RECP 150PP, 2 LUNCHES, WED LGR REC/DIN DANCE SPOUCES PROG,
                                                MON OPENING BKFST, BIG PROBLEM HISTORICALLY IS ACCOMMODATING WED BQT, SPOUCES PG
 MTG TYPE    CONF        FREQUENCY   ANNUAL     RM,PAST PRGM ON FILEIMPORTANT: RMA IS THE NAT ASSN OF BANK LOAN & CREDIT OFFICE
 DECISION    LOCAL       LAST UPDATE 11/88      S/WKSHOPS..60/75 ANNUALLY...10 TO 150PP EA/BD MTG-25PP..PIC K TOP SITE ANNUALLY.
 COMMISSION  N

 MAX ROOMS 1200   MAX MEET    1500   MAX F&B 1700   EXH STYLE        S   M   T   W   T   F   S   S   M   T   W   T   F   S
 # SUITES     0   MTG SET-UP    TS   F&B TYPE  D    # BOOTHS    0
 % DBL OCC    5   # BRK SESS     3             MOVE DAY IN-  OUT-  0%  0   0   0   0   0  20 100 100 100  80   0   0   0

 (05) MS TINA SHAFFER                 MEETINGS MANAGER          215-665-2872          MAJ DAY IN  SU        HOTEL PREF   DTN CIT
                                                                                     MONTH PREF  10 11 09  GEOG PREF    DO

                                                     DEFINITE
 ARRIVE    SEQ DEPART   Y/B L/S HOTEL      DEF CITY     ST DATE SENT SUN  MON  TUE  WED  THU  FRI  SAT  TOTAL  S/R  D/R
 10/30/83 (1) 11/02/83  80  O  FAIRMONT    Y  SAN FRAN  CA  /  /                        12   54  217         0    0
                                                              413  408  406  357   36    0    0  1903
 10/26/84 (1) 10/30/84  81  O  CONDADO     Y  SAN JUAN  PR  /  /    0    0    0    0    1    7   25   92         1    0
                                                              148  147  143    0    0    0   89  548   563
 09/19/85 (1) 09/26/85  82  O  SHERATON    Y  BOSTON    MA  /  /                        25   89  548         1    1
                                                              913  921  912  718   46    0    0  4172
 09/28/86 (1) 10/01/86  83  O  HYATT       Y  HOUSTON   TX  /  /    0    0    0    3   18   52  321         0    0
                                                              699  703  688  528   19    5    4  3040
 11/01/87 (1) 11/04/87  84  O  HILTON      Y  HONOLULU  HI  /  /    0    0    0    0    0    0    0         0    0
                                                                0    0    0    0    0    0    0    0
 11/00/88 (1) 11/00/88  85  O  HYATT       Y  CHICAGO   IL  /  /    0    0    0    0    0    0    0         0    0
                                                                0    0    0    0    0    0    0    0
 11/00/89 (1) 11/00/89  87  O  WESTIN      Y  ATLANTA   GA  /  /    1    0    0    0    0    0    0         1    1    1
                                                                0    0    0    0    0    0    0
 11/00/90 (1) 11/00/90  87  O  SHERATON    Y  SEATTLE   WA  /  /    0    0    0    0    0    0    0    0    0    0
                                                                0    0    0    0    0    0    0
 11/00/91 (1) 11/00/91  87  O  HILTON      Y  ATLANTA   GA  /  /    0    0    0    0    0    0    0    0    0    0
                                                                0    0    0    0    0    0    0

                                                     TENTATIVE
 ARRIVE    SEQ DEPART   Y/B L/S HOTEL      DEF CITY     ST DATE SENT SUN  MON  TUE  WED  THU  FRI  SAT  TOTAL  S/R  D/R
 11/00/92 (1) 11/00/92  00  S  MARR BOSCO  N  BOSTON    MA 11/17/88   0    0    0    0   25   90  550         1    1
          NN12880315                                           950  950  950  750   50    0    0  4315
 11/00/93 (1) 11/00/93  00  S  MARR SFOMO  N  SAN FRAN  CA 06/28/88   0    0    0    3   18   52  321         1    1
          NN07880353                                           699  703  688  528   91    5    0  3108
 11/00/93 (2) 11/00/93  00  S  MARR BOSCO  N  BOSTON    MA 11/17/88   0    0    0    0   25   90  550         1    1
          NN12880316                                           950  950  950  750   50    0    0  4315
```

FIGURE 6-7 (cont.) Sample printout from a computerized client history system. (Courtesy of Marriott Hotels.)

FIGURE 6-8 Manual filing and record-keeping systems (left) are gradually being replaced throughout the industry by the faster, more accurate, and more efficient computerized systems.

manual systems will still have their place, especially for backup purposes (Figure 6–8).

ACCOUNT EXECUTIVE'S WORK FORMS

The final major category of sales and marketing forms and records are those that can be used by the sales executive to gather information and data that can be both professionally and personally helpful. Proper usage can help the individual salesperson sell more efficiently and professionally, and thus more profitably.

These forms in effect recap most of the information discussed in Chapters 2 through 5 and include:

1. Property Profiles
2. Employee Hobbies and Skills Inventory
3. Product Analysis SWOT* List
4. Features Appraisal Checklist
5. Features Into Benefits Chart
6. Competitive Services and Amenities Analysis
7. Key Business Source List
8. Airline Survey
9. Daily Occupancy Summary
10. Monthly Market Mix Report
11. Segment and Source Room Nights Analysis
12. Monthly Forecasts and Revenue Projection
13. Annual Revenue Forecast
14. Market Segment Goals, Strategies, and Tactics
15. Sales Action Plans
16. Package Plan and Special Promotions Forecast
17. Sales Tool Cost Analysis

Each of these forms is illustrated in Figure 6–9.

The first eight forms from the previous listing concentrate on the types of information a sales executive should have access to for direct selling purposes. The remaining nine forms relate more to business projections and marketing management considerations. Nevertheless, they should be available to all members of the sales and marketing "team." One of the more prevalent needs of hotel sales executives is for financial information and forecast data that can offer additional direction toward the goal of *booking profitable business at the time the property needs business the most.*

---

*The acronym "SWOT" stands for an especially useful tool for evaluating one's competitors as well as studying your own property. The "S" and "W" stand for "strengths" and "weaknesses" (of one's product, competition, personal skills, etc.). The "O" and "T" represent "opportunities" and "threats" and are basically external factors over which one has little if any control (legislation, highway construction, taxes, etc.).

WORK FORMS

PROPERTY PROFILE (Tangibles)

LOCATION: _____

_____
_____
_____

ROOMS: (No.) Singles ____ ; Doubles ____ ; Twins ____ ; Suites ____

        (Rates) Sgl $ ____ ; Dbl $ ____ ; Tn $ ____ ; Suites $ ____

FOOD: (No. of Seats) Coffee Shop _____ ; Dining Room _____

       (Hours Open) Coffee Shop _____ ; Dining Room _____

BEVERAGE: Seats in Lounge _____ ; Hours Open _____

ROOM SERVICE: Hours _____ ; Type _____

MEETING SPACE:	Name of Room	Capacities:				
		Theatre	Schoolroom	Reception	Dining	Exhibits

ON-PREMISE AUDIO-VISUALS: _____

OTHER REVENUE-PRODUCING OUTLETS: _____

SPECIAL FEATURES & FACILITIES: _____

SPORTS & RECREATION FACILITIES: _____

OFF-PROPERTY ATTRACTIONS: _____

PROPERTY PROFILE (Intangibles)

ATMOSPHERE: _____

_____
_____
_____

DECOR & AMBIENCE: _____

_____
_____

STAFF PROFILE	Age Category	Main Employment Sources	Special Training	Average Length of Employment
Front Office				
Dining Room				
Kitchen				
Housekeeping				
Maintenance				
Security				
Accounting				
Management				
Other (_____)				

ADDITIONAL COMMENTS: _____

_____
_____
_____
_____
_____
_____

EMPLOYEE HOBBIES & SKILLS INVENTORY

NAME & DEPARTMENT	LANGUAGES SPOKEN (Read)	HOBBIES/ SPORTS	TALENTS (Music, etc)	CIVIC/SOCIAL CLUB MEMBERSHIP

FIGURE 6-9 Work forms used to profile both the physical and the human resources of the property.

PRODUCT ANALYSIS "SWOT" LIST

STRENGTHS	WEAKNESSES	OPPORTUNITIES	"THREATS"
Location:			
Rooms:			
Food:			
Beverage:			

PRODUCT ANALYSIS "SWOT" LIST (cont'd):

STRENGTHS	WEAKNESSES	OPPORTUNITIES	"THREATS"
Other Revenue Outlets:			
Special Features & Facilities:			
Sports & Recreation Facil.:			
Off-Property Attractions:			

FEATURES APPRAISAL CHECKLIST:

FEATURE	BENEFICIAL TO	NEGATIVE TO	INCONSEQUENTIAL
Location:			
Rooms:			
Food:			
Beverage:			

FEATURES APPRAISAL CHECKLIST (cont'd):

FEATURE	BENEFICIAL TO	NEGATIVE TO	INCONSEQUENTIAL
Other Revenue Outlets:			
Special Features & Facilities:			
Sports & Recreation Facil.:			
Off-Property Attractions:			

FIGURE 6–9 (cont.) "SWOT" form used to analyze a property's strengths and weakness (left) can then be combined with a features appraisal checklist to determine which strengths and weaknesses are most consequential to which market segments.

FEATURES INTO BENEFITS CHART   Target Market: _____

FEATURE	GENERAL BENEFIT	MONEY-SAVINGS	TIME-SAVINGS	CONVENIENCE-PROVIDING	PROCEDURES-SIMPLIFYING
Rooms:					
Food:					
Beverages:					
Location:					
Function Space:					
Rec./Sports Facilities:					
Special Features:					
Special Services:					
Other:					

COMPETITIVE SERVICES &
AMENITIES ANALYSIS (Individual Leisure Traveler)

ITEM	Us	A	B	C	D	E	F	Remarks
Connecting Rooms								
Double-Doubles								
Recr. Facilities								
Pool								
Health Club Fac.								
Childen's Programs								
Info. Center								
Nearby Attractions								
Baby Sitters								
Family Menus								
24-Hr. Snack Svc.								
Gift Shop								
Game Room								

COMPETITIVE SERVICES &
AMENITIES ANALYSIS (Individual Business Traveler)

ITEM	Us	A	B	C	D	E	F	Remarks
Quick Checkin								
Instant Checkout								
Corporate Rate								
Guaranteed Res.								
Fast Breakfast								
Room Service								
Reliable Wakeup								
Limo Service								
Health Facil.								
Exec. Floor								
Writing Desk								
DD Phones								
Radio								
Cable TV								
Good Lighting								
King-size Beds								
Business Services								

FIGURE 6-9 (cont.) Some additional work forms, prepared on a market segment basis, pinpoint specific benefits and compare services and amenities with those offered by the competition.

AIRLINE SURVEY:

Date Completed: _____

AIRPORT: _____

Airport Manager: _____
_____
_____
_____

Phone: _____

Other Airport Contacts: _____
_____
_____
_____

Airline	Daily Flights	Key Cities of Origin	Key Contacts	Business Potentials (crew, etc.)

DAILY OCCUPANCY SUMMARY:

Month of _____, 19____

WEEK BEGINNING	Sunday OR % ADR	Monday OR % ADR	Tuesday OR % ADR	Wednesday OR % ADR	Thursday OR % ADR	Friday OR % ADR	Saturday OR % ADR
TOTALS							

Month Recap:　　　　　　This Year　Last Year　2 Years Ago

OR (Occupied Rooms)　　　_____　_____　_____

% (Percentage of Occupancy)　_____　_____　_____

ADR (Average Daily Rate)　_____　_____　_____

MONTHLY FORECASTS AND REVENUE PROJECTIONS:

Month & Year _____

MARKET MIX GOALS	%	# ROOM NIGHTS	AVERAGE ROOM RATE	ROOM REVENUE	F & B REVENUE	OTHER INCOME	TOTAL REVENUE
Ind. Business Tr.							
Ind. Leisure Tr.							
Assoc. Convention							
Corp. Meetings							
Group Leisure							
TOTALS							

MONTHLY MARKET MIX (BY %):

For The Year _____

MAJOR MARKETS	JAN.	FEB.	MAR.	APR.	MAY	JUNE	JULY	AUG.	SEP.	OCT.	NOV.	DEC.	YEAR AVERAGE
Ind. Business Travel													
Ind. Leisure Travel													
Assoc. Conventions													
Corp. Meetings													
Tour Groups													

MONTHLY MARKET MIX (BY ROOM NIGHTS):

MAJOR MARKETS	JAN.	FEB.	MAR.	APR.	MAY	JUNE	JULY	AUG.	SEP.	OCT.	NOV.	DEC.	TOTALS
Ind. Business Travel													
Ind. Leisure Travel													
Assoc. Conventions													
Corp. Meetings													
Tour Groups													
TOTALS													

ANNUAL REVENUE FORECAST:

Year: _____

MARKET MIX GOALS (%)	Jan	Feb	Mar	Apr	May	June	July	Aug	Sep	Oct	Nov	Dec	TOTAL YEAR
Ind. Bus. Trav.													
Ind. Leisure Trav.													
Conv./Mtgs.													
Group Tours													

DOLLAR FORECASTS	Jan	Feb	Mar	Apr	May	June	July	Aug	Sep	Oct	Nov	Dec	TOTAL YEAR
Available Rooms													
Average Occupancy													
Occupied Rooms													
Average Room Rate													
ROOM REVENUE													
F& B Revenue													
Other Income													
TOTAL REVENUE													

FIGURE 6-9 (cont.) Sample survey, summary, and forecast forms that record information for use in a property's annual marketing plan.

GOALS, STRATEGIES, AND TACTICS:

TARGET MARKET: _____   YEAR: _____

GOALS	STRATEGIES	TACTICS	SALES TOOL SUPPORT

PACKAGE PLAN AND
SPECIAL PROMOTIONS FORECAST:

For the year: _____

TYPE OF PLAN/ PACKAGE	Target Markets	Applicable Dates	Special Features	Price	Proj. Rm.Nigts	Proj.Total Revenue	Prom/Mktg Methods	Budget
TOTALS								

KEY BUSINESS SOURCE LIST:

TARGET MARKET: Individual Business Traveler

COMPANY OR FIRM NAME	FILE #	ROOM NIGHTS PREVIOUS YEAR	EXPECTED R.N. THIS YEAR	PROJECTED R.N. NEXT YEAR	OTHER POTENTIAL REVENUE (Mtgs, F&B)
Local Area					
Primary Outside Market Area					
#2 Outside Market Area					

SALES ACTION PLANS:

Year: _____

TARGET MARKET: _____   OBJECTIVES & GOALS: _____
_____

ACTION STEPS	Responsibility	Jan	Feb	Mar	Apr	May	June	July	Aug	Sep	Oct	Nov	De

SALES TOOL COST ANALYSIS:

TARGET MARKET: _____

ITEM:	QUANTITY REQUIRED	DATE AVAILABLE OR USED	COST	REMARKS

SEGMENT & SOURCE ROOM NIGHT ANALYSIS:

Year: _____

SEGMENTS	Jan	Feb	Mar	Apr	May	Jun	Jul	Aug	Sep	Oct	Nov	Dec	Total	% of Annual R.N.
Ind. Bus. Tr.														
Ind. Leisure Tr.														
Conv./Mtgs.														
Group Tours														
Govt/Mil./Ed.														
Air Crews														
TOTAL R.N.														

SOURCES	Jan	Feb	Mar	Apr	May	Jun	Jul	Aug	Sep	Oct	Nov	Dec	Total	% of Annual R.N.
Direct Reserv.														
800 Number														
Reserv. System														
Mtg. Planner														
Travel Agent														
Walk-ins														
TOTAL R.N.														

FIGURE 6-9 (cont.) Some additional records that relate specifically to the planning of actions to be undertaken by the sales executives.

ACCOUNTS ANALYSIS

For example, information from the preceding work forms and records should be coupled with data from such accounting office reports as the daily report, monthly profit and loss statement, and other financial information. This can be of substantial help to sales executives in tracking their efforts on both an individual and a departmental basis. To do this, each sales executive should prepare a personalized *financial analysis* and a *sales analysis,* similar to the following questionnaire guide:

Financial Analysis

1. Who are your top five market segments in order of monetary importance (i.e., both volume and contributions to profit)?
2. Who are the top five accounts within each segment in terms of gross sales?
3. How many room nights and total room revenue does each account represent annually [and the amount of increase (decrease) of each] compared with each of the past five years?
4. How much food and beverage revenue and other income revenues does each account bring in annually?
5. Combining items 3 and 4, what total annual revenue does each account represent, what percent does this represent compared to all other accounts in the segment, and what percent does it represent compared with total annual revenue from all business sources?
6. What is the cost of soliciting, securing, servicing, and maintaining each market segment?

Sales Analysis

1. How often do you call on your top 25 accounts?
2. What are you doing to retain as well as increase their business potential?
3. What appeals and benefits can you offer to counter any benefits offers by your competitors?
4. Have you lost any previous top 25 accounts during the past year, and why?
5. What would it take to get them back?

FIELD USE

We are sure you must have some questions at this point, such as:

1. How and where does one gather all of this information?
2. How and where are all these data recorded and updated on the many records and forms used in the modern sales/marketing office?
3. What does one do with all the information one can obtain from these records?
4. When and where is all the information used in practice?

The answer to each of the above is: *in the field.*

Information laying around in files or on computer disks and not used is totally worthless. There is a point to gathering, maintaining, and updating all these data—and that is to use it intelligently to book business. The only way to book business for most sales executives is to go out and actively *sell,* which is the subject of the next chapter.

seven

SELL

DEFINING COMMUNICATIONS

Before defining communications (which we must in order to define *selling* properly), it might be appropriate to give you another definition of marketing. This one is from W. W. "Bud" Grice,* who looks at marketing as the:

Powerful
  Persuasion of
    People to
      Purchase your
        Product or
          Property at a
            Predetermined
              Profit.

Each of these words "carries its own weight" within the definition, but the ones we focus on in this chapter are "persuasion" and "purchase"—because this is what the selling function is all about.

In hotel sales, the selling function is also a *buying* function for the person with a need, want, or desire for accommodations, facilities, and services.

The exchange between a buyer and seller, especially where there is face-to-face personal contact, should be an interchange of information, ideas, and suggestions, leading to a sale or purchase where each party feels it will benefit. In negotiations, this positive environment is called a *win–win* situation. To best accomplish this, both parties must follow the *basics* of effective communications.

One of the more popular working definitions of communications that bears this out is: "the *unaltered exchange* of information, ideas, and concepts *between* two or more people." There are several key words in this definition which are extremely important to the sales executive, regardless of whether the communication takes the form of a personal call, a letter, or an advertisement in a newspaper or magazine.

Unaltered. Many of you have undoubtedly played the game "Whispering Down the Lane." This is where someone whispers a story to the next person, that person in turn whispers it to another, and so on. The fifteenth or twentieth person down the line (or lane) then relates the story to the group, and then the first person tells the original story. In most cases, the two tales have little if any similarity. That's alteration—and that's what you don't want to happen in any type of sales communications.

To illustrate what could happen, let's set up a scene where a hotel sales executive is discussing VIP accommodations with a meeting planner and agrees to set aside *nine adjoining two-room suites.* In the minds of many hotel executives, a two-room suite is one bedroom with an adjacent parlor; to the buyer, however, it may be a two-bedroom setup with a parlor in between. Many customers also say "adjoining" when they really mean "connecting." (All connecting rooms are adjoining, but not all adjoining rooms are necessarily interconnected.) So right there we have two initial alterations, and as the old saying goes, right there we have a "failure to communicate."

---

*W. W. "Bud" Grice, CHSE, was the first vice president of marketing for Marriott Hotels. He is a past president of the Hotel Sales and Marketing Association International and a member of HSMAI's Hall of Fame.

Additional (or secondary) alteration could happen further down the line as the account executive transmits this request to the rooms division manager, who in turn passes it over to the reservations department, who in turn passes it down to the front office. What we could end up with is a practical but unfortunate example of our "Whispering Down the Lane" game.

Similar situations can occur in print and broadcast advertising and in direct mail. With these media, there is the added disadvantage that communications at the time the message is being received is only "one way." The reader cannot immediately ask the hotel executive, "What exactly do you mean by a set of adjoining two-room suites?"

Exchange and Between. These two words are directly interrelated and emphasize the key concept that effective communications must be "two-way," with opportunity for reply. The response by a buyer, for example, can either be a "Fine . . . set aside those dates right now for us" response, or a request for clarification, additional information, more time to consider, and so on. The very nature of certain types of communications affords a "natural" opportunity for an immediate "two-way" dialogue. These include personal calls on a client, telephone calls, "FAM" (familiarization) trips, site inspections, or exhibit booths at a customer convention or trade show.

With other sales or communications tools, there will be a response time lag, such as in the use of print, broadcast, and direct-mail advertising. In these cases you must make sure that a *response vehicle* is clearly indicated and that such a response on the part of the reader or listener is easy to make. This "make it easy for the customer to buy" action step is essential in establishing an effective communications exchange opportunity between seller and potential buyer. This concept can also form a practical working definition of the term *selling*.

SALES TOOL SELECTION

The hospitality industry can utilize a wide variety of different means of communications to sell effectively and productively. Each type of sales tool has significant advantages, disadvantages, and limitations, and some of them have just been described.

Among the key communications sales tools are:

1. Personal selling (face-to-face contact)
2. Telephone selling (also called telemarketing)
3. Direct mail
4. Collateral materials (folders, brochures, flyers, etc.)
5. Print advertising (newspapers and magazines)
6. Broadcast advertising (radio and TV)
7. Outdoor and transit advertising (posters, signs, billboards, and displays)
8. Public relations (especially the component known as "publicity," which takes such forms as news kits, press releases, interviews, and feature stories)

The relative effectiveness of each medium or selling tool will depend on such key factors as:

1. Type and location of the property
2. The history, image, and reputation of the facility

3. The property's objectives and goals
4. The nature and promotional activity of the competition
5. Profiles and characteristics of key target markets
6. The promotional budget
7. Staff capabilities and limitations

Which sales tools to select for a given activity may also depend greatly on where you are located in relation to your key market areas. For example, if you are located in Washington, D.C., New York City, or Chicago and want to call on locally headquartered association executives, *personal sales calls* (using your geographic card files) can be productive and cost-effective because there is a concentration of potential customers in your immediate vicinity. But if you are located in Honolulu, Hawaii, and you want to contact the same association executives to discuss "offshore" meetings and incentive trips, you would use the *telephone* for most of the initial contact activity, perhaps supplementing it with concentrated sales blitz* activity on the mainland once or twice a year.

EVALUATION CONSIDERATIONS

A common question with respect to sales tools relates to the "ideal" mix of advertising, personal selling, and other means of promotion. The query is commonly stated: "How much or what proportion of my overall advertising and promotion efforts and budget should be devoted to personal selling, to the various individual forms of advertising, to public relations, and so on?"

From a business perspective, the question is really an ill-advised one because the most honest answer would be a somewhat curt return question: "Well, what are you planning to promote and to whom, and what will it cost you to effectively do the job and thereby reach your objectives and goals?"

The corollary question which then often follows is: "What percentage, or how much, of my advertising and promotion budget should I spend on developing convention and group business," or "on developing travel and tour business," or "on expanding my individual business travel market?" Here again, the answer must be the same as above. There are no magic formulas or ratios that can be pulled out of a hat.

COORDINATED PROGRAMS

The utilization of sales tools for a particular market segment or for a specific campaign often follows a specific sequence. It is rare that one particular sales tool stands totally by itself.

In the industry one hears of the sales director who works in a unique property with little competition, who personally handles 300 to 400 very specialized group accounts, who has a 90 percent repeat business factor, and who doesn't leave the property to make any sales calls, rarely uses direct mail, does no media advertising, and relies exclusively on the phone for all customer contact. That's the utopian situation every hotel may be striving for; it certainly represents the epitome of cost-effectiveness. Realistically, though, nearly every

---

*A *sales blitz* is a concentrated program of making as many sales calls as possible by as many people as possible in as little time as possible in a specific set of locations. In our Hawaii illustration, it would usually be conducted when another activity would bring the sales staff to the mainland (such as a hospitality industry convention or customer trade show).

property must rely on the combined, coordinated, and integrated usage of *multiple media* to gain maximum exposure and sales impact.

THE PERSONAL SALES CALL

While virtually all forms of sales tools can be utilized for most solicitations and follow-ups, there is a general ranking as far as potential effectiveness. For most properties, *personal calls* would get top billing, primarily because large amounts of volume business can be generated through direct face-to-face dialogue with clearly identifiable decision makers.

For conventions and group business, for example, one sales call could have the potential of developing thousands of room nights, high-volume food and beverage sales, and other departmental income revenues, all of which in just a few years (assuming repeat business) could represent many hundreds of thousands of dollars. It would be highly unlikely that this type of "high ticket item" commitment would usually be made solely on the basis of the decision maker looking at an ad, a brochure, or a form letter.

This is not to state or imply that these other forms of customer communications do not have their place and value. Their effective use will be discussed later. But if not initially, then somewhere close to the decision-making point, both buyer and seller generally must personally meet, particularly if the business involved is what might be termed a "big ticket" sale.

How does one make an effective sales call? What type of preparation is necessary? How does one make a winning presentation? How does one overcome objections? How does one effectively "close" and make the sale? These are certainly key questions that everyone in sales has asked at one time or another. Before developing some potential answers to these, a few initial observations about sales calls in general.

ENVIRONMENT

Sales calls used to be thought of primarily as the process of leaving your property and on a preplanned appointment basis, visiting a specified number of prospects in their offices. But there are also other types of environments that can prove productive, especially as they would relate to the main objective or purpose of the contact:

1. As an *attendee* at a national or state customer convention or trade show (ASAE, MPI, ICP, etc.). Visibility—getting known and establishing contacts—would be among the main objectives here.
2. As an *exhibitor* at a customer convention or trade show. Visibility, contact, and the distribution of brochures and other take-home literature would be among the key objectives.
3. At a *neutral* location—neither customer office nor hotel. May be prearranged ("Let's play golf Saturday") or unplanned (striking up a conversation with a person sitting next to you on a plane).
4. *Planned visit* by a customer to the hotel's sales/marketing office, often in conjunction with a site inspection or "FAM" trip.
5. *Drop-in visit* to your sales office by a potential customer who is on the property for another reason (a meeting planner on a vacation, or on a company business trip, or attending a civic/service club luncheon).

6. *Prearranged gatherings* of potential customers who may have dual functions. This could include inviting those guests on business trips to a special "manager's reception" or "manager's breakfast," where sales executives informally search out those business executives who may also have meeting planning responsibilities. This could be followed up by offering a tour of the property's meeting facilities at the guests' convenience.

7. *Unannounced site inspection.* Not really a sales call initially since you as the hotel sales executive may be unaware that the innocuous-looking vacationer with full family, or the business executive who wanders all over the property as though totally lost, are both also there to inspect your facilities for other potential uses. Later, when and if they make their presence known, the situation becomes an on-property sales call.

8. *Cold calls* (including sales blitzes and student blitzes). These situations are different from the others in that the main intent at that time is not to book business but to determine "what's out there" in a given area or office building. It is more or less a "search and evaluate" mission for purposes of creating or updating prospect files and qualifying "suspects." The process basically is one of introducing yourself, exchanging business cards, handing out a folder or brochure, possibly but not always asking a few essential questions (e.g., general types of meetings, size of largest group, names of key decision makers who make individual travel arrangements) and generally leaving without attempting to make the sale at that time. That will be done in a follow-up. In the basic cold call, where you are canvassing an area without appointments just to see if you have overlooked any possibilities, bookings could be made. But in the blitz* situation, where you have large numbers of people "on the road" for a specific period of time, the objective is to get essential information as quickly as possible from as many contacts as possible, to be used to update files and records for follow-up calls.

9. *In-house prospecting.* This procedure can perhaps best be illustrated through a story of a well-known sales director some years ago who came from England and knew that Americans generally have a fascination for a British accent. Periodically he would sit in the hotel lounge, usually on a Monday or Tuesday when the house was filled primarily with commercial business, and strike up casual conversations along the following lines: "Do you stay here often? . . . What company do you represent? . . . Are you in any way responsible for meetings in your firm? . . . You are; have you seen the meeting space in this hotel? . . . You haven't; well I just happen to be the sales director here and I'd be delighted, at your convenience, to show you around." Needless to say, he booked considerable business at virtually no cost (except, perhaps, to pick up an occasional beverage tab).

CALL OBJECTIVES

Every personal call should have a main objective, which could be any one or a combination of the following:

*Blitzes have become extremely popular during the past two decades. They usually take one of three forms: (1) use of operating department personnel who have guest-contact experience (room clerks, bartenders, etc.) during low occupancy periods; (2) use, in chains and franchise systems, of the sales staff of sister properties who may be in your hotel or area attending a regional sales meeting of the hotel chain; and (3) the ever-growing use of students from the nearly 1000 two- and four-year schools of hotel administration in North America, as well as students from the hundreds of other hospitality schools around the world.

1. To establish a positive image (or overcome a previously "negative" one)
2. To establish visibility (either or both for the property and for the sales executive)
3. To qualify business by separating "suspects" from "prospects" (i.e., files and records maintenance)
4. To check on the current and potential future requirements of specific customers
5. To "whet the customer's appetite" by showcasing the property and its facilities*
6. To obtain future commitments
7. To close a sale and get a definite contract
8. To rebook an account that could not make a rebooking decision when it was last on property
9. To "save" a cancellation
10. To reopen a lost or "neutralized" account

Once these objectives have been established, one does not immediately run out and call on the contacts or decision makers. As the next pages will illustrate, there is a systematic sequence of actions before, during, and after each set of sales calls, which can help ensure their successful completion.

KEY COMPONENTS

The majority of sales calls involves a visitation by the hotel sales executive to the client's or potential customer's office. Also, a substantial number of people start their sales careers as account executives "pounding the bricks." So, let's run through the basic procedures of making effective sales presentations using this type of environmental situation. There are three main components in nearly every type of sales call:

1. The preplanning or preparation stage
2. The presentation
3. The follow-up

BASIC PREPARATION

We have done our homework on the client, we are knowledgeable of their past performance, we have a good idea of current needs and requirements, we know the type of meetings and other functions the company or association holds, we know the first available open dates for each type of meeting, we have studied their individual travel housing needs, and we have identified all the decision makers. So we're ready to go . . . right? No: Not yet!

That is only part of the preparation. There are, for instance, a number of other factors in preparing *yourself* to ensure the maximum potential for a favorable reception by the client.

---

*Some properties make a tactical error by inviting association executives, travel agents, tour operators, and travel writers to their properties only during a downtime or low-occupancy period (when it might be easier to get them "comps"). Most volume decision makers, however, prefer to see the property "in action," especially if one or more conventions or tour groups on the property have profiles or requirements similar to theirs.

Some of these will be more consequential than others, depending on whether or not a prior relationship has been established with a particular prospect. If the decision maker knows you and the property, the sales presentation will take on a different "flavor" than if the two of you had never met.

There are some key attributes for successful personal selling that cannot be established overnight. But continuous cultivation of the following characteristics can be helpful in establishing the proper rapport with various types of business potentials.

Visibility

Are you known in the marketplace; do you attend customer meetings, especially joint sessions between buyers and sellers? Do you volunteer for leadership positions in organizations that interface with potential business decision makers? Are you active in local, state, and national hospitality industry organizations as well as being a working "allied" member of key meeting planning and travel and tour groups?

Signature

Meeting planners, travel agents, tour operators, and other volume buyers meet hundreds, sometimes thousands, of hotel executives during the course of a year (and sometimes in one or two days at a major convention or trade show!). Is there something about you that can make you stand out in a positive way from the rest?

A personal "signature" can be beneficial in establishing and maintaining recognition. It could be an item of clothing (a distinctive belt buckle or pipe or the fact that you wear "Western-style" boots), or it could be some giveaway that might be representative of your area or property, or it could be an unusual skill, hobby, or background not necessarily connected to your business life. It's not an absolute necessity but it helps if some type of personal signature can be established and maintained in a natural, nonoffensive, and positive manner.

Reputation

Are customers, or even prospects who haven't met you before but have heard of you, glad to see you because of your known dedication, honesty, reliability, commitment, and ability to follow-through? Do you have the reputation as one who can be counted on? This is something, of course, that you cannot build overnight. But it is a trait you can prepare for and constantly refine.

Creativity

A skills area that can be a significant part of your reputation is innovation and creativity. The customer is often buying your problem-solving ability, your flair and showmanship capabilities, and your creative talents for suggesting something different or out of the ordinary.

Sense of Humor

A proper sense of humor can be an extremely helpful attribute, if only that it allows you to put things in their proper perspective. When utilized properly it can be most useful, for example, in alleviating potentially stressful situations or possible confrontations with customers.

As you look back at the preceding checklist, you might well ask, "What does this have to do with the preparation of a sales call?" Yes, these are long-range personal characteristics. But they are also key traits and attributes that one should cultivate and improve upon constantly since they can substantially influence the initial reception and subsequent impact of your sales presentation.

PHYSICAL PREPARATION

Now, let's look at some considerations that relate to the more "physical" aspects of preparing yourself for the sales call. These include positive appearance, dress, grooming, and general deportment and bearing. All of these can combine to give off the "right signals," especially when you are dealing with people who do not know you. The positive signals in effect say to a potential client or customer: "You will be dealing with confident, knowledgeable professionals who care enough about themselves to care about you."

Appearance and Dress

What you wear can certainly make an impact, especially during a first contact. But as fashions keep changing and casual informality becomes more prevalent, it is sometimes difficult, if not confusing, to figure out what will get the most positive acceptance. Some hotel companies have specific guidelines or dress codes, especially for men. (Women have much more fashion flexibility and choice.) Other companies merely indicate "suitable or appropriate business dress." (Make sure that they specifically tell or show what they mean by suitable or appropriate.)

Here are some general guidelines that would seem to be appropriate in nearly all situations:

1. Clothing is somewhat like a uniform and should therefore reflect the *tone* of the property or company. If the hotel is a traditional landmark and positions itself as the flagship of history and nostalgia, it would not be too appropriate for its sales executives to envelop themselves in the latest fashions direct from London, Paris, or Rome. By the same token, if the hotel is a five-star property, casual slacks and an open sports shirt would not be reflective of its more "formal" image.

2. The operating *style* or philosophy of the property also has some bearing. If the atmosphere and ambience, together with the overall "pace" of the operation and the staff, is relaxed and laid back, bright, flashy, and overly "trendy" clothing might be somewhat out of place.

3. Appearance and dress, on the other hand, should reflect the *message* the property is trying to convey to a specific recipient. If you are selling your southern resort as a place for a group's board of directors to hold a combination "work and fun in the sun" January meeting, it may not always be appropriate to wear a dark black suit and solid gray tie, even if the group's headquarters are in a major northern city. There could be a "credibility gap" between the image you are trying to convey and your appearance while conveying it.

4. Then you also have to be concerned about the *type* of people you are soliciting. Are they conservative or liberal in their outlook, philosophy, and general lifestyles? Here's where your knowledge of demographic and psychographic profiles can have direct, practical application. What you would wear when calling on an association of bankers could differ from what you might select when calling on a group of creative designers.

5. You should also consider *where* you are making calls, so that you are not completely out of style with what is suitable or appropriate for the area. Business executives in Honolulu generally dress more casually than their counterparts in Boston. And what would be considered formal wear in Manila could be thought overly casual in London. Businessmen in Tucson, Arizona, usually do not wear ties during the day in the summer because of the climate and the more laid-back lifestyle.

6. You must also consider the *utility* aspect of your clothing. The latest "fad" for men might be suits without pockets; if so, where do you keep your business cards? Speaking of business cards, they're next on the preparation checklist.

Business Cards

These are included in the preparation stage since there are two major considerations before you go into the field: (1) how many should be brought along, and (2) what should be included on them? Nothing can be more embarrassing than to run out of business cards just before what might be the most potentially important call. Although there is no hard and fast rule, the minimum number to take with you can be related to the WPS (worst possible scenario).

For sake of illustration, assume that you represent the Center City Hotel. You have just been hired as a senior account executive, and you are going to Hartford, Connecticut, for a week to call on 30 key insurance company meeting planners whom you know from your previous hotel experience.

What is the minimum number of cards? Well, the worst possible scenario would be that you would have to give one to each of your contact's receptionists, one to each of their secretaries, and one to each meeting planner. You'll also need nine or ten more cards to hand out to people you did not necessarily expect to meet at the airport, in restaurants, in elevators, on the street, and so on. So at least 100 cards for the 30 contacts should protect you from the WPS.

What should be included on a business card; which is in effect a sales tool, as well as a means of introduction? It goes without saying: property name, hotel or chain logo, address, phone, telex, fax, and so on, as well as your name and title. If you are doing considerable business internationally, or if your property is located overseas (particularly in the Far East), the reverse side may have the same information in another applicable language.

This sounds simple enough, yet there is a very key point to be emphasized here, which is often overlooked. What do you think is the most consequential element on the business card? Or to put it another way, what would many of your contacts consider to be the key element? Surprisingly, perhaps—it is very often the *title*.

In cases where buyers do not know you, your title immediately indicates your positioning in your hotel and your comparative positioning with respect to their own responsibilities and authority. All things being equal, people usually prefer to deal with their peers.

Unfortunately, the hospitality industry tends to do two things with titles that can prove detrimental, especially to the younger or new account executive.

First, the title may be too impressive: vice president and director of marketing—when in fact, the person (who is a one-person sales department of a small property) has little if any decision-making authority that such a title infers. Or the opposite occurs. A person with a title such as assistant sales representative is sent out to book an account that could be worth hundreds of thousands of dollars. However, the title says to the prospective buyer: "We really don't think that much of you at this point, so we're sending our newest and rawest trainee out in the field to get some 'combat experience' with you!" Not very flattering to the prospective customer, and not very helpful to the success of the new sales executive.

It really comes down to a question of whether the sales executive has the *authority commensurate with the responsibility* indicated by the title. If not, the seller—the hotel representative—may find himself or herself at a disadvantage during any negotiations that may take place prior to concluding the presentation.

A number of hotel companies have developed titles for their starting salespeople that are somewhat "neutral." They do not imply that the person has unlimited authority, but at the same time they do not give the impression that he or she is the "newest person on the totem pole." Such generic titles as "senior account executive" and "key accounts supervisor" seem to strike a practical compromise for many operations. Avoiding the subordinate term "assistant" in favor of "associate," "coordinator," or "executive" can also be helpful. The selection of titles on business cards can be considered a seemingly small but often significant aspect of the preparation stage.*

Promotional Literature

In addition to business cards, consideration should also be given in the initial preparation stages to the type and quantity of other promotional and/or informational literature to be taken on the sales call. These could include:

1. Folders and brochures (both general all-purpose rack folders and convention brochures)
2. Floor plans and audiovisual equipment lists (if not part of the brochure)
3. Color photos of meeting rooms, food and beverage functions, special theme-party events, and entertainment activities
4. Area maps and outside attractions folders
5. Transportation schedules (airlines, buses, trains, limos)
6. Testimonial letters. If used, care should be employed in selecting them so that they represent groups who have requirements or membership profiles similar to the groups on whom you are calling.
7. Audiovisual materials, such as the ever-growing use of both audio tapes and videocassettes

Finally, make sure that you bring along some materials that can help you *personally,* such as a street map of the city. In some localities, a subway map can also be quite useful in going from one business area to another, especially in inclement weather. (We are making the assumption, of course, that you have

---

*A personal observation about business cards. The present authors wonder why so few people put their picture on their cards. Consider how many hotel executives a meeting planner, a tour operator, or a corporate travel manager meets in a year, how many cards are collected, and how difficult it is for so many of us to put a face to a name. Of course, we may be somewhat biased! (See Figure 7–1.)

DAVE DORF ASSOCIATES

333 N. Gladstone Avenue
Margate, NJ 08402 USA
Phone: (609) 823-2132
FAX: (609) 823-0139

DAVID C. DORF, CHSE

ASassociates

RD 2, BOX 454
SHANDELEE ROAD
LIVINGSTON MANOR, NY 12758

(914) 439-4391

ANDREW R. SCHWARZ
PRINCIPAL DIRECTOR

FIGURE 7-1 Sample business cards.

plotted out your sales call schedule, based on appointments and on the principles of effective time and territory management.)

All of these items can be categorized as *visual aids*. But bear in mind that the most important visual aid you have is *you*. How you look (appearance), how you stand or sit (posture), how you use your hands and eyes (gestures), and how you move (bearing) are key components of your presentation. Their effective employment can be learned and practiced ahead of time.

APPOINTMENTS

This brings us directly to the subject of *appointments*, which is the "bridge" between the preparation and presentation stages. Should you make them, or should you rely on the supposition that good potential clients will be delighted to see you because you are bringing such fantastic information which will be so crucially important to their critical needs and decision-making responsibilities?

While that last phrase has a nice-sounding positive philosophical ring to it, one must be aware of the realities of modern business life:

1. No appointment—and you are liable to be turned away from many industrial parks and commercial buildings because of the emphasis on "safety and security."
2. No appointment—and you may find that your contact is deeply involved with high-priority internal matters, such as finishing up a report due for presentation in 20 minutes, and justifiably, cannot see you at that time (see Figure 7-2).

FIGURE 7-2 One possible "danger" of drop-in calls without appointments. Our happy sales executive is eager to tell his story; unfortunately, his contact has a departmental report that is due for presentation in 20 minutes!

3. No appointment—and during certain times of the year, you are likely to find a good percentage of your contacts on vacation. With the growing tendency for minivacations (such as four one-week vacations spaced throughout the year rather than the traditional four-week summer get-away) there is just that much more chance that "Mrs. Smith left just yesterday for a week in the Islands!"

4. No appointment—and you also face the possibility that your contact, Mrs. Smith, who runs 85 meetings a year, is out of the office at one of them . . . 2000 miles away.

5. No appointment—and if your contacts are in, they may be at a department head or staff meeting, "tied up at the moment" with someone else, or waiting for one of your competitors who has an appointment for just about the time you walked in. So you run the risk of either sitting and waiting or returning later, neither of which is good time and territory management.

One must also bear in mind that meeting planning or travel arrangements may often be just a small part of the total responsibilities of your contact. In companies or associations where there are no centralized meeting departments or no full-time convention or meeting managers, you may also run the risk of "catching Mrs. Smith" at an inopportune time, when she is concerned with other responsibilities and priorities. "I'm terribly sorry but Mrs. Smith will be tied up all day with a finance meeting today, and she'll be with the auditors all day tomorrow."

We recognize that many salespeople do not necessarily *like* to make appointments. This is especially true among those who prefer to sell "visually" and whose "in the flesh" personalities and styles are more suited to face-to-face situations. Their main concern is that if they call ahead for an appointment, they may run the risk that the prospect will say, "It's not really necessary for you to take up your time to visit me; why don't you tell me what you would like to discuss right now over the phone."

One of the ways to avoid this is to have your sales secretary make appointments—and as far in advance as possible. For the most part, you do know when and where you are going for the next year; it should be right in your action plans. After appointments are made, update your tickler or trace system and be sure to reconfirm as appointment times get close.

THE PRESENTATION STAGE

OK—you have done your homework, prepared yourself both mentally and physically, and have your appointment schedule in order. Now it's time to go out and sell (whoops! . . . time to go out and *motivate* the contact to make a *purchase*). It has been said (especially by many customers) that the best sales presentation consists of three parts: (1) the opening, (2) the middle, and (3) the closing, and that success is directly related to how near you bring the closing to the opening.

There is a classic story, repeated many times in many versions, concerning a salesperson selling portable computers. He saunters into a prospect's office, accompanied by a trainee. Sitting "junior" down, he proceeds to start his presentation, trying to impress both the client and the trainee with his selling prowess.

He is immediately interrupted by the prospect, who says: "Before you start, I have bought other products from your company in the past, and they have always been very good. But what I specifically need to know about your new line of portable computers before making any purchase commitments is:

1. How much do they weigh?
2. How long can they go on batteries before recharging?
3. Are they IBM compatible, and to what extent?
4. And what type of discount can you offer on various quantity purchases?"

"Those are excellent questions, Mr. Prospect," says our fearless salesman, "and during my presentation, I will cover each in depth!"

In this situation, the closing certainly should have been offered in virtually the same breath as the opening. But in other situations, where the prospect is not that eager (or does not have a direct need) to make an immediate purchase, the presentation stage can involve considerable time and effort as the sales executive details the benefits of the product or service.

Much has been made in many books on sales of the relationship and proper etiquette between the sales executive and the receptionist and/or contact's secretary. We will make the assumption right here that those engaged in hospitality industry sales do know the commonsense fundamentals of courtesy and deportment—so we won't rehash what should be basic to any industry, including ours.*

The Reception Area

There often is an interim period when the sales executive may have to spend a few minutes in a reception area or lounge before being shown into the prospect's office. In fact, some veteran sales executives will show up earlier than their appointment time to take advantage of a short waiting period.

This waiting period can prove extremely beneficial if one keeps one's eyes and ears open. A great deal of last-minute information can be gained from casual observation and discussion. For example, a corporate receptionist excuses herself by saying, "I hope you don't mind but I have to get right back to work; things have really been jumping since we merged with the XYZ Company earlier this week." Or you glance at the latest membership newsletter on the reception desk in a trade association office and note the prominent front-page headline, "ABC Association to Schedule 60 Additional Training Sessions Next Year."

These are the types of situations that can give you key last-minute information which can very well open up new sales opportunities. Psychologically, it can impress prospects who may not know how you got the information; all they know is that you must be very interested in helping them since you seem to know so much about their organization. It also gives you an excellent and timely opening line: "Mr. Prospect, I'm delighted to learn that you will be conducting a new series of additional training sessions in our area next year. We are currently building a specially designed conference center that will open in six months. I would be delighted if you would be among our distinguished guests for a special opening reception and tour the weekend of November 10–11. In the meantime, let me show you the floor plans and sketches of the facility so that you can see how it can serve your future needs."

Flexibility

This ability to be *flexible* in your presentation can be an important attribute at the very beginning, right after you have been ushered in to see the prospect. "Canned" sales presentations (rehearsed 10 times in front of a full-length mirror) are, or should be, a thing of the past.

The sales presentation should be a dialogue between buyer and seller. The discussion should focus on ways each can help the other satisfy needs and requirements by presenting a series of relevant benefits. Each is (and rightly so) hoping to come out a "winner" (the win–win negotiations position referred to at the start of this chapter). But it should not be at the expense of the other party.

The seller (the hotel sales and marketing executive) wants and needs to come back to the property and report, "I made a great *sale* today." The buyer (meeting planner, travel agent, tour broker, or corporate traffic manager) needs to report back and say, "I made a great *purchase* today."

KEY DEFINITIONS

There are many definitions of the word *sale,* but the one we'll use here because of its direct pertinence is:

---

*But we do recommend that you use your library to read up on proper sales call etiquette and procedures.

The securing (or booking) of the right

Type of business . . . at the right

Time, into the right

Space—at the right

Price.

By one of those strange but deliberate coincidences, one of many definitions of a "purchase" is the securing of the right *type* of product, service, or facility, for the right *time*, with the right *space*, for the right *price*. When both parties are more or less using the same basic criteria, it opens the door for *negotiations* (a formal name for "trade-offs"), which can become an integral part of the presentation and final closing process.

But let's go back to the beginning of the presentation stage. Following the introductions and other preliminaries,* a naturally occurring, conversational dialogue should take place, based to a large degree on the main purpose of the call.

THE ABILITY TO LISTEN

One of several difficult attributes that hotel sales executives must acquire is the ability to *listen*. Someone once said that you cannot make mistakes when your ears are open and your mouth is shut. That can be hard at times for many sales/marketing personnel, who because of the inherent nature of the selling function, tend to be somewhat extroverted.

Listening is indeed necessary—to a point. It is one of the best ways of finding out what is important to the buyer. But if the customer takes complete control of the interview, you no longer have communications because the situation then reverts to a one-way flow.

PROBING QUESTIONS

The basic working technique in most sales presentations is, indeed, to let the customer or potential buyer talk, but in terms of responses to a series of probing questions or statements. The six key factors of market profiling (borrowed from journalism)—*who, what, when, where, why,* and *how*—can be a useful guide to formulating probing questions.

Here are a few examples:

"*Who* is responsible for selecting the headquarters hotel after the city has been chosen?"

"*What* type of additional information may I send you to help get a favorable consideration for our property?"

"*When* can I show you our videocassette?"

"*Where* would be the best place to show this . . . at your next convention or at your headquarters office?"

"*Why* do you believe that there might be some resistance to meeting outside the country?"

*These preliminaries, many of which are social in nature, can be extremely consequential to the success of the sales presentation. In many countries, social customs and formalities must be observed that have little, if anything, to do with business. It is essential to check this when soliciting business from outside your country.

"How could we best work with you in developing an attractive program to help you increase attendance by spouses?"

PROBING STATEMENTS

Not all probes need to be in the form of questions. Many can be blanket statements, often based on your research as well as observation. The key is to state them in a helpful yet matter-of-fact manner and then wait for the prospect's reactions.

Here are some examples of such probing statements:

- "Now that each department in your company is to conduct its own training meetings, I'm sure you'll find our smaller multimedia rooms ideally suited to your needs."
- "Since check-in has always been a main concern of your group after their rather lengthy travel time, we can now offer you a new and special time-saving preregistration system."
- "If you can guarantee 1000 room nights a year, we'll be able to give you a very special corporate rate and protect that rate during the entire year."
- "While our main ballroom can easily accommodate your annual meeting, we have 20 smaller, totally redesigned conference rooms that could be ideal for your new sales training programs."
- "Our new corporate rate plan will not only guarantee that your traveling executives will be assured of preferred accommodations no matter what time they arrive, but this program can directly assist you in the planning and budgeting of your company's travel expenditures."

THE ART OF PEOPLE WATCHING

The ability to observe and respond to the actions and reactions of people in a selling situation (particularly when using both probing questions and statements) can be one of the most effective attributes that any executive can cultivate. This is especially important when confronted with a difficult or tense situation, as we'll soon see. This is another of the reasons why *flexibility* is so important and why "canned" or totally memorized presentations are usually so ineffective.

HANDLING TENSE SITUATIONS

Sometimes, observation can assist you greatly before the presentation even takes place. Let's say that you are calling on Mr. John Adams, finance director of the ABC Corporation, who is responsible for the preparation and conduct of two financial planning meetings and one budget review session, which are held away from the company premises each year.

You have an 11:00 A.M. appointment, but his secretary informs you that the department head meeting that he is attending has gone long past its scheduled ending time. But she indicates, with some concern in her voice, that Mr. Adams will be down in 10 or 15 minutes. Mr. Adams finally comes storming through the reception area muttering about "damn hotels who cause you to ruin your budgeting plans!"

Here is a situation where you are now going to have to face a person who is in an obviously negative frame of mind. Depending on your established relationship with Mr. Adams, you might suggest to him that "I'm sure you're going to be rather busy right after your meeting. Perhaps it might be best if we reschedule our appointment for a more convenient time for you." He may very well say, "No, come right in . . . I need some relief after that session," or he may agree to rearrange the appointment. In either case, you have helped establish a more positive relationship.

Sometimes a circumstance beyond one's control can be personal rather than professional. Let's say that Mr. Adams seems rather agitated and keeps glancing at his phone right from the start of your presentation. After he mumbles several times, "I wish she would call," you might suggest that "perhaps this is not the most opportune time for us to get together," and that you would be glad to check with his receptionist to schedule another appointment either later that day or at some other time.

THE BENEFITS OF OBSERVATION

There are a number of other common situations where observation can play an important role in enhancing your presentation. Objects on the prospect's wall or desk can be one such indicator, and virtually every book on selling seems to make this a key issue.

"Ah, Mr. Adams, I see from that trophy-sized bass and plaque on your wall that you are a member of Bass Fisherman's Anonymous. I just love to fish for largemouths myself and I just might be persuaded to divulge the location of my favorite secret lake." *(Now that I've established a common interest and spiced it up with a little flattery, booking his business should be a cinch!)*

Wrong . . . don't think that you have "hooked" Mr. Adams with that corny line. However, his love of fishing might be more subtly worked in later in your presentation.

"Mr. Adams, in addition to the fact that the location of our resort can free you from any unneeded distractions during your financial planning meetings, you might also be interested to know that we just purchased exclusive fishing rights on the 10-acre lake that fronts our property." (A pause as you observe Mr. Adams raising his eyebrows and smiling to himself.) "And we also provide fishing tackle and boats at no additional charge to our special guests."

PERSONALITY TRAITS

Observation of the *personality* of a customer, especially one with whom you have had no previous contact, can also be helpful in determining what *style* of presentation you should employ. You have your own style in selling, the customer has a specific style of buying, and what you are trying to do is to avoid a conflict situation between the two styles.

Most sales executives can be categorized as either *hard sell* (every contact is a confrontation) or *soft sell* (every prospect is "my very dear friend"). On the other end is the customer counterpart: the hard buy ("I've been in this business 30 years, sonny boy!") or the soft buy (every hotel sales executive is "my very dear friend").

Buyer Styles

Some further explanation about each type of buyer. *Hard buyers* generally come in two major varieties: (1) the ones who have come up through the "school of hard knocks" and know the business (theirs and yours) inside out, and (2) those who know very little about either business but feel that they can hide that fact by overpowering you.

Soft buyers are sometimes overly easygoing by nature and upbringing, but many of them also react to a possible lack of knowledge by developing a highly cordial personality. Many of them are "amateurs" (and meeting planning is only a very minor part of their responsibilities) rather than full-time trained professionals (see Figure 7–3). They are eager to listen to you, but they cause "challenges" by purposely avoiding any situations where they must make immediate decisions. They hate to say "no" to anyone. On the other hand, they rarely take the initiative to say "yes."

Seller Styles

Which type of sales executive are you: hard sell or soft sell? What type *should* you be?

Well, for those of you who may have heard that the hospitality industry is really *show business,* here's a very practical application of this concept. The answer in nearly all situations is that one cannot afford to be either a hard-sell or a soft-sell sales personality. You must be flexible and react according to your observations of the type of buyer you are facing. The general rule is: "Be an actor . . . and for the most part, play the *opposite* role."

When facing the hard buyer, you may have to back down a little and offer a set of choices that in effect will give the prospect the decision-making prerogative. But this technique often results in prospects "selling themselves." When facing the soft buyer, you may have to exercise a little more direct control, gradually ease in and take over, and indicate that there are a number of options to a given situation, any one of which will well serve the needs of the buyer. Often, the sales executive must lead or steer this type of buyer to a specific decision.

Buyer–Seller Style Situations

How does this work? The situations seem similar in that with either type of buyer, you are offering a set of choices and asking each to make a decision. The distinction lies in *how* you direct the prospect toward a choice.

FIGURE 7–3   Amateur vs. professional.

Amateur vs. Professional

Corporate
  Amateur: Meeting planning is an added duty (often viewed as an imposition).
  Professional: Chief function is planning; is usually well trained.

Association
  Amateur: Only a small part of many different functions (often viewed as an annoyance and inconvenience).
  Professional: Primary function is meetings management; is usually well trained.

Here is a set of examples. The setup situation is that you are trying to *extend the sale* by suggesting an "ice-cream break" in the afternoon during a group training session. The first illustration is directed at the hard-buy prospect.

Hard-Buy Prospect

Hotel sales exec: "Mrs. Jones, with this widespread revival in nostalgia and the good old days, we can offer your group an old fashioned ice-cream bar, complete with hand-dipped ice cream and turn-of-the-century soda fountain. This can be set up either in the back of the meeting room or outside in the adjacent corridor. Which would you prefer?"

"Hard-Buy" Jones: "What kind of a fool do you think I am, Mr. Hotel Sales Executive, I didn't fall off the haytruck yesterday! If my people go out wandering in your corridor at 3 in the afternoon, it'll take a typhoon to get them back into the meeting room."

Soft-Sell Reply

Hotel sales exec: "You're absolutely right, Mrs. Jones, I must have left my thinking cap home. Of course, we will set up the ice-cream bar and soda fountain in the back of the room. What's more, you might announce that there will be a 10-minute 'hygiene break' before we start serving; that should get them all back into the room."

Soft-Buy Prospect

Now for the same ice-cream break setup, but in this case, Mrs. Jones will be representing a soft-buy type of customer:

"Soft-Buy" Jones: "Do you really think a break would be necessary?"

Hard-Sell Reply

Hotel sales exec: "Well, your people will have gone through a rather full day and I'm sure they would appreciate *your* suggestion of a break which would be at the same time somewhat novel as well as most welcomed. Now, would you like me to set up the ice-cream service in the corridor?"

"Soft-Buy" Jones: "But if you do that, don't you think I'd lose most of the people?"

Hotel sales exec: "That could be a possibility and to prevent that from happening, let's set up the ice-cream bar in the back of the room."

Note that in each scenario, the prospect was given a choice that could not be answered by a flat "yes" or a "no." In fact, in neither situation was the prospect directly asked if she wanted an ice-cream bar set up in the first place. But the difference in the presentation to the two different types of buyers was in the style and the technique of presenting the choice.

Now, what would likely happen when a hard-sell hotel sales executive knocks heads with a hard-buy meeting planner and won't adjust the style of presentation? The phrase "knocking heads" just about says it all in describing the probable effect. It will end up being one of negative "confrontation."

On the other hand, the soft-sell hotel sales executive with the soft-buy customer won't get anywhere either. You will probably end up with an "after you, my friend; no after you, kind sir" waltz-around-the-room scene where everybody becomes good friends but no one dares to pin the other person down to a decision.

Determining the customer's buying style may require the hotel sales executive to then role-play and adjust the presentation style accordingly.

OBSERVABLE HUMAN BEHAVIORAL TRAITS

A further refinement in this adjustable role-playing relates to a skill known as *observable human behavioral traits* analysis. The basic technique involves the seller's observation of both physical and mental characteristics of the buyer and then determining the presentation style that would tend to be most effective in dealing with the other person. This approach is often suited to situations where you have never met the other party and therefore must use observation and listening as tools to get an initial "handle" on the prospect.

The foundation of this diagnostic tool is built around two main considerations:

1. Is the other person more prone to *tell*—or to *ask?*
2. Is that person more likely to be *open* as far as displaying emotions, feelings, and reactions—or *closed* by keeping them hidden?

The closed-emotion teller is called a *driver;* the open-emotion teller is termed an *expressive.* The closed-emotion asker is known as the *analytical;* and the open-emotion asker is categorized as an *amiable.** The physical, mental, and work habits characteristics of each are indicated in Figure 7–4 and are portrayed in a photo montage in Figure 7–5.

As with other diagnostic tools, *both* the buyer and the seller can be included under any of the four classifications. To obtain the best rapport with a prospect, hotel sales executives may have to "jump out" of their own personal classifications and assume the ones that will more effectively interrelate with the buyer. For example, let's say that you are trying to book an association of accountants. Because of the very nature of their line of work, both the membership and staff would tend to be in the *analytical* category. And let's assume you categorize yourself as an *expressive,* proud of your creative problem-solving abilities.

A freewheeling *creative* person could conceivably clash with an *analytical* person who is more comfortable behind systems and structure. In this situation you might have a better chance with your presentation if you move over to the characteristics of a *driver* and in a strong and decisive way present a detailed program with a wide variety of safeguards and contingencies specifically spelled out. The end result of your presentation will probably be in the form of a 20- to 30-page letter of agreement or contract.

You will note from Figure 7–4 that the *analytical* is basically task oriented, while the *expressive* is more likely to be people oriented. This basic difference is often the cause behind any clashes in personality, which can adversely affect the potential for making the sale.

Handling Different Styles

To prevent such clashes (which would, of course, negate or severely minimize the opportunities for making the sale), sales executives, regardless of the sell-

---

*In some presentations the driver may be called a *commander,* the expressive a *performer,* and the amiable an *adapter.*

OBSERVABLE HUMAN BEHAVIORAL TRAITS

Conflicting Social Styles
- Analytical
- Amiable
- Driver
- Expressive

Closed Emotions

Analytical   Driver

Asks   CONFLICT / CONFLICT   Tells

Amiable   Expressive

Open Emotions

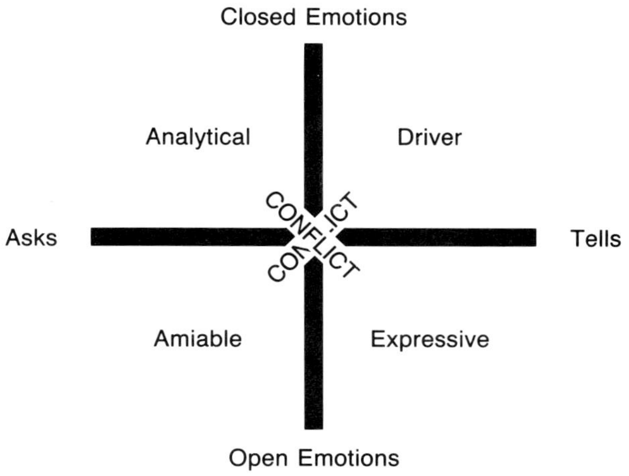

ANALYTICAL
- Task, detail, and data oriented
- Poor on people relationships
- Logical and orderly
- Slow paced
- Probes and questions
- Looks for both sides
- Tends to be suspicious
- Wants safeguards and guarantees
- Non risk-taker
- Retreats in "pools of detail"

AMIABLE
- Highly personable
- Business with friends
- Warm and open
- Easily approached
- Low keyed: dislikes pressure
- Looks for suggestions
- Expects others to be open
- Not decision-prone
- Manages tension by "giving in"
- Can build up hostilities

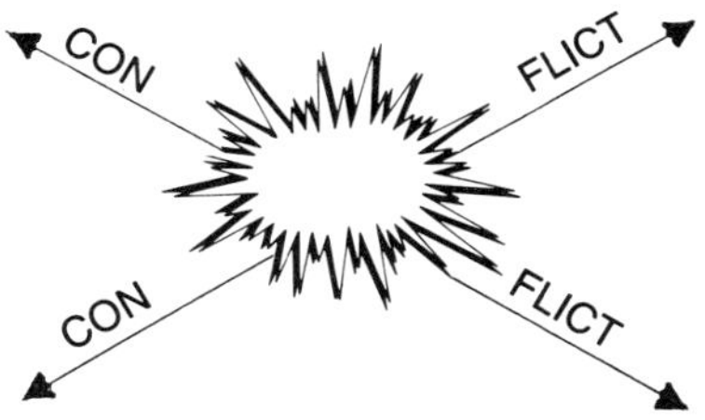

DRIVER
- Highly professional
- Down to business
- No small talk; no jokes
- Time-conscious; quick results
- Task-oriented
- Self-controlled
- Neat; no loose papers
- Risk-taker
- Wants options
- The decision-maker

EXPRESSIVE
- People-oriented
- Take-charge person
- "Doer and teller"
- Intuitive
- Dislikes time pressures
- Appears to be disorganized
- Risk-taker
- Open and emotional
- Not good on details
- Highly creative

CON   FLICT

CON   FLICT

FIGURE 7–4 Characteristics of the four "players" in the observable human behavioral traits analysis technique.

ing style they prefer, must be prepared to be actors. There are a number of adjustment techniques one could make, such as becoming a "minimodel" of the buyer. As mentioned earlier, if a seller's style is diagonally opposite that of the buyer (see Figure 7–4), one can try "moving around the chart" to determine which selling style will be more compatible with the prospect's style. The use of probing questions and the way the prospect responds to them is one way of ascertaining this.

FIGURE 7–5 Photo-montage highlighting the general appearance and surroundings of each of the four personalities represented in the observable human behavioral traits analysis.

Here are some basic procedures for reacting to each buyer style:

With a Driver:

1. Do more listening than talking.
2. When talking, try to pick up your pace.
3. Do not introduce or dwell on personal matters.
4. Do not expect praise or positive feedback.
5. Present choices and options (and let the prospect do the choosing).
6. Never tell "drivers" what they—and you—*cannot* do.

With an Analytical:

1. Make sure that you know all your facts cold.
2. Have them readily available in writing (or in chart or graph form).
3. Take copious notes.
4. Slow down your speaking pace.
5. Expect criticism, nit-picking, and cross-examinations.
6. Be prepared to take action and to push the person toward a decision.

With an Expressive:

1. Key in on your *new* features, services, and amenities.
2. Summarize frequently (creative people often lose track as they jump from one idea or thought to another).
3. Recognize and acknowledge their thoughts and opinions.
4. Compliment frequently; such people thrive on "stroking."
5. Be prepared to do all *their* paperwork.

With an Amiable:

1. Be prepared to dwell on personal matters.
2. Give them personal feedback.
3. Encourage them ("stroking").
4. Be firm but gentle when trying to close the sale.

TRANSACTIONAL ANALYSIS

Another diagnostic technique that came into vogue some years ago is *transactional analysis* (TA). Although it was somewhat "trendy" at the time and subject to considerable opinion and even controversy, certain aspects of the process are particularly suited to improving the buyer–seller relationship.

The basis of TA is that in a given "problem" situation, initially the people involved will play one of three roles: the "child," the "parent," or the "adult" (see Figure 7–6). As a seller, your reactions to the buyer's actions will also fit into one or more of these categories.

Here is a rather simplified illustration. Assume that you are again talking with Mrs. Smith, finance director of the XYZ Corporation. She happens to mention that her two previous meetings were "totally screwed up by those two incompetents I have on my staff who are supposed to handle all details and make sure that all points are covered!"

She is in effect passing blame "down the line," which is a "child" reaction. You could initially counter with a somewhat authoritative "parent" response: "But Mrs. Smith, as an experienced department head, you do have the *authority,* along with the responsibility, to make sure that you have proper staff support for these important service details."

Then, to offer a solution to the problem, you can quickly shift to an "adult" role by stating: "I know we can work together on this and solve your problem when you next meet with us. We have just hired three experienced as-

FIGURE 7–6 Practical transactional analysis.

Practical Transactional Analysis

Child: "It's not my fault! The other person did it!"
Parent: "I don't care whose fault it is; you do what I tell you!"
Adult: "It doesn't really matter now whose fault it might be; let's first solve the problem."

---

sistant convention managers whose sole functions will be to work directly with the customer to ensure the success of all meetings. They would be happy to shoulder these service details for you." Note also that the seller is indirectly *asking for the order* by using the expression "when you next meet with us."

VOLUNTARY AND INVOLUNTARY REACTIONS

By now, this must all sound like an exercise in practical psychology—which is exactly what it is intended to be. In a sales presentation, we assume by now that you know your product and how it can be used; you know your customers and their needs and requirements; and you know something about how they do business. If the presentation stage was restricted to a cold recitation of facts and figures on the needs of a buyer, and a similar counter recitation of the available space/time units of accommodations, facilities, and services that could be provided by the seller, the entire buying process could probably be done by two linked computers.

Fortunately for buyer and seller alike, the decision-making process is based largely on "human" factors which cannot be encased in a microchip. Similarly, the selling process must make use of flexible, nonprogrammable factors. This is one of the main reasons that we have been stressing the importance of observation—and in fact, have made it the key component of the entire presentation process.

Perhaps there is no better example of the utilization of the powers of observation (both sight and sound) than in the evaluation of your customer's reactions to what you are saying during the sales presentation.

There are basically two types of customer reactions:

1. *Voluntary:* The customer deliberately and with full awareness responds to what you are saying.
2. *Involuntary:* The customer does not consciously realize that he or she has made an observable response.

Each type of reaction can then additionally be viewed by the seller as being *positive* or *negative,* as diagrammed in Figure 7–7 (see also Figure 7–8).

Voluntary Reactions

Voluntary reactions are generally the easiest to observe and to respond to. They do not have to relate directly to the subject being discussed: "I really like your new ballroom renovation." It could be a positive call to the secretary: "Hold all my phone calls for the rest of the morning." Or it could be a very negative, "Bring in my mail; I'll have plenty of time in a minute or so to look it over."

FIGURE 7–7 Customer reactions.

	Positive	Negative
Voluntary		
Involuntary		

FIGURE 7–8   Various types of voluntary and involuntary reactions. Clockwise, from the upper left: positive voluntary (prospect calls secretary to "hold all calls"); positive involuntary (prospect leans over and handles brochure); negative voluntary (prospect overtly pushes sales executive away); and negative involuntary (prospect stares at the ceiling).

Involuntary Reactions

Involuntary reactions can be especially significant in that they may offer subconscious indicators as to how the prospect *really* feels. They can also be potentially dangerous if you rely too heavily on them since they are open to misinterpretation. Also, differing social customs in different areas of the country, as well as in different areas of the world, may (for example) make a certain gesture a positive indicator, while elsewhere it may be totally negative.*

Doodling

There is one additional type of reaction that must be considered because it is so widespread. It is basically *involuntary*, but is in a sense "ambivalent" in that it

*One of the classic examples: In the United States, touching your thumb to your index finger and forming a circle usually means "A-OK." In certain other areas of the world, it is a rather offensive and vulgar gesture.

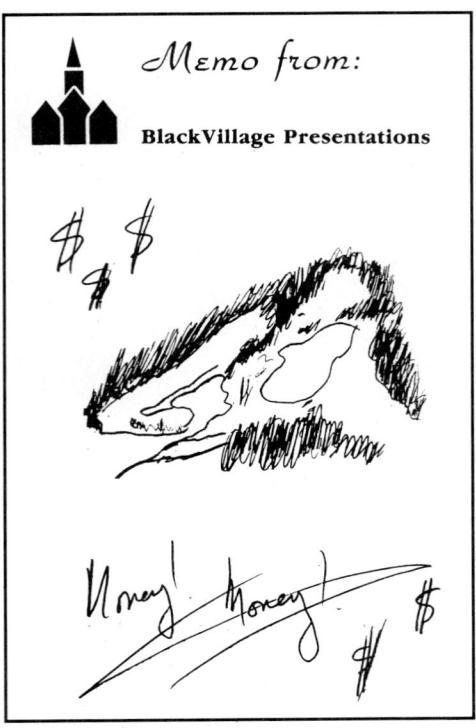

FIGURE 7-9 Negative doodling.

FIGURE 7-10 Positive doodling.

can be either positive or negative. This is *doodling*, which the dictionary describes as the act of drawing or scribbling in an aimless, preoccupied way.

You are telling John Adams, the finance director of the ABC Corporation, about your recreational facilities and how much you have spent the past year upgrading your golf course to make it the very finest in the area. You note that Mr. Adams is unconsciously but emphatically scribbling on a pad of paper in front of him (see Figure 7-9). It would seem that Mr. Adams is concerned about whether or not he will be bearing a good part of the costs of your renovation as they might be reflected in your rates and prices. So the best course would probably be to change the subject immediately.

However, suppose that as you glance down at Mr. Adams' doodles, you note the scene depicted in Figure 7-10.

In this case, Mr. Adams seems to have unconsciously but very positively placed himself on your golf course and is hoping to beat his previous best score. You could then continue with the golf course as part of the presentation, adding information about your special golf tournament program for groups, invite Mr. Adams and his staff for a weekend of golf, or whatever you feel will be necessary to finalize a booking.

HANDLING OBJECTIONS

The most noticeable customer reactions, of course, occur when specific *objections* and *complaints* are voiced. Such overt actions may be aimed at a past negative experience the customer may have had at your property or at a sister hotel (or heard that someone else has had). Or it might be focused on a specific point you are detailing in your presentation.

Some of the methods of handling complaints have already been discussed earlier in this section, especially as part of some of the illustrative dialogues between the customer and the hotel sales executive. Following is a recap checklist of these and a few other points relating to the concept of *converting objections into positives.*

1. Don't view an objection as a personal affront; don't get into a personality "war"; and above all, don't argue with the customer, especially as to the validity of the complaint.

2. Mentally key yourself to the philosophy that an objection is usually a positive signal that prospects are interested in you and your facilities. Otherwise, they wouldn't have taken the time and effort to bring up the subject in the first place.

3. However, bear in mind that some types of prospects (such as the "hard buy") may make a minor objection as a test to see *how* you respond (in TA terms, do you respond as a "child," "parent," or "adult?"). This is especially true when there has been no previous personal contact or prior use of the property.

4. Recognize that different types of people have different reasons for making objections. Going back to the "observable human behavioral traits" analysis technique, the "driver" often introduces a minor complaint to let you know right off that he or she is "the boss." The "analytical," on the other hand, may make the very same objection for the purposes of having you counter with a protective guarantee or safeguard.

5. Relax and above all *listen.* Let the customers have their "day in court." Do not interrupt (the worst word you can use is a defensive "but . . . "). Very often, people raise objections to get something off their chests which may be only remotely related to you and your presentation. Their concluding statement often ends up, "But I really don't know why I'm bothering you with all this past history; you certainly weren't involved at the time so it's not *your* fault!"

6. Take notes when the customer issues a complaint. Besides its functional use for follow-ups, it can have positive psychological impact. It indicates to the client that you feel that what is being said is highly important.

7. Decide whether you should let the subject "die" or whether you should take direct action. If you feel that the complaint or objection is critical to the success of your future dealings with the client or to making the sale, you might possibly probe for any additional details, write them down, and indicate that you will investigate further. Above all, make sure that you do report back—one way or another.

8. If the objection is related directly to some detail that might affect the setup or servicing of a future meeting, try to offer the client a set of alternatives. Here again, depending on your observations of buying style and other behavioral indicators, you would either let the customer alone make the decision or would steer the customer toward a specific choice.

SOLVING OBJECTIONS

Depending on the type of customer you are dealing with, one can often counter objections by offering positive options or "solutions."

If, for instance, a meeting planner objects to the *time* of the year you are suggesting she move her convention (and you have a good idea that costs are among her principal concerns), you might respond along these lines:

- "You don't like meeting during summer weekends in a city . . . but aren't you concerned about getting the best possible facilities and service for the most economical price? Yes—and the time of the year isn't as important to you as costs . . . right? Well, let me show you what we can offer you during summer weekends which can save you and your group as much as 40 percent."

On the other hand, you might counter an objection about the *location* of your property in this manner:

- "But is central location that important to you? Isn't the *total cost* of your sales meetings critical as far as your budget is concerned? Thus our airport location will save you considerable surface transportation expenses—as well as valuable time."

Since you cannot always anticipate what types of objections you may face, this is another good reason why presentation flexibility is so essential.

COMPENSATORY SELLING

Some sales executives, especially those with the authority to negotiate, may use a technique called *compensatory selling* to counter certain types of objections. This is in effect a trade-off offer in which the sales executive offers the customer an additional service or facility to satisfy a potential buyer's objection.

It may take the form of sponsoring a cocktail reception, providing additional complimentary rooms, and so on. Since it may not necessarily take care of the objection, this method is more of a "pacifying" technique, although there are occasions when it can be useful.

Let's say, for example, that your property is located in an outside area, away from the center of town and you perceive that the meeting planner prospect is somewhat concerned about its accessibility. You normally charge for parking, but in this case you might offer complimentary parking to the attendees as a compensation.

However, the compensating factor must be meaningful and beneficial. Offering free parking to a group where 90% of the attendees will be flying in would be meaningless; providing complimentary shuttle bus service to and from the airport would be a more appropriate gesture.

CLOSING CONSIDERATIONS

In the late 1950s and early 1960s, there were many books on the general theme, "How I Made a Million Dollars My First Year of Selling by Utilizing 500 Secret Closing Techniques."* However, selling hotel facilities and accommodations is quite different from selling common consumer goods and services (soap, vac-

---

*These were invariably written by insurance salespeople—who if they did make a million, probably did it largely from the sale of their books and related seminar presentations.

uum cleaners, and insurance), which is what most of these super salespeople were offering.

Perhaps the most important consideration as one finishes the presentation is to determine whether or not one should "push" for a decision at that particular time. There are a number of factors to consider in your decision to initiate any type of closing action:

1. Does the person you are talking with have the sole and final say on selecting the location and/or the property?
2. Who else, if anyone, must that person consult as a matter of "policies and procedures"? (Does the staff of a centralized meeting planning department contact the individual department heads before making a final decision, to bring them into "the act"?)
3. Does the decision maker seek the advice and council of specialists for certain "sensitive" areas, such as financial or legal, before making a commitment?

It is, of course, helpful if you have this information already documented in your files. But even then, you would want to check to see if policy has been changed or if the authority area of your contact has been increased or decreased since you last met.

Timing

Assuming that the sale can be made during the interview, at what point should one strive for a commitment? The "pat" answer is, "Whenever the customer is ready to buy" . . . which, believe it or not, is not only true but constantly seems to be ignored.

Remember our "portable computer" story earlier in this chapter. Well, one of the common hotel counterparts, related by more than a few meeting planners, takes on one or more variations of the following scenario:

Young eager sales executive: "Good morning, Miss Meeting Planner, my name is Betty Johnson from the Center City Hotel and Conference Center, and. . . ."

Meeting planner (breathlessly interrupting the YESE): "Am I glad to see you! The property in your area where we had scheduled a three-day meeting for next month just told us they are temporarily closing*—and I desperately need 100 rooms for August 3 to 6; and one major meeting room for 175 people. Do you have accommodations and space available on those dates?"

YESE: "Oh, I'm sorry to hear about that, and I'll check our availability and let you know. However, the reason I'm here today is to tell you some good news. We are planning to add another 75 rooms to our fine property, including two special floors of VIP executive suites. These will be available in about six to eight months—and I'm really excited about this addition. I'm sure you'd be interested in these floor plans and sketches."

Sure she would . . . the "meeting without a home" for next month will take care of itself!

Recall our opening paragraph that introduced the material on presentation. It was mentioned that a presentation consists of the opening, middle, and

---

*It can and does happen, for a number of reasons: strikes, fire, hurricanes, a new owner who does not want the group, double bookings, and other causes with or without legal implications.

closing and that success was often determined by how close you bring the two end parts together. The preceding illustration is certainly a prime example of where the closing should immediately be substituted for the opening. The middle (the presentation stage) should then be eliminated as far as what you *wanted to say,* in favor of what the *customer needs to hear* to solve an immediate and most apparent problem.

But let's take a more prevalent situation. You are in your presentation stage working toward a "windup" or summary. How do you know when and if to ask for the order?

THE CLOSING

We are now at the stage where the main purpose of the sales call has arrived. It is to positively "close," make the sale, get the booking, sign the contract, block the dates and space, and so on. *Right? Not necessarily.*

First, not every call has the objective of making a sale. The call could be for purposes of determining the prospect's future needs, but not necessarily done at the time that the prospect would normally make any decisions. The call might be for the purpose of getting to know the new decision makers of an association or company with whom you have never done business before. Or it might be part of a sales blitz to travel agencies where you are merely initiating a contact and perhaps leaving off some new literature or information, such as a new brochure on your 250-room addition.

Indicator Signals

Here again we go back to the importance of *observation.* There are both verbal and nonverbal signals which can serve as indicators that a closing situation is approaching—or, conversely, that the prospect does not seem to be in a positively responsive mood. These may include:

Negative

1. Lack (and even deliberate avoidance) of eye contact
2. Fidgeting
3. Clenched fists (a sign of mental rather than overtly physical "hostility")
4. Constant looking at watch or clock
5. Random and constant shuffling of papers
6. Slouching and staring at the ceiling
7. Bobbing and "falling asleep"

Positive

1. Nodding of head in agreement
2. Hands on chair and smiling
3. Sitting up at the end of the chair and leaning toward you
4. Handling your brochures and other literature

Bear in mind that these are not absolutes. Staring at the ceiling may be negative (i.e., shutting you out) or in a few cases, positive (i.e., shutting out all distractions and carefully reflecting on what you have said). But what you are looking for is the cumulative impact of all types of buying signals and the determination of when to try to "close the sale."

CLOSING TECHNIQUES

Let's again assume that the person you are dealing with does have the authority to make a decision (at least a tentative one) and that you feel the time is right to bring your presentation to its purposeful finish. What type of closing technique is best? The answer, as with so many other responses involving sales and marketing, is, "It depends."

Some of the more common techniques that have been given specific identifying names include:

1. *Prestige or status close:* This technique is used when the sales executive calls the attention of the potential buyer to other groups who have used the property. In such instances the sales executive selects previous customers who are looked upon as being equally or more prestigious than the prospect. In the presentation, the sales executive implies that the prospect should utilize the property since he or she is "equal" in status with these previous customers.

2. *First-timer close:* Here the sales executive concentrates on the fact that the prospect will be the first to use a new or redecorated facility, or have the opportunity to be the first to utilize some other service of the property.

3. *Fear of rejection close:* This is the situation where the sales executive informs the prospect that unless immediate affirmative decision can be reached, the facility may not be available since other prospects are interested in booking the same dates. The implication is that the customer better act quickly or could be "left out."

4. *The affirmative close:* Under this procedure, the sales executive asks the prospect a series of questions (not necessarily related to the possible booking) from which an affirmative response is anticipated. The prospect is being conditioned psychologically to establish an affirmative state of mind. Then the prospect is asked to give an affirmative response to the question of selecting the property.

5. *The minor point close:* In this situation the sales executive, utilizing a positive approach, endeavors to have the prospect make a commitment on a decision regarding some minor detail. It might be a matter of asking the prospect how he or she wishes the hotel to handle the billing, how many bars should be available for a particular reception, how many people are to be seated at the head table for the banquet, and so on. The sales executive assumes that when the prospect agrees to a minor point, the prospect is making a commitment.

6. *The alternate choice close:* In utilizing this technique, the sales executive requests the prospect to make a decision where a choice is offered. For example, local, service, or civic club prospects may be asked if they would prefer the Blue Room reserved for the reception and the Gold Room set aside for the luncheon, or the reverse. Again, a presumption is made: If the prospect makes a decision (or set of selections) involving alternatives, he or she has probably already made a favorable decision toward your property.

7. *The summary close:* In this procedure the sales executive reviews the prospect's needs and outlines the manner in which these needs can be accommodated. The sales executive then summarizes how any objections can readily be overcome and gives particular emphasis to the features and services of the property in which the prospect has indicated special interest. After summarizing the features in terms of customer benefits, the sales executive asks for the order.*

8. *The price close:* Although there are a number of ways of closing on the basis of price, the traditional one is to inform the prospect that prices being quoted can be guaranteed only if the prospect confirms immediately. If the prospect must wait for a period of time before making a decision, there is a possibility that the prices will have to be adjusted.

Trial Closing Techniques

The most effective closing techniques (singly or in combination) will reflect back to many of the "personality" characteristics discussed earlier, for which some examples of trial closings were given. One of the most effective trial closes was originated by Jim Jones,† president of James E. Jones Associates. Known as the "Listen to the Music" trial close, here is a sample dialogue:

> *Sales executive:* "In your opinion, do you feel our hotel can be of service to you?"
> *Potential buyer:* "No."
> *Sales executive:* "Apparently, you have some reason for feeling that way. May I ask what it is?" (And then listen.)
> *Potential buyer:* "Your prices are too high."
> *Sales executive:* "If you could change your dates to August, I'm sure we could work within your budget."

Within this trial closing framework, potential buyers may in turn do some trial probing of their own. One such probing technique is known as *looping.* For example, looping occurs when a potential customer says, "I'd love to bring my group to your property but we are on a real tight budget next year."

But you have to determine whether the buyer is really saying:

1. "Your prices are too high," or
2. "I really don't want to do *any* business with you or your hotel," or
3. "If you sponsor our opening reception, do not charge us for audiovisual equipment, and do not charge us for coffee breaks, I think we can live with your room rate structure."

As you reach for the opportunity to close, be prepared for such stalling tactics. They often signal that while the potential customer is highly interested, further negotiation may be likely before the customer is ready to sign a contract.

---

*This procedure is often effective when dealing with both the analytical and expressive types of buyers.

†Jim Jones spent over 24 years in meeting planning with Connecticut General Life Insurance Company, Hartford, Connecticut, and is a founder of such important customer groups as Meeting Planners International, the Society of Corporate Meeting Planners, and the Insurance Conference Planners Association. Our thanks to him for permission to use his material here for illustrative purposes.

If you decide that you cannot effectively book at a particular time, you should determine what the next step of the process would be. This could be done by specifically asking, "What would be my next step in getting a favorable commitment from you?", or even, "What do I need to do next to get your business?" The one tactic to avoid, and it seems one that is unfortunately all too common (especially on a Friday in the summertime), is to say, "Well, I'm sure you have other things on your mind for this weekend; why don't you think it over for a few days and we'll get together within the next week or so."

THE FOLLOW-UP

If the prospect cannot commit at the time of your sales presentation, you must determine the next step necessary to get a booking or pursue further action leading up to a sale. It might be to send additional information, brochures, folders, or other literature; reschedule a follow-up sales call to make a presentation before a small group of people or before a larger site selection committee; or schedule a mutually agreed upon time for the potential customer or a committee to visit the property.

These follow-up steps may not be the most glamorous. But more potentially available business has been lost because of follow-up negligence (sometimes known as sheer laziness) than possibly for any other single reason. The very act of "following up," and how quickly and accurately it is done, serves a dual selling function:

1. It gives the decision maker the "ammunition" to make a favorable recommendation on your behalf, especially when presenting your "case" to the attention of a committee or board.
2. It offers the customer a sampling of how well you would follow through and ensure the fulfillment of their requirements and servicing details, especially those who have not previously conducted any business with you.

Along with the sending of required information or materials, a short thank-you note, especially to those whom you contacted for the first time, can have positive customer relations value. Such public relations can even be productive later with accounts whom you did not book. A brief follow-up letter such as the one shown in Figure 7-11 could be helpful in maintaining a positive, open line of communications with a prospect who for one or more reasons did not (or could not) book with you.

FIGURE 7–11 Follow-up letter.

Dear Miss Meeting Planner:

Thank you so much for discussing your meeting plans with me last week.

Though we could not be of direct assistance to you this time, I look forward to keeping in touch.

Please remember the Center City Hotel any time we may be of any possible service to you and your fine group.

Cordially,

Young Eager Sales Executive

TELEPHONE SELLING

Personal sales calls, of course, are not the only means of customer contact. In fact, many people are taking a second look at a more expanded use of the telephone, since it can have a most positive impact not just on making a sale but also on time and staff management and cost-effectiveness.

Next to face-to-face contact, the phone offers the best opportunity for a running dialogue between buyer and seller. It sets up an environment for *two-way* "give and take" communications and the immediate countering of objections. But realistically, most of the skills that can be employed by the observant, flexible, positive role-playing sales executive are lost or unavailable over the phone, since there is currently* a lack of visual contact through the use of this medium.

Telephone Challenges

One of the key challenges of selling by phone is that you cannot supplement your oral presentation with such hands-on visual support as folders, brochures, floor plans, and so on. Many meeting planners, for instance (especially those who do not know your property), like to "walk" their program through your facilities, event by event, room by room. If they do not, this is often a good technique for the sales executive to employ, especially since many organizations and companies have the same basic meetings format from year to year. But it is rather difficult to utilize this "let's see how we fit" technique over the telephone (unless you have mailed folders and brochures in advance).†

Another challenge that must be recognized with respect to the phone is that it is probably the most misused and abused communications tool around. When improperly employed, it can be inconvenient, annoying, intrusive, and even resented by the receiver.

A potential customer can put aside a direct-mail piece or a newspaper/magazine that carries your advertising, and look at it during a more convenient time. Even a "drop in" sales call can be diverted by a skilled receptionist. But phone calls, even under most office screening procedures, can reach receivers during times when their minds are occupied with matters that relate to other important aspects of their jobs.

This situation can cause a great deal of buyer resentment, particularly when so many calls concern matters where the information could be obtained more readily by other means or from other people. Let's take a situation where a hotel sales executive has indicated to the buyer's secretary or phone receptionist that it is vitally important to immediately contact Joan Smith, finance director of the XYZ Corporation, even though she advises that Mrs. Smith is "tied up at the moment in a most important budget meeting." What do you think Mrs. Smith's reaction will be after being summoned from the meeting to hear the sales executive's opening line:

"Mrs. Smith, I'm delighted to be able to talk with you. I know you are a busy person, but I need some essential information so that we can more readily assist you with your future meeting plans. Have you decided on Chicago yet for next year's main finance committee meeting, and if so, to whom should we send a proposal for consideration as the host hotel?"

In this situation, which, unfortunately, is all too real, the telephone only

---

*We say "currently" because we are still awaiting the final breakthrough in the concept of "videophones" to make them a feasible and economic means of visual as well as audio communications.
†However, the increasing use of fax equipment allows one to transmit printed matter to a prospect while conversing by phone.

heightened the sales executive's apparent lack of knowledge of even the basic fundamentals of customer research.

Decision Forcing

The telephone can, unfortunately, easily be misused as a means of trying to force a customer decision. Much has been made in the last several years on the

FIGURE 7–12 Editorial on telemarketing that first appeared in the January 1989 issue of the *HSMAI Student Bulletin* distributed by the Hotel Sales and Marketing Association International.

COMMENTARY

WHAT'S IN A NAME . . . ? TELEMARKETING

Marketing is the key component of the word *telemarketing,* yet it almost seems an oxymoron in that one seems to find very little of the marketing concept in most telephone sales and promotional efforts.

Many of you will be involved with selling by phone when you enter the industry. And I'm sure many of you have already been exposed to this medium during student telephone "sales blitzes" or intern practicums.

Thus it would seem timely to mention a few considerations about the use (as well as the misuse and abuse) of this medium.

For introductory illustrative purposes, let me recount a conversation (virtually verbatim since I had a tape machine on) between myself and a real estate "salesman."

Salesman: Let me introduce myself, I am . . . with the real estate firm of . . . I have great news for you. This is the time to sell your property. Selling prices have never been higher, there is a great demand for housing, and I'd like to help you make as much money as possible.

Me: Hold on a second. Who said I was in the market to sell? Have you ever seen my house; do you know where it's located; do you know how long I've lived in it; do you know my age, my profession, my household? Do you know whether I just bought it—or whether I've already had a mortgage burning party? Do you know anything about me at all?

Salesman: No, not really, but . . .

Me: Well, since you haven't done a single bit of homework, if I were in the market to sell, what makes you think I'd trust the sale of my home to a complete idiot like you!

Needless to say, that ended the call. I should also add that this so-called salesman had left three previous messages during the course of a week (I was out of town) requesting that I contact him immediately upon my return.

Telemarketing has its place; I'm not "knocking" its selective and proper use. But extra care and caution should be exercised in its use because it is probably the most *intrusive* form of sales communications.

It's not like a personal call, where prior appointments are often required or where a receptionist or secretary can readily screen you. It's not like a piece of direct mail, which can either be read or immediately tossed away. It's not like print advertising, which can similarly be ignored if not properly prepared and presented. And it's not like radio or TV, which can be either turned off or zapped.*

Too many amateurs have entered the field, abusing and misusing the telephone, to the detriment of those who do their homework, use it appropriately, and recognize its limitations and its advantages.

The result is that most people have a very negative view of telemarketing. A major corporate meeting planner recently told me that it is company policy that each incoming call is screened by the receptionist, who tells the caller, where applicable, "I'm sorry but we do not accept telemarketing calls in this office."

While that may seem rather arbitrary, it is indicative of the way this medium is looked upon.

We are, as stated previously, flooded with amateurs who feel that because they can talk—and have used a phone all their lives, they can easily become an expert in telemarketing.

And that's why people get 6:00 P.M. Sunday nuisance calls from telephone "hucksters" trying to sell a subscription to a magazine one already has. And in our industry, that's why a meeting planner will get telephone calls from a hotel trying to get a piece of business which the property already has on the books.

All of which means that when you are out in the industry, you can't pick up a phone, call some names you have on a list, and begin making a proper, persuasive sales presentation. It does mean that you need to do your homework (which means research), know the advantages and limitations of the phone as a sales medium, know the best techniques of selling where you don't have the advantage of either visual contact or movement, and be receptive to what the other person on the other end is saying (or not saying).

Then, perhaps, we can all justifiably emphasize the *marketing* portion of the telemarketing approach.

*Zapped. A term indicating that a channel or station has been changed by the viewer listener (usually by remote control) as soon as a commercial comes on.

David C. Dorf

David C. Dorf, CHSE

merits and the disadvantages of telemarketing (see Figure 7–12). However, what can be accomplished over the phone in the way of selling a magazine subscription for $20 a year, or soliciting a $10 charitable contribution, is significantly different than trying to pin down a meeting planner (who may not even know you, your property, and your area) to make a five- or six-figure financial commitment.

This is not to imply that sales cannot be made by phone. But in most cases when this happens, much of the groundwork had already been laid through the coordinated use of other communications tools, such as advertising, direct mail, and personal sales calls. The telephone was then used to make the specific booking conveniently. The use of the telephone can be particularly helpful in supporting other aspects of selling, and in particular it can be most effective as part of the *sales management* function, especially in properties using a specific system of *qualifying accounts*.

QUALIFYING ACCOUNTS

As an illustrative example, the Center City Hotel has divided its convention and group business accounts into three basic classifications, according to their value to the property:

1. *A Accounts* numerically represent 15% of the total number but 65% of the business volume.* (These are often called *"key"* or *"priority"* accounts.)
2. *B Accounts* represent 25% of the accounts by number, and 20% of the volume.
3. *C Accounts* represent 60% of all accounts numerically but only 15% of the volume. (Many of these, incidentally, are at best marginal, and upon further review may be inactivated in favor of more promising business potentials.)

The management of these accounts must be predicated on their number, business potential, the number of staff available to cover them, and the selection of the best combination of sales tools to get bookings on a cost-effective basis.

To continue with our example, as a preliminary planning guide, the marketing director of the Center City Hotel might decide that:

1. *A accounts* will receive four calls a year, at least two of which will be personal calls.
2. *B accounts* will receive two calls a year, one of which will be a personal call.
3. *C accounts* will receive one call a year, not necessarily a personal call.

The remaining calls or contacts within each classification will be done by phone or a personalized letter—or both. This will then be coordinated later within the specific action plans for each target market segment, and then ultimately into such working sales office systems as the geographic files and the trace files.

---

*These percentage breakdowns are for illustration only and are not necessarily representative of industry practice.

CUSTOMER-ORIGINATED CALLS

Yes indeed, buyers do call sellers, and in the hospitality industry, for a variety of different reasons that can be highly productive for hotels.* Here are some common examples:

1. A tour broker with whom you may not have had any business in the past hears favorably about your property from a fellow broker and calls to get additional information and literature.

2. A business traveler sees your ad in an in-flight magazine and calls the special telephone number you have highlighted (and in some planes, can do it directly in flight with on-board phones).

3. Potential meeting clients have received advance word (often via the "grapevine") of a new addition or facility to be added to your property and call for further and more direct information.

4. A long-time friend calls to congratulate you on your new affiliation and wants some information on the facility for her company's end-of-the-year social functions.

5. An executive who stays with you for individual business travel purposes has just been promoted to a new position which includes added responsibilities for planning and placing various meetings. You receive a call for meeting facilities information and assistance.

6. A meeting planner needs other or additional accommodations and facilities for an event that had previously been booked in your area. This can happen, for instance, in long-term booking situations where the group has significantly increased in size and has in effect outgrown the facilities booked previously. Your counterpart in the other hotel may call you saying, "Help, I have a group that I can no longer handle," or "Do you have 60 double-bedded rooms for the nights of August 17 and 18?" Irrespective of who actually places the call, these are still buyer-originated sales opportunities.

7. A personal friend calls you to let you know that his daughter has set her wedding date and wants to look at your property as a possible site for the wedding reception.

8. A potential prospect suddenly has an emergency need for rooms and space. This often occurs due to a crisis situation within the company or within the field or profession represented by a trade association. A hastily called meeting or series of meetings may result. Generically termed *reaction meetings,* these often produce an immediate need on the part of the buyer to find properties for planning sessions, strategy conferences, and board of directors meetings.

These and similar situations are particularly important because since the prospective buyer initiated the contact, customer interest has been evidenced from the very start.

Handling Incoming Calls

However, somewhere way up front in a hypothetical best-seller *Murphy's 100 Laws of Innkeeping* one would find that these calls will invariably come in

---

*Although we are discussing buyer-originated calls made by phone, the same principles hold for personal calls originated by the buyer, as described in the section on personal calls.

when most, if not all, of the sales staff is out making calls! One is hesitant to even think of the value of potential business that may be lost to a particular property because of situations similar to the following:

Prospect: "I'd like to speak to Bob Brown,* please."

Switchboard operator: "I'm sorry, sir, we do not have a Bob Brown registered in this hotel."

or

Prospect: "I'd like to speak with someone in your sales office."
Operator: "Oh, you must have the wrong number, sir. This is not a real estate firm."

or

Prospect: "I'd like to talk with someone about a company Christmas party for 100 people."
Operator: "I guess that would be somebody in the sales department, or would it be the banquet office? Well, it really doesn't make any difference; they're all out of town attending our chain's annual convention. Could you call back next week?"

Now, we are not picking on the poor switchboard operator. In fact, any blame for situations such as these often lies with those responsible for teaching the proper procedures of handling and routing incoming calls, and part of that training responsibility assuredly rests with the sales/marketing department.

To sum up, and to add a thought concerning the future, the telephone can certainly be an effective communications and selling tool when effectively employed. But its inherent limitations must also be recognized. Too many people seem to utilize the phone for purposes beyond its present capabilities, especially as it relates to the booking of a "big-ticket item" such as a 1500-person convention for four days or for a contract with a company for 3000 room nights a year.

On the other hand, there are a number of technological advances that can add to the importance of the telephone as a potentially key sales tool. These include:

1. *Conference calls:* Different decision makers in different locations can be connected up to listen to a sales presentation.
2. *Linked facsimile transmission (FAX):* The same people can instantaneously receive printed items (floor plans, diagrams, proposals, contracts, etc.) from the seller.
3. *Computer links:* These can supplement fax transmissions for conveying printed information and data.
4. *Closed-circuit TV hookups:* Decision makers in various locations can view a video presentation on the property and its facilities.

These and many other possibilities may soon change the relative positioning of the telephone. It may indeed soon become an equally effective partner with personal sales calls for soliciting and booking many types of both individual and group business.

Note: For this illustrative example, Bob Brown is an account executive who has been with the property for six months.

HOSPITALITY SUITES AND EXHIBIT BOOTHS

As described in this chapter, the usual verbal sales presentations are made on either an individual basis or before a group such as a site selection committee; and they can be made either in person or by phone. However, there are a number of other opportunities for sales executives to interface directly with potential customers. Attendance at customer conventions and trade shows, for example, offer the opportunity to meet potential clients, especially during social sessions such as receptions and meal functions. In addition, there is often the opportunity to specifically arrange for *meeting points,* such as by being an exhibitor or by sponsoring a hospitality suite (see Figure 7–13).

The guidelines described earlier in this chapter on the preparation stages of a sales call are equally applicable to the manning of an exhibit booth or hosting a hospitality suite. Even though the setting is more informal and often largely social, it is essential to bring along plenty of business cards, brochures, and other pictorial literature. In turn, the business cards of all booth and suite visitors should be collected for prompt follow-up back in the sales office.

To conclude this chapter on selling, the recaps in Figure 7–14 outline the basic characteristics of each major type of sales call. In the next chapter we discuss other types of promotional activity which can be used both independently and in cooperation with personal selling.

FIGURE 7–13 An exhibit area (often termed a "marketplace") can be arranged to offer a variety of opportunities to initiate contacts, distribute promotional literature, and exchange information between sellers and potential buyers. (Courtesy of the Council on Hotel, Restaurant, and Institutional Education.)

Out-of-Town Sales Trip

1. Advance planning is the key. Secure a map of the city if it is unfamiliar. Grid out the city into sections.
2. Assign files by city sections to underwrite intracity efficiency.
3. Prioritize your files to make certain that you secure your most important appointments first.
4. Make up a grid by time slots, by day of week. As you secure an appointment place it in the grid. Build your lesser appointments in by section around your important appointments.
5. Maintain a list of other customers that you could call on but are not necessarily important. Do a letter to these people indicating that you will be in town and that you would be interested in seeing them if possible.
6. Send a letter confirming your appointments to all preset appointments.
7. Develop an objective list for each account you will be calling on.
8. After the trip follow up with a letter.

Outside Sales Call—Cold Call

1. This is the most difficult of all sales situations. The customer is not expecting you. You do not know what to expect, nor does the customer.
2. You are generally disrupting plans of people in the office by your presence.
3. You must first qualify who in an office might even be responsible for planning or routing business.
4. As the initial purpose is to qualify business, it is not important that you speak directly with the decision maker. Often an assistant can give you all the information you need.
5. In the event you cannot see the planner, leave your business card and then follow up to set an appointment.
6. Never tell a person, ''I just happened to be in the area and thought I would drop in.''

Outside Sales Call—Appointment

1. The purpose of this type of call is either to solicit or to qualify.
2. Solicitation should be addressed after qualification has been accomplished. This could be done on the same appointment.
3. The customer has not asked to see you or shown any interest in your property. The appointment has been at your request with only a potential benefit to the customer.
4. Always finish the appointment with an indication of the next step to be accomplished.

Outside Sales Call—Sales Blitz

1. The purpose of a sales blitz is generally to contact a great volume of accounts within a very brief period of time.
2. The blitz may occur to promote and/or qualify accounts as part of a new hotel opening or to address a property shortfall.
3. Occasionally, a chain may organize a blitz team to canvass a specific city to qualify potential business for no specific property.
4. The key to the sales blitz lies in the organization of the overall plan. Files should be separated by specific geographic areas. There should be a premeeting of the blitz team members to explain the purpose and to address any specific questions that they may have.
5. It is critical that the results of a blitz be measured. Call reports/business leads should be handled on a daily basis.

FIGURE 7-14 Types of sales calls.

Telephone Solicitation/Qualification

1. Review file to understand customer's business.
2. Based on analysis of business, empathize as to what would be customer's primary interests in planning meeting (i.e., price, recreations, location, etc.).
3. Before making call, set objective to be accomplished in making call.
4. If purpose is to qualify meetings, either qualify over telephone or if numerous, set up an appointment for a personal call.
5. Always state your purpose in calling to the customer.
6. If your purpose is to solicit known business, your objective should be to set up an appointment with the customer for a specific reason/benefit to the customer. Preferably, this should be at your hotel.
7. Always finish the conversation with some other action you will take.
8. If the customer is busy, have the customer indicate some other time for you to call that would be convenient.

The Hospitality Suite

1. Depending on the convention agenda a hospitality suite game plan should be established. This should incorporate the extent of suite activities, theme or no theme, hours of operation, size of suite, and extent of food and beverage.
2. If a game is incorporated into the suite concept, it should be one that does not retard business conversation or ties down all team players to working the game as opposed to mixing with customers.
3. Each evening there should be a designated suite manager whose responsibility it is to police the suite for competitors who linger too long in your suite. Competitors should be made welcome if they drop in for a drink but should not be allowed to spend the evening working your suite.

Seminars

1. Most salespeople do not attend the "organizations" meeting sessions. This gives you excellent exposure to many planners with little or no competition.
2. You also become conspicuous as a professional salesperson with an identified interest in the matters that affect customers.

Off-Convention Activities

1. Often, it is to the team's advantage to line up group dinners in advance with top customers to go to a top restaurant in the city where the convention is being held.
2. This is an excellent way to isolate customers away from your competition as well as to introduce other members of your team to top clients.

Trade Show

1. The key to working a trade show is to have a game plan going in. Trade show activities encompass (1) the booth, (2) the hospitality suite, and (3) the seminars.
2. The objective of any trade show should be to qualify potential business for your property or to generate leads for other properties.
3. A trade show chairman should be designated to coordinate preparation, show, implementation, and recap. Results should be measurable either by bookings or by leads generated.
4. From the standpoint of individual preparation the property attendees should compile a "hit list" of customers they want to meet at the show.

Preshow Meeting
1. Upon arrival at the convention a team meeting should be called to review the objectives. Assignments should be made as to who will be scheduled in the

FIGURE 7–14 *(cont.)*

booths and at what time. The same applies to the hospitality suite.
2. It should be indicated that at the end of each day before the evening activities there should be a lead-writing party. These leads should be turned in daily to the team coordinator.
3. Daily results should be tabulated and posted each morning at the trade show booth.

The Trade Show Booth
1. Booths should have some sort of a hook to draw potential customers out of the aisle and into the booth for business discussions, perhaps a drawing for a television set. The concept is to stop customers in the aisle to ask them if they have entered the drawing, then to ask for a business card to enter, and then to talk about the planner's organization and potential meeting.
2. As time is limited, you should make quick notes on the back of the business card to hold for the lead-writing party. Later the card is placed in the "hopper" for the drawing.

Inside Property Visitation

1. When a customer contacts you to visit the property, it is generally with the intent of booking a specific program at your hotel.
2. Your questioning should follow with both fact-finding questions and feel-finding questions. It is of paramount importance that you get as much information as possible in order to make your most effective presentation.
3. What the customer is buying and you are selling is space and time at a stated price. Any of these can be varied to arrive at the final contract.
4. Examples of fact-finding questions:
   a. What are your preferred meeting dates?
   b. What is your arrival and departure?
   c. How is the decision made for this meeting?
   d. Who or where else are you considering?
   e. Pattern for sleeping rooms? How many singles, twins, and suites do you require?
   f. Do you have any exhibits? What type? How many? What are setup and teardown requirements?
   g. Where have you met in the past?
   h. Do you have any flexibility on your meeting dates?
   i. Where do most of your people come from?
5. Examples of feel-finding questions:
   a. What are you trying to achieve with this program?
   b. What do you feel are the most important aspects of your program?
   c. What went well at your last meeting? Why? What could have gone better? Why?
   d. What gave you interest in considering our property for this program?
6. A major advantage with a property visitation is that you can demonstrate and show the quality of your product and services to the customer on a firsthand basis.

FIGURE 7–14 *(cont.)*

eight

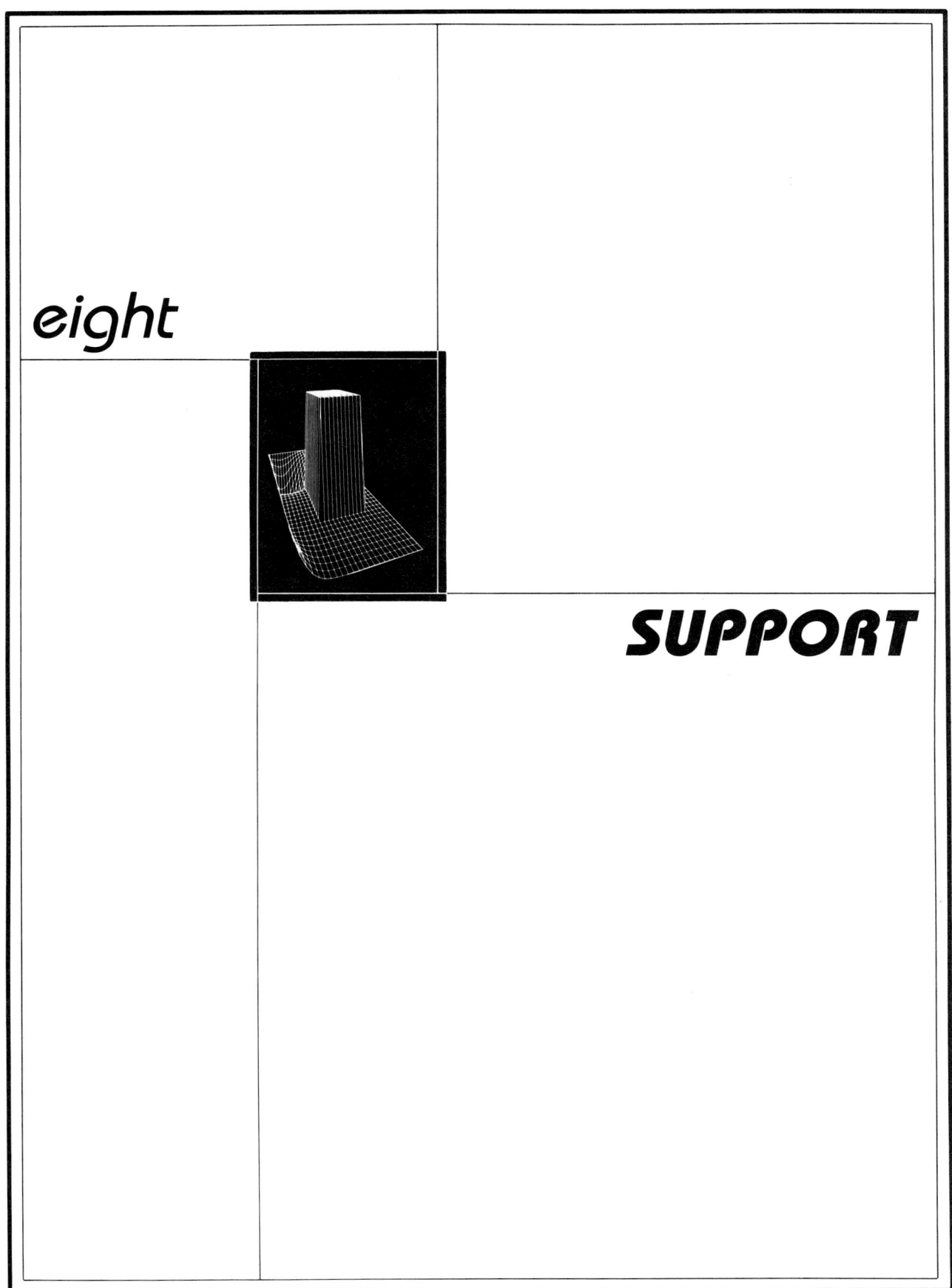

SUPPORT

Although personal contact is the chief method of customer communications, there are many other *support* tools and cooperative agencies that can assist the sales executive in determining business potentials, communicating with them, and aiding in ultimately making the sale. Although they can in themselves effect a direct purchase, their chief use by a property is to lend support to the main promotional activities. Such supportive *tools* include:

1. Direct-mail advertising
2. Collateral materials (printed items supporting the main direct-mail letter)
3. Media advertising
4. Public relations (including publicity)

Some of the more common supporting *agencies* include:

1. Government tourist boards and ministries of tourism (see Figure 8–1)
2. State, regional, county, and local departments of tourism
3. Convention and visitors bureaus
4. Chambers of Commerce
5. Airlines, bus companies, cruise lines, and other transportation companies
6. Third parties, such as wholesalers, retail travel agents, tour operators, hotel representation firms, and multiple management companies

There is a direct tie-in between the supporting sales tools and the supporting agencies. Because their promotional budgets are generally much larger than that of an individual property, many tourist boards, convention and visitors bureaus, and airlines can reach a wider audience with greater frequency and with greater use of both print and broadcast advertising. These agencies may also do direct selling, such as making sales calls during a blitz campaign to sell a destination, the manning of exhibit booths at customer conventions and travel-oriented trade shows, and cooperative participation in area familiarization programs (FAM trips) and site inspections.

DIRECT-MAIL ADVERTISING

Because direct mail is in most cases the most widely used of the supporting sales tools, we will take a look at this medium first. Direct mail has been loosely defined as "anything that is conveyed by one party to another through a postal system."* *Direct-mail advertising* is a further refinement of this definition. It excludes personal correspondence and focuses on the type of mail contact that is designed to acquaint recipients with a new or improved product or service, or to continue to remind them of an existing one, for purposes of making a sale. This, incidentally, would also be the main purpose of other forms of advertising, such as newspaper, magazine, TV, and radio.

Another term one may run across is *direct marketing,* of which direct mail advertising is a primary example. This term refers to the targeted methods used to reach a specific recipient or closely defined audience. This is in contrast

---

*This definition, however, does not take into account the rapid growth of private mail carrier systems, or the new technology, such as fax and computer link-ups, which has given birth to the term *electronic mail.*

FIGURE 8–1 National tourist boards can lend a wide variety of both support and direct promotional services. These collateral materials were sent in response to an inquiry to the Norwegian Tourist Board in New York. The items include 4-color brochures promoting the scenic, recreational, and cultural attractions of the country to both the leisure and group business travel markets, as well as folders from specific cities and individual hotels directed at conference planners and incentive group organizers. (Courtesy of the Norwegian Tourist Board, New York.)

to *broadcast marketing,* which is directed at a wide audience, such as the readership of a newspaper or magazine or a radio or TV station audience.

Direct-Mail Uses

Direct mail is one of the most versatile of all possible sales tools, and can be used for such diverse selling purposes as:

1. *Prospecting:* often done by sending out questionnaires with return reply cards. This method of turning "suspects" into "prospects" is a form of "qualifying" business potentials.
2. *Updating:* also using the questionnaire reply card approach to obtain new or revised data on existing accounts, to update files.
3. *Introducing:* announcing a new, expanded, or improved service or facility to a select group of people to whom such information would be important and meaningful. It could also mean introducing a new key staff member of the property (general manager, executive chef, sales director), as is done in the mailing of press kits or press releases.
4. *Selling:* asking directly for a buying response, such as the return of a room reservation card.
5. *Supporting:* such as sending letters to preregistered attendees for a customer trade show, inviting them to visit your booth or hospitality suite.
6. *Replying:* response to customer-originated requests for information or action. This reply function can also be tied directly into other forms of selling, such as the follow-up for information after a personal sales call, a request for information generated by "coupon" advertising, or the use of tip-ins and business reply card insertions in magazines and newspapers. This process is also termed "fulfillment"; that is, the magazine ad generates interest and inquiry, the direct-mail reply fulfills the request.
7. *Reminding:* periodic mailings to selected lists of frequent users, very often done by resorts on a seasonal basis, to encourage repeat business.
8. *Creating:* developing special packages (generally centered around a theme) and mailing out promotional literature to "create" new business.
9. *Following through:* patronage appreciation correspondence which can aid in rebooking.

This same usage guide, which is only a starter list, can also be employed when considering the uses of other supportive sales tools: folders, brochures, and other collateral; media advertising; and public relations, especially the publicity component of PR.

The preparation of newspaper and magazine ads and broadcast commercials is generally left to advertising and marketing directors, in coordination with the advertising agency of the property or chain. However, anyone selling on any level, even a new account executive who has just entered the industry, will be involved with the preparation of direct mail, even if it is just a short "thank you" follow-up to a personal sales call.

So we now take a look at the preparation of direct mail copy, including the copy that would appear on supporting collateral. You may note that there is a great deal of emphasis on preparing copy as it relates to market segmentation. Thus the concepts of segmentation as discussed in Chapter 5 can now be readily observed in their practical everyday applications.

DIRECT-MAIL COPY*

One of the classic stories of our industry (which has been told and retold at many an educational seminar) concerns the mother mouse and her little brood who were walking down a dark alleyway. All of a sudden, they came face to face with a large, ferocious, and obviously very hungry cat.

The cat was ready to pounce on the hapless family (a full meal: main course and all those succulent appetizers) when the mother mouse looked the cat squarely in the eyes and barked, "bow-wow, bow-wow!" Being a rather intelligent cat, the hungry feline immediately hightailed it out of the alley.

The mother mouse turned to her offspring and said, "See kids, what I've been preaching to you all your lives . . . how important it is to speak a second language."

To be successful, hospitality industry executives must also be conversant in a second language: in our case, the language of the customer. Hotel sales and marketing executives, for example, have learned that you do not merely attempt to *sell* the *features* of your product. Instead, to be effective, you must try to *motivate* your prospects to *purchase benefits* that will satisfy their specific needs and wants or fulfill their particular objectives and goals.

The basic "mother tongue" of our industry is primarily product-oriented. We write and speak in glowing terms of our rooms, food and beverage outlets, public space, convention and function facilities, and recreational/fitness program capabilities. We couple the hard facts with such superlatives as "the finest," "the most convenient," "the most exciting," and so on. But people do not buy variations on brick, stone, glass, wood, and steel, no matter how creatively we may describe them.

They are, first, seeking "solutions to their problems" (i.e., fulfillment of goals and objectives). Second, they are looking for an appropriate mix of experiences, change and escape, adventure, romance, activities, educational opportunities, recreational outlets, and similar benefits that will contribute to and enhance their mental and physical well-being.

Not only must we learn the basic language of our customers, we must also learn many different "dialects." The marketplace is composed of many different types of people living a wide variety of different lifestyles, and looking to the hospitality industry for many different uses and purposes. The sales language used to attract the meeting planner varies from that directed at the travel agent or tour operator, which differs from that aimed at the business traveler, especially in terms of the benefits they are seeking.

The ability to transmit our capabilities to provide these benefits to different types of individuals and groups having varying needs, wants, hopes, and desires—in their specific "language"—is what we would call *communications.* One of the key forms of communications (customer contact, if you wish) is *direct-mail advertising.* The correct copy approach—the way we utilize words in terms of the audience—and the word pictures we paint in terms of our audiences' lifestyles are especially critical when utilizing direct mail as a promotional medium.

Advantages versus Challenges

The written word has many advantages (*permanency,* for one), but it also offers many challenges. *Clarity,* for example, is one of the prime concerns in direct-

*The following material on direct-mail copy has been adapted from an article originally prepared by the present authors for the HSMAI publication, *Marketing Your Hotel Through Direct Mail.*

mail copy. At the time of the reading of a letter or a brochure, the situation is strictly that of "one-way communications" (a term that is actually an oxymoron, since the word communications implies a *two-way* condition). However, the reader at that stage cannot ask the writer, "What do you mean by?" or "Can you give me further details?" or "Can you suggest an alternative?"

Add to this the *confusion* caused by differing interpretations of the technical jargon of our trade (do you and your customers know and agree on the difference between a confirmed reservation and a guaranteed reservation, between a lectern and a podium, between connecting rooms and adjoining rooms?) and the importance of clarity in direct-mail copy becomes even more consequential.

Another key consideration in direct-mail copywriting is that the words themselves must bear the brunt of conveying the full intent of the message. With the spoken word—personal sales calls, telephone conversations, audiovisual sales presentations, and radio and TV advertising—changes in pitch, inflection, and pacing ("vocal variety" as Toastmasters International teaches) can add not only dramatic impact but can help reinforce the purposes and objectives of the message. With direct mail, *italics,* underscoring, **boldfacing,** and use of additional colors can add a nominal degree of emphasis but cannot approach the flair and drama capable with that most flexible of all instruments, the human voice. So with direct mail, more than with any other form of customer contact, care in the *selection* of words becomes a primary concern in relation to ensuring the highest degree of effectiveness.

Marketing Considerations

We are not going to concentrate here on fixed rules of grammar and syntax, and all the other letter-writing "mechanics" so near and dear to the hearts of English teachers. Rather, we stress the basics of copy selection based on marketing considerations.

Here are some fundamental guidelines that relate to the overall concept defined earlier: "Speak the language of your customers":

1. *Copy should reflect the tone and convey the positioning of your property.* An informal, breezy, conversational tone is fine for a rustic resort or a sportsman's lodge. But a more elegant verbal eloquence would be appropriate for a property positioning itself along the lines of a "Five-Star, Deluxe Continental Excelsior Grand Palace." The words should fit the desired image. Otherwise, your description may establish a "credibility gap" between the actual product and the public's expectations.

2. *Copy should fit the demographic compositions of your target audiences.* Demographics refer to the measurable and quantifiable characteristics of your market segments, using such criteria as:

• Age	• Occupation or profession
• Sex	• Family income
• Marital status	• Nationality
• Family size	• Point of origin
• Education	• Prior travel experience

As discussed previously, the public is conveniently incorporated within one or more of the above. In addition, people tend to form organizations directly related to each of the groupings. Thus you can readily reach specific demographic segments through a wide variety of list sources. Some examples:

- *AGE:* senior citizens (AARP)
- *SEX/OCCUPATION:* women business executives (ZONTA)
- *POINT OF ORIGIN:* ZIP code occupant lists
- *PROFESSIONS:* mailing-list brokers

and many other sources, such as trade association and professional society membership rosters, magazine and newspaper subscription lists, and your own customized lists developed from names gleaned from your registration cards and guest history records.

Since you know the key demographic characteristics of the people comprising a specified mailing list, you can tailor your copy to speak their language and in many cases, the very specific "dialect" of the group.

3. *Copy should similarly relate to the psychographic profiles of your target audiences.* Psychographics can be a valuable analytical tool that groups people into qualitative lifestyle segments. One of many techniques is to set up profiles initially based on the general characteristics commonly associated with an "upbeat" liberal lifestyle, as compared with a more traditional conservative outlook. Some of the characteristics of each profile could include:

Liberal	Conservative
Extroverted	Introverted
Romantic	Realist
Futurist	Traditionalist
Active	Passive
Leader	Follower
Participant	Spectator
Nonconformist	Conformist
Creative	Structured
Impulsive	Planner
Allocentric	Psychocentric

Psychographic characteristics are not as specific as demographic ones, and there are considerable variations and crossovers where people may jump from one style to another, depending on circumstances and the roles they are assuming at a particular time. However, copy considerations here are perhaps more consequential than with demographic differences. We are talking about words, verbal images, and word pictures that can directly "turn on" or "turn off" the reader, depending on personality, upbringing, opinions, beliefs, attitudes, and other lifestyle factors that may influence acceptance of the message.

Earlier we talked about not only understanding the language of the customer but also the different "dialects" spoken by subsegments of a target market. Let's combine several demographic and psychographic characteristics to illustrate this:

Suppose that you are packaging a tour and want to attract a *young, active, highly confident* portion of the group travel market. The initial day's program might be described in these terms:

"Following your noon arrival at the unique Last Resort, you will have plenty of free time to explore the fascinating and exotic charm of this mysterious and romantic 'fun in the sun' hideaway. The sensuous Pirates Port area then awaits you for an exciting evening of adventurous dining, followed by an inexhaustible choice of 'on your own, til-the-sun-comes-up' pleasures and delights."

Now let's direct the same description at a more *senior-aged, passive, nonconfident* travel market. Appropriate changes of adjectives and similar modifiers would result in a rewrite more compatible with this segment's lifestyle, such as:

"Following our noon arrival at the world-renowned Last Resort, we will meet in the lobby at 1:00 P.M. for a buffet lunch, followed by a tour of this historic area. The famous Pilgrims Port area will be our traditional seafood dinner setting—after which we will board our modern air-conditioned bus for the return trip to our hotel."

Note the substitution of all those "shelter, safety, and security" words. The basic components of the two tour packages are the same. But the descriptive modifiers have been changed to reflect the predominant lifestyle features of the two different segments. In other words, same language, different dialects.

One of the techniques of copywriting, especially when directing similar messages to different audiences, is to prepare a "word equivalent chart" similar to the following:

Active, Self-Confident	**Passive, Nonconfident**
• You, your	• We, our
• Free time, on your own	• Guided, planned
• Free to roam, to explore	• Guided (lectured) tour
• Exotic, sensuous, sensual	• Charming, historic
• Mysterious	• Famous, well-known
• Adventurous dining	• Traditional dining

You can then utilize the applicable terminology to describe an all-inclusive "closed" tour (right column), which will differ from the description of an on-your-own "open-ended" tour package (left column).

4. *Copy should put the reader in the picture.* One way to do this is to "tag line" your features in terms of user benefits. This enables your recipients to visualize themselves in benefit-providing situations.

There's nothing wrong, for example, in mentioning your "express check-in and check-out service," but remember that this is only a feature. Personalizing this in the form of a benefit could prompt an additional tag line such as "No need to waste valuable time standing in long lines," a circumstance the reader can readily visualize.

5. *Copy must be truthful.* Very often it is not what you say as much as the assumptions made by the reader because of what you did not say. (Is the "sin of omission" worse than the "sin of commission"?) To highlight "majestic, panoramic views of the ocean" when only 80 of your 300 rooms in your courtyard-style resort face the sea is hardly in accord with the inference that all rooms have sweeping ocean views.

6. *Copy should avoid "puffery."* Grandiose statements about your accommodations and facilities are usually easily recognized as meaningless, and thus detract from the impact of the rest of the message. Copy should basically

inform and then persuade, and offer assistance to the reader in evaluating where to go, where to stay, where to meet, and where to eat. The chief offenders in this regard—the statements that sound good but offer nothing—are such meaningless superlatives as:

- ''The most central location in town''
- ''Located in the heart of all activities''
- ''The most modern accommodations in the area''
- ''The finest continental cuisine''
- ''The latest state-of-the-art meeting facilities''

Reliance on these and similar industry clichés is simply mental laziness and offers nothing concrete in terms of reader benefits.

So what is *good* copy? Well, it's really a combination of many factors, much like a good recipe. Mix equal parts of the following:

- Attention
- Truthfulness/honesty
- Empathy (with the reader)
- Creativity/innovation
- Pertinent information/data
- Helpfulness/usefulness

Add a dash of humor (where appropriate), mix carefully, blend and stir, heat or cool, and deliver the final product to an audience whose appetite you have whetted for your specific product.

To Recap

Direct mail, by its very nature, has many unique advantages. It can readily be targeted to a single person or to a select group of people sharing common characteristics, attributes, and interests. Thus specific words and verbal pictures can be selected that will have maximum impact because they relate personally and professionally to the reader's lifestyles, needs, wants, hopes, desires, anticipations, expectations, dreams, daydreams, and fantasies.

On the other hand, there are limitations that must be recognized and compensated. Direct mail ordinarily does not employ *motion* as does TV, *sound* as does TV and radio, *dominating size* as do outdoor posters and billboards, or on-the-spot immediate *dialogue response* as do telephone and personal contact.

Thus the written word must bear the responsibility for the effectiveness of that form of sales communications known as direct-mail advertising. One of the key definitions of effective communications (presented initially at the start of Chapter 7), which also defines the role of copy in direct-mail advertising, is the ''unaltered transferring of an understandable message between two or more people.''

COLLATERAL MATERIALS

The term *direct mail* usually implies a letter or printed self-contained message, or a cover letter that serves to call attention to the enclosure materials contained in the envelope.

These enclosure materials can take the form of folders, brochures,* reprints of newspaper/magazine feature stories, advertising reprints, testimonial letters, rate cards, and many other items, often largely pictorial, which serve to support the objectives of the mailing.

Collateral materials are also multiple-purpose sales and marketing tools. They can be distributed by hand when making sales calls or when "manning" an exhibit booth. They can also be displayed internally in the sales office, at the registration desk, and in guest rooms as "take-home" items. They can even be "tipped in" or inserted into trade magazines and consumer publications. They can even "ride" along with a magazine as an enclosure, especially with the increasing use by publications of clear shrink-wrap as a protective mailing cover.

Multiple Use and Distribution

A unique aspect of folders and brochures is that distribution is often *made by the customer.* Association meeting planners, for example, traditionally use brochures from the convention headquarters hotel in mailings to stimulate attendance from both members and their spouses. This folder is either the regular pictorial rack folder or "shell" folders, provided in quantity so that the group can customize its mailing by imprinting its name, logo, name of the event, and the time and place. In some instances, other information, such as a program, can also be imprinted. The group mails them (generally paying for postage and handling) to its membership, together with accompanying registration forms.

Another example is the display of brochures and folders in travel agency offices. A word of practical caution: Too many hotels blindly send hundreds of folders to every travel agency on their list. In far too many cases, most are tossed into the trash (the agency, after all, is not a distribution center for the property). So one should contact agencies ahead of time and ask specifically how many they could use. Additionally, the hotel's sales executives or travel and tour representatives should spot-check agencies to make sure that the materials are indeed on display.

Both of the preceding examples illustrate how certain customers can in effect act as an intermediary "sales office" for the property. There is a significant difference, though: Association meeting planners can act as *distributors*, whereas travel agents act primarily as *displayers*.

Effective Brochures

Unfortunately, there can be a great deal of abuse and waste in the preparation, production, and distribution of folders and brochures. They are the most commonly used *pictorial* sales tools of the hospitality industry. However, in most instances, professional advice should be sought, to maximize their impact and effectiveness. To merely ask someone to "print me a bunch of folders that I can use to promote my hotel" can be costly and unproductive.

At the 50th Anniversary Convention of the Hotel Sales Management Association, guest speaker Jane Maas, then vice president of Wells Rich Greene

---

*The distinction between a folder and a brochure is often somewhat blurred. A folder generally contains multiple panels and is prepared so that it fits directly into a standard #10 envelope (size approximately 4 by 9 in.) or in a travel agent's display rack (which is why they are sometimes called *rack folders*). A brochure generally measures 8½ by 11 in., is staple-stitched, lies flat, and fits a 9- by 12-in. envelope as well as the sales office's standard manila file folder. There are many size variations among brochures, often depending on style and layout and the attempt to look "different" and attract attention.

Advertising, New York, offered attendees the following working checklist for developing better folders and brochures:

1. Decide on your positioning—place the product a certain way into the consumer's mind.
2. Agree on a creative strategy and put it in writing—what you will say and how.
3. Set objective, identify target audience, include a consumer benefit(s), and support the benefit(s) with proof. Give your product a distinct personality.
4. Collateral should be consistent with advertising and have the same family feeling.
5. Put your selling message on the cover—like a headline in an ad.
6. Put your positioning on the cover.
7. Put a benefit on the cover.
8. Use one illustration on the cover instead of many small ones.
9. Set yourself apart.
10. Avoid clichés—visual and written.
11. Use photographs rather than drawings.
12. Demonstrate your point of difference from your competition.
13. Show activity, not just scenery.
14. Show food close up.
15. Caption your photographs.
16. Don't be afraid of long copy.
17. Spotlight the important facts.
18. Tell the truth.
19. Be helpful, not clever.
20. Maps get high readership.
21. Understand the new consumer—talk to important segments, such as people who like the outdoors, culture seekers, fishermen, single women, and so on.
22. Don't stint on quality.
23. Include several pieces in a mailing.
24. Break the rules for a reason.

Looking back at the preceding checklist, item 24 could be viewed as an "escape clause." On the surface, it seems to offer a reason or "excuse" for ignoring any of the other 23 guidelines. However, there certainly can be valid circumstances where innovation, creativity, and special situations may fully justify preparing brochures and folders that "break the rules."

For example, let's go back again to our Center City Hotel. In this case we'll expand our example to create a "parent company" known as the National Center City Hotel Corporation, with 20 properties throughout the nation. They are located in many different settings: center city, suburban, airport, mountain resort, seaside resort, and so on.

In this situation one could devise a corporate brochure which on the cover would have separate pictures of each property, four across and five down. This total of 20 separate photos would seemingly violate checklist item 8.

However, a marketing rationale could readily justify this design: namely, that the positioning goal (item 6) of the chain is to emphasize to various markets that the company can offer a wide variety of different types of properties in a wide variety of environments.

What types of brochures or folders are best? That's another of those questions that can always be legitimately answered, "it depends."

Purpose of Collateral Materials

The primary factors in determining copy, illustrations, layout, and design must relate to the main purpose of the collateral materials. In turn, and of equal importance, is consideration of the recipients and how they will be using the materials.

Convention and meeting organizers, for example, need specific quantitative information about guest rooms, particularly connecting rooms, suites, and other combination accommodations. Their records on past meetings should show how many singles, twins, club floor accommodations, and suites are customarily used by their attendees.

FIGURE 8–2 A category breakdown of the types of guest rooms, as well as a detailed listing of guest room facilities and services, can be useful in the collateral materials prepared for convention organizers and other meeting planners. (Courtesy of The Drake, Chicago, Illinois.)

FIGURE 8–3 A listing of on-premise audiovisual equipment should be an integral part of the descriptive literature sent to meeting planners, especially those responsible for training sessions and other educational programs. (Courtesy of Lyford Cay Club, Nassau, Bahamas.)

ROOM INFORMATION

Number of rooms	535	Check-out time	12:00 p.m.
Number of floors	10	New day begins	7:00 a.m.
Bedrooms		*Combinations: connecting rooms*	
Single	41	Two bedroom	30
Twin	199	Three bedroom	48
Queen	116	Four bedroom	18
King	152	*Boardroom Suites:*	
Vista Floor	27	Two bedroom suites	4
Suites		One bedroom suites	1
Junior Suite	21		
One bedroom	15	Rooms with 2 bathrooms	20
Sico Parlors	16		

ROOM FACILITIES

- Air-conditioning with individual controls
- Heating with individual controls
- 2 direct dial phones in each room
- Clock radio with alarm
- Remote control TV (network and cable)
- Electric current: 110 Volts
- Non-smoking floors
- Minibars
- Bathroom scales
- Complimentary *Chicago Tribune* weekdays

- Views of Lake Michigan, Michigan Ave and Walton Place
- Private bath (tub and shower)
- First-run movies/all sports and news channels
- Bathrobes
- Rooms available for the disabled
- Flowers and fruit in rooms daily
- Turn down service with chocolates

Vista Executive Floor

Situated on the top floor of the hotel, the Vista Executive floor offers the discriminating traveller and business person 24 spacious, designer decorated guest rooms, including three luxurious lakeview suites. Included among the numerous amenities and services are pre-registration, special check in/check-out, lounging robes, special bath conveniences, fresh fruit, floral arrangements, complimentary Chicago newspaper and the *Wall Street Journal*. Complimentary continental breakfast is available in the Vista Executive Lounge.
From 4:00 p.m.-12:00 a.m. guests can enjoy complimentary drinks and hors d'oeuvres. Soft refreshments are available throughout the day in the Lounge.
Two deluxe boardrooms for meetings of 12 and 24 respectively, with magnificent views of Lake Michigan are contained within the Vista Floor complex.

TRANSPORTATION TO HOTEL

From	Distance		Time	Via
	Km	Miles	Mins	
O'Hare Airport	32	20	30-45	Taxi/Bus
Midway Airport	25	14	30-45	Taxi/Bus
Union Railroad Station	4	2.5	10	Taxi/Bus
Northwestern Railroad Station	3.2	2	7	Taxi/Bus

CHICAGO

The Drake
Operated by
HILTON INTERNATIONAL

LYFORD CAY CLUB
CONFERENCE PLANNERS' GUIDE

Audio-Visual Equipment

MOTION PICTURE PROJECTORS
16mm Sound – Built-in Speaker
16mm Sound – Separate Speaker
16mm Sound – Self threading
Dual 8mm – Self threading
Super 8mm – Sound Projector

SLIDE PROJECTORS
35mm Kodak Carousel, remote control
35mm Kodak Ektagraphic Deluxe
Dissolve Control–Kodak Model 2, for 2 slide projectors
Cassette Sync Recorder/Player for slide sync, auto advance

OTHER PROJECTION EQUIPMENT
Overhead Projector – for transparencies
Opaque Projector – for typed or printed material on solid paper
Filmstrip Projector – Sound
Projection Table – Adjustable

AUDIO EQUIPMENT
Cassette Tape Recorder – (tape extra)
Portable PA System

VIDEO EQUIPMENT
Video Cassette Recorder, ¾" with 4' x 4' screen
Video Cassette Recorder, VHS ½" with 4' x 4' screen
19" Color TV Monitor
Color TV Camera

PROJECTION SCREENS
50" x 50" – Tripod
60" x 50" – Tripod
70" x 70" – Tripod
96" x 96" – Tripod
12' x 12' – Conference Room Only

ADDITIONAL ITEMS
Flip Chart Pads
Cassette Tapes (60 minutes)
Extra Microphones
Easels
Xerox-copying machine
NCR Word Processor
IBM Typewriters

This breakdown, either numerically or by percentage, can be most helpful to them in forecasting the mix of guest rooms required for future meetings. Figure 8–2 illustrates how a detailed itemization of room inventory and room facilities information can be incorporated in a meeting brochure.

Meeting planners must also have detailed floor plans, room capacity information, and lists of available equipment (see Figure 8–3). They very often use this information to "walk their program" through the facility, event by event, to see if the property can physically accommodate their program needs. Pictorial folders are nice but not necessary at that decision-making stage. However, after the property has been selected, the association meeting planner would then usually request a supply of either pictorial or shell folders as visual help to promote attendance.

The same pictorial folders would also be appropriate for the individual leisure traveler (and in many cases the individual business market as well). However, the detailed convention and meeting brochure would normally be a waste of time, effort, and money if distributed to the average vacationer or commercial traveler.

For most folders directed at the individual leisure traveler, at least three common elements should be included:

1. An 800 or other toll-free number for making direct reservations
2. A detailed road map showing the location of the property relative to the main highways, airports, points of interest, and so on (see Figure 8–4)
3. A space for a travel agent imprint (generally on the back panel of the folder)

FIGURE 8–4 These detailed transportation and location maps not only aid guests in getting to and from the property, but also assist them by providing directions to key area attractions and business sections. (Courtesy of Hotel New Otani, Osaka, Japan.)

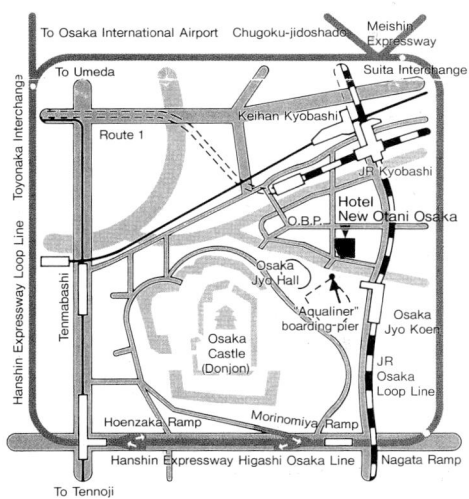

By car
- Approx. 10 min. (3.2km) from Yodoyabashi.
- Approx. 15 min. (4.5km) from Umeda.
- Approx. 15 min. (4.4km) from Honmachi.
- Approx. 20 min. (6.0km) from Namba.
- Approx. 25 min. (7.3km) from Shin Osaka.
- Approx. 30 min. (19.3km) from Itami International Airport.

*When taking the Hanshin Expressway from the above places, get off at the Hoenzaka Ramp.
*When taking the Hanshin Expressway from Higashi Osaka, get off at the Morinomiya Ramp.

Conveniently located near Osaka's business and entertainment centers.

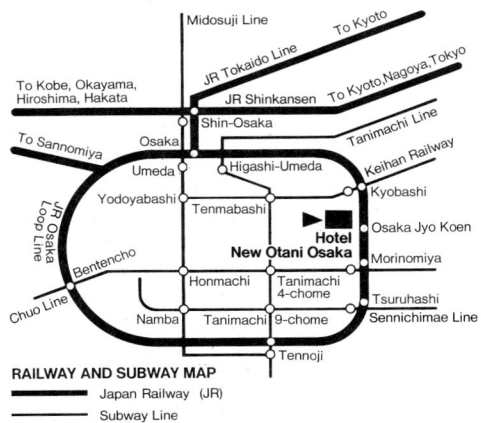

RAILWAY AND SUBWAY MAP
——— Japan Railway (JR)
——— Subway Line

By train
- 9 min. from Umeda to Osaka Jyo Koen Station on the JR Osaka Loop Line.
- From Namba: Take the Sennichimae Subway Line to Tsuruhashi and transfer to the Osaka Loop Line. 10 min. from Tsuruhashi to Osaka Jyo Koen Station.
- Only three minutes on foot from Osaka Jyo Koen Station (JR Osaka Loop Line).
- Limousine bus service between the Hotel and Osaka International Airport. Ten trips daily.

Folders and brochures can be highly effective in supporting direct selling efforts by creating impressions and images. As the illustrations in Figure 8–5 indicate, when distributed to the appropriate markets, they can draw the reader into the picture by emphasizing specific benefits that relate to the particular market segment's needs, wants, and lifestyles.

FIGURE 8–5 *Pictorial folders, directed at specific markets, focus on each segment's distinctive lifestyle needs or wants. (Courtesy of Bill Bard Associates, Monticello, New York.)*

Intimate Dining
(Romance)

Group Dining
(Social Interaction)

FIGURE 8-5 *(cont.)* Some additional examples of folders geared to different lifestyle needs.

Casual Outdoor Enthusiasts
(Informal ''Escape'')

Upscale Outdoor Enthusiasts
(Casual Elegance)

FIGURE 8-5 *(cont.)*

Upscale Elegance-Seekers
(Status)

Spectator Sports Enthusiasts
(Outdoor Activity Sharing)

FIGURE 8–5 *(cont.)*

Family Activities
(Social Togetherness)

Indoor Social/Recreational Participants
(Social Interaction)

The relationship of pictures to your recipients' lifestyles (psychographic profiles) is an essential consideration in selecting illustrations (note Figure 8–6) as well as the choice of words when writing copy. Folders and other collateral materials can also be extremely effective in promoting specialized packages, holidays, theme promotions, and other special interest group activities, as illustrated in Figure 8–7.

FIGURE 8–6 Swimming pool scenes from four different folders, directed at four different psychographic segments. The selection criteria should relate to the predominant lifestyles of the guests each property is trying to attract and whether those guests can readily put themselves into the picture. (Courtesy of Bill Bard Associates, Monticello, New York.)

Applied Psychographics

Active nonconfident   Active self-confident

Passive nonconfident   Passive self-confident

FIGURE 8–7 Folders and other collateral materials are well suited to promoting an ongoing series of special activities targeted at hobbiests and other special-interest groups and organizations. (Courtesy of Mohonk Mountain House, Lake Mohonk, New Paltz, New York.)

MEDIA ADVERTISING

Direct-mail and collateral materials are in many instances a specific part of the personal selling process. They can be mailed out ahead of time to prospects to acquaint them with the property, making it easier for the sales executive to discuss features and benefits with the prospect clients. During the sales presentation, they can be used as specific visual references.

It has been said so many times that it almost seems too elementary, but it is particularly relevant here: Those who sell in the hospitality industry have an additional challenge in that they cannot bring the product along for demonstration purposes. Thus brochures and folders have to carry the brunt of product portrayal, especially when the sales executive is making a presentation in a prospect's office.

In the case of media advertising, the purpose generally is somewhat different. The tie-in when it is received by the recipient is not related that directly to the *immediate* selling process. Advertising's overall objectives are twofold: (1) to *tell* and (2) to *sell.* As such, it will very often set the stage for acceptance of the sale executive later when in direct contact with a prospect.

For example, a prospect's recall of your ad can make your direct selling job much easier. In some cases, prospects may already be more than "half sold" and are looking for additional information, such as illustrated in the following dialogues, which are directed at Mrs. Nelson, the hotel sales executive:

Corporate traffic manager: "By the way, Mrs. Nelson, I saw your ad the other day in several trade journals. I was really intrigued about your new corporate upgrade discount program. Tell me more about it."

or

Travel agent: "Delighted to see you, Mrs. Nelson. Say, that was quite a spectacular commercial your chain had on TV the other night. You know, the one that pictured 15 of the most economical yet upbeat hideaway islands in the Caribbean. Just what my clients would love! You wouldn't happen to have some brochures with you?"

or

Meeting planner: "I've been following your ad campaign about the construction and opening of your new convention center. I think it mentioned something about a videocassette that accompanies your meeting planner packet. Do you happen to have one with you?"

This last illustration, incidentally, offers the sales executive the opportunity for an immediate pickup and possible extension of the sale.

"I certainly do, Mr. Meeting Planner. As a matter of fact, I have two versions with me. One is more functional and is intended for meeting planners such as yourself. It walks you through setups and arrangements, A/V and staging, and other areas that you are responsible for—and emphasizes our special features which can be particularly beneficial to you. The other video focuses on our recreational facilities and area attractions. This would be particularly suited for your use in promoting attendance."

TYPES OF MEDIA

The preceding examples illustrate some but not all of the various forms of media, and as you will also note, they were directed at several, but not all, types of markets. For comparison purposes, Figure 8–8 charts the more prominent forms of media that can be selected for use in the hospitality industry.

Advantages and Limitations

Because of the characteristics of each medium, each will have certain inherent advantages and limitations. Here are some examples:

Three Leading Types of Media

AUDIO (RADIO)	VIDEO (TV)	PRINT
Network	Network	Newspaper
Local	Local	Magazine
Public service	Public service	Special interest/trade publications
Audiotape (learning tapes	Satellite	Billboards, signs, posters, car cards
with commercial	Cable network	Direct mail
messages)	Videocassette	Collateral (folders and brochures)
	(with commercials)	Desktop publishing

FIGURE 8-8 *Some advertising and promotional vehicles grouped within broad-based media classifications.*

1. Newspapers generally have a short shelf life (often less than a day). On the other hand, messages or ads can be changed daily or inserted quickly as needed.

2. Magazines have a longer retention life, can offer better utilization of color, but their circulation generally represents a small percentage of the potential decision-making prospects. Trade magazines, especially those directed at a particular segment (i.e., meeting planners, tour operators, etc.) generally have less "waste" than do consumer-oriented magazines.

3. Radio offers the additional appeal of sound and can be localized through time slotting to reach specific segments at specific hours (i.e., business executives during "drive-time" periods). However, it has an extremely short "life" (heard and gone).

4. Television, which combines sight, sound, and motion, would seem, on the surface, to be the ideal medium. But national TV can be expensive, is short-lived (seen and gone), and can involve considerable initial production costs. However, local broadcasting and cable stations are beginning to bring some costs down to a more feasible level. A variation of TV advertising that has repeat-showing value is the emerging use of advertising on rented or purchased videocassettes.

ACTION PRINT ADVERTISING

One of the traditional limitations of print advertising is that it in effect just lays there waiting to be noticed and read. In personal selling as well as in TV advertising and certain types of "moving" outdoor billboards and flashing neon signs, motion plays an important part in focusing attention and stimulating interest.

In face-to-face selling, the sales executive can employ motion (such as gesturing or directly handing an item to the prospect) to directly influence the recipient to actively react or respond. Even direct-mail advertising can cause physical reader involvement, as the recipient handles supporting collateral materials, fills out questionnaires, and returns reply cards.

With some ingenuity (and admittedly, a suitable budget), there are methods of creating "action" and reader involvement in newspaper and magazine advertising. Several examples are illustrated in Figure 8-9.

FIGURE 8–9 Some examples of getting the reader to become actively involved with printed ads. On the top, both a brochure and a business reply card have been tipped in between a two-page center spread. On the bottom, the pop-up cardboard Roledex contains a business card that can be removed and filed.

AN ADVERTISING SAMPLER

Most of the principles of writing copy in terms of specific target audiences (outlined in the discussion of direct-mail advertising) apply as well to media advertising. These include researching the demographic and psychographic profiles of the designated target audiences and speaking the language of the reader or listener.

Because newspaper, magazine, and TV advertising also incorporates pictures (and in the case of TV, sound, and motion), it is also important in many forms of hospitality industry advertising that the audience can readily place themselves visually in the picture. This also puts added emphasis on compatibility of words and pictures; that is, each should reflect and support the other.

A variety of different types of print advertising are shown in Figure 8–10. These are directed at different audiences, with messages specifically tailored to a variety of different needs, wants, and desires. They are also related to specific objectives and goals of the individual properties.*

*Not all of the ads pictured are currently running. They were selected among those over the past four or five years that were particularly effective in reaching specific markets.

A Great Way To Wrap Up Your Week.

When you stay at the Sheraton North Shore Inn this weekend, you get more than a $10 gift certificate for shopping and free transportation to Northbrook Court. After you've found the perfect gift, we'll wrap it for you while you relax in a brand new guest room, take a swim in the pool or dine in our restaurant. All for only $55* per night from December 2 through January 1, 1989.

*Per room, per night, plus tax. Friday, Saturday and Sunday nights only. No charge for children under 18 sharing room with parent(s). Rate does not apply for groups. Limited availability. Reservations recommended.

Sheraton North Shore Inn
933 Skokie Boulevard ◆ Northbrook, IL 60062 ◆ 312/498-6500

The hospitality people of **ITT**

Some Key Principles of Effective Hotel Advertising

FIGURE 8–10 *Attention:* Gaining the readers' attention and then compelling them to read on are key advertising challenges, especially in trade magazines which may carry several hundred hospitality industry messages in each issue. From left to right: Two methods of gaining attention: (left) a "play on words" headline (courtesy of Gardner, Stein & Frank, Inc., Chicago), and (right) a spectacular illustration (courtesy of Warren/Kremer Advertising, New York).

Make any size meeting a landmark event.

All the advantages of meeting in New York come together in one spectacular hotel. Where a glass elevator ride takes you through the world's tallest atrium. With magnificent views of Manhattan. Revolving rooftop restaurant and lounge. 1,877 oversized guest rooms and exquisite large suites. A 1,500-seat Broadway theatre. New York's largest ballroom. And an immense yet flexible complex of 57 meeting, banquet and exhibition rooms—an awesome 80,000 square feet in all. The New York Marriott Marquis. A colossal step forward for intimate meetings or large conventions. For information and reservations call 212-398-1900.

Marriott People know how.

NEW YORK **Marriott** MARQUIS

1535 Broadway at 45th Street New York, NY 10036-4017

On land or sea, the fun never sets.

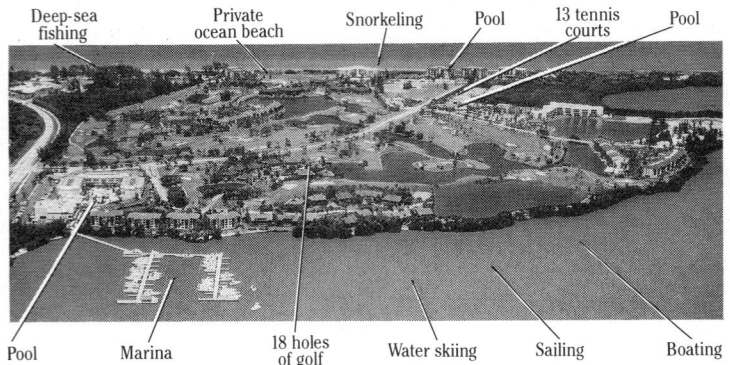

Deep-sea fishing · Private ocean beach · Snorkeling · Pool · 13 tennis courts · Pool

Pool · Marina · 18 holes of golf · Water skiing · Sailing · Boating

Come to southeast Florida's newest resort. All these are the pleasures awaiting you, along with dining, casual or continental, and dancing and entertainment.

The *Island Funaway.* Our special package is only $55* and includes a deluxe room and two-hour Intracoastal waterway cruise aboard the *Island Princess.* See your travel agent or call 800/444-1432.

*Per person, per day, double occupancy, eff. Dec. 18. Minimum two-night stay. Limited number of rooms at this rate.

INDIAN RIVER PLANTATION
RESORT AND MARINA
Hutchinson Island ◆ Stuart, Florida 34996

FIGURE 8–10 *(cont.)* *Humor:* Another way of gaining attention is through humor, especially puns and other wordplays, in the headline. (Courtesy of Gardner, Stein & Frank, Inc., Chicago.)

A million isles from the ordinary.

The Island Funaway. $55.*

Come to southeast Florida's newest resort. Our $55 package includes a handsome guest room *and* a two-hour cruise on the luxurious *Island Princess.* Also awaiting you are all these a la carte pleasures — 18 holes of golf ◆ 13 tennis courts ◆ 3 pools ◆ 1,700-ft. private ocean beach ◆ marina ◆ deep-sea fishing ◆ boating ◆ water sports ◆ fine dining ◆ dancing and entertainment. See your travel agent or call 800/444-1432.

*Per person, per day, double occupancy, eff. Dec. 18. Minimum two-night stay. Limited number of rooms at this rate.

INDIAN RIVER PLANTATION
RESORT AND MARINA
Hutchinson Island ◆ Stuart, Florida 34996

PUT A "SUITE" IN YOUR VALENTINE'S DAY

Spend a night of romance in the heart of Chicago.

We'll pamper you with champagne in your beautiful studio or one-bedroom suite. Special late dinner reservations are available at **Lawry's The Prime Rib Restaurant** across the street. On Saturday and Sunday we've extended your check-out so you can browse through galleries and shops on the Magnificent Mile just one block away.

Only $59* for studio suites, **$89*** for one-bedroom suites, each with fresh brewed coffee and tea, Perrier and juice in the refrigerator, fluffy towels, hairdryer, and free in-room movies. Adjacent parking is available.

For *your* Suite Valentine's Night, call 312/337-1000.

*Per suite, per night, plus tax, Friday, Saturday and Sunday nights (Feb.12-14) only. One night advance deposit required.

LENOX HOUSE
AT THE MAGNIFICENT MILE
616 North Rush Street at East Ontario • Chicago, IL 60611 • 312/337-1000

FIGURE 8–10 *(cont.)*   *Key word emphasis:* Capitalizing on a key word is another form of attention getting, which also may use humor, especially puns. Here the word "suite" ("sweet") is appropriately used by all-suite property to promote both holidays and summer weekends. (Courtesy of Gardner, Stein & Frank, Inc., Chicago.)

SUITE CHICAGO SUMMER WEEKENDS.
At Chicago's new all-suite hotel.
LENOX HOUSE

FABULOUS LOCATION. Just one block from the Magnificent Mile. The best shopping, restaurants, nightlife, galleries and museums are footsteps from our door.

SUITE VALUE. All of our studio and one-bedroom suites have coffeemakers, Perrier and juices in the fridge, fluffy towels, hairdryer, morning newspaper and free in-room movies. Adjacent parking is available.

$59* per night for studio suites. **$89*** per night for one-bedroom suites.

For your Suite Chicago Weekend, call (312) 337-1000; from outside Illinois, 1-800-44-LENOX or your favorite travel agent.

*Per suite, per night plus tax (up to four persons), Friday, Saturday and Sunday nights only. Advance reservations required. Limited number of rooms available. Rates do not apply during conventions or for groups. Effective through September 30, 1988.

LENOX HOUSE
YOUR CHICAGO HOTEL
616 North Rush Street at East Ontario • Chicago, IL 60611 • (312) 337-1000

FIGURE 8–10 _(cont.)_ _Action:_ The showing of people "doing things," rather than just posing, is particularly suited to hospitality advertising, where readers can readily place themselves in the picture. (Courtesy of Gardner, Stein & Frank, Inc., Chicago.)

FIGURE 8–10 _(cont.)_ _Position and image:_ Advertising can be particularly helpful to the sales executive in establishing a position and image for a specific property. In these examples the emphasis is on developing an image appealing to the "escape" market seeking the four "S's" of Seclusion, Space, Silence, and Solitude. (Courtesy of Lithographics, Altamonte Springs, Florida.)

A Memorable Occasion Deserves An Unforgettable Celebration.

A Bar Mitzvah. The celebration of a boy becoming a man. It's a once in a lifetime event and at Headquarters Plaza Hotel we help you and your family celebrate the moment with a party that is created especially for you. Enjoy award-winning cuisine, imaginative menus, and superior service for a reception of 40 to 400 guests. Celebrate your special occasions with us. Plan the day you'll always remember by calling Brenda, toll free at
800-225-1941

HEADQUARTERS PLAZA HOTEL
3 Headquarters Plaza • Morristown, New Jersey • (201) 898-9100

A Memorable Occasion Deserves An Unforgettable Celebration.

Celebrate a very special 16th birthday with a party that your daughter will always cherish. Whether it's dancing to top 40 tunes in our Hurricane Alley nightspot, or a "summer sun" theme party in our ballroom, Headquarters Plaza Hotel will help you create a moment to remember. Good fun, fabulous food, and friendly staff are all yours to enjoy. Celebrate your special occasions with us. Plan a Sweet Sixteen she'll never forget by calling Brenda MacDowell toll free at
800-225-1941

HEADQUARTERS PLAZA HOTEL
3 Headquarters Plaza • Morristown, New Jersey • (201) 898-9100

A Memorable Occasion Deserves An Unforgettable Celebration.

The recognition of personal milestones. A night to remember, shared with friends, family, and colleagues. Celebrate the occasion with a party created especially for you. Headquarters Plaza Hotel. Award-winning cuisine, imaginative menus, and superior service for 40 to 400 guests. Spend your special moments with us. Plan the party you'll always remember by calling Brenda MacDowell toll free at
800-225-1941

HEADQUARTERS PLAZA HOTEL
3 Headquarters Plaza • Morristown, New Jersey • (201) 898-9100

A Memorable Occasion Deserves An Unforgettable Celebration.

The special moment when two are joined together as one. It's a once in a lifetime event where every detail should be perfect. At Headquarters Plaza Hotel we help you capture the moment with a celebration that is created especially for you. Choose from a variety of elegantly appointed surroundings accommodating 40 to 400 guests. Complemented by award-winning cuisine, imaginative menus, and superior service. Celebrate your special occasions with us. Plan the wedding day you'll always remember by calling Brenda MacDowell toll free at
800-225-1941

HEADQUARTERS PLAZA HOTEL
3 Headquarters Plaza • Morristown, New Jersey • (201) 898-9100

FIGURE 8–10 (cont.) *Targeting:* This ad series was specifically targeted to introduce a new property to the local community. It utilizes people, rather than "bricks and mortar," to describe various types of group occasions and celebrations that can be held in a hotel for people of all ages. The series also illustrates the principle of consistency of appearance and style. (Courtesy of Irma S. Mann Strategic Marketing, Inc., Boston.)

FIGURE 8–10 (cont.) *Targeting:* For some market segments, advertising can also be aimed obliquely at the real decision makers, such as those who are responsible for making travel arrangements for others. (Courtesy of Warren/Kremer Advertising, New York.)

FIGURE 8–10 (cont.) *Coordination and consistency:* The principle of "coordinated appearance" can be an important element in conveying an overall image relationship between corporate advertising and advertising done for an individual property within the chain or franchise system. The corporate ad on the left is specifically directed at the incentive group market; the property ad on the right uses a modern-day reenactment of an historical event to catch the attention of meeting planners. Despite the differences in both product and target audience, both ads have a similarity of style and tone that can reinforce reader awareness and recognition. (Courtesy of Robinson, Yesawich & Pepperdine, Maitland, Florida.)

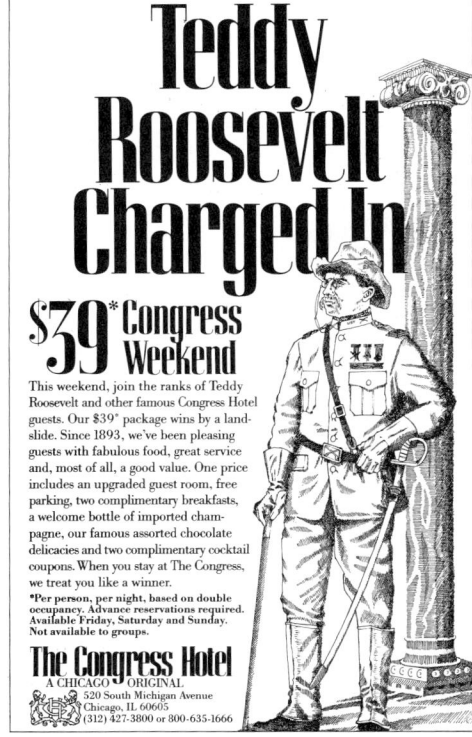

FIGURE 8–10 (cont.) *Nostalgia:* Nostalgia and images of "the good old days" are particularly suited to hotels with a history. This series (which also illustrates the concept of coordinated appearance), focuses on the variety of celebrities who have enjoyed the hotel in the past, and also employs humor and wordplay in the headlines. (Courtesy of Robinson, Yesawich & Pepperdine, Maitland, Florida.)

"MEMORABLE."

"Thanks to your fine staff for providing us with a memorable, productive sales meeting."

Johnson Wax

Americana Lake Geneva Resort

Lake Geneva, Wisconsin
**Call 414/248-8811.
In Illinois, call 312/939-1078.**

"EASIER."

"Everyone was pleased with every aspect of our meeting. Your attention to details made my job easier."

Mobil Chemical Company

Americana Lake Geneva Resort

Lake Geneva, Wisconsin
Call 414/248-8811. In Illinois, call 312/939-1078.

"PRAISE."

"The quality of food, service, audio-visual and activities earned your people meaningful praise."

Midwest Agricultural Chemicals Association, Inc.

Americana Lake Geneva Resort

Lake Geneva, Wisconsin
Call 414/248-8811. In Illinois, call 312/939-1078.

"RAVES."

"Our 50th anniversary meeting was a great success and rave reviews are pouring in."

Gingiss International, Inc.

Americana Lake Geneva Resort

Lake Geneva, Wisconsin
Call 414/248-8811. In Illinois, call 312/939-1078.

FIGURE 8–10 *(cont.)* *Testimonials:* Let others help sell for you. Potential customers can often identify themselves with similar users and tend to more readily believe their statement or opinions. This series also illustrates the principles of ''coordinated design'' and is an example of ''reverse plate'' printing—white on black rather than the customary black on white. (Courtesy of Gardner, Stein and Frank, Inc., Chicago.)

Sink your teeth into this!

Stamford Marriott's Hungry Hour. Featuring an incredible 24 foot buffet for only $3.99. Your favorite frozen drinks. The latest videos and music. Every night Monday thru Thursday from 4:30 p.m. to 7:30 p.m. at Stamford Marriott's Forum.

An excellent choice for after work fun and entertainment, with the finest collection of old friends and new. Finally, a whole new forum to satisfy your appetite for evening entertainment. Don't forget about our Pool Party on Fridays. Free Parking Available.

Marriott People know how.

THE FORUM

STAMFORD **Marriott**®

2 Stamford Forum, Stamford, CT 06901
(203) 357-9555

All you can eat for just $2.00

Marriott's *Hungry Hour*℠

Watch how far your dollars can go Sunday thru Friday from 5 pm to 8 pm. At the Long Island Marriott's Hungry Hour℠ you can fill your plate as many times as you like for just $2.00. With selections from our elaborate buffet. Hot and cold favorites. Assorted cheeses. Fresh fruit. Salads. And more. Hungry Hour℠ at the Long Island Marriott. We've just increased the value of a dollar.

Ask about Doolittle's Flying Aces Club. Members enjoy discounts on rooms and food. No waiting in line. And complimentary admission to special parties and events. Ask for details and a registration form. Doolittle's. Long Island's favorite nightclub.

Marriott People know how.

Doolittle's

At the Long Island Marriott. Adjacent to the Nassau Coliseum
101 James Doolittle Boulevard, Uniondale, NY 11553   AAA ◆◆◆◆ Hotel (516) 794-3800

Marriott Fever Catch It!

Whatever your pleasure—deluxe accommodations, superb dining, a relaxing Health Club, indoor pool, the popular Empire Lounge—you can be sure the La Guardia Marriott will do it right.

A great home base for dining.

Our cuisine bats a thousand every time! Whether it's our fabulous Cassel's Restaurant where you'll find a winning selection of your favorite steaks and seafood. Or Benjamin's Restaurant for a delicious Sunday brunch. You're sure to be served generous portions of our legendary Marriott hospitality...catch us today. For more information or reservations call (718) 565-8900

Marriott People know how.

LA GUARDIA **Marriott**®

La Guardia Marriott, 102-05 Ditmars Blvd., East Elmhurst, NY 11369

FIGURE 8–10 (cont.) *Multipurpose:* Although in general most ads should concentrate on a single purpose, there are instances when multipurpose messages can be appropriate. This advertising series is aimed primarily at building up food and beverage business, but it can also aid in stimulating general room sales and special package programs. A key aspect of both ads is also significant: the current concern over third-party liability. What traditionally has been an emphasis on "happy hour" beverage promotion has been changed to a "hungry hour," featuring a variety of attractively priced food service promotions. (Courtesy of Warren/Kremer Advertising, New York.)

EFFECTIVE ADVERTISING

As you'll note from the preceding samples, advertising can take on many different roles. In some cases it may be to inform the public about a new or improved service, it may be to introduce a new type of lodging facility to a specific target segment (see Figure 8–11), or it may urge the reader to take a prescribed set of actions in order to receive a particular set of benefits. In addition to often being a soft-sell medium to convey an image, it can serve as a hard-sell medium to stimulate a direct purchase, especially when it utilizes a "return action" mechanism such as a coupon or reply card.

In many cases it is used (as stressed previously) to support the direct selling efforts of the hotel's outside sales executives. Some key principles for developing effective advertising, irrespective of its objectives, are outlined in Figure 8–12.

FIGURE 8-11 Advertising messages, particularly in the form for a continuing series, are especially suited to creating *awareness* of a specific type of lodging facility. (Courtesy Habitat Corporate Suites.)

> **Effective Advertising . . .**
>
> - Relates to other promotional activities
> - Has clear objectives and goals
> - Reflects the image and tone of the product
> - Is aimed at specific markets
> - Speaks the language of the target markets
> - Motivates the recipient by stressing benefits
> - Offers solutions to customer "problems"
> - Follows the basics of two-way communications

FIGURE 8–12 Effective advertising.

AREA AND COMMUNITY SUPPORT

"No man is an island entire of itself," said the poet John Donne many years ago, and the same is true of each component of the hospitality industry. Frequently, hotels do not make fullest use of the sales support staff of state, regional, area, and local facilities, who are also in the overall travel and tourism business.

Unless restricted by regulations (such as state government groups who may have to meet within their state), size, or specific business obligations, decision makers usually select the destination first. They then look for suitable sites and properties within these boundaries. This is true for leisure travelers, incentive groups, most professional and trade associations, and many company meetings.

Most countries, states, and provinces in the United States and Canada, and many regions within them, have departments or offices (either wholly or in part municipally funded) that are charged with destination promotion. Cities also may have convention and visitors bureaus that promote the community and often provide support services.

All of these can be helpful to the sales executive initially by promoting the visibility of the area or city to the general marketplace, and second, by cooperatively participating in a variety of promotional efforts, such as:

1. Exhibit booths at customer trade shows
2. Participation in area familiarization (FAM) trips for travel agents, tour operators, travel writers, and meeting planners
3. Preparation and distribution of promotional folders and brochures, especially those that are recreation, sports, and activities oriented (and which generally have a much longer shelf life than general hotel brochures)
4. Preparation of area directories and travel guides that contain hotel and attractions listings
5. Matching or participating funds for joint venture area advertising
6. Cooperative advertising ventures, where there may be the added benefit of more coverage per advertising dollar
7. Creating, developing, and promoting cultural events, festivals, and social and recreational activities, many of which are group oriented
8. Special area promotional tie-ins with brand-name consumer products, for wider and more constant visibility

A Cooperative Illustration

How does this support cooperation work, and how can it assist the individual sales executive? Here's an illustrative example. Let's say that you are representing a resort property and have called on travel agents located in a feeder city 250 miles away. You have met with and left a supply of folders with your key agency contacts. A client visits one of the agencies and says that he is interested in a fall foliage weekend vacation for himself and family.

He generally will ask for, or the agent will hand him, a selection of *area* promotional folders. The client will then select the destination area that seems most appealing to him and then ask to see brochures and other information on properties in that area. So in this case, your chances of obtaining business from that person will initially be related directly to the efforts of those responsible for promoting the destination.

There are many outstanding examples of destination selling in countries around the world and in states and provinces throughout North America. The ongoing program that has perhaps been cited most often as a role model is the highly successful "I Love New York" campaign. Figure 8–13 illustrates some of the cooperative advertising and promotional materials used in this program on the statewide, regional, and local levels.

FIGURE 8–13 *Representative statewide promotion materials from the "I Love New York" campaign. (Courtesy of the New York State Department of Economic Development.)*

Four-Color Magazine Advertising

Seasonal TV Advertising (30-Second Spots)

Regional

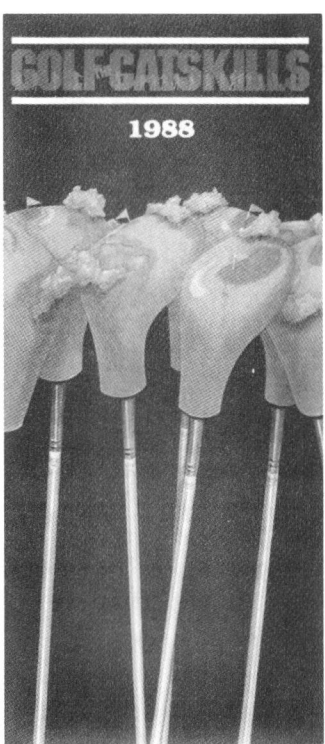

FIGURE 8–13 (cont.) Representative regional and local area promotional materials are tied in with the overall ''I Love New York'' campaign. (Courtesy of the Catskill Association for Tourism Services and the Sullivan County Public Information Office.)

Local

FIGURE 8–13 *(cont.)*

Cooperative Convention Promotion

As stressed previously, most customer decisions involve selecting the destination first, followed by the selection of the hotel. This is particularly true with the great majority of association conventions. This is one area where the hotel sales executive can especially utilize the cooperative approach and the support of area and community tourism and promotional agencies.

In soliciting convention accounts, the sales executive will often use support materials from a variety of municipal agencies and tourism organizations (see Figure 8–14). Often, especially for larger groups, such as national trade associations, supporting letters of invitation or welcome will be written by such officials as:

1. The county executive
2. The mayor
3. The president or executive director of the convention and visitors bureau
4. The head of the chamber of commerce
5. The president of the local chapter of the national association

FIGURE 8–14 One way of employing area promotional materials to help secure a convention. Before focusing on the features and benefits of his particular property, the sales executive first tries to sell the meeting planner on the destination, using promotional literature supplied by area and community tourism agencies.

INTERMEDIARY AGENCIES

The hotel sales executive also has the opportunity to enlist the support and cooperatively work with a variety of intermediary (or third-party) agencies. Selection of these will often depend on the property's market mix and which types of business are considered the primary or base markets.

Key intermediaries for specific market segments include:

1. *Group leisure market:* wholesalers, tour packagers and operators, and wholesaler/retailers—to develop domestic and international tour business, as well as incentive packages
2. *Individual leisure traveler:* travel agents
3. *Individual business traveler:* travel agents (although most companies traditionally have had their own travel department, or arrangements were made through a key executive or secretary, an increasing number of companies now use the services of a travel agency)
4. *Group business traveler:* hotel representation firms and, increasingly, multiple management companies

ADVERTISING TO TRAVEL AGENTS

There is a very key difference in advertising to travel agents, compared with advertising to such markets as individual business travelers, meeting planners, or to the leisure-oriented public via consumer magazines. The latter groups are the *buyers* and the users (i.e., the direct consumers). Travel agents, on the other hand, are in effect salespeople for the property and are actually supporting *sell-*

ers on behalf of the property or chain. Thus advertising to them must carry additional and very specific information, which will give them the ammunition, the ability, and the motivation to sell for you.

So what is a good ad to a travel agent? *Hotel and Travel Index* annually conducts the "Harvey Advertising Excellence Awards," which honor the advertising achievements of those who have most effectively reached U.S. travel agents. The Harvey Research Corporation surveyed travel agents to determine what type of advertising was most meaningful to them in the booking of a property, and the feedback was used in formulating the following Harvey Awards Checklist for Effective Advertising:

1. Give factual information on your location, accommodations, facilities, rates, packages, meeting rooms.
2. Advise agents that reservations are positively honored.
3. Include photographs of the hotel, guest rooms, and facilities as space permits.
4. Sum up services, sports activities, and other sales points in concise, easy-to-read paragraphs.
5. Identify nearby attractions, such as sightseeing, theme parks, shopping, etc.
6. List rates and specials, such as "children under 18, free."
7. Show any packages in effect and cite their availability.
8. Include 800 or other direct reservations number.
9. Include commission payment (or prepayment) policy, plus any special commission rates for low season or weekends.
10. Include proximity to major corporation, industrial parks, and airports.

According to Melinda Bush, publisher of *Hotel & Travel Index:* "An effective ad will be carefully positioned to meet the specific needs of travel agents. In the case of trade and directory advertising, you must show the travel agent, corporate travel, or meeting planner why he or she should sell your hotel. Thus, positioning is the standard by which an advertisement succeeds or fails."

PUBLIC RELATIONS

Another somewhat all-inclusive support component of the sales function is a rather broad category called *public relations*.

Basically, the term refers to all of the actions taken on a soft-sell, "nice guy" basis with those who are in a position to assist you, both professionally and personally.

This includes:

- *In-house guests:* How often do you "stroll the house" to meet with them; does your sales office have an "open door"?
- *Your employees:* who fulfill the promises you make to the customer or guest
- *The trade:* especially your counterparts in other properties who can refer business to you—or work with you on joint selling efforts
- *Industry associations:* both your own and those representing your buyers and their members

- *The general public:* their image and perception of both you and the property or chain you represent
- *The community:* your contacts with local professional, political, social, civic, religious, and educational organizations and members, especially those who are in positions to influence business; another aspect of community relations is involvement in charity organizations
- *Support industries:* your relationships with travel agencies, tour operators (especially those in your community), sightseeing attractions, theme and amusement park operators, owners of independent restaurants and lounges, transportation company officials, taxi companies and drivers
- *Purveyors and suppliers:* those who provide you with supplies and services, and who could also be customers or could influence business
- *The press:* both local consumer and industry trade publications editors and columnists

PUBLICITY

The last item on the preceding checklist (the press) leads into the subject of publicity. *Publicity* is a component of public relations and is basically defined as "the gratuitous mention of a product or service—usually in a public outlet such as newspapers, magazines, radio, and TV."

Publicity can offer indirect soft-sell opportunities such as editorials, feature stories, and so on. Hotels generally send information on expansion programs, renovations, new facilities, newly hired key staff, famous guests, and other potentially newsworthy items in either "release" or "press kit" form to their contacts in the media.

There are at least three key aspects to be aware of concerning publicity:

1. The fact that you may be advertising in a publication should not be used to *force* editors to include a feature story or article.
2. Publicity is *not* "free." There are investment expenditures such as the preparation and mailing of press kits, releases, and photographs.
3. Although an occasion that generates publicity may sometimes occur "on the spur of the moment," a specific publicity program should be planned a year in advance (often as an integral part of the "action steps" of a marketing plan).

Some of the key steps in the general planning of a publicity program include:

1. Studying all available outlets—newspaper and magazine, radio and TV, motion pictures, and public speaking—to determine which are best suited for a particular property
2. Deciding on the best methods of reaching these outlets
3. Establishing procedures for obtaining news coverage, as well as acceptance of releases
4. Creating proper and cordial relationships with editors and station managers, particularly local ones
5. Establishing a budget, to include photography costs and press entertainment expenses

ADVERTISING—PUBLICITY TEAMWORK

Although we cautioned against using advertising as "blackmail" to get free space in a publication, there is a natural relationship between the two, particularly from the point of enhancing effectiveness. So if the feature story is newsworthy to begin with, there is often a good chance that it can be coupled "hand in hand" with a pertinent advertisement, as illustrated in Figure 8–15.

MISCELLANEOUS SUPPORT OUTLETS

In recent years, a number of new support outlets have appeared primarily in TV and movies. Although they are not necessarily suited (or affordable) for most hotels, they should be recognized—and include:

- *Product presentations:* the featuring of a hotel in a movie or TV drama, as either a background or an integral part of the plot. A flat fee is usually paid to the producers.

FIGURE 8–15   A feature story in an Icelandic newspaper about a country-western theme party is coupled with an advertisement promoting that special function. (Yes, the people and their names surprisingly resemble those of the present authors!) One especially important point about publicity photos: Try to have the name of the property in view, as shown above. Also, make sure that you have established proper relationships with the editors and feature story writers so that the name will not inadvertently be "cropped" out.

Bandarísku prófessorarnir, sem verða gestir á Sælkerakvöldinu í kvöld, fyrir utan Hótel Loftleiðir í „Kántrý-gallanum".

Texas grill og Tortillas á Sælkerakvöldi í kvöld

Í KVÖLD, fimmtudag, verður Sælkerakvöld á Hótel Loftleiðum. Gestir kvöldsins verða 2 bandarískir prófessorar, Andrew Schwarz og David Dorf.

Í fréttatilkynningu frá Hótel Loftleiðum segir, að þeir félagar kenni hótelrekstur, veitingamennsku og matargerð vestanhafs, og séu því langt frá því að vera byrjendur í faginu. Þar segir ennfremur að þeir hafi verið leiðbeinendur á sérstöku námskeiði fyrir starfsmenn íslenskra veitingahúsa undanfarna daga. Mælst er til þess að gestir þeirra mæti í „kántrí-gallanum", þ.e. í skyrtu og léttum buxum eða gallabuxum og með klút um hálsinn, á Sælkerakvöldið í kvöld.

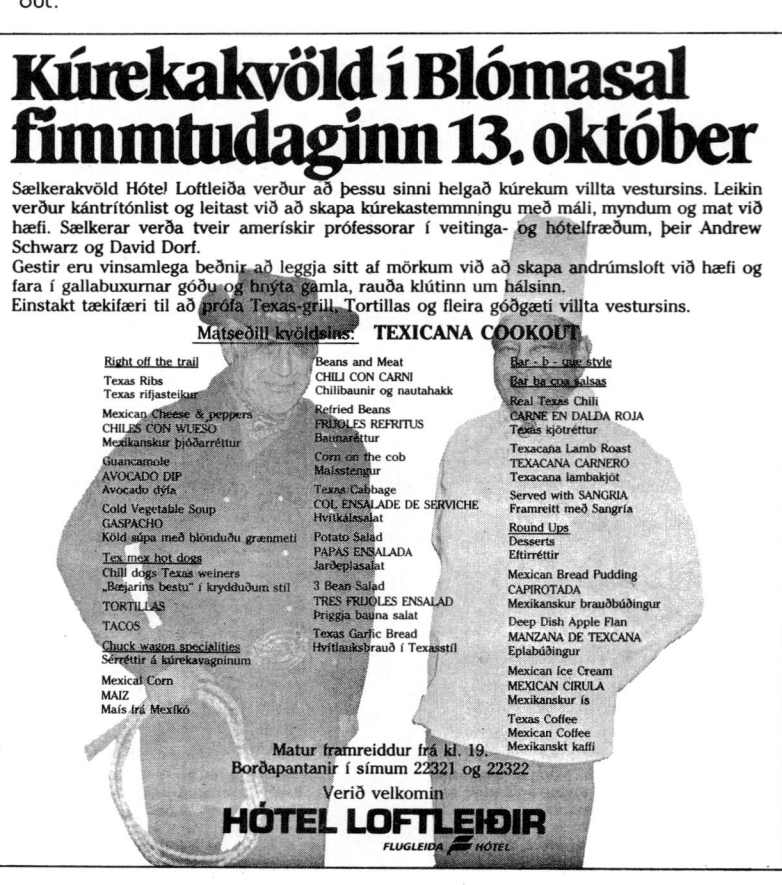

- *"Hitchhiking":* the coupling or tie-in of two usually unrelated products. A classic example is the long-running TV commercial that had as its tag line: ". . . the coffee served at the [name of famous hotel]."

- *Promotional consideration:* an exchange of accommodations for the mention of your name, with or without a short sales message. Although this is sometimes done in movies (usually at the closing "credits crawl"), it is most commonly seen on TV quiz programs and talk shows (e.g., "guests and contestants of our show stay at the fabulous Center City Hotel; 300 modern rooms in the heart of beautiful downtown Center City!").

Now to bring you all up to date in this study of contemporary hotel sales practices: so far, you've done all of your research and analysis, set up your sales office records and files, made your sales calls, and utilized all of your applicable promotional support resources. So you must be all done with the overall selling function.

Not quite! As Chapter 9 will show, *selling starts at the door.*

nine

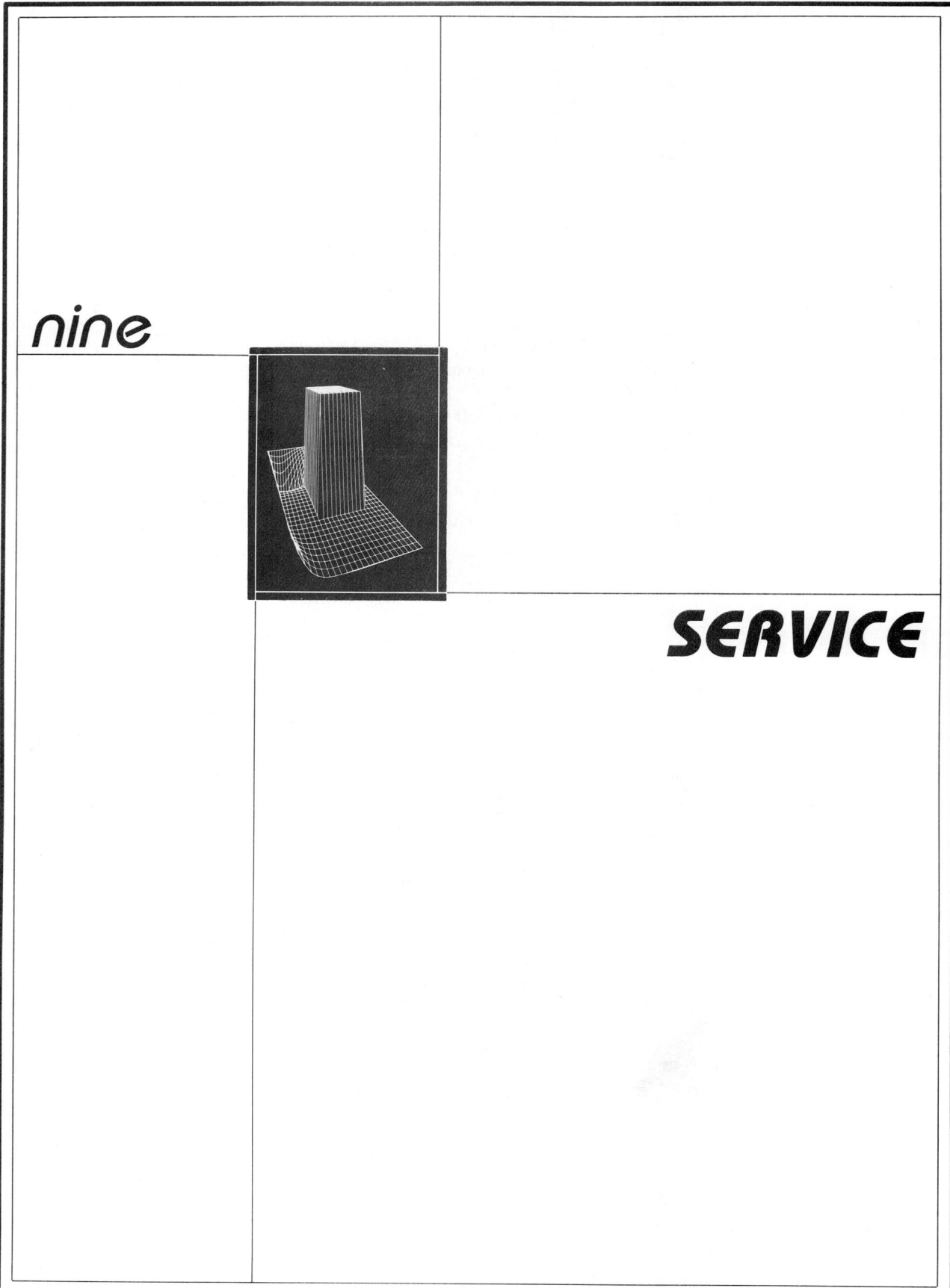

SERVICE

SERVICING CONCEPTS

As defined in its practical application, *servicing* is the delivery or fulfillment of all of the promises and commitments that were made to obtain the business of the customer. A secondary definition, but perhaps in the long run of even more consequence, is that servicing is all of the positive actions taken to maximize guest satisfaction, which in turn leads to high-volume, high-profit repeat and referral business.

A potential guest just doesn't wake up in the morning and say, "Gosh, I've got to go to a hotel this week; my life just wouldn't be complete without it!" Rather, as we have seen in previous chapters, there is an entire "menu" of needs, wants, and desires, and so on, that motivate potential users to select particular destinations and properties to fulfill specific objectives and goals.

The servicing "delivery system" goes into action the moment a guest arrives, from the greeting of the doorman or bellman, to the reception at the front desk (which in most parts of the world is called just that—the "reception" desk), and throughout the stay—in dining rooms, lounges, recreational facilities—concluding with checkout.

Servicing is an entire subject in itself, and its scope is further broadened when coupled with *internal selling*. In the combined area of *internal sales and servicing,* a property has four main categories of responsibilities:

1. Fulfilling the commitments of the booking (or to put it in a legal context, "honoring the contract")
2. Ensuring maximum guest satisfaction
3. Increasing the average expenditure per guest
4. Increasing the potential for referrals, recommendations, and repeat business

Some of the various methods of achieving these objectives can include:

1. *Training:*
   a. Attitude, courtesy, and awareness training
   b. Point-of-purchase sales training
   c. Techniques of extending the sale
   d. Preventive maintenance (how to anticipate and handle complaints)
   e. Quality assurance programs

2. *Internal Sales Literature:*
   a. Guest room directories, tent cards, menus, etc.
   b. Laundry and valet lists
   c. In-house TV (special channels, lobby TV monitors)
   d. "On hold" and "wake-up call" telephone sales messages
   e. Lobby and elevator posters
   f. Rack folder display racks
   g. Marquee signs and window displays
   h. Promotional messages on bills and statements

3. *CrissCross Interdepartmental Promotion:*
   a. Direct personal referral (bellmen telling guests about special dining room buffet)
   b. Table tent cards and other announcements
   c. Laundry and valet "wrapper" messages

The person booking a particular piece of business may not be totally involved in each of the preceding areas. But the success of subsequent follow-up rebookings, as well as the property's reputation in the marketplace, can be significantly influenced by each. In addition, the sales executive is, in the minds of the customers, responsible for the fulfillment of all servicing details.

Surveys indicate that the reason most guests do not fully utilize all of the facilities of a property is that they are largely unaware of all that is available for them to use and enjoy. Account executives and other outside sales personnel obviously cannot be on hand to point out all of the outlets in a property that are available to the customers and clients they have booked or influenced.

Printed literature in guest rooms is often overlooked by the guest. So it is chiefly up to the guest-contact employees of the operating departments to ensure positive guest servicing, both by their attitudes and by the ability to "sell" once the guest steps through the lobby doors.

In fact, there is a saying or motto used as the theme of the "Selling Starts at the Door" seminars conducted by the present authors which states:

> *The sales department may not be the whole hotel*
> *but the whole hotel must be a sales department.*

The Sales—Servicing Relationship

At this stage some of you may be wondering why all this sudden focus on *service*. Isn't this a book on contemporary hotel *sales?* Yes, it is—but sales and service are so inexorably tied together that it is difficult to separate the two. It recalls that old question: "Which came first, the chicken or the egg?"

There's a classic story, probably apocryphal, about automotive pioneer Henry Ford visiting one of his first dealerships. He noticed a prominent sign in front of the building that read "Ford Sales and Service." He promptly ordered the dealer to change the sign to read, "Ford Service and Sales," advising that without proper service, it would be difficult to make sales. This highlights the fact that the relationship of service to the selling effort is a primary factor in obtaining, maintaining, and expanding a profitable volume of business.

Follow-Through Capability

Sales executives must be especially aware of their property's ability to properly service the accounts they book. This relates specifically to the capability of staff to properly prepare for and service the business commitments made to the customer. Promises are sometimes made in order to get a booking, on the "hope" that the operating staff can do the job.

What you sometimes end up with, to repeat an oft-quoted example used by more than one meeting planner: "The sales executive sold us on an outdoor chicken barbecue for 500 people and said, 'No problem . . . we can handle it!' " Unfortunately, instead of getting 500 baked half-chickens, we ended up with 500 half-baked chickens!"*

SERVICING "POLITICS"

Another area where selling and servicing are welded together relates to the "politics" of group business. Both association and corporate meeting planners generally have a variety of organizational needs that must be satisfied when

---

*This, incidentally, is usually then followed up by another old saying: "Fool me once, shame on you; fool me twice, shame on me." Not wishing to appear foolish in front of their members or business associates who are paying their salaries, the meeting planners will simply go elsewhere next time.

planning and conducting their meetings, especially their annual conventions or national sales meetings. These needs (which relate to both the organization and the individual attendees) generally fall under the following three categories:

1. *Program needs:* a variety of educational and informative subject matter so that there will be "something for everyone"
2. *Social needs:* group interaction and networking opportunities through food and beverage functions, theme parties, organized team sports, and free-time recreation (see Figure 9–1)
3. *Political needs:* recognition of achievers and volunteer leaders who are "moving up" in the organization

FIGURE 9–1 Solving the social and recreational needs and desires of guests, especially convention and meeting attendees, is largely a function of the creative servicing abilities of the hotel and its staff. This portion of a group activities guide folder also contains suggestions for a variety of spouse, children, and theme programs. (Courtesy of The Breakers, Palm Beach, Florida.)

The Breakers is unparalleled in providing the finest Sports and Recreation facilities and programs for our guests. The versatility, planning and professionalism of our services ensures that each meeting is provided with activities and events that meet your particular interests and objectives. Sports and recreation scheduled as part of a meeting provides conference attendees the total resort experience and enhances all other components and objectives of the meeting. Our superior leisure service professionals, services, facilities and innovative menu of activities enables you to select those extra touches that make your meeting special and memorable. Let us do the work for you. Choose from the selection provided or ask for a unique custom designed program. We look forward to meeting your needs.

SPECIAL EVENTS FOR CONFERENCE ATTENDEES

Sun Sports

Great fun for everyone on the beach. Team competition in six events from the list below for a two-hour event or 12 events for a four-hour event. The emphasis is on having a good time! Sun Sports can also be scheduled at sunrise or sunset for an extra special activity in a beautiful natural setting. Events include:

Volleyball	*Dizzy Lizzy Relay*
Sand Skis	*Centipede Shuffle*
Water Balloon Toss	*Letter Scramble*
Back to Back Relay	*Beach Ball Volleyball*
Chariot Race	*Fish Out of Water Relay*
Obstacle Course	*Ping-Pong Shot Put*
	Frisbee Golf

Lawn Olympics

Team competition in your choice of traditional lawn activities. Teams compete for the best scores in each event and are awarded points for their respective placings. Lawn activities are adapted to facilitate team scoring in which everyone participates. The following events may be scheduled:

Putting	*Lawn Bowling*
Horseshoes	*Croquet*
Shuffleboard	*Ping-Pong*
	Bocce Ball

Team Builders

A program with a purpose, Team Builders assists in creating a team camaraderie, increasing communication skills, motivating participants, and building leadership. Cleverly designed events and activities help achieve these objectives. Sample events include:

Skills Course	*Skin the Snake*
Silent Numbers	*Team Spell*
Group Skis	*40-Legged Relay*
Chariot Race	*Scavenger Hunt*

That's the Breaks

Olympics for wimps! Invite everyone to make an equal fool of themselves in non-threatening and zany events for all skill levels. It's mostly for fun with a good sense of competition where losers can be winners. Suggested events include the following or you can create your own:

Wimp Obstacle Course	*Water Balloon Toss*
Dizzy Lizzy Relay	*Ping-Pong Shot Put*
Coconuts Relay	*Crab Crawl*
Balloon Stomp	*Run-around-the-CEO Relay*
Chugathon	*Barbershop Balloon*
Soccer Ball Relay	*Poker Fun Run*
	ETA Fun Run

Breaker Beach Party

Beach party activities will enhance your dinner and help guests get in the right mood for fun. Any or all activities may be incorporated in your theme party. Try these:

Beach Blanket Bingo	*Lei Making*
Beach Breakers	*Sand Sculpture*
Beach Volleyball	*Limbo*

Water Sports

H_2O, in we go! Wake up your group with a competition in the pool. It's wet and wild and a great way to cool off after a long day of meetings. Choose from these events:

Beer Dive	*Over and Under*
Ping-Pong Ball Stuff	*Lifeguard Sez*
Disrobing Relay	*Belly Flop Contest*
Inner Tubing	*Raft Relays*

Champagne Croquet or Putting

A cocktail party with a twist on our croquet or putting lawns. Our professional will instruct your group on the finer points of social croquet or putting, and run a mini-tournament. It's a Palm Beach tradition.

Sailboat Regatta

Regatta race using 16-foot Hobies on the waters of Lake Worth, located 15 minutes from The Breakers.

Tournaments

Serious competition for the sports-minded in volleyball, croquet, shuffleboard, horseshoes, ping-pong or putting alone or as a combination.

Scuba

Diving instruction for all levels and interests is now available at The Breakers. From a Discover Scuba course to offshore dives, our diving professionals ensure a successful and exciting activity.

Fitness Breaks

Let us help your group relieve stress and tension without even leaving the meeting room. We'll bring the props, instructors and music for a 15-minute stress break including stretches and energizers.

Fun Run

A two-and-a-half-mile path starts and ends at The Breakers and is routed entirely on Palm Beach. We will provide maps for all participants and traffic patrolmen at appropriate locations for your group's safety.

Aerobics

Professional workouts for any level are available for your group in our dance studio, by the pool or on the beach. A walking or biking workout tour of the area is good exercise and informational, too.

Snorkeling

One of the best reefs in Florida is just a swim off our private beach. Snorkeling instruction and guided tours are available for the adventurous guest.

Fitness Seminars

Choose from a variety of topics on fitness and health for a hands-on seminar. Presented by professional training and exercise consultants, lectures provide the foundation for starting a wellness program.

Croquet Events

Wicket shooting contest, Croquetathon or Golf-Croquet tournaments are special events conducted on our beautiful courts by a USCA professional.

Rainy Days

When the weather is inclement and regular activities must be cancelled, we have many alternatives for groups. We can schedule any options in advance on a tentative basis for your convenience. A few suggestions are as follows:

Indoor Olympics	*Movies*
Financial Seminar	*Card and Game Room*
Golf Clinic with our pro	*Horse Racing*
Tennis Clinic with our pro	*Fitness Activities*
Simon Sez for Adults	*Indoor Putting*
Breakers Orientation	*Indoor Scavenger Hunt*
Bingo	*Quick Draw*

It is relatively easy for the sales executive to gain and maintain current information on the program and social needs of the group, as well as their educational goals. These are documented in the sales files on each group, and updated periodically through direct-mail questionnaires, telephone calls, and personal contacts. However, it is very often the "political" aspects of a meeting that may suddenly and unknowingly surface when face to face with a potential client. It is therefore essential that the sales executive recognize that proper servicing of the group business market will often involve assisting the meeting planner with "ticklish political situations" (without, of course, getting involved with the internal politics of the organization).

Meeting planners must often deal with the pressures of granting special (and legitimate) favors or attention to certain members of their organizations, without alienating others. This can, in turn, be reflected in the types of "can you do me a favor" requests they make of the hotel, such as room upgrades, special amenities, airport pickups, and the like. These may surface initially during the negotiations stage, but many will occur at the last minute at the start of or during a particular session. Many of these "special servicing" requests, incidentally, are for speakers, panelists, special guests, and members of the press who may be covering a particular convention or meeting—and the meeting planner is actually serving as a "go-between," which makes the requests even more important.

Some Political-Servicing Examples

For example, the policy of your hotel might be to provide one complimentary room for every 100 persons in attendance, for use by the meeting planner for staff, speakers, and key officers. You are negotiating with a group with which you have previously done business and which also represents a good prospect for the future. In prior meetings, the "one comp per hundred" posed no problem; however, this time the meeting planner indicates that he *must* have an additional complimentary room for their next meeting of 225 attendees.

He then tells you that his company has just hired a new finance director who will be attending this meeting. So he needs the customary two complimentary rooms for himself and for the president of the organization, plus an extra one for the "new guy on board."

The meeting planner readily admits that it would make him "look good" as well as "stroke" the new finance director if the hotel could offer the extra accommodations without charge, especially since the finance director was especially hired to review and tighten the company's financial operations. Your ability to work out an arrangement with him will be an indication to him of your ability to service his *political needs,* which as you may note, are a combination of professional and personal.

Meeting planners face many similarly sensitive internal political decisions, which in turn are passed on to the hotel. Some of the more common ones include:

- Who gets complimentary accommodations, who gets suites and what type, and who is to be housed on special VIP or executive club floors?
- Who should be put at the head tables; who is to be seated at the up-front reserved tables?
- Who in the organization will be selected to be speakers, group discussion leaders, moderators, and introducers of special guest speakers?

- Who is to make verbal reports at board meetings (and thus take "center-stage"), and who just hands in written ones?
- Within the organization, whose recommendations carry the most weight with respect to program content, outside speakers, and other activities?
- Who gets preferred exhibit space, that is, the locations that will naturally get the heaviest traffic? What can be done to divert or force traffic flow to other key exhibitors?

Although these may seem on the surface to be internal concerns of the buyer, the sales executive is often asked to assist, especially with regard to any special servicing requirements that affect each of the above.

SERVICE SEGMENTATION

One of the key aspects of servicing is that it represents different things to different people. The procedures followed in analyzing market segments and their varying needs, wants, and decision-making priorities have their counterparts in determining who gets what type of service and to what degree.

One can "overservice" guests who, for example, may be staying at a relatively remote and isolated resort for the sole purpose of getting away from it all, who want to "escape" from their normally hectic business and social lives. In fact, the activity/confidence psychographic profile matrix introduced earlier can also be applied as a basic guide to servicing. In Figure 9–2, "staff en-

FIGURE 9–2 The servicing levels of the guest-contact staff should be related to a market segment's psychographic profile.

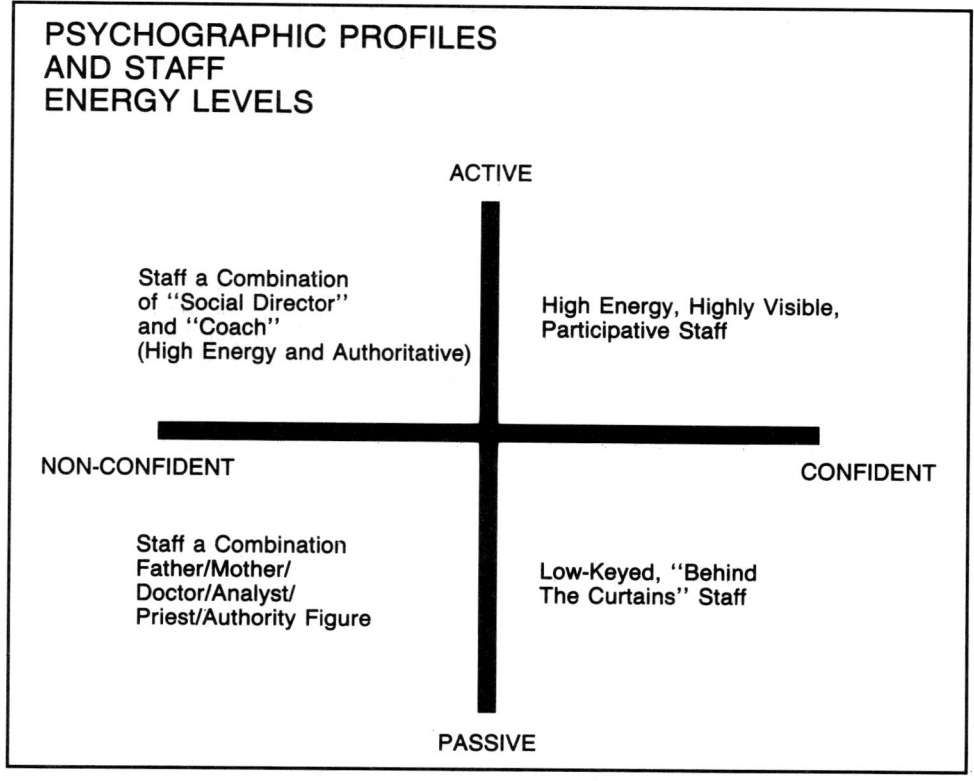

PSYCHOGRAPHIC PROFILES
AND STAFF
ENERGY LEVELS

ACTIVE

Staff a Combination
of "Social Director"
and "Coach"
(High Energy and Authoritative)

High Energy, Highly Visible,
Participative Staff

NON-CONFIDENT

CONFIDENT

Staff a Combination
Father/Mother/
Doctor/Analyst/
Priest/Authority Figure

Low-Keyed, "Behind
The Curtains" Staff

PASSIVE

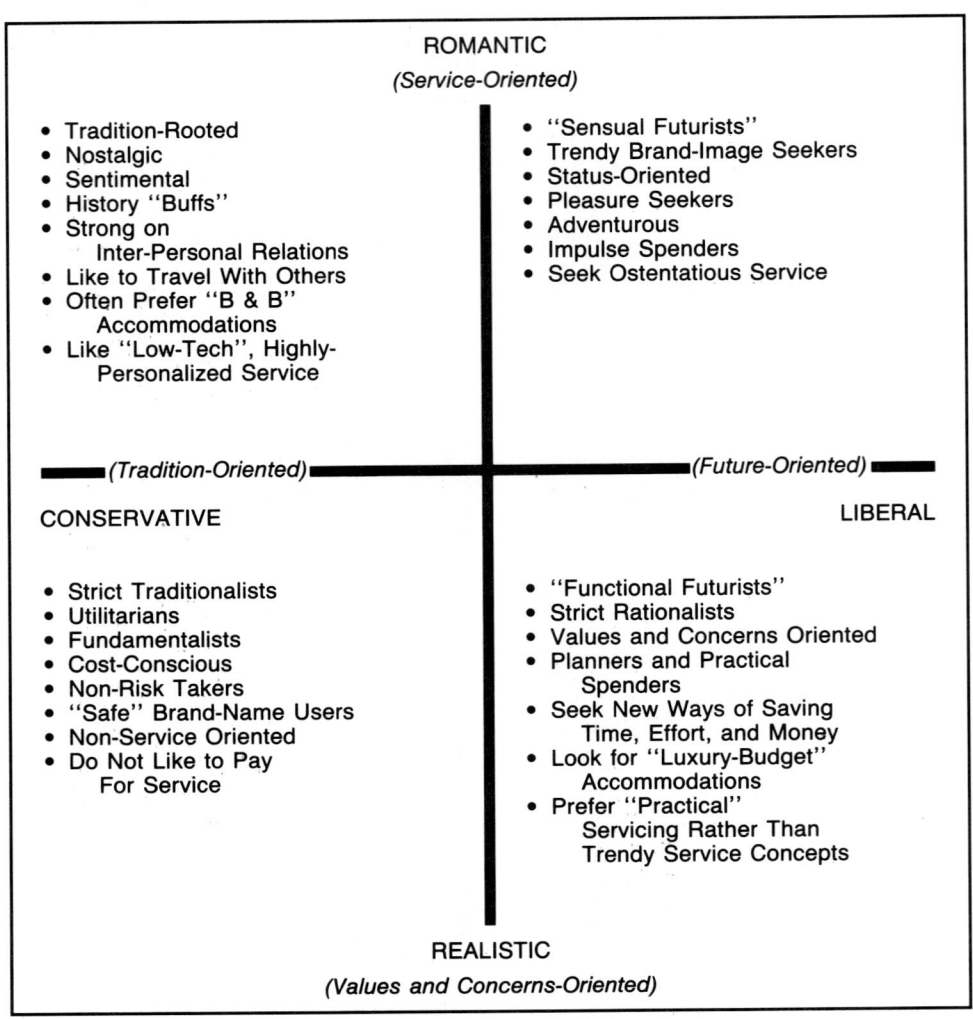

FIGURE 9–3 Another psychographic profile system emphasizes different perceptions of servicing as determined by lifestyle outlooks and preferences.

ergy levels" are related to specific psychographic profiles, which in turn describe the general type of service generally preferred by each group.

Another system of psychographic profiling uses a different set of parameters. It relates servicing to whether a person is primarily a "romantic" or a "realist" on one axis, a "conservative" or a "liberal" on another. As can be seen from Figure 9–3, there is a considerable distinction as to what constitutes "good service" between a non-service-oriented "realistic conservative" and a somewhat ostentatious service-seeking "romantic liberal."

ADVERTISING–SERVICING RELATIONSHIPS

Another consideration in servicing are the perceptions people may obtain from their interpretation of your advertising message. There must be a direct correlation between what the property is trying to convey, what the audience perceives, and what the property will actually deliver. This, too, can be tied directly into the psychographic profile illustrated previously. For example, several ads intended to reach totally different psychographic markets are illustrated in Figure 9–4. Note the difference in the way in which services, or the lack of them, are presented.

The Walker's Cay "getaway" ads are directed at those leisure travelers who are seeking low-key "hideaways." The type of service that will most appeal to them will be of a subdued, unobtrusive nature. What they will *not be getting* can be just as important in a positive way as what they will be receiving. On the other hand, the Biltmore ad highlights the type of service that is highly visible, highly energetic, upscale, and styled along the lines of "European elegance."

FIGURE 9–4 Different sets of services are highlighted in these ads, which are directed at different target audiences. (Walker Cay, courtesy of Lithographics, Inc., Altamonte Springs, Florida; The Biltmore, courtesy of Gardner, Stein & Frank, Inc., Chicago.)

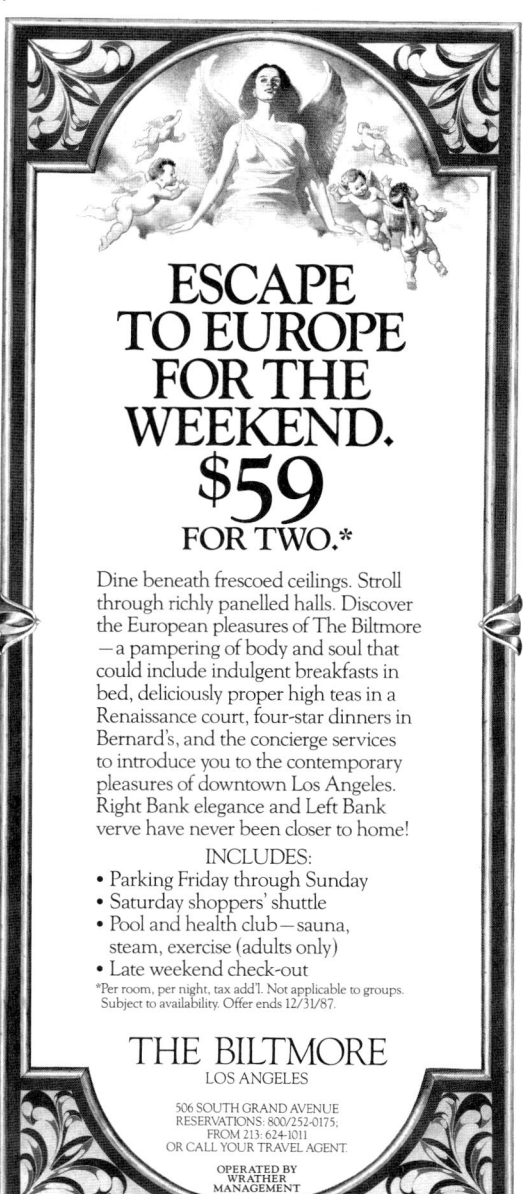

SERVICING SPECIFIC MARKETS

The concept of market segmentation is not only a useful tool in the selling process; it is also another important key in supplying an appropriate mix of service features and details to specific groups of people with specific needs. A general servicing checklist that relates to the specific needs and wants of the individual business traveler is shown in Figure 9–5. These generalized servicing considerations can be further "fine tuned" when directed at a subsegment of the business travel market: for example, the *extended-stay* market. Whether utilizing hotels because of company relocation or because of a lengthy business trip in a "hub" area, extended-stayers (generally defined as those who stay 10 or more days at a time) require and desire more than the customary hotel services.

In fact, the old promotional concept of a hotel being a "home away from home" is for this market an essential consideration and should be incorporated within the overall servicing philosophy of any property going after this market segment. The very name of the property, and the features highlighted in its sales and advertising, should emphasize this philosophy, as illustrated in Figure 9–6.

COMPARATIVE ANALYSIS

The consideration of the servicing elements that most appeal to specific market segments can start with a self-analysis. This evaluation, done on a market segment basis, would analyze internal *strengths* and *weaknesses*—and external

FIGURE 9–5 Service checklist of those items most needed and appreciated by the individual business traveler. These items are not in any particular order; in fact, item 20 on the list is often number 1 in the minds of many business travelers.

Target Market: Individual Business Traveler

1. Quick check-in and check-out
2. Rooms available upon arrival
3. Quick breakfast service
4. Easily accessible transportation
5. Efficient reservation service
6. Convenient recreational outlets and health facilities
7. Writing desks
8. Good lighting; desk lamps should be 75 to 100 watts, depending on color of room decor
9. King-size wastepaper baskets
10. King-size soap and bath towels
11. Full-size mirrors and "make-up" mirrors—for *both* men and women
12. Direct-dial phones (DD "credit card" phones if at all possible)
13. Radio
14. Cable TV (especially HBO, Showtime, and ESPN)
15. Listings of local activities and events
16. Knowledgeable staff: front-desk people who know the area and the community
17. Room service or "late nite" snack bar nearby (possibly even microwave vendors in lobby)
18. Convenience or sundries shop
19. Availability of photocopy equipment, typewriters, and similar business amenities
20. Reliable wake-up service

You're right. It doesn't look like a hotel.

The Residence Inn by Marriott offers suites so inviting, so affordable, they're more home than hotel.
Located just minutes from the parkway, we offer a list of amenities unmatched in comfort and relaxation – all for about the same price as a standard hotel room.

COMPLETE WITH:
- Complimentary Breakfast Buffet
- Complimentary "Evening Snack" Tuesday and Thursday
- Complimentary Grocery Shopping Service
- Complimentary Morning Newspaper
- Fully Equipped Kitchens
- Separate Living Room Area
- Private Entrance
- Most Suites with Fireplaces
- Daily Maid Service
- Outdoor Barbecue Grills
- Outdoor "Sportcourt"
- Outdoor Pool and Jacuzzi
- Coin Operated Guest Laundry
- Same Day Valet Service
- Frequent In-house Guest Functions
- Room Service provided by a local Restaurant
- Health Club Privileges
- Airport Limousine Service Available
- Car Rental Available at Discounted Rates

**THE RESIDENCE INN MONMOUTH-TINTON FALLS
90 PARK ROAD
TINTON FALLS, NJ 07724
(201) 389-8100**

Take Exit 105 (Rt. 36) off the Garden State Parkway through the first traffic light and take the jughandle onto Hope Road. Take first left turn onto Park Road.

FIGURE 9–6 A special services checklist is featured as part of this ad directed specifically at the extended stay market. This is also an example of multiple use of a promotional piece. Reprints of the ad can be used as direct-mail enclosures and are also distributed to those nearby Roy Rogers, Bob's Big Boy, and Sbarro interstate highway food service outlets, which are part of the Marriott Corporation. (Courtesy of Residence Inn by Marriott.)

*o*pportunities and *t*hreats. Figure 9–7 offers an example of this type of servicing SWOT analysis, again directed at the individual business travel market.

This information can be particularly useful when the hotel sales staff is out selling to executives who are responsible for arranging individual business travel for their companies. It also has practical value in designing advertising to be placed in business-oriented publications. A similar SWOT listing should be made for other market segments, such as the individual leisure traveler, travel and tour business, conventions and meetings markets, and even for such specialized groups as senior citizens and international visitors.

FIGURE 9–7 Portion of a servicing "SWOT" list, analyzing a property's service situation with respect to the individual business travel market.

Servicing "SWOT" List Analysis: Individual Business Traveler

	STRENGTHS	WEAKNESSES	OPPORTUNITIES	THREATS
Rooms	In-room TV check-out system	Limited number of two-room suites	TV cable companies reducing charges and fees	Two all-suite properties opening
Food and beverage	Full 24-hour room service	Rapid staff turn-over in dining rooms	Four-year hotel school 2 miles away	Four fast-food outlets within two blocks
Fitness and recreation	Located on 2 acres of land	No indoor pool or sauna	City to release land adjacent to property	Commercial health spa leases space with competitor

COMPETITIVE SERVICES ANALYSIS

After plotting out an analysis of servicing features that are especially meaning-ful to a particular market segment, the sales executive should then compare them with what's available in the key competitive properties for this specific form of business. There are a number of fairly easy ways to do this:

1. Read your competition's advertising. What are they stressing as key ser-vicing benefits? Do they focus on a particular USP (unique servicing prop-osition)?

2. Study your competitors' folders, brochures, and collateral materials. Walk through their lobbies and observe internal literature and signage. Are they directed specifically at one or two key services, such as the avail-ability of fax equipment or a special health club facility?

3. Stay overnight at your competitors' operations, and role-play a specific market segment. What do they have that would be particularly important to you as you look at it from the user's viewpoint?

4. Survey your current business, asking which services are most important to them, which services are becoming more consequential to them, and which services they wish you had.

5. Read the trade press, especially articles and case studies on servicing.

6. Attend industry conventions and trade shows, especially those featuring exhibitors who supply service items (see Figure 9–8).

As soon as you determine which services are currently "hot items" among each of your key market segments, which you have, and which your competi-tors do—or do not—have, you can draw up a comparison chart similar to that illustrated in Figure 9–9.

FIGURE 9–8 Industry trade shows are an excellent source of servicing ideas, especially where the exhibitors are introducing new or improved ser-vicing concepts and products. Because shows and other types of exhibits are often held on an annual basis, it also offers long-term "networking" opportunities between buyers and sellers. (Right photo courtesy of Earle Tunick, Resort Photo Service, South Fallsburg, New York.)

Competitive Services Analysis: Individual Business Traveler

Item	Center City Hotel	A	B	C	D
Airport limo	×	×	×	×	
Free parking	×				×
Quick check-in	×		×	×	
VIP (concierge) floor		×	×		
24-Hour room service		×	×	×	×
No-charge local calls					
Fax facilities	×				
TV checkout	×		×		

Key: A, Outlaw Inn C, Empty Arms
 B, Last Resort D, Action Hotel

FIGURE 9-9 Competitive comparison chart, focusing on the services and amenities most desired by the individual business traveler. Similar evaluations should be made for other market segments, bearing in mind that your competition for one particular market may differ from those properties competing with you for other types of business.

This comparison is useful for upgrading service. The example shows that we are the only property in the "competitive arena" for the business traveler that does not offer 24-hour room service. Should we consider it—or is it a service element that really is not that necessary at the moment as far as it affects the decision-making process of this market segment?

We can find this out through a variety of means:

- Check with some of your regular, repeat business guests as to whether they wish or miss this particular service at your facility.

- Ask your counterparts at the competitive properties how effective this service is for them. (In most instances, they will be willing to share and exchange information.)

- Read articles in the trade magazines, both hospitality and customer, which relate to servicing the business traveler.

- Attend sessions at hospitality industry (as well as customer group) conventions that focus on or include discussion sessions on servicing.

- Attend industry trade shows, exhibitions, and convention "market places" and make it a point to visit booths of service suppliers.

UNIQUE SERVICING PROPOSITION

As you look back at the comparison chart (Figure 9-9), you will note that in this example, virtually every property features airport limo service. So while it is a key service obviously in demand by the business traveler, having it does not give one any competitive advantage. On the other hand, you are the only property to currently offer fax facilities and only one of two offering the convenience of TV check-out. These unique servicing propositions can readily be turned into unique selling propositions—and provide "ammunition" for use in personal selling, advertising, and other direct promotion.

The preceding examples were, for illustrative purposes, directed primarily at the business traveler. The same technique could be applied to studying the servicing needs and desires of other market segments, with a comparative analysis of how you "match up" to the competition. However, the complexity of conventions and meetings offers additional servicing challenges, which the sales executive must be concerned with, especially during the selling process. So we'll now take an in-depth view of them.

SPECIALIZED SERVICING

The primary task of the hotel is to provide, properly and efficiently, the housing, function space, food and beverage, and social and recreational facilities needed by the meeting planner or organizer to ensure a successful event. However, the meeting planner is also involved with other people who require their own sets of services (many of them specialized or unique), such as:

1. The individual attendees and their families
2. Special groups of attendees, such as students, overseas guests, and allied or affiliated members
3. Decorators, staging specialists, and audiovisual technicians
4. Exhibitors
5. Hospitality suite hosts
6. Members of the press

Although the special needs of each of the previous groups may be arranged through the meeting planners, they are basically "middlemen" and the hotel is often the primary supplier of the requested or required services, especially those that are to be secured locally.

It is in the area of providing specialized services that the meeting planner will so often depend on the property, especially for a proper response to the request "please help me." It is essential to remember that we are first and foremost in the problem-solving business. The checklists in Figures 9–10 and 9–11 offer examples of the key servicing needs of meeting planners and the counterpart key servicing needs of program speakers.

FIGURE 9–10 "Baker's dozen" listing of key servicing needs of the typical meeting planner. Note that while most of them are "tangibles" in that they can be quantified by number or time, others are "intangibles," such as the last two on the list.

A Dozen Key Servicing Needs of the Meeting Planner

1. Proper notification of when and where
2. Accuracy in time postings
3. Designation of in-house executive with authority
4. Ability to get to meeting rooms *early*
5. Truly soundproof rooms
6. Simplified procedures for getting additional equipment
7. System of checking master account daily
8. Fast and efficient check-in and check-out procedures
9. Accurate system of obtaining figures and statistics
10. Safety, security, and emergency procedures
11. Creative ideas, especially from food and beverage staff
12. Evidence of management visibility and support
13. Positive support-staff attitudes

Ten Very Basic Needs of Speakers

1. Ability to get to the room early
2. Microphones that really work, and plenty of cord for roving mikes
3. Easily accessible light switches near the lectern, not on the other side of the room
4. Noncurling, proper-size audiovisual screens
5. Proper projection tables
6. Large chalkboards in top condition
7. Plenty of chalk and magic markers
8. Lecterns in top condition
9. Modern equipment (cordless mikes, cordless slide-advance units, VCRs)
10. Service staff that knows the difference between lectern and podium, overhead and opaque projectors, etc.

FIGURE 9–11 Basic needs of speakers that are either brought directly to the hotel or filtered down through the meeting planner.

The first two items in the meeting planner's "wish list" really reflect on the needs of the attendees as well. "Where's the meeting? and What time do we start?" are common questions by delegates far too often directed at meeting planners at times when they are preoccupied with more essential details (such as when the speaker wants the room setup changed and there is only 15 minutes in which to do it!).

So the question to the hotel, particularly where conventions and meetings are the key market, could be: "Should we invest in an in-house TV system where meeting information can be presented on a special channel in each room as well as in the lobby and other public areas of the hotel, and thereby provide a service to both the meeting planners and the attendees?" (See Figure 9–12.)

FIGURE 9–12 Meeting program listings through an in-house TV system are becoming a standard service feature in many convention hotels.

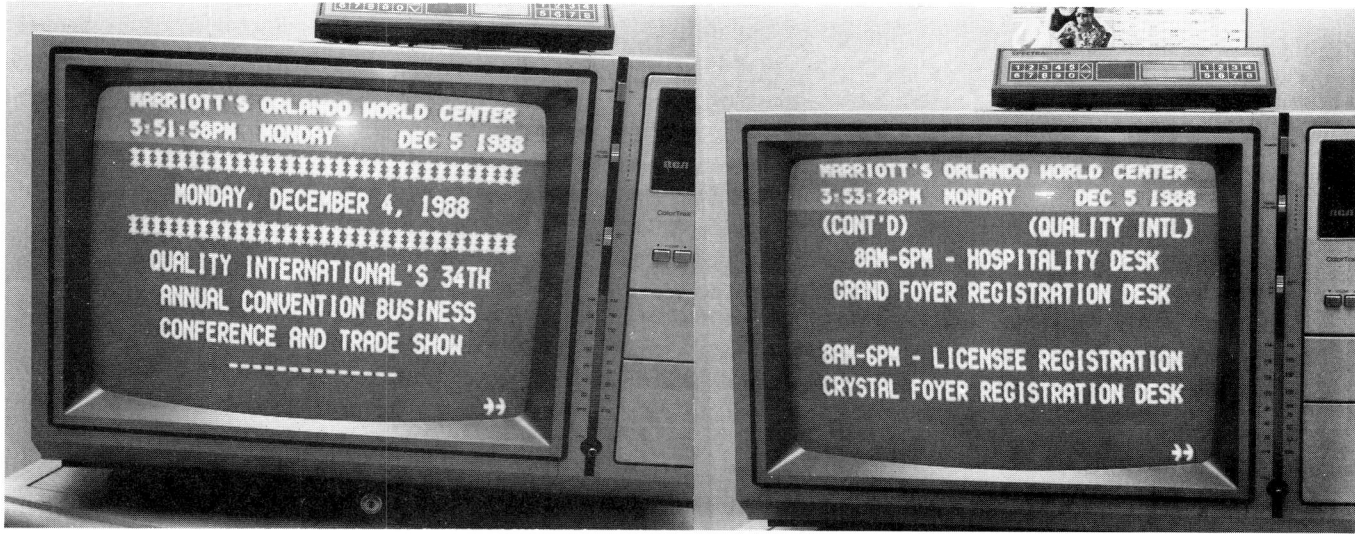

SERVICE AND PRODUCT UPGRADING

A similar review should be made of the relative importance of other services as they relate to the needs of various other market segments. This is necessary so that the property can properly "deliver the goods," especially in these days of constantly changing customer needs and wants.

Periodic product and service audits should be keyed to performance objectives of the property. This can help pinpoint areas, for example, where upgrading may be necessary. A similar audit of competitive properties can also be productive, especially any new operations that may have the latest servicing features and amenities.

Let's assume for illustrative purposes that a property wishes to concentrate on the top of the market, affluent individual business traveler as well as the upper strata of the meetings market.

This could very well involve capital expenditures (investments) to bring the property up to the quality that these markets anticipate and expect. This could include installing or upgrading the following:

- Check-in and check-out procedures (in-room TV check-out)
- Concierge service
- Special VIP floors, with floor staff
- 24-hour "club-style" VIP lounges
- Upgraded 24-hour room service
- Health spa facilities
- Limousines and drivers (for transportation to and from the business district as well as the airport)
- Special guest room design and furnishings (business suites)
- In-room computer terminals
- Wide selection of satellite and cable TV
- Photocopy and fax equipment
- Secretarial and translation services
- Paging service, voice mail, etc.

We have been bouncing back and forth between various market segments in this discussion of servicing. But remember that we have stressed before that no one person is locked into a particular segment. Travelers play many different roles and demand different sets of services and amenities.

The convention delegate may have need for specific types of services relating to the meeting program. However, the same person may have a changing viewpoint as to what constitutes good service when the meeting is over but stays over for an extra day or two. That person changes from a group business attendee to an individual leisure traveler.

Or a company may schedule a training session for its sales personnel in a city where the company has many clients. Many of the attendees will stay over to conduct business at the conclusion of the sessions. They then become individual business travelers, and here again, will have a changing set of servicing priorities. But since, as we have mentioned previously, the conventions and meetings market is the most complex, as well as for many properties the most profitable, we now take a more detailed look at the many factors that constitute *convention servicing.*

CONVENTION SERVICING

During those "early days of hotel sales," most on-the-road hotel sales representatives were responsible primarily for *booking* group business. They were largely evaluated on the volume of business obtained and were not usually accountable for its servicing.

Many of these pioneering hotel sales executives were salespeople who came from other industries. They often had little, if any, knowledge of hotel operations. So they stayed clear of any direct in-house involvement once they made the sale. Therefore, the responsibility of servicing the booking was usually left to the manager, assistant manager, banquet manager, or catering director.

As the importance of group business emerged, and as more sales executives came "up through the ranks," there was more of a tendency for the person booking the account to be on property to ensure that it received proper attention and service.

The client also felt more secure in dealing directly with one person from start to finish. On the other hand, there was the possibility of "friction" between the sales executive and the operating departments, particularly if the salesperson had little in-house knowledge or visibility. This could be further compounded in cases where to get the booking, the sales executive may have made commitments that could be challenging for the property to fulfill.

But the pendulum never swings in just one direction. Today, with the increasing sophistication of meeting requirements and the increasing specialization within the sales and marketing functions, we do see a noticeable swing back to the separation between sales and servicing as to defining responsibilities. But there is also a growing trend toward combining convention servicing and catering.*

Convention Servicing Functions

At first, convention servicing was an added duty for the catering or banquet department (often in conjunction with the housekeeping staff). But it has grown in stature to become a distinct and multifaceted function.

A high degree of managerial abilities and skills are essential to properly fulfill all the details relating to the proper servicing of a 500-person, three-day, intensified educational conference, with its numerous food and beverage functions, meeting room setups and changes, staging procedures, multimedia audiovisual equipment, and sports, recreational, and entertainment requirements.

In some large convention hotels, there may be 30 or more meetings of varying sizes and complexities going on at the same time! To further intensify the challenges, many of the facilities and services of the hotel may also be sought after by representatives of other market segments in the house, such as business travelers, tour groups, or individual leisure travelers. Long lines at the front desk and at lounges and dining rooms can even cause "conflicts" between the various types of business, each blaming the other on the lessening of service.

Meeting planners generally prefer dealing with one hotel executive rather than numerous department heads (see Figure 9–13). This, combined with all of the other facets just mentioned, will make the hotel convention service man-

---

*In effect, there appears to be a greater tendency to separate external and internal functions and to combine what formerly were separate internal responsibilities.

COMMENTARY

WHAT SERVICING "IS NOT"

A few years ago, I was asked to do a seminar for department heads in a major convention hotel (whose name will not be mentioned to protect the guilty).

The subject was to be on "Interdepartmental Co-operation As It Relates to the Servicing of Convention and Group Business"—not easy to say in one breath, but certainly clear as to what was to be covered.

Because of traffic conditions, I arrived some 15 minutes late, found my way up to the room where the department heads were seated—and noticed that there was no flipchart or chalkboard (though both were ordered).

After apologizing for being late, I asked how I could get a chalkboard—and was told by the convention services manager in attendance to call extension —- on the house phone on the wall directly (and conveniently) behind me.

Up came the chalkboard, with four (yes, 4) husky housemen, one for each corner. And they carefully leaned it against the back wall.

"Where's the easel or some other support to place it on?" "Oh," said another attendee, "you have to call the housekeeping department for that." This time, it took only two persons to bring up a wooden easel which probably weighed all of 5 pounds.

"You know what else is missing?" I asked. "Chalk . . . I usually bring my own supply, but forgot this time."

"Oh, chalk and erasers are maintained in the accounting department; they have supply accountability for all such small items," I was informed by another attendee. And after calling there, chalk (two small pieces; nubs, we call them) and an eraser were brought up (only one person needed this time!).

"Well," I said, somewhat facetiously, "do I need to really expound on the subject . . . I would say that in the three phone calls and 25 minutes that it took to get a simple item which had been previously ordered and should have been here to begin with, I think we visually made a rather dramatic illustration of what servicing IS NOT."

David C. Dorf, CHSE

FIGURE 9–13 Example of what can happen if a planner or speaker has to deal with numerous departments rather than a centralized convention servicing department.

FIGURE 9–14 A convention coordinator must be as skilled as a circus ringmaster, "juggling" the requirements of the sales department, the operating departments, and the meeting organization in a way that satisfies all parties.

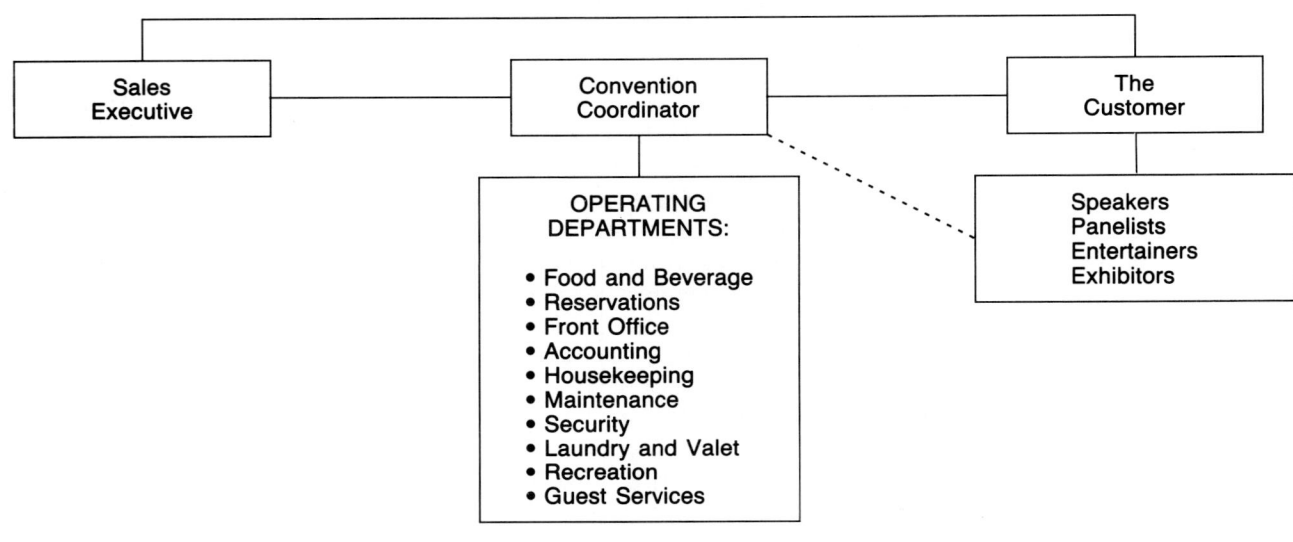

THE THREE-WAY COMMUNICATIONS ROLE
OF THE CONVENTION SERVICE COORDINATOR

Sales Executive

Convention Coordinator

The Customer

OPERATING DEPARTMENTS:

• Food and Beverage
• Reservations
• Front Office
• Accounting
• Housekeeping
• Maintenance
• Security
• Laundry and Valet
• Recreation
• Guest Services

Speakers
Panelists
Entertainers
Exhibitors

ager or coordinator feel like a ringmaster in a three-ring circus (see Figure 9–14).

Convention Servicing Organization

For the servicing function to run smoothly and efficiently, some revisions to traditional tables of organization may be needed. An "ideal" organizational chart of the marketing department for a large convention hotel is suggested in Figure 9–15.

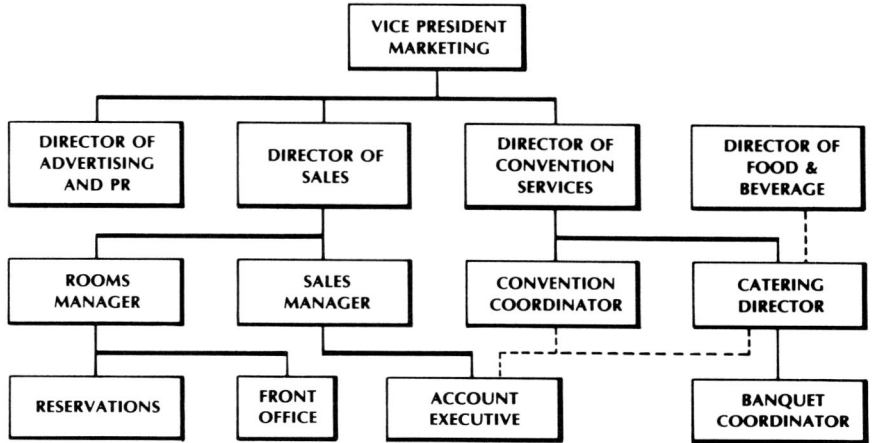

FIGURE 9–15 Portion of an organization chart for a large hotel, coordinating all selling and servicing functions under the marketing department umbrella. The dashed lines between the sales executive and the convention coordinator and the catering director indicate liaison and training coordination, not reporting responsibilities.

SERVICING SPECIALIZATION

Some (but not all) hotel executives feel that those who have been trained to be professionals in the techniques of selling should spend as much time as possible in the marketplace. And many salespersons agree. Often being extroverted, they are more comfortable out in the field making contacts and bookings rather than remaining on property to handle and check constantly on a myriad of details.

Similarly, after the booking, many people find it more expeditious to turn an account over immediately to the in-house servicing professionals, who will then take on the direct responsibilities for all housing, food and beverage, and function room setup arrangements.

The internal servicing staff, however, usually does have a key selling responsibility: to try to rebook the account on conclusion of the convention or meeting. This is, of course, the most cost-effective means of selling available to any property.

CUSTOMER CONCERNS

There are some concerns even with the system of "specialized coordination" (or "coordinated specialization"). Some customers feel somewhat insecure after developing a good working relationship with the sales executive, only to be turned over to a "stranger" as soon as the contract is signed. The big question: "How well will that other person fulfill the promises and commitments originally made by the sales executive?"

A second major concern on the part of the customer (and even on the part of the hotel sales executive) is the ability, knowledgeability, and authority of the key convention servicing executive, variously called a convention manager, convention service manager, convention servicing coordinator, or other.

CONVENTION SERVICE TRAINING

In the past this was a position for which little if any training was available.* Many, if not the majority, of convention service managers and coordinators still come up from the ranks, such as from banquet and catering or from the sales department. However, more attention is now being placed on making this position a career goal, especially among those entering the hospitality industry. This, in turn, can offer additional opportunities for those eventually wishing to forge a career in hotel sales.

Many schools of hotel administration now offer courses in the servicing of group business. A variety of programs on convention servicing are also available from summer school programs and from various industry trade associations for those already in the industry, and new certification programs are being directed at upgrading their professionalism.

SPECIALIZED SERVICING COMPANIES

Another growing area in the servicing of group business relates to the specialized services required by meeting planners, for setups, staging, and decorating, as well as for the more sophisticated audiovisual needs of speakers, trainers, and other program presenters. Many hotels can no longer afford to maintain all of the variety of equipment and staging apparatus needed to service the needs of so many different types of groups. Therefore, more and more reliance is being placed on the support capabilities of professional outside sources.

The relationships that the hotel must establish with these outside sources adds a "fourth ring" to our convention coordinator's former three-ring circus. The article in Figure 9–16 relates some of the key aspects and challenges of this relationship, as seen from the service supplier's viewpoint. Unfortunately, the negative situations described in the article can occur in the simplest of operations, involving just a few hotel departments. You would think there could not be a single problem involved with bringing a chalkboard into a meeting room. However, the "What Servicing Is Not" commentary (Figure 9–13) shows how complicated the most basic servicing routine can become. Fortunately, as hotel convention servicing departments become more sophisticated and better trained, the positive example highlighted in Figure 9–16 will become the rule and not the exception.

---

*Unfortunately, what happened in far too many cases was that this position was occupied by a long-time houseman who no longer was able to do as much physical work as in the past. But his knowledge as well as his contacts still made him valuable to the hotel, so he was given a new title, an office, and some supervisory responsibilities, but unfortunately no comparable administrative training.

A TALE OF TWO HOTELS

John's Journal

In many ways this is a common story, but it needs telling because the points need to be made once again. It is a story of two hotels in San Francisco. In one everything went wrong; in the other, everything went right.

In the right one, the hotel allowed us to move in and begin construction on Sunday evening for a Monday morning event. The display went together without a hitch. We even had time to reposition the tables that were set up for the luncheon and to get extra tables and screens for items we wanted to display in the eating end of the room.

We finished our task in three hours and retired. The next morning we arrived at 9 well-rested, not the 5 A.M. we were expecting if we had not been able to set up the night before.

Maintaining a strong color scheme was critical and the hotel was willing to change, move, and get anything we needed. We asked that the buffet table skirt be changed to gray. Although it needed to be straight-pinned rather than clipped on, a more time-consuming process, that it was taken care of simply added to the impression we were forming about the hotel.

For the evening presentation some people had not responded, so we reduced the place settings from seven to six at each five-foot table. Thirty minutes later we discovered we had our full complement of guests, so we had to ask that the table settings be increased to seven per table. To our surprise, there was no grumbling from the staff, no attitude except one of graciousness. The entire event was a success for the client and thoroughly enjoyable for all of us who worked on it.

During our use of the room, the catering office brought several prospective clients through. Our unsolicited comments about the hotel may have cinched those sales. A few weeks later I had occasion to speak to a UPI reporter doing a story on holiday entertaining and I mentioned the hotel with enthusiasm.

The impression the hotel staff left with us was probably worth at least $20,000 in revenue and publicity. What hotel have we been describing? The new and elegant *hotel nikko san francisco*. Our thanks to Karen Kinoshita and to her staff.

The second tale is one of narrow hallways, late setup, and "don't give-a damn" service. This hotel will not be named.

First, the room was not available until mid-afternoon even though it was promised just after lunch.

Elaborate displays were to be created on each buffet table and we had asked for only one thing—to position the buffet tables and put the top cloth in place. The tables were placed, but not draped because "we do it later."

A quick visit to the banquet manager got us a little attention and that problem was solved. Then she disappeared.

We were now about 90 minutes from the event. While most of the displays were prefabbed, a lot of detailing was going to be done in place. My hot glue gun was plugged in and I was ready to roll.

Midway along the assembly process the glue gun went cold. One of the setup people needed an extension cord for a food warmer, so mine seemed like a good choice. Once I got the glue gun fired up again, only a few minutes went by before it was unplugged once again.

I noticed some of the idle setup people playing with the props—including a $50 handmade Japanese parasol. I recovered that only to notice that the matching cover had been crumpled up and thrown into the trash.

While the hotel's staff was making life difficult for me, the banquet manager was nowhere to be seen. The client's guests probably didn't even notice anything was amiss by the time the doors opened, but we were "done in."

I will not mention the name of the hotel. My experience might be an exception, I don't know. I do know that I will never recommend the property and I will not point them out as a hotel that knows how to do things right.

This is the lesson: While hotels may be function factories, turning out events all day long, each client has invested money, time, creativity, and planning into his/her event. The client is worried, anxious, and hopeful. To the client it is very important; it is not just another function.

Note to hotels: You may want to photocopy this article and give it to each and every person who comes in contact or works with planners and clients. The real impact might be worth thousands of dollars to your property.

FIGURE 9–16 A tale of two hotels. John Cailleau is the owner of Event Design & Production, San Francisco, and we thank him for permission to use his article.

INTERNAL SALES TRAINING

A rapidly growing area of responsibility for sales executives involves training of guest-contact employees, so that they can willingly, courteously, efficiently, and effectively follow through on all the overall promises and detailed commitments made with their clients or customers. This "training for sales-minded servicing" approach relates very strongly to the concepts of cost-effective sales. The least costly and most profitable sale is the one the customer makes: repeat business, referral business, recommendations, and other forms of what has begun to be called *radiation advertising*.*

Proper servicing gives the guest specific reasons for recommending a property to others. On the other hand, there is also a "preventive maintenance" concept here: A person is likely to tell two to three times as many people about a negative experience as about a positive one.

SERVICE FOLLOW-THROUGH

Constant checking and reevaluation are necessary to ensure that both physical and personal service standards are maintained and enhanced. This is an age of constant product and service changes. This can become particularly critical whenever improvements or new features are introduced to the hotel in general or specifically within one of the guest-contact departments.

For example, a change in *checkout hours* might be considered because of changing airline schedules from the key feeder cities bringing the majority of business from a certain property. This may be beneficial to the frequent guest who flies in on business, but its impact on others must be considered:

1. What will be the impact on other guests who do not travel by air?
2. What provisions may have to be made to accommodate luggage?
3. Under what situations will extensions to the new checkout hour be granted?
4. What will be the impact on staff and on possible rescheduling of shifts?

Figure 9–17 illustrates some other situations that could occur when changes are made without considering their impact on servicing.

SUMMARY FROM STATLER

Ellsworth Milton Statler was one of the most significant pioneers in the hospitality industry, particularly in the area of sales promotion. He was also a great innovator in establishing principles and practices of guest servicing. The following advice, which Mr. Statler sent in 1917 to the managers of all his properties, really captures the essence of what service is all about:

> From this date you are instructed to employ only good-natured people, cheerful and pleasant, who smile easily and often. This ought to go for every job in the house, but at present I'll insist on it only for people who come in contact with guests.
>
> And it isn't only a case of hiring. That policy is to govern all promotions; and you are to begin, right now, to measure your present staff by it.
>
> If it's necessary to fire some people, do it. Get rid of the grouches, and the people who can't keep their tempers, and the people who act as if they were always under a burden of trouble and feeling sorry for themselves. You can't make that kind of

---

*So called because the concept is that the customer will "radiate" good words about your property. Not the best term in the world, but perhaps better than the old expression, "word-of-mouth advertising."

COMMENTARY

FOLLOW-THROUGH
(or, The Whole Should Be Equal to the Sum of Its Parts)

Back in those other "good old school days" when we were introduced to the basic concepts of algebra, one of the first axioms we learned was that "the whole is equal to the sum of its parts."

This was obviously more than just an intellectual concept, but its practical applications often seem lost in many of today's major industries—including our own.

For example, sometimes a change is initiated in a component of a product or service which on the surface appears to offer a genuine convenience to the customer and consumer.

Yet, the effect this change will bring on the other parts of the overall product somehow gets lost in the shuffle. The result of this lack of follow-through is that the desired positive impact on the customer is negated. In fact, the customer may feel doubly aggravated.

To illustrate, during one of my recent seminar trips I stopped off at one of those ubiquitous fast-food operations which dot virtually all of our main highways. In this particular operation, there was a sign by the take-out coffee station indicating that as an extra convenience, customers could now get coffee in three different sizes, including a new giant 16-oz cup.

The challenge, however, was that they still stocked the same small plastic stirrers which could not be used in the larger, obviously taller cups—without burning one's fingers.

The reply, when asking one of the supervisors if they had a larger stirrer, was "no, not yet; we still have thousands of regular ones which we have to use up before ordering new ones!"

Packaged products are particularly susceptible to this lack of follow-through. I'm sure we're all familiar with the hot dogs and rolls "game." One year hot dogs may come packaged in sixes, but rolls come separately in packages of eight. Another year, hot dogs may come 10 to a package and rolls are reduced to six in a package.

You would think that this would not happen in a purely service industry such as ours. Unfortunately, here are a few classic examples:

• The hotel which underwent a sudden and speedy renovation and expansion program of its meeting rooms. While prominently featured in its presentations to new prospective customers, the sales department neglected to tell those meeting planners who were already booked that the changes might possibly affect the number and types of rooms needed for their various sessions.
• The hotel which moved its specialty dining room facilities, which attracted a great deal of local business as well as guest patronage, from the lobby to the rooftop. Management neglected to consider the impact of the increased traffic on their already overworked elevators.
• The "center of town" dining facility which doubled its size and capacity, did extensive and very effective local newspaper and radio advertising, but neglected to take into account the result the increased business would have on its already inadequate parking facilities.

After graduation, many of you will be entering this industry in important supervisory capacities. Much of your responsibility will involve making sure that product and servicing changes, additions, and innovations are carried through to your specific department or function, especially those of a guest-contact nature.

So, remember the importance of follow-through—and that the total guest experience must *at least* equal the sum of all of the parts.

David C. Dorf, CHSE
HSMAI Student Bulletin

FIGURE 9-17 Some examples of the importance of a proper servicing follow-through.

person over; you can't do anything with him profitably, but get rid of him. Let the other fellow have him, and you hire people who can be taught.

This is to be our basic principle! Hire pleasant, cheerful people, people of good disposition, and reject everyone who isn't.

It isn't enough to be courteous to 74 patrons and pert with the 75th. It won't do to be cheerful 58 minutes of the hour and disgruntled the other 2. It isn't sufficient for 10 employees to give service and the 11th to go slack on his job.

In another hotel another clerk could have sold the guest just as comfortable a room, another bellman could have handled his bag just as well, another waiter may have served him piping hot dinner just as promptly, but the thing that will make the impression on guests is that our employees seemed "glad to do it," they seemed interested in him personally.

Gracious service means more than "perfect" service. Every hotel employee is a salesman. He must satisfy customers with the only thing he has to sell—service—and he must please them with the way he sells it. I believe that a majority of the complaints in a hotel are due more to the guest's state of mind than to the importance of the thing about which he complains.

E. M. Statler

This sound and practical advice is as timely today as when it was first published. The results when properly followed can lead to the highest degree of guest satisfaction, which is what the next chapter is all about.

ten

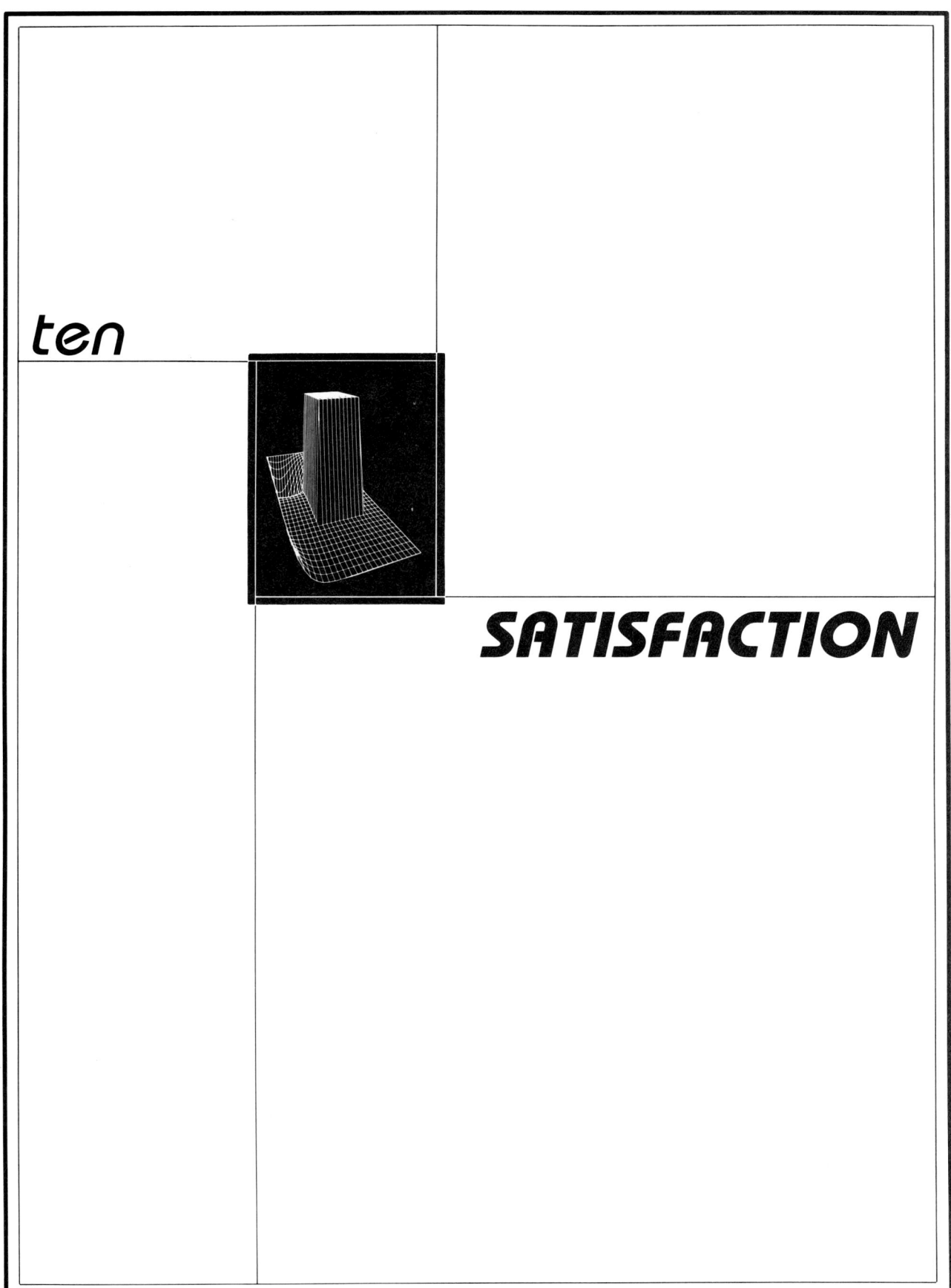

SATISFACTION

After the previous rather lengthy discourse on servicing, one might assume that the hospitality industry has become about as altruistic as one could be. And indeed, some shortsighted hotel operators have "accused" sales and marketing executives of "working for the customer" rather than for those who pay their salaries. In reality, a sales executive should "work" for the satisfaction of both the property and its guests. Being part of a service industry, every lodging establishment's objective should be to fulfill the anticipations and expectations of its guests through proper service. This, in turn, leads to the highest possible degree of customer satisfaction.

Satisfaction is basically determined by how well each guest's needs and preferences are met as they relate to that person's objectives and goals. To find this out, the sales executive must follow through after the sale to find the answers to such fundamental questions as:

1. What did you like about your hotel experience, and why?
2. What did you dislike, and why?
3. Would you come back?
4. Would you recommend us to your friends and business acquaintances?
5. If you had a negative reaction or experience, what might we do to turn it around?
6. To put it more directly, what can we do to get you to come back?

SATISFACTION AS A SALES TOOL

Can satisfaction be a workable sales tool? Certainly, especially in the areas of referrals and recommendations, as well as both direct and indirect reselling. For example:

- Satisfied guests will often recommend your property to friends and business acquaintances, and this often has more "credibility" than many other means of direct promotion.
- A satisfied leisure traveler may also have a reason to return to your area as a business traveler or a convention/meeting attendee. In essence, this offers a "recommendation to one's self," another way of asking, "Would you come back to this property under different circumstances or roles?"
- A satisfied business traveler may also be a meeting planner or carry substantial weight in recommending sites for his or her department's meetings. And the commercial guest may also be in the position of recommending the property to other departmental planners in the company.
- The individual guest, at your property for either business or for leisure-related reasons, may also serve as a volunteer member of an association's site selection or time-and-place committee.
- Positive feedback by guests about your hotel, made to your counterparts at other properties, can lead them to recommend you for business they could not accommodate.
- They would also be more likely to send you overflow business if they receive favorable comments from satisfied guests.

- Satisfaction feedback can also help determine which properties would want to work with you for joint or cooperative promotions.

Many of the above are variations of what has been referred to earlier as radiation advertising.

RELATIONSHIP TO MARKETING

Since this is a book on selling, we should clarify the very direct relationship satisfaction has to the rest of the marketing functions. As you have undoubtedly noticed throughout the book, we have presented a number of different definitions of marketing, from a number of different sources. So here's yet another, tying together three main components of marketing concept: selling, servicing, and satisfying (Figure 10-1).

Specific Actions

There are some very specific actions that sales executives can take to check on key factors affecting the satisfaction level of the business they book. Many of these actions might even be considered operational in nature. However, they affect the potential for repeat business as well as possible impact on the reputation of both property and staff. These could include:

- Suggesting improvements and additions to the physical property, including rooms, function space, meeting room equipment, amenities, and services ("product enhancement")
- "Walking the house" periodically to observe guest conduct, guest–staff interaction, and any evidences of guest dissatisfaction
- Reviewing outstanding bills before they are sent by the accounting department to major customers and volume account executives

FIGURE 10-1 Definition of the all-inclusive term "marketing," in which "servicing" and "satisfaction" are key components, along with "selling."

Marketing is all the things you do to selectively	COMPONENT	FUNCTION OF:	RESPONSIBILITY OF:
↓			
Attract and secure the highest volume of business of all types;	Selling	1. Advertising 2. Public relations 3. Publicity 4. Personal selling	Director of marketing (or sales)
↓			
Properly service such business; and	Servicing	1. Convention service department 2. Banquet department 3. Operating departments (especially front office and accounting) 4. All guest-contact employees	1. Sales director 2. Convention service manager 3. All department heads
↓			
Encourage this business to keep returning	Satisfying	Everyone	Everyone
↓			
At a profit			

- Reviewing all compliment and complaint letters, irrespective of the department at which they are directed

IMPACT OF COMPLAINTS ON SELLING

The last item on the checklist above is one of the most critical, since a complaint related to a previous experience may unexpectedly surface during a sales call and catch the account executive completely "off guard." The executive may be prepared for complaints relating to available dates, types of accommodations, meeting room charges, room rates, food and beverage prices, and other "negotiable items" that often surface during the course of a buyer–seller dialogue. The handling of these situations was discussed and dramatized in Chapter 7. In that chapter we also presented the concept of compensatory selling, which has a counterpart: compensatory servicing and satisfaction. The principle is the same: offering a substitute feature, benefit, or service to "make up" for the lack or unavailability of another.

However, the compensation must be meaningful in terms of the needs and objectives of the guest. For example, let's take a business traveler who orders room service for breakfast. The hotel "guarantees" that it will be delivered in under 20 minutes or "breakfast will be on us." If it comes late, 40 minutes or an hour later, for instance, the compensatory "free breakfast" will usually not satisfy the customer, whose concern at the time was related to being on time for the first business appointment.

As has been stressed so often, the fact that the customer may be assuming several different roles is again a critical concern to the sales executive. That very same unsatisfied business executive may also be responsible for meetings or social events as well, as the sales executive may later find out when making a call to the executive's company. The "unexpected complaint" has a good chance of surfacing during the sales presentation.

The unexpected complaints that we are referring to here are more "internal" and "operational," yet can ultimately affect the marketing program in general and sales efforts in particular if not taken care of to the satisfaction of the guest, client, or customer. Here is a negative "shopping" list of some of the more prevalent complaints (not in any particular order) that might come up in a discussion with a prospect and substantiate customer dissatisfaction:

- Discourteous, inattentive, and poorly informed employees
- Lack of cleanliness, repair, and refurbishing
- Undelivered messages and wake-up calls
- Exorbitant charges for room service, soda and snack machine products
- "Gouging" in telephone surcharges and both incoming and outgoing fax messages
- Clogged shower heads, low water pressure, unreliable temperature controls (both water and heating/air-conditioning)
- Room service trays left overnight in hallways
- Meeting room light switches and other controls located 100 or more feet away from where speakers would normally stand
- Worn-out blackboards, flipcharts, and screens, which should have been replaced years ago

That's just for "openers." One could readily add two or three more dozen items that are wide open to potential complaints, especially where properties have become complacent and lax in conducting periodic quality control inspections.

RESPONDING TO COMPLAINTS

Regardless of where a possible service infraction occurred, after proper investigational procedures have been taken, a prompt response should be made. It will be up to the property's policies and procedures who sends the "apology" letter or phone call. But in cases where the guest involved is a VIP contact or responsible for volume business, the marketing or sales director may be the one to respond.

A sample response letter may take the form shown in Figure 10-2. Another variation of this letter might be the more direct approach, substituting the wording shown in Figure 10-3 for the first paragraph.

CAUSES OF DISSATISFACTION

To minimize the likelihood for dissatisfaction, one should recognize its three major overall causes and the relative percentage of occurrences:

1. Poor design, packaging, and marketing of the product or service (40%).

Dear Mr. _____:

I have just received your letter concerning your disappointing experience last month in our Last Chance Motel.

While nothing can change the unfortunate situation which has already taken place, I do want to personally let you know how distressed I am at the treatment you received at the Front Desk. I most sincerely apologize for any inconveniences this may have caused.

Please let me know in advance when your travels again take you to this area—and I will do everything possible to make your return visit a pleasant and enjoyable one.

Cordially,

FIGURE 10-2 Sample response to a complaint letter.

FIGURE 10-3 Response letter variation.

Dear Mr. _____ :

I was most distressed to learn of your disappointing experience at our Front Desk during your visit with us last month.

---

2. Discourteous, untrained, uncaring, nonmotivated employees (20%).

3. The customers themselves (30%). Some customers need to be educated on the how's and the why's.* Back in 1921, the Hotels Statler Service Code manual rather daringly noted that "Almost every day a Statler Hotel has a complaint from some guest, about a detail or service. Every complaint has conscientious attention. Each Statler Hotel is operated on the theory that the guest is always right. But—quietly, now—sometimes we find out, whether we admit it or not, that the guest was NOT right in that particular instance."

Despite the tremendous increases in travel and hotel use by all segments of the public since that was written some 70 years ago, the industry is still subject to many "the guest is always right . . . sometimes" types of complaints. Right or wrong does not matter. If not properly handled, they can lead to considerable dissatisfaction and resulting loss of business.

BEHAVIORAL ANALYSIS

Part of the reasons for such reactions can be traced to plain, ordinary "human nature." To put it perhaps a little more scientifically, *behavioral analysis* can be used as a diagnostic tool in determining why people act and react. It is basically a study of the ways people seem to be reacting to life in general; their attitudes and opinions; and the ways they face potential challenge areas which could affect their relationships with, for instance, guest-contact hotel employees and staff.

In this fast-paced, highly stressed, electronic age, people seem to exhibit the following characteristics, many of which relate directly (and all indirectly) to their satisfaction level when traveling and when staying at a hotel:

1. Less willingness to be uncomfortable—both physically and mentally

2. More stress

3. More loneliness

4. More fear of the future (look for reassurances that things will not change)

5. More loyalty (tied into a desire for the predictable)

6. Higher expectations (because of greater travel experiences and sophistication)

7. More demands (rather than simply "requests")

8. Greater concerns about rights (What if I change reservations? How can I change my room or seat?)

9. Less concern about their responsibilities and obligations

10. Less conscience in their behavior (try to see how much they can "get away with," especially in a "win–lose" situation)

11. Greater tendency to go over another's head, seeking out the "person in charge" (reflects on the importance of titles)

12. Become more honest in that they will let you know their likes and dislikes

13. A desire to let others fight their battles (third-party intervention)

*This is sometimes called the "When all else fails, try reading the instructions" syndrome.

14. A tendency to be more testing (they will ask questions they already have answers to, to find out if you know)

15. A habit of labeling other people quickly (snap judgments)

16. Less courtesy—but are more appreciative (they don't say "thanks" as often, but really mean it when they do)

17. Less inclination to wait (hate to stand in line)

18. Greater tendency to lose track of time (exaggerate the time it takes to get service)

19. A habit of viewing large or big in a negative way

20. More individuality (they are looking for "customizing")

THE POSITIVE APPROACH

So far, it may seem that the emphasis has been put on the negative side of satisfaction: complaints, stressful behaviors, and so on. However, by its very definition, satisfaction is a positive trait and one that can be developed in a positive manner. One of the first steps would be for a property to target specific areas for satisfaction improvement. These might include the following objectives:

1. To improve the *quality* of our product

2. To enhance the *consistency* of our service

3. To increase the *professionalism* of our employees

4. To advance our *knowledge* and *understanding* of our customers

Product design technology ("build a better mousetrap") can be one way of developing higher customer satisfaction. For example, where hotels use a plastic key-card, it could be so designed that inserting it would turn on the lights, TV, and air-conditioning, or whatever else was preset. Closing the door as one leaves would turn them off. Results: happier guests who don't have to stumble all over the room trying to find switches. To the property, cost savings through energy conservation.

You will note that most satisfaction elements are people oriented; and they relate not only to the customer but to the staff as well. A hotel with highly dissatisfied personnel will hardly be one with satisfied guests.

The Marriott Corporation has prepared a film, *The Spirit of Success*, which focuses on the following principles of satisfaction:

1. Treat employees fairly.

2. Listen to your customers.

3. Evaluate and challenge regularly what you are doing.

4. Maintain high standards of quality.

5. Provide promotional and career progression to hard-working employees.

Some of these may not immediately seem to relate to the concept of satisfying the guest. But take item 5: If employees know that they can advance readily if they do the best possible job, they will make the extra effort to provide the best possible service as it relates to satisfying the needs and wants of the guest.

THE ROLE OF TRAINING

The training function (now often termed HRD—*human resources development*) offers a key method of instilling the concept of servicing for maximum guest satisfaction. The expanded working definition of training shown in Figure 10–4 highlights the attributes that should be cultivated by all guest-contact personnel.

Training

*T*olerant . . of the fact that many people in the hotel are not necessarily at "their best" . . . they are on strange and unfamiliar "turf."

*R*eceptive . . to the needs, wants, hopes, desires, expectations, and anticipations of the guests, which may vary substantially according to who they are, why they are here, prior travel experience, etc.

*A*nticipative . . of potential wants or needs . . . "How may I help you?"

*I*nnovative . . ready to offer options or variations where appropriate.

*N*egotiative . . the ability to "work with" the guest, especially if their specific needs cannot be precisely met . . . to offer suitable alternatives; to be able to handle complaints.

*I*nspirational . . to give the guest the feeling of active confidence and reassurance . . . to inspire the guest with the feeling that he or she has made the right choice.

*N*eeds-oriented . . to be empathetic to the needs of the guest.

*G*oals-oriented . . to be similarly empathetic to the needs and goals of the hotel, the department served, and fellow employees.

FIGURE 10–4 The letters of the word "training" can form a practical guide to the traits desired in all guest-contact employees.

EMPLOYEE COMMUNICATIONS

A constant flow of communications to all employees stressing the importance of the satisfied guest is another method of assisting the overall sales effort. This can be done in internal newsletters, posters and signs in employee dining areas, and through messages in pay envelopes, generally known as *payroll stuffers* (see Figure 10–5). More formalized training programs can use a variety of audiovisual presentations as well as specific courses which are often developed at the chain or franchise headquarters for unit property use.

Another sometimes overlooked source of training materials is the trade press, where editors and feature columnists often focus on subjects relating to guest satisfaction. Figure 10–6 shows two "editorial" examples, written over 20 years ago. But they are just as (if not more) timely today. Each could be the basis of at least a one-hour training session.

METHODS OF MEASUREMENT

Most hotels use one or more devices in an attempt to measure guest satisfaction. Perhaps the most common is the in-room guest questionnaire, which asks the customer to evaluate the property's features and services from poor to excellent (Figure 10–7). The basic challenge with this method is that the responses

Thought of the Week

WE WANT OUR GUESTS TO HAVE A FAVORABE OPINION OF YOU,
OUR HOTEL, OUR SERVICE.
ARE YOU DOING YOUR BEST TO HELP KEEP OUR
GUESTS SATISFIED?

LET'S BLOW OUR HORN!

Let's tell the world about ourselves and our organization. Let's prove to our Guests that we appreciate their patronage. Let's show the public that we realize that our security—our jobs and our pay-rolls—are builded upon the SATISFACTION that comes from dealing with us.

Let's do all this by offering our Guests the kind of SERVICE that will bring them back to us time after time.

Let's Blow Our Horn! But let's remember that ACTIONS speak louder than WORDS.

32

THE ONE THAT GOT AWAY . . . .

Is always the biggest one, of course. Ask your friend, the fisherman. But the "One That Got Away" isn't the one that gave the flavor to that breakfast he talks about.

★ The Guest who gets away—because some one of us had failed in courtesy or friendliness or helpfulness—is our "biggest one," too. We will want to "fish that pool" until we get the "strike." And after we've "landed" him, we'd best put our gear in order.

There's not much satisfaction in merely TALKING about "The One That Got Away."

30

THE BIG BROADCAST

● The SATISFIED GUEST tells us that he likes us by continuing to do business with us.

● The DISSATISFIED GUEST frequently isn't content with discontinuing his patronage. He "takes to the air and tells the world" about our mistakes, thereby advertising our competitors.

● That isn't the sort of "Big Broadcast" that helps anyone in our business.

● Let's not have Dissatisfied Guests!

38

FIGURE 10–5 One of the earliest examples of payroll stuffers that focused on customer satisfaction was a series of over 50 messages used in the 1930s by Atlantic City's Traymore Hotel.

EDITORIAL

THE "WALL OF SILENCE"

The need for proper communications among hotel/motel management, department heads, and employees seems to be receiving more and more attention these days; yet one of the most vital areas of communications, that between the hotel and the guest, seemingly is all too frequently overlooked or else taken for granted.

In particular, the lack of proper verbal communications between guest-contact employees and the customer often creates a "wall of silence"; evidenced, for example, by the room clerk who bluntly points to the stack of registration cards as a guest prepares to check in, the bellman who mutely turns on the lights, air-conditioning, and TV as he rooms a guest, or the waitress who silently hands a customer a menu without a single word of recognition.

The guest who complains to others of the "cold" atmosphere of a particular property usually is not talking about physical characteristics or a lack of decor—instead, he probably is referring to the "silent treatment" he seems to receive from the various employees with whom he comes in contact. To the average guest, these guest-contact employees represent "the hotel," and they can create more lasting impressions (either positive or negative) than all the colorful brochures or letters with the manager's signature he may have previously received.

Friendly, helpful, courteous, and timely communications between employees and guests seems elementary, but it is vital from the standpoint of public relations, sales-minded servicing and in the final analysis—profits.

—D. C. D.
HSMA Bulletin
July 1967

EDITORIAL

THE ART OF SAYING "THANK YOU"

The hotel–motel industry is still basically an industry comprised of people whose main purpose is to fulfill the personal requirements, needs, and desires of other people. Yet too many operators, surrounded by new or renovated edifices of steel and glass, and utilizing the most up-to-date equipment, sales, and managerial methods, have seemingly lost a great deal of the "personal touch" which is so vital to both securing and keeping a profitable level of business.

"Cold"—"without atmosphere or class"—"impersonal"—"like an office or factory"—these are but a few of the adjectives we have heard long-standing hotel–motel customers use in describing certain operations. These people undoubtedly will be "shopping around" to find other facilities where they still will be accorded the genuine hospitality which is supposedly so traditional in our industry.

The basic yet ever so simple art of saying "Thank you" to departing guests, for example, unfortunately seems to be on the wane—and far too often, a Mr. Smith in room 402 seems to be considered merely as a body occupying and paying for a certain accommodation, rather than being treated as a distinct human being.

One particular comment from a steady user of hotel–motel accommodations seems to sum it all up, when he recently remarked, "In far too many properties, I have the feeling they could care less whether I was there, was leaving, or ever coming back. And when the hotel was particularly busy, I've even had the impression that the desk couldn't wait till I checked out!"

A bellman's sincere, "We hope you enjoyed your stay, Mr. Smith—glad to have had you with us"; a cashier's, "Thanks for staying with us, Mr. Smith . . . hope to see you again soon"; or some other sign of personal recognition and appreciation by guest-contact employees may seem like a rather small point. But to Mr. Smith and the millions of other travelers like him, this simple gesture (or the lack of it) very often determines where he will be staying during his next return visit.

The art of saying "Thank you" requires no physical or mental effort . . . in fact, it isn't really an art. It should be nothing more than just ordinary, everyday, common courtesy and common sense. The lack of it most certainly will negate much of the overall sales and marketing efforts made by any hotel or motor inn.

—D. C. D.
HSMA Bulletin
June 1968

FIGURE 10–6 Editorials on guest satisfaction.

Dear Guests,

Thanks for staying at the Claridge Casino Hotel. We're sure you're going to enjoy yourself.

Simply fill out this questionnaire. Tell us what's right, what's wrong or where we can use some help. Then leave the completed form with our hotel cashier, or mail it to us. Postage is paid. As an incentive, we're offering a 20% room rate discount* next time you visit us. We'll send back your 20% coupon together with our gratitude.

(*This offer applies Sunday through Thursday only and is subject to availability. Not valid in July or August. This offer cannot be used in conjunction with any other discount or promotional offer.)

ROOMS

How would you rate your room?

	Excellent	Good	Fair	Poor
Ready	☐	☐	☐	☐
Clean	☐	☐	☐	☐
Comfortable	☐	☐	☐	☐
In proper working condition (TV, Bathroom facilities, etc.)	☐	☐	☐	☐
Properly supplied (Towels, soap, ashtrays, coat hangers, etc.)	☐	☐	☐	☐
Adequately furnished	☐	☐	☐	☐

Comments: _____

HOTEL SERVICE

How would you rate the following hotel services:

	Excellent	Good	Fair	Poor
Room Reservation	☐	☐	☐	☐
Valet Parking	☐	☐	☐	☐
Bell Service	☐	☐	☐	☐
Front Desk	☐	☐	☐	☐
Housekeeping/Maids	☐	☐	☐	☐

Comments: _____

CASINO SERVICE

Please rate our casino services.

	Excellent	Good	Fair	Poor
Casino Cashier	☐	☐	☐	☐
Dealers	☐	☐	☐	☐
Change Handlers	☐	☐	☐	☐
Security Officers	☐	☐	☐	☐
Hosts/Pit Personnel	☐	☐	☐	☐
Cocktail Service	☐	☐	☐	☐

Comments: _____

RESTAURANTS

How would you rate the quality of:

	Food				Service			
	Excellent	Good	Fair	Poor	Excellent	Good	Fair	Poor
Martino's	☐	☐	☐	☐	☐	☐	☐	☐
Twenties Supper Club	☐	☐	☐	☐	☐	☐	☐	☐
Garden Room	☐	☐	☐	☐	☐	☐	☐	☐
Stadium Deli	☐	☐	☐	☐	☐	☐	☐	☐
Great American Buffet	☐	☐	☐	☐	☐	☐	☐	☐
On A Roll	☐	☐	☐	☐	☐	☐	☐	☐

Comments: _____

ENTERTAINMENT/LOUNGE

Please rate the quality of:

	Service				Entertainment			
	Excellent	Good	Fair	Poor	Excellent	Good	Fair	Poor
Palace Theater	☐	☐	☐	☐	☐	☐	☐	☐
Celebrity Cabaret	☐	☐	☐	☐	☐	☐	☐	☐
Lucky's Bar	☐	☐	☐	☐	☐	☐	☐	☐
Twenties Lounge	☐	☐	☐	☐	☐	☐	☐	☐

Comments: _____

FIGURE 10–7 Guest survey form. The questionnaire portion of a guest comment card. These evaluation sheets are often in the form of a multi-panel self-mailer, so the guest can either hand it to the cashier upon check-out or mail it postage paid. (Courtesy of Claridge Casino Hotel, Atlantic City, New Jersey.)

OVERALL

How do you rate the overall quality of Casino/Hotel services and facilities:

Excellent ☐   Good ☐   Fair ☐   Poor ☐

Comments:_____

_____

_____

GENERAL INFORMATION

What is the primary purpose of your visit? (check one)

☐ Business   ☐ Corporate Meeting/Convention

☐ Pleasure/Vacation   ☐ CompCard

How did you select the Claridge?

_____

_____

How did you arrive?

☐ Private Auto   ☐ Bus   ☐ Airplane

On the average,

Number of visits per year_____

Length of stay each visit_____

	Yes	No
Have you been our guest before?	☐	☐
Would you return to the Claridge Casino Hotel?	☐	☐

On the average how many hours per day do you spend gambling at the Claridge? _____ hours.

Other Atlantic City Casinos?_____hours.

List in order of preference, the three (3) casino games you play most often (Slots, Video Poker, Blackjack, Craps, Roulette, Big Six, Baccarat.)

1. _____

2. _____

3. _____

Which type of slot machine do you play most often?

	5¢	25¢	50¢	$1.00
Regular (reel type)	☐	☐	☐	☐
Video	☐	☐	☐	☐
Credit	☐	☐	☐	☐

Your opinions and answers will be treated with strict confidence. We sincerely appreciate your interest in our hotel and casino and hope to have the pleasure of serving you again.

Arrival Date _____ Departure Date _____ Room Number _____

Name: Mr.
        Mrs.
        Ms. _____

Address: _____

City:_____

Phone: (   )_____

Have you any remarks that may help us improve our services?

_____

_____

_____

Have you met an outstanding employee? Please let us know his/or her name

_____

Department _____

```
THANK YOU

YOU MAY LEAVE THIS COMPLETED FORM WITH
OUR HOTEL CASHIER, OR MAIL IT TO US,
POSTAGE PAID.
```

Claridge
Atlantic City
THE FRIENDLY GAMBLING HOUSE.

FIGURE 10–7 (cont.)

generally follow a reverse "bell-shaped curve." There is usually some response from the negative end of the curve ("I hate everything") and also from the high end ("I love everything"). But there often is very little return from the vast majority of guests who would represent the middle portion of the curve. However, when responses are evaluated periodically, they can offer information on trends—such as areas of improvement, particularly if the property has initiated specific quality service and guest satisfaction programs.

Another method of measuring guest satisfaction is by comparing the ratio of compliment and complaint letters, or to put it into simpler terms, "fan mail" versus "pan mail." Additional techniques have been described elsewhere in this book, such as random sampling among specific market segments, and direct discussions between the sales staff and the guests at such opportune times as the "manager's reception" or "manager's breakfast."

Another means is to have a friend or relative stay at your hotel for a couple of days and offer candid opinions on everything from the physical layout of the property to attitudes of the staff. This type of evaluation can be very similar to the way a meeting planner or travel agent may conduct an "unannounced site inspection."

THE DIFFERENCE IS TREATMENT

Looking at it from the guest's viewpoint, satisfaction is the positive end result of the hotel's ability to solve needs, hopes, desires, expectations, and so on. So this subject directly relates to the sales function.

It is obviously easier to rebook business from a happy patron, or to initiate a first-time sale from someone who has a positive impression of the property because of recommendations and referrals by other satisfied users (radiation advertising). The key to satisfaction lies in a property's emphasis on constantly checking and improving guest relations. The checklist in Figure 10-8 spells out a positive philosophy that can be a useful guideline in this area.

FIGURE 10-8 Philosophy of guest relations. (Courtesy of Raymond A. Dault, Professor Emeritus of the Department of Restaurant, Hotel, and Institutional Management, Purdue University, and Executive Director of the Indianapolis Hotel and Motel Association.)

The only difference between hotels
is the way they treat guests

Eleven Commandments of Guest Relations

Guests . . . are the most important persons in our business.

Guests . . . are not dependent on us—we are dependent on them.

Guests . . . are not an interruption of our work—they are the purpose of it.

Guests . . . do us a favor when they call—we are not doing them a favor by serving them.

Guests . . . are a part of our business—not outsiders.

Guests . . . are not a cold statistic—they are flesh and blood human beings with feelings and emotions like our own.

Guests . . . are not someone to argue or match wits with.

Guests . . . are persons who bring us their wants—it is our job to fill these wants.

Guests . . . are deserving of the most courteous and attentive treatment we can give them.

Guests . . . are the people who make it possible to pay your salary and the salaries of all others here at our hotel/motel.

Guests . . . are the life-blood of this and every other hotel/motel.

Some years ago, a poem made the rounds of the hotel industry. While we do not know the original source, we certainly know its message, which pretty well sums up this important subject.

My Store

If I possessed a shop or store
I'd drive the grouches off my floor
I'd never let some gloomy guy
Offend the folks who come to buy.
I'd never keep a boy or clerk
With mental toothache at his work,
Nor let a man who draws my pay
Drive customers of mine away.
The reason people pass one door
To patronize another store,
Is not because a busier place
Has better silks, or gloves, or lace,
Or cheaper prices, but it lies
In pleasant words and smiling eyes;
The only difference, I believe
Is in the treatment folks receive.

Walter Duckwall

eleven

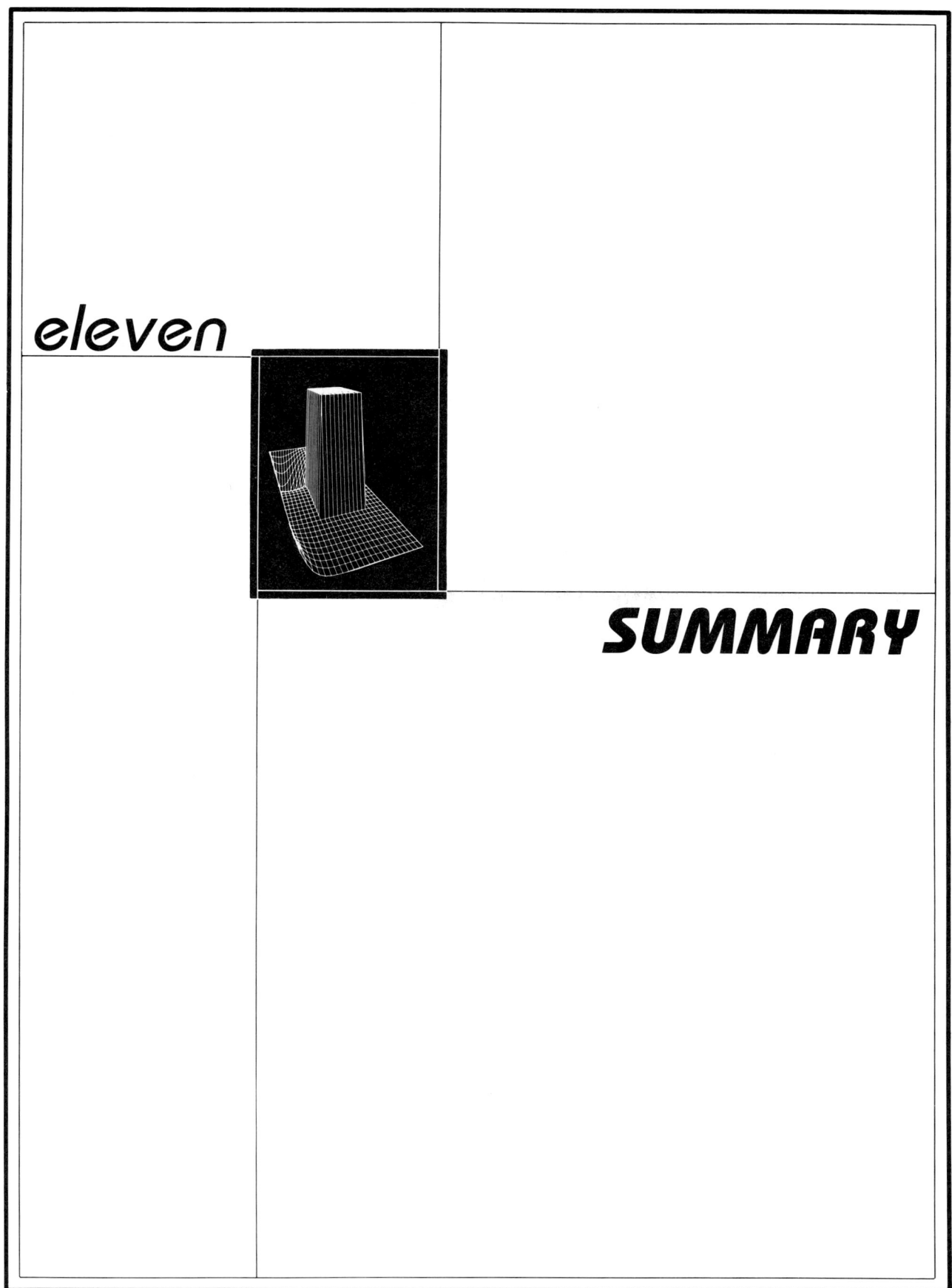

SUMMARY

For many of you, this may have been your introduction to the concepts of promotional research and analysis, sales administration, selling, advertising, and customer service and satisfaction. Those of you in school will in many instances find that there are a number of additional and more specialized courses available (for which this may have been a prerequisite). Each will undoubtedly delve more deeply into its particular area. Such courses might include "Convention Sales and Servicing," "Banquets and Catering," "Hospitality Advertising," "Marketing Strategies," and others that focus on a specific aspect of hospitality sales and marketing.

Because of this, we thought that a good way of summarizing this book might be in the form of a personal message rather than the traditional point-by-point recap. It is more in the style of a philosophical recap instead of a "nuts and bolts" review. But then we have been stressing throughout that selling, servicing, and marketing are both personal and professional philosophies.

Throughout this book we have placed emphasis on tools, techniques, and traits that help make a sales executive a success, both personally and professionally. Some of the major attributes include:

- *Empathy:* the ability to see things as your customers would view them
- *Awareness:* the recognition of how conditions are and how they are likely to change
- *Flexibility:* the ability to see the other viewpoint and to offer alternatives when necessary
- *Creativity:* the answer to the challenge, "Do something different for me!"
- *Visibility:* who knows you—and what do they think of you?
- *Sense of humor:* so as to be able to put things in their proper perspective

To elaborate on this, we now offer a summation centered around the philosophical guideline that "success is spelled with a dozen 'I's'."

INDUSTRY UNIQUENESS

To put success in its proper perspective, you must relate it to the quality called *uniqueness*. The hospitality industry offers a highly fascinating and most challenging career field. It is one that is open to you 24 hours a day, seven days a week, 365 days a year—in every corner of the globe and every spot in between.

It is also a field with a rather unique product: *hospitality*. You can't see it, hold it, feel it, smell it, taste it, wear it—and you can't have a prospective customer "take it for a spin around the block." Yet, whether you are in sales or in operations, you have to sell it continuously, at a profit—24 hours a day, seven days a week, 365 days a year.

This product is also rather unusual in that it is extremely *perishable*. It cannot be sold on the usual unit basis. You have to sell it—and constantly resell it—without any opportunity to say, "Hey, I've sold out; I've 'maxed' my quota . . . I've done all I can do . . . I'm going on vacation for the rest of the month!"

Our industry seems to offer proof positive of Einstein's theory of relativity. In hospitality marketing, you exist in a variation of a "space-time continuum" because you are involved with a specific number of rooms, seats, and square feet of function/meeting space—on a per day basis. In the case of food and beverage outlets as well as banquet and meeting space, your product may even be defined in units per hour.

There is more to the uniqueness of the lodging product. You cannot *shelve* it on a bad day and then sell twice as much on a good day to make up for it. You cannot sell today's vacant room twice tomorrow; you cannot look at your empty main banquet room at lunch and say, "No problem, I'll put two groups in that space at the same time for dinner and make it up!"

SUPPLY AND DEMAND

Those of you who have studied economics will also discover that the hospitality industry does not always follow the usual laws of supply and demand.

For example, let's say that you have a 300-room mountain resort hotel. You cannot tell your "factory" to hold back on 100 rooms because your forecast for next Wednesday indicates a demand for only 200 accommodations. Nor can you tell them to send you the other 100 rooms, plus an additional 200 for the following weekend (to take care of back orders), because your forecasts indicate a peak demand for weekend leisure family travel. You also cannot call your "distributor" and ask him to rush 10 additional rooms when you're full because a bunch of people just walked in off the street without reservations. So hotel sales executives, unlike salespeople in many retail hard-goods industries, face the challenge of selling a fixed product, which cannot be shelved, which is highly "perishable," and which cannot generally operate under the concept of fluctuating inventories based on variable demand.

A DIFFERENT PRODUCT

Now, just what is this product . . . rooms, food and beverage, public space? No way! As has been stressed throughout, we do not sell features. We provide (and motivate customers to purchase) benefits that are designed to satisfy very specific, yet changeable needs, wants, and desires of very specific segments of the public.

What we offer are the *intangibles* that are incorporated within the steel, brick, and glass of our structures. We offer escape, atmosphere, glamour, romance, intrigue, dreams, luxuries, conveniences, opportunities—and a certain number of necessities. Compared with many other industries, especially those offering tangible, "hold in your hand" products that can be taken into and consumed in the home, we are indeed different!

We are not saying that you cannot use the business and management principles employed by other industries. What we are emphasizing is that we have to *adapt* them to fit the special character of the hospitality industry. This in turn calls for a somewhat different set of personal characteristics for building and ensuring success in our particular field.

A STARTER LIST FOR SUCCESS

What attributes, characteristics, qualities, personality traits, and abilities does one need to be a success in today's (and tomorrow's) hospitality industry? We have come up with a starter list of a dozen (not in any particular order or rank).

Each starts with the letter "I"—so we can call this "success is spelled with a dozen 'I's' ":

1. Involvement
2. Intelligence
3. Initiative
4. Incentive
5. Instinct
6. Imagination
7. Ingenuity (innovation)
8. Inspiration
9. Integrity
10. Independence
11. Individuality
12. Infectiousness

What we will do now is look at each characteristic—and pass along some thoughts, concepts, ideas, suggestions, philosophies, and a bit of practical commonsense advice that may offer some guidance as to what may be important in the advancement of your hospitality industry career goals. We presuppose that your goals are directed at eventually achieving a management position either in operations or sales and marketing (or if you really want to get ahead, both). This, in turn, can additionally provide a review of the preceding 10 chapters.

INVOLVEMENT

We have stressed that we are in the problem-solving business and that the three main reasons why people travel and use hotels, motor inns, or resorts are (1) business, (2) leisure, and (3) health and fitness—or increasingly, a combination of two or all.

For the most part, people do this not to acquire material goods, but to improve their *minds,* their *bodies,* and their *professional position.* They have "problems" relating to both professional and personal objectives. For them, we are in the problem-solving business because we are viewed as being in the satisfaction business.

To be good managers—and that term, as you know, includes general managers as well as sales/marketing managers—we have to be a combination parent figure, psychologist, priest or minister, and physical therapist.

This means that we have to be involved with our customers on a mind/soul/body basis. In short, we have to care. In this business, you should never have the opportunity to say, "I don't have time, Mr. or Mrs. Guest, for your problems"—because involvement with, and the satisfaction of, customer problems are the reasons we are in business.

INTELLIGENCE

To involve ourselves effectively with our guests, we must learn to communicate effectively. The ability to communicate properly is a principal measure of a person's intelligence. Intelligence does not necessarily mean making the dean's list, or "creaming" the finals in food chemistry, or getting straight "A's" in accounting. All of that is fine and good, but in the field, intelligence means understanding your product (property and services), what it can and cannot offer in terms of benefits, and what you can and cannot do with it in terms of satisfying customer needs. It also means understanding the ever-changing needs and wants of the people who purchase your products. It means "doing your homework"—for real! It also means learning how to convey an appealing and understandable sales message to bring your product and potential customer together for everyone's benefit and profit.

It also means understanding and speaking another language: that of your customers. Successful optometrists do not sell glasses; they provide better vision. A perfume company does not sell smells; it offers hope. A number of years ago there was a famous ad from a chain-saw company. It pictured a man with a saw and some trees in the snow, a house and smoking chimney in the background. The message said nothing about the features of the saw; it simply stressed the benefit with the brief caption, "Take Home Some Warmth Today."

In the same light, we don't sell beds, breakfast, and booze: the *three "B's" industry*, as we are sometimes called. Instead, we offer the benefits of restful sleep, an enjoyable dining experience, and a relaxing social ambience.

INITIATIVE

The nature of our business often makes certain attributes more important than others as to their influence on success. For example, people in sales never have the luxury of completing a job. They must therefore take the initiative to strive constantly to do more and better. This could include extending the sale, rebooking business, seeking new and more profitable business sources, offering new services and amenities, concentrating on building up soft periods, and devising ways of overcoming newer and perhaps more modern competition.

If a hotel runs at 100% occupancy, the sales or marketing executive must focus on increasing the average daily rate and the average daily expenditure per guest. In most cases, no one is standing over the shoulders of those in the sales departments; such efforts are usually self-generated. Even general managers must look beyond their operational duties and take the initiative to sell.

To offer a very specific example, some years ago the Sheraton Corporation had an outstanding sales training film describing how to effectively sell four different types of customers who had four distinctively different sets of problems and objectives. In one segment, a business traveler checks into the hotel, and the general manager sees him, goes over, and introduces himself and welcomes him to the property. In the course of conversation he asks the guest if he was familiar with the company's new corporate rate plan. When the guest said that he wasn't, the general manager immediately handed him a folder and explained the procedures for applying. That's taking the initiative, above and beyond what might be specifically spelled out in a job description.

Everyone in selling must be able to seize the opportunity. When an opportunity does not present itself, people must go out and look for it. To put it simply, a person has to be a self-starter.

INCENTIVE

To take the initiative effectively, there must be some sort of realistic incentive. Incentives come in many forms: money, advancement and promotion, titles, prestige, awards and honors, and so on. But these are given out primarily as rewards for that which has already been accomplished.

There are also incentives (some of them variations on the above) that people must provide for themselves. Self-esteem and pride of accomplishment, for example, are types of incentives that must be started from within. In sales and marketing, we often have to provide our own incentives. We have to be self-starters, self-actuators, self-pushers, self-motivators.

One of the greatest incentives can be pride in our jobs. One of the reasons that this can work so well is that a sales executive cannot do the job to the "very max." Let's say that you look at your occupancy forecasts for next week: 83%. Fantastic! Close the office; hang out the "gone fishing" sign.

Not really. 83% occupancy means 17% vacancy, which in a 500-room hotel means 85 vacant rooms per day, a total of 595 rooms per week. Using a $200 per day folio charge per room night, this adds up to a potential loss of $119,000 for the week. Extending that for the year, assuming the same relative figures, this comes to $6,188,000 worth of "lost income" for an operation whose occupancy is more than 15 points above the national average!

When both of the present authors were growing up (instead of growing out), one of the pop songs of the day was "I'm Never Satisfied." That should be the theme song of every hotel sales/marketing executive. If you adopt it personally, it should go a long way toward providing the self-incentive that you need to continue to ask yourself: "What else should I be doing to improve the profit picture of this operation today, next week, next year, and five years down the road?"

INSTINCT

Instinct is another important but somewhat undefinable attribute that all successful hotel executives seem to have developed. It is not something that you can learn from a book. It comes about from a marriage of experience and common sense. A working word for instinct is "fieldwise"; another, perhaps not very scientific but one you can all relate to, is "gut feeling."

One particular area of our business where instinct often plays a key role is in the evaluation of business potentials. The marketplace keeps changing, new groups of customers emerge, and the demographics and psychographics of our current primary markets keep adjusting. We have to be able instinctively to evaluate the business potentials of this ever-shifting market. Should we adjust our marketing strategies with our current business? Should we try to develop some of the newly emerging segments, or try to cultivate more fully the ones we already attract? Should we change our image? Should we add new facilities, services, or amenities, or should we upgrade what we already have to offer? Facts and figures help, but despite in-depth research, a great deal of critical decision making must often be done with some degree of intuition and instinct.

IMAGINATION

One of the challenges of our industry (and there seem to be so many!) is that we cannot offer direct samples to a prospective customer. We are not like the car salesperson who can hand prospective customers the keys and suggest they take it around the block to see how quickly it accelerates and how smoothly it handles corners. Imagine saying to a potential guest: "Take the keys and go up to room 510 and lie down on the bed for 20 minutes. If you like it, why not take it for the night!"

We cannot make the "try it" type of commercial you so often see on late-night television. Imagine a commercial for a hotel along these lines: "People are our most important product. So I'll tell you what I'm going to do. For a limited time and a limited time only, I'm going to send you a room clerk and a maid—and if you're not entirely satisfied at the end of one week, just return the unused portion!''

Because nearly everyone in the lodging industry, at least on the surface, seems to offer the same three main products (rooms, food and beverage, and space), we have to be imaginative in the way we present our product. We have to package it with romance, glamor, intrigue, atmosphere, anticipation, and so on. We have to sell with flair. We must merchandise the difference (to those to whom such differences will be meaningful). If we do not have any distinguishing characteristics, we must create them.

Imagination means using your brain, sometimes in new and different directions. It also can mean the simpler yet significant things, such as changing the concept of "off season" to "value season" and then using your imagination to create programs and packages to entice those market segments that are perhaps budget-sensitive but rebel against being classified as cheap, second-class citizens.

Imagination means coming up with ideas to satisfy one of the most prevalent customer requests, especially from those involved with bringing in and managing conventions and other forms of group business. These requests usually are in the form of a challenge: "What can you do for us that will be different from that which was done in the past?" and "What can you offer that is different from what your competition is promoting?"

Imagination means: "What can we do to serve both groups whom we inadvertently booked into the same space at the same time? Just found out about it the day before they are coming in, no other space is available at ours or any nearby property—and neither group can change dates at the last moment."

INGENUITY

Imagination is fine—it is necessary—but basically it is a mental process. You have to translate the mental thoughts of imagination into the physical results through ingenuity—or if you like, innovation. Take the double-booking problem just stated. Imagination can lead you to say "What if we . . . ?, but it will take some ingenuity to actually do it.

Ingenuity is part of the problem-solving process, and since we are in the problem-solving business, it becomes one of the most important and essential abilities a sales or marketing executive can acquire. Here are a few thoughts to review when faced with a challenge:

1. *Don't try to invent the wheel.* There are really no new ideas, no new problems, no new solutions, just variations or new twists. To put it succinctly: The only constant is change; the only changes are variations on the constants.

2. *Don't try to solve a complex problem all at once.* Divide it up into components and work on each in a logical sequence (although sometimes, reassembling it and working at it from a different perspective may actually stimulate a creative approach). One past president of HSMA International, "Bud" Grice (quoted at the beginning of Chapter 7), had a great response to the age-old question "How do you eat an elephant?" His reply: "One bite at a time!"

3. *Use a checklist* to aid you in solving problems. But rather than a static checklist, use one that will spur the imagination. Here is a simple one used

in introductory creative thinking sessions which is particularly applicable to hospitality challenges. When faced with what seems a difficult problem, ask yourself:

- What can be added or extended?
- What can be deleted?
- What can be substituted?
- What can be rearranged or reorganized?
- What can be reversed?
- What can be combined?
- What other uses for the product or service (in addition to what was originally intended)?
- What negatives can be turned into positives (or, if you have a lemon, sell lemonade)?

Answering the applicable set of questions can start you on the road to having a reputation among your customers for innovation and ingenuity.

INSPIRATION

Inspiration is a management tool that can be of great importance toward reaching a hospitality career goal. It is a threefold responsibility. You have to:

1. Inspire yourself (self-motivation).
2. Inspire those who work with and for you (team spirit).
3. Inspire the customer (to become a salesperson for you).

If we had to pick out the component of inspiration that counts the most, a good case could be made for *confidence*.

We are a people industry, giving those we come in contact with the feeling that we can solve their problems, that we can offer them the best answers to their challenges or needs. The incidence of success in making the sale will be heavily influenced by how well we as people inspire confidence in other people.

INTEGRITY

Sincerity, believability, and integrity are the "confidence-inspiring yardsticks" with which our guests and clients are most likely to measure us. They are also the scales with which we are judged by our peers, our employees, and even our friendly competitors.

In our relationships, especially with customers, we must know what we can or cannot deliver. We need to know our property's limitations, our staff's capabilities, and our ability operationally to fulfill sales/marketing promises.

We work under the constraints of a buyer's market. Customers, clients, and guests have full choice as to where—or where not—to bring their business. They are the decision makers, and decisions are largely made according to an evaluation of how well we live up to promises and commitments.

As more and more properties come on line throughout the world, and as transportation makes it easier and quicker to reach all corners of the world, the user has more and more choice in the selection of both leisure and business destinations and properties. *Integrity* becomes one of the major products both a destination and an individual property has to offer within this highly competitive industry. Hotel executives make their reputation not on the features of the particular facility they happen to be associated with at the time, but more on the fact that regardless of where they are or have been, they have a track record of delivering at least—and very often *more*—than what they promised.

INDEPENDENCE

Most sales and marketing executives generally prefer to be as independent as possible. They want to be able to sit down with a customer, make decisions on behalf of the property, and have the freedom to negotiate, if needed, to make the sale without having to check back with "headquarters" every few minutes. And this is the way it should be. Operations staff should have confidence in their sales and marketing personnel that they can make the right decision for the good of the property. The sales and marketing staff should, of course, be given a framework of authority, commensurate with their responsibilities, to allow this independence. In addition to being a motivating factor that can be an inspirational incentive, such confidence on the part of operations can lead the customer to feel that there is maximum teamwork between operations and sales and marketing. This in turn makes the sales executive "look good" in the eyes of the potential client.

Ours is the type of business where the individual sales executive is considered by the customer to be a major part of the product. Thus it is essential to strive for independence by first establishing a reputation for ability ("earning your wings"). Then fight for increased authority. When you become the top person in the department or the organization, be sure to allow your people the same appropriate amount of independence—within a framework that spells out what they can and cannot do on their own. Under modern management concepts, one must be able to delegate both responsibility and authority.

INDIVIDUALITY

Independence can be looked upon as a partner with individuality. This is a rather personal trait—sort of a "personal identity" characteristic which in so many industries seems to be lost within the "corporate image, corporate uniform, corporate clone syndrome."

In the hospitality industry, however, we are people dealing with people. It is, therefore, particularly important that one be a recognizable individual (rather than a faceless robot), with a specific personality and a specific identity. This is especially true when out in the marketplace, since we usually do not carry our physical products with us. This specific identity and personal positioning statement must be incorporated within the dictates of good taste and a flexible corporate policy.

The most important product you will have to offer to the user of hospitality goods and services will be yourselves. So, to boil it down to basic, understandable terms, determine early in your career to:

- Stand out, in a positive way.
- Work on developing a unique personal and professional profile.

- Become highly visible among your customers, the hotel staff and employees, and among others in your industry.
- Develop a specific, memorable "personality."

In our business, especially when selling the intangibles, and even more so when selling the "product" to first-time users on a totally untested, unsampled basis, we must be aware that people will buy from us largely on the basis of personal impressions. It can be an added sales advantage to cultivate something distinctive, expand your best attributes, stress a personal feature, and stand out in some area personally and/or professionally. It could be something distinctive in dress or appearance, a gimmick, gadget, or giveaway with which you become associated, an unusual avocation or hobby, or some other characteristic that makes you, in a very positive way, a distinctive individual—in short, one who is easily remembered and sought after by your customers and potential clients.

INFECTIOUSNESS

Initially, this last success trait, infectiousness, may sound horribly negative. But among various definitions of this word is one that can be very positive: "tending to excite similar reactions on others."

Basically, this is a form of teamwork. When selling, one makes all sorts of promises and commitments to the customer. But one does not (and realistically could not) carry them all out by one's self. All the operating and service departments within the property share the load within their specialized areas of follow-through and fulfillment. All of what has been detailed so far in this summary chapter has been presented in terms of ourselves. But that's only part of the challenge of success. We then have to positively *infect* all who work with us with the traits of intelligence, initiative, incentive, imagination, integrity, and so on. Call it motivation, call it establishing "espirit de corps," call it acting as a role model, call it promoting teamwork—it is all of these and more. It brings to mind one of the classic definitions of motivation: "the creation of proper job attitudes so people will willingly perform to their fullest abilities."

THE 13TH "I"

Over the years, both authors have been privileged to visit hundreds of campuses around the world and, in one form or another, have presented these 12 "I's." We now realize that we have shortchanged our audiences. They should have been given a "baker's dozen." In fact, the one word left out may be more important than many of the others. This overlooked positive trait so essential to success in the hospitality industry, especially in the sales/marketing area, is *inquisitiveness*.

Those of you in college have a unique opportunity, especially during internships and other "in-field" training programs, to come in contact with those already in the hospitality industry. But perhaps even more important, you will have many opportunities to meet those who represent our many varied customer markets: the guests or the buyers.

So, when out on a practical exercise such as a student sales blitz, or when working between terms or perhaps even full-time while going to school: be *in-*

quisitive. Ask questions; talk with as many people as possible; never be afraid to ask the same types of questions that customers and guests ask you about your products and services: who, what, where, when, why, and how.

Don't be afraid that someone will jump on you with: "What kind of a dumb question was that? How many years did you go to school?" People are usually flattered to be asked questions or their opinions.

The George Bernard Shaw statement about communications seems to be making the rounds these days. It is to the effect that: "The danger of communications is the illusion that it has been accomplished." Let's paraphrase this: "The danger of *education* is the illusion that it has been accomplished."

Many of you now in school cannot wait to get out. Graduation is the ultimate goal; the completion of one's education is how so many look at it. Well, remember that the graduation exercise is called "commencement," which means that you are just *beginning* your education.

So when you finally enter the field, continue and expand your inquisitiveness. Those of you already in the industry: *Never give it up!*

THE CHALLENGE OF THE FUTURE

Many of you who are studying this book are currently preparing yourselves for a career in a field you will be entering within the next two or more years. Because the industry is such a rapidly changing one, such study must continue, particularly in a constantly changing competitive environment and an ever-increasing customer awareness, sophistication, and selectivity.

To meet the challenges of the future, it is important to the success of hotel executives (sales as well as operations) that they have a sound *background understanding* of:

- The history of the general growth of the hospitality industry
- The immediate past history of the industry, especially the trends that have taken place within the past decade or two
- The changing product, especially that representative of the type of property or chain/franchise with which they are currently affiliated
- Changes in competitive operations, especially new types of properties, or properties that formerly were not considered competitors
- Changes in the market, especially growth of specific market segments
- Changes in customer needs and wants, preferences and demands

This type of knowledge becomes particularly vital whenever one enters a transition period, which is what we seem to be in as we approach the twenty-first century.

THE FINAL THOUGHT

We are sure that by now all of you recognize that the authors enjoy alliteration (as portrayed by presenting a propensity for promulgating polysyllabical profundity). In addition to "success spelled with a dozen 'I's,' " you may have noted that each of the 11 chapters of the book started with the same letter: "S." Sounds like a game, but this was done for a very specific reason.

If we take the letter "S" and combine it with another letter, "U" (i.e., *you*), we end up with

As we indicated toward the end of Chapter 1, *profit production* defines both the responsibilities of the hospitality industry and the specific role of contemporary hotel sales.

appendix a

SAMPLE DEMOGRAPHIC AND LIFESTYLE PROFILES

Glossary of Terms

ADI
(Area of Dominant Influence)
A market defined as a television viewing region based on measurable viewing patterns of individuals making up the area. Each county in the U.S. is allocated exclusively to one ADI. ADIs are defined by the Arbitron Ratings Company.

Adults
Individuals age 18 or over living in households within the continental 48 states of the U.S.

Age
The current age in years of the adult head of household.

Children at Home
Indicates whether children age 18 or under are members of a household. Children's ages are represented by seven age ranges.

County Size "A"
A county located within the 25 largest metropolitan areas.

County Size "B"
A county which does not qualify as an "A" county but has population over 150,000 or is located within a metropolitan area with population over 150,000.

Credit Card Usage
The classification of a household as a regular user or non-user of particular credit cards.

Dual Income Household
A household which contains at least two sources of employment income.

Education
The highest level of education achieved by adults age 25 and over. This is a 1980 Census Bureau-based estimate.

Head of Household
The person in whose name the home is owned or rented. For homes owned or rented jointly by a married couple, the "head of household" is determined by the household members. The terms "head of household" and "householder" are interchangeable.

Home Ownership
The classification of a household as either owner occupied or renter occupied. Owner occupied households include owners of a house, townhouse, or condominium.

Household
A single dwelling unit occupied by a person or persons. Persons which make up a household can be individuals living alone, roommates, married couples or families.

Household Income
The combined income of all individuals living in a household. Income sources include employment, pensions, dividends, interest, etc.

Income Earners
The classification of a household as either containing one or two sources of employment income. All households which contain a single resident are automatically assigned one source of employment income.

Index
A measure of the over or under representation of a characteristic within a market area or segment. The base of reference for deriving an index is the population of U.S. adults or the collection of U.S. households. An index greater than 100 indicates an over-representation. An index less than 100 indicates an under representation.

Lifestyle
The types of interests and activities in which a single or married adult member of a household regularly participates.

Marital Status
The classification of a household as either married or single. Single includes divorced, separated or widowed.

Mean Number of Interests
The average number of lifestyle interests reported per household out of all households representing an ADI, county, lifestyle or consumer segment.

Median Age
The age at which half of all adult heads of household are younger and half are older.

Median Income
The income at which half of all households earn less and half earn more.

Occupation
The employment status of an adult.

Population
An aggregation of adults.

Race
The racial/ethnic origin of an adult. This is a 1989 Census Bureau-based estimate.

Rank
The arrangement of ADIs by degree of household participation in a lifestyle, or by the concentration of households in a consumer segment.

Stage of Family Lifecycle.
The classification of a household into a distinct category based on specific characteristics of the household. These characteristics include marital status, adult age, presence or absence of children, and children's ages.

Total U.S. Adult Population
(Population: 183,483,753   Households: 92,129,039)

	U.S. Population	U.S. Percent	U.S. Index		U.S. Households	U.S. Percent	U.S. Index
Occupation				**Stage in Family Lifecycle**			
Administrative	21,284,115	11.6	100	Single, 18 - 34, No Children	12,345,291	13.4	100
Blue Collar	15,045,668	8.2	100	Single, 35 - 44, No Children	5,435,613	5.9	100
Clerical	15,045,668	8.2	100	Single, 45 - 64, No Children	7,278,194	7.9	100
Homemaker	27,339,079	14.9	100	Single, 65+, No Children	8,291,614	9.0	100
Professional/Technical	44,953,519	24.5	100	Married, 18 - 34, No Children	5,067,097	5.5	100
Retired	33,761,011	18.4	100	Married, 35 - 44, No Children	3,500,903	3.8	100
Sales/Marketing	10,275,090	5.6	100	Married, 45 - 64, No Children	14,187,872	15.4	100
Student	6,238,448	3.4	100	Married, 65+, No Children	10,594,839	11.5	100
Other	9,541,155	5.2	100	Single, Any Child at Home	5,343,484	5.8	100
				Married, Child Age Under 13	11,516,130	12.5	100
Education (1980 Census)				Married, Child Age 13 - 18	8,568,001	9.3	100
Elementary (0-8 years)	24,257,635	18.3	100	**Household Income**			
High School (1-3 years)	20,280,973	15.3	100				
High School (4 years)	45,864,161	34.6	100	Under $20,000	33,074,325	35.9	100
College (1-3 years)	20,678,639	15.6	100	$20,000 - $29,999	15,017,033	16.3	100
College (4+ years)	21,473,972	16.2	100	$30,000 - $39,999	13,266,582	14.4	100
				$40,000 - $49,999	10,686,969	11.6	100
Race/Ethnicity				$50,000 - $74,999	12,805,936	13.9	100
				$75,000 and over	7,186,065	7.8	100
White	142,199,909	77.5	100				
Black	20,550,180	11.2	100	Median Income: $28,622			
Asian	1,467,870	0.8	100				
Hispanic	15,596,119	8.5	100	**Income Earners**			
American Indian	550,451	0.3	100				
Other	2,935,740	1.6	100	Married, One Income	33,350,712	36.2	100
				Married, Two Incomes	20,084,131	21.8	100

	U.S. Household	U.S. Percent	U.S. Index		U.S. Households	U.S. Percent	U.S. Index
				Single	38,694,196	42.0	100
Age of Head of Household				**Dual Income Households**			
18 - 24 years old	5,251,355	5.7	100	Children Age Under 13 Years	5,067,097	5.5	100
25 - 34 years old	20,636,905	22.4	100	Children Age 13 - 18 Years	4,145,807	4.5	100
35 - 44 years old	19,992,001	21.7	100	No Children	10,871,227	11.8	100
45 - 54 years old	14,095,743	15.3	100				
55 - 64 years old	12,805,936	13.9	100	**Age by Income**			
65 years and older	19,254,969	20.9	100				
				18 - 34, Income Under $30,000	14,556,388	15.8	100
Median Age: 45.1 Years				35 - 44, Income Under $30,000	7,554,581	8.2	100
				45 - 64, Income Under $30,000	10,871,227	11.8	100
Sex/Marital Status				65+, Income Under $30,000	15,201,291	16.5	100
Single Male	17,412,388	18.9	100	18 - 34, Income $30,000 - $49,999	7,646,710	8.3	100
Single Female	21,281,808	23.1	100	35 - 44, Income $30,000 - $49,999	6,541,162	7.1	100
Married	53,434,843	58.0	100	45 - 64, Income $30,000 - $49,999	7,278,194	7.9	100
				65+, Income $30,000 - $49,999	2,487,484	2.7	100
Children at Home							
At Least One Child	26,256,776	28.5	100	18 - 34, Income $50,000 - $74,999	2,763,871	3.0	100
Child Age Under 2	3,961,549	4.3	100	35 - 44, Income $50,000 - $74,999	3,961,549	4.3	100
Child Age 2 - 4	6,725,420	7.3	100	45 - 64, Income $50,000 - $74,999	5,159,226	5.6	100
Child Age 5 - 7	6,725,420	7.3	100	65+, Income $50,000 - $74,999	1,013,419	1.1	100
Child Age 8 - 10	6,817,549	7.4	100				
Child Age 11 - 12	4,698,581	5.1	100	18 - 34, Income $75,000 and over	921,290	1.0	100
Child Age 13 - 15	6,541,162	7.1	100	35 - 44, Income $75,000 and over	2,026,839	2.2	100
Child Age 16 - 18	7,093,936	7.7	100	45 - 64, Income $75,000 and over	3,593,033	3.9	100
				65+, Income $75,000 and over	644,903	0.7	100
Home Ownership				**Credit Card Usage**			
Owner	60,252,392	65.4	100	Travel/Entertainment	14,832,775	16.1	100
Renter	31,876,647	34.6	100	Bank Card	55,738,069	60.5	100
				Gas/Department Store	31,692,389	34.4	100
				No Credit Cards	26,072,518	28.3	100

Good Life Activities	U.S. Household	U.S. Percent	U.S. Index
Attend Cultural/Arts Events	15,385,550	16.7	100
Career Oriented Activities	11,239,743	12.2	100
Community/Civic Activities	12,068,904	13.1	100
Fashion Clothing	12,529,549	13.6	100
Fine Art/Antiques	9,581,420	10.4	100
Foreign Travel	12,161,033	13.2	100
Gourmet Cooking/Fine Foods	15,846,195	17.2	100
Home Furnishing/Decorating	18,517,937	20.1	100
Money Making Opportunities	9,489,291	10.3	100
Real Estate Investments	6,909,678	7.5	100
Stock/Bond Investments	12,068,904	13.1	100
Wines	11,055,485	12.0	100

High Tech	U.S. Household	U.S. Percent	U.S. Index
Electronics	7,738,839	8.4	100
Home Video Games	9,673,549	10.5	100
Personal/Home Computers	14,556,388	15.8	100
Photography	20,360,518	22.1	100
Science Fiction	7,278,194	7.9	100
Science/New Technology	8,015,226	8.7	100
Stereo/Records/Tapes	39,154,842	42.5	100
VCR Recording/Viewing	36,390,970	39.5	100
Watching Cable TV	37,680,777	40.9	100

Sports/Leisure	U.S. Household	U.S. Percent	U.S. Index
Bicycling Frequently	13,727,227	14.9	100
Boating/Sailing	12,621,678	13.7	100
Bowling	14,648,517	15.9	100
Golf	16,306,840	17.7	100
Physical Fitness/Exercise	30,218,325	32.8	100
Racquetball	6,633,291	7.2	100
Running/Jogging	11,424,001	12.4	100
Snow Skiing Frequently	8,015,226	8.7	100
Tennis Frequently	6,633,291	7.2	100
Walking for Health	37,220,132	40.4	100
Watching Sports on TV	35,561,809	38.6	100

Outdoor	U.S. Household	U.S. Percent	U.S. Index
Camping/Hiking	20,821,163	22.6	100
Fishing Frequently	22,571,615	24.5	100
Hunting/Shooting	14,740,646	16.0	100
Motorcycles	6,356,904	6.9	100
Recreational Vehicles/4-WD	7,646,710	8.3	100
Wildlife/Environmental	14,372,130	15.6	100

Domestic	U.S. Household	U.S. Percent	U.S. Index
Automotive Work	13,266,582	14.4	100
Avid Book Reading	35,561,809	38.6	100
Bible/Devotional Reading	17,136,001	18.6	100
Coin/Stamp Collecting	7,923,097	8.6	100
Collectibles/Collections	10,226,323	11.1	100
Crafts	24,229,937	26.3	100
Crossword Puzzles	19,899,872	21.6	100
Current Affairs/Politics	15,569,808	16.9	100
Entering Sweepstakes	15,385,550	16.7	100
Gardening	31,231,744	33.9	100
Grandchildren	18,425,808	20.0	100
Health Foods/Vitamins	14,003,614	15.2	100
Home Workshop	21,097,550	22.9	100
Household Pets	28,836,389	31.3	100
Needlework/Knitting	19,162,840	20.8	100
Self-Improvement	15,201,291	16.5	100
Sewing	18,794,324	20.4	100
Shopping by Catalog	23,308,647	25.3	100
Veterans Benefits/Programs	5,712,000	6.2	100

Mean Number of Interests: 9.4

POPULATION counts are used to determine the projected counts for RACE/ETHNICITY, OCCUPATION and EDUCATION.

HOUSEHOLD counts are used to determine the projected counts for all other categories.

Footnotes:
1. Education population counts are based on 1980 census population data for adults 25 years and older.
2. Race/Ethnicity population counts are based on 1989 census population updates.
3. All other population/household counts are projected to the 1989 census updates.

Salt Lake City, UT

Demographics
Base Index US = 100

Occupation	Population	%	Index
Administrative	118,116	10.3	89
Blue Collar	108,942	9.5	116
Clerical	82,566	7.2	88
Homemaker	184,628	16.1	108
Professional/Technical	290,129	25.3	103
Retired	182,334	15.9	86
Sales/Marketing	61,925	5.4	96
Student	67,659	5.9	174
Other	50,457	4.4	85

Education (1980 Census)

	Population	%	Index
Elementary (0-8 years)	58,317	7.4	40
High School (1-3 years)	103,238	13.1	86
High School (4 years)	287,647	36.5	105
College (1-3 years)	186,773	23.7	152
College (4+ years)	152,098	19.3	119

Race/Ethnicity

	Population	%	Index
White	1,048,135	91.4	118
Black	6,881	0.6	5
Asian	6,881	0.6	75
Hispanic	59,631	5.2	61
American Indian	9,174	0.8	267
Other	17,201	1.5	94

Age of Head of Household	Households	%	Index
18-24 years old	52,202	8.9	156
25-34 years old	154,845	26.4	118
35-44 years old	128,451	21.9	101
45-54 years old	81,528	13.9	91
55-64 years old	66,278	11.3	81
65 years and older	103,817	17.7	85
Median Age	**41.7 years**		

Sex/Marital Status

	Households	%	Index
Single Male	99,711	17.0	90
Single Female	109,095	18.6	81
Married	377,728	64.4	111

Children At Home

	Households	%	Index
At Least One Child	228,748	39.0	137
Child Age Under 2	48,682	8.3	193
Child Age 2-4	78,596	13.4	184
Child Age 5-7	81,528	13.9	190
Child Age 8-10	83,874	14.3	193
Child Age 11-12	58,653	10.0	196
Child Age 13-15	66,865	11.4	161
Child Age 16-18	61,586	10.5	136

Home Ownership

	Households	%	Index
Owner	422,891	72.1	110
Renter	163,643	27.9	81

Stage in Family Lifecycle	Households	%	Index
Single, 18-34, No Children	79,769	13.6	101
Single, 35-44, "	26,394	4.5	76
Single, 45-64, "	27,567	4.7	59
Single, 65+, "	39,298	6.7	74
Married, 18-34, "	36,365	6.2	113
Married, 35-44, "	17,009	2.9	76
Married, 45-64, "	75,663	12.9	84
Married, 65+, "	61,586	10.5	91
Single, Any Child at Home	35,779	6.1	105
Married, Child Age Under 13	107,922	18.4	147
Married, Child Age 13-18	79,182	13.5	145

Household Income

	Households	%	Index
Under $20,000	208,806	35.6	99
$20,000-$29,999	113,201	19.3	118
$30,000-$39,999	101,470	17.3	120
$40,000-$49,999	69,211	11.8	102
$50,000-$74,999	66,865	11.4	82
$75,000 and over	26,981	4.6	59
Median Income	**$27,454**		

Income Earners

	Households	%	Index
Married, One Income	254,556	43.4	120
Married, Two Incomes	123,759	21.1	97
Single	208,806	35.6	85

Dual Income Households

	Households	%	Index
Children Age Under 13 years	37,538	6.4	116
Children Age 13-18 years	32,259	5.5	122
No Children	53,375	9.1	77

Age By Income

	Households	%	Index
18-34, Income under $30,000	131,970	22.5	142
35-44, "	49,855	8.5	104
45-64, "	54,548	9.3	79
65+, "	85,634	14.6	88
18-34, Income $30,000-$49,999	58,653	10.0	120
35-44, "	50,442	8.6	121
45-64, "	49,855	8.5	108
65+, "	11,731	2.0	74
18-34, Income $50,000-$74,999	12,317	2.1	70
35-44, "	20,529	3.5	81
45-64, "	29,913	5.1	91
65+, "	4,106	0.7	64
18-34, Income $75,000 and over	3,519	0.6	60
35-44, "	7,625	1.3	59
45-64, "	13,490	2.3	59
65+, "	2,346	0.4	57

Credit Card Usage

	Households	%	Index
Travel/Entertainment	64,519	11.0	68
Bank Card	340,776	58.1	96
Gas/Department Store	158,364	27.0	78
No Credit Cards	198,835	33.9	120

Lifestyles
Base Index US = 100

Salt Lake City, UT

The Top Ten Lifestyles Ranked by Index

Snow Skiing Frequently	254	**Racquetball**	175
Camping/Hiking	218	**Personal/Home Computers**	142
Recreational Vehicles/4-WD	211	**Fishing Frequently**	140
Hunting/Shooting	180	**Self-Improvement**	132
Motorcycles	177	**Golf**	129

The "Good Life" Activities	Households	%	Index
Attend Cultural/Arts Events	121,999	20.8	125
Career-Oriented Activities	75,663	12.9	106
Community/Civic Activities	76,836	13.1	100
Fashion Clothing	69,211	11.8	87
Fine Art/Antiques	58,067	9.9	95
Foreign Travel	76,249	13.0	98
Gourmet Cooking/Fine Foods	85,634	14.6	85
Home Furnishing/Decorating	117,893	20.1	100
Money Making Opportunities	58,067	9.9	96
Real Estate Investments	36,365	6.2	83
Stock/Bond Investments	69,798	11.9	91
Wines	55,721	9.5	79

High Tech Activities			
Electronics	54,548	9.3	111
Home Video Games	73,903	12.6	120
Personal/Home Computers	131,384	22.4	142
Photography	147,220	25.1	114
Science Fiction	53,375	9.1	115
Science/New Technology	58,067	9.9	114
Stereo/Records/Tapes	266,286	45.4	107
VCR Recording/Viewing	244,585	41.7	106
Watching Cable TV	210,566	35.9	88

Sports/Leisure Activities			
Bicycling Frequently	99,124	16.9	113
Boating/Sailing	96,778	16.5	120
Bowling	96,192	16.4	103
Golf	134,316	22.9	129
Physical Fitness/Exercise	213,498	36.4	111
Racquetball	73,903	12.6	175
Running/Jogging	83,874	14.3	115
Snow Skiing Frequently	129,624	22.1	254
Tennis Frequently	43,990	7.5	104
Walking for Health	233,441	39.8	99
Watching Sports on TV	222,296	37.9	98

Outdoor Activities	Households	%	Index
Camping/Hiking	288,575	49.2	218
Fishing Frequently	200,595	34.2	140
Hunting/Shooting	168,922	28.8	180
Motorcycles	71,557	12.2	177
Recreational Vehicles/4-WD	102,643	17.5	211
Wildlife/Environmental	102,057	17.4	112

Domestic Activities			
Automotive Work	104,403	17.8	124
Avid Book Reading	241,652	41.2	107
Bible/Devotional Reading	136,662	23.3	125
Coin/Stamp Collecting	51,028	8.7	101
Collectibles/Collections	56,894	9.7	87
Crafts	182,412	31.1	118
Crossword Puzzles	88,567	15.1	70
Current Affairs/Politics	97,951	16.7	99
Entering Sweepstakes	90,326	15.4	92
Gardening	232,854	39.7	117
Grandchildren	130,797	22.3	112
Health Foods/Vitamins	88,567	15.1	99
Home Workshop	146,634	25.0	109
Household Pets	182,999	31.2	100
Needlework/Knitting	146,634	25.0	120
Self-Improvement	127,864	21.8	132
Sewing	151,326	25.8	126
Shopping by Catalog	135,489	23.1	91
Veterans Benefits/Programs	29,913	5.1	82

Mean Number of Interests		10.7	114

appendix b

OTHER SELECTED SOURCES FOR MARKET INFORMATION

In recent years, there has been a rapid growth in the number of journals, newsletters, magazines, and newspaper feature sections that offer a wide variety of sources for obtaining market, product, and competitive information.

Some of these have been mentioned in various chapters throughout the text. Others are included in the listings of the trade press and industry trade associations that follow this appendix.

Some further sources are listed here as a guide to the *variety* of information outlets that can be useful to the student and the industry executive alike. This list is by no means intended to be all-inclusive.* Rather, it is representative of the *different types* of resources one can utilize in obtaining important sales and marketing information, especially that related to industry trends, projections, and forecasts.

Some publications are included whose names may not at first glance seem pertinent to hotel sales. Though they may have titles indicating their main topic area is food service or training, they often carry articles and commentaries on the lodging industry or feature general topics relating to key aspects of sales, such as human resources development and communications skills.

GOVERNMENT SOURCES

U.S. Commerce Department
Bureau of the Census
Center for Demographic Studies
Washington, DC 20233

U.S. Government
Superintendent of Documents
Washington, DC 20402

*One must reconcile the "sins of commission" with the "sins of omission." No matter how extensive the listing, there are bound to be some inadvertent omissions. Besides, all texts have space limitations. So, the publications listed here are representative of those regularly received by your present authors.

State Government
Each state has a number of agencies and bureaus that collect and furnish market analysis information—as do state, area, and municipal government travel and tourism offices.

Example: New Jersey has several State Data Centers, such as the Office of Demographic & Economic Analysis, the Department of Community Affairs—Division of Housing, and the Bureau of Economic Research, Rutgers University. A full state-by-state, city-by-city listing of over 600 similar sources is contained in "The Insider's Guide to Demographic Know-How," published by the American Demographic Press, P.O. Box 68, Ithaca, NY 14851.

COLLEGES AND EDUCATIONAL ORGANIZATIONS

Arizona Hospitality Trends
Arizona Hospitality Research and Resource Center
Northern Arizona University School of Hotel
and Restaurant Management
Flagstaff, AZ 86011

The Cornell Hotel and Restaurant Administration Quarterly
20 Thornwood Drive, Suite 106
Ithaca, NY 14850

Hospitality Research Journal
CHRIE Publications Department
1200 17th Street, NW, 7th Floor
Washington, DC 20036–3097

Hosteur Magazine
CHRIE Publications Department
1200 17th Street, NW, 7th Floor
Washington, DC 20036–3097

The Journal of the Canadian Hospitality Institute
8 Lomond Drive
Etobicoke, Ontario, Canada M8X 2W3

Tourism Today
College of Tourism & Hotel Management
81 Aglanjia Avenue, P.O. Box 281
Nicosia, Cyprus

MAGAZINES AND NEWSPAPERS

Valuable and up-to-date sales and marketing information, particularly consumer profiles, new products and services, and hospitality industry surveys and forecasts, can be found in many business magazines such as *Newsweek* and *Time Magazine*. In addition, their travel departments often have reports, usually in handy chart and table form, on current market and tourism trends, based on demographic and psychographic surveys of their subscribers.

Newspapers also offer localized information on new property construction, area growth, travel and tourism growth, and in some instances include detailed financial data on individual properties as part of feature stories.

Among international newspapers, *USA Today* (especially the Business Travel Section) and the *International Herald Tribune* (now available in the United States) regularly showcase articles on tourism, travel, and the lodging industry.

NEWSLETTERS

Here is a potpourri sampling of some representative periodicals that are printed in newsletter format. In addition to offering sales and business administration information, techniques, examples, and case studies, they can be sources for sales-idea stimulation and adaptation.

Bottom Line Personal
P.O. Box 58446
Boulder, CO 80322

Communication Briefings
(A Monthly Idea Source for Decision Makers)
700 Black Horse Pike, Suite 110
Blackwood, NJ 08012

The Competitive Advantage
(The Newsletter for Sales and Marketing Professionals)
P.O. Box 10092
Portland, OR 97210

Creative Training Techniques
(A Newsletter of Tips, Tactics, and How-Tos for Delivering Effective Training)
Lakewood Publications, Inc.
50 S. Ninth
Minneapolis, MN 55402

The Executive Speechwriter Newsletter
(A Newsletter of Quotes, Jokes, Stories and Ideas for the Executive Speechmaker)
Words Ink
Emerson Falls

St. Johnsbury, VT 05819

Practical Supervision
Professional Training Associates, Inc.
210 Commerce Blvd.
Round Rock, TX 78664

Restaurant Personnel Management
(Serving the Total Hospitality Industry's Human Resource Needs)
Fairfield Research, Inc.
5620 South 49th Street
Lincoln, NE 68516

REPRINTS

A number of magazines and journals have compiled reprints of articles either written by a featured columnist or on a common topic. These can be particularly helpful as sources of information on specific sales and marketing subjects.

A Decade of Howard Feiertag's Sales Clinic
Hotel & Motel Management Magazine
7500 Old Oak Blvd.
Cleveland, OH 44130

The 50 Best Hotel Slogans You've Ever Heard
100 Creative Packages
50 Sales and Promotion Ideas
750 Guest Services Ideas
c/o Innkeeping World
P.O. Box 84108
Seattle, WA 98124

How To Increase Occupancy
(A Guide to Profitable Markets)
HSMAI Marketing Review Reprint Series
Hotel Sales and Marketing Association International
1300 L Street, NW, Suite 800
Washington, DC 20005

ADDITIONAL SOURCES

There are other miscellaneous but useful sources of information such as credit card companies, particularly American Express. They conduct periodic surveys of the hospitality industry and publish reports on the habits and preferences of different travel market segments.

A comprehensive listing of books and other publications devoted to marketing in general, and the selling and servicing of specific market segments, is contained in the monthly "Marketing Tools Alert," a special news supplement to *American Demographics* magazine, P.O. Box 68, Ithaca, NY 14851.

appendix c

SAMPLE JOB DESCRIPTIONS

One of the challenges in the sales and marketing area of hotel management is the preparation of job descriptions—and the equating of job titles and specifications within the industry.

The functions of a sous chef, or a night auditor, or a waiter in one property are basically the same as those of their counterparts in similar properties around the world.

However, a sales manager in one hotel may be the "top" person and head of the department, responsible for all promotional as well as servicing activities, including advertising, public relations, internal merchandising, and convention and banquet servicing.

In another operation, the sales manager may be positioned on a relatively low rung of the departmental organizational ladder. There may be a considerable hierarchy above that title, including assistant sales director, sales director, advertising director, convention services director, assistant marketing director, marketing director, and vice president–marketing.

In another property, the sales manager may spend most of the time out on the streets making sales calls and booking business. And in yet another facility, the sales manager may serve as an on-property departmental administrator, primarily responsible for such functions as accounts allocation and records management.

For purposes of illustration, therefore, we will present two basically generic descriptions which represent (1) the common entry-level position and (2) the top-level position that many "entry-levels" will aspire to reach.

ENTRY-LEVEL POSITION

Position Title: Account Executive

Reports to: Sales Manager

Supervises: Sales Interns

Primary Function:

Develops, solicits, books, and rebooks business from those accounts within the designated market segment

(and/or geographic area) assigned by the sales manager.

Specific Duties:

1. Maintains periodic contact with and calls upon the decision-makers within all currently assigned accounts.
2. Seeks out, qualifies, and develops new accounts within the assigned market segment or geographic area.
3. Refers other potential business from existing accounts to the proper departments, other sales specialists, and, where applicable, to affiliated properties within the chain or franchise system.
4. Contacts and maintains liaison with such third-party or intermediate decision-makers as travel agents, wholesalers, tour operators, transportation company officials, incentive travel managers, and multiple management company administrators.
5. Within the established weekly quota, conducts at least the minimum number of required outside sales calls, telephone calls, and on-site inspections.
6. Maintains individual booking quotas as they relate to sales department forecasts and goals.
7. Prepares and submits sales activities log, report-of-interview forms, booking and lost-business reports, and similar forms as determined by sales office procedures and systems.
8. Maintains proper liaison with competitors, particularly in situations involving joint sales efforts and community promotion. Periodically "shops the competition" to determine comparative strengths and weaknesses.
9. Supervises sales interns and student sales and phone-blitz program participants.
10. Serves as MOD (Manager on Duty) in accordance with established schedules.
11. Participates in community activities through membership in local organizations, civic, and service clubs.

NOTE: At one time it was a fairly standard industry philosophy that the person booking a piece of business would be on property to service the account. However, it has become more prevalent for account executives to be strictly "outside" sales specialists. After a booking, the account is turned over to an "inside" convention service specialist who then takes on the responsibility of coordinating the fulfillment of the booking requirements.

For this reason, the preceding job description does not include any specific servicing duties.

TOP-LEVEL POSITION

Position Title: Vice President–Marketing

Reports To: The Company President

Supervises: Director of Sales
Director of Advertising & Public
   Relations
Director of Convention Services
Banquet & Catering Manager

Coordinates With: General Manager
Food & Beverage Director
Rooms Division Manager
Comptroller

Primary Function:

Overall responsibility for researching, planning, implementing, directing, evaluating, and controlling the market activities of the property, as they relate to the attainment of the annual fiscal forecast for total revenue from all outlets. Additionally responsible for providing marketing support to such operating departments as rooms and food & beverage, towards achieving their specific departmental goals.

Specific Duties:

1. Within the framework of established policies, develops annual marketing plans and supporting action plans, to include:
   a. Evaluation of sales trends, competitive developments, and changes in market and customer-segment demand.
   b. Identification of opportunities for (as well as challenges to) profitably increasing sales in all rooms, food, beverage, and other income-generating outlets.
   c. Recommendation of appropriate annual sales and revenue goals, including appropriate sub-goals for each market mix segment.
   d. Establishment of sales quotas for each individual sales executive.
   e. Preparation of specific programs to achieve targeted goals.
2. Recommends and prepares detailed task basis annual budget necessary to carry out marketing programs, including appropriate "benchmarks" and controls to ensure that expenditures conform to established forecasts and limits.
3. Supervises all personnel involved in outside solicitation of travel agents, tour operators, incentive buyers, association and corporate meeting planners, traffic managers, and other prospects, clients, and customers.
4. Coordinates and evaluates the marketing activities of all sales and servicing personnel to insure that sales commitments are fulfilled through proper servicing follow-through.
5. Works with the designated advertising agency and public relations firm to create, develop, and implement media advertising, direct mail and supporting collateral, and public relations programs and campaigns consistent with the marketing goals of the property.
6. Supervises preparation and distribution of all internal sales and merchandising literature and in-house advertising messages, including those placed in the rooms, food & beverage outlets, lobby areas, and public space.
7. To provide a basis for future planning, maintains an effective system of reporting sales and advertising results for use in measuring progress towards marketing goals, including measurement of the individual performance of sales personnel.
8. Recommends changes in the organization and administration of marketing activities, including review of policies, systems, and procedures.
9. Actively aids in the selection, training, assignments, review and evaluation, salary adjustments, and re-assignment of sales and marketing personnel.
10. Responsible for the training and human resource development programs of sales and marketing personnel, ensuring that they are given the knowledge, tools, and techniques necessary for proper job performance as well as for potential career advancement. Additionally, ensures that all sales and servicing personnel are familiar with all applicable policies, procedures, and regulations, as well as specific responsibilities and equivalent frameworks of authority.
11. Develops and conducts selling and servicing training programs for the guest-contact personnel of the operating departments.
12. Similarly aids in the human resources management of all personnel engaged in the on-property servicing of business.
13. Ensures that statistical data and financial information used in sales and marketing activities are properly maintained by the operating departments where they originate, including accounting, reservations, front office, guest credit, and guest history.
14. Through department head meetings and participation on the property's executive or management committee, keeps all sales and operations personnel informed of planned advertising cam-

paigns, public relations programs, special promotions, and changes in sales and marketing objectives.

15. Advises the company president of competitive and customer market developments and challenges, interprets their significance and likely impact, and recommends appropriate changes in facilities, services, amenities, rate and price structures, and promotional methods and outlets.

16. Promotes the image of the company and property through applicable personal and professional visi-

bility within the community and among suppliers, competitors, customers, and potential clients.

17. Represents the company within the industry through membership in the Hotel Sales and Marketing Association International, Meeting Planners International, and other hotel and customer organizations.

18. Represents the company and participates where appropriate at trade shows, exhibitions, and cooperative promotional and familiarization programs.

appendix d

KEY HOSPITALITY TRADE ASSOCIATIONS

Trade associations and professional societies offer members of the hospitality industry a wide variety of benefits, including education and other career advancement assistance.

The following list is a selective representation of those organizations in the hospitality and travel field, including hospitality educators and customer groups. Most of them hold annual conventions, seminars, and workshops. In addition, they publish books and journals, newsletters, and other periodicals containing articles on current topics and issues; in effect, they are a primary means of continuing education for those in the field.

We wish to thank the Council on Hotel, Restaurant, and Institutional Education (CHRIE) for providing the basic listings.

Note: A number of associations are totally "volunteer leadership" organizations, with no paid staff or permanent office. In such cases, the addresses shown are those of the current president or secretary and will often change from year to year.

Air Transport Association of America
1709 New York Avenue, NW
Washington, DC 20006

American Correctional Food Service Association
304 West Liberty Street, Suite 301
Louisville, KY 40202

American Culinary Federation
10 San Bartolla Road
St. Augustine, FL 32084-3466

American Dietetic Association
216 West Jackson Blvd., Suite 800
Chicago, IL 60606-6995

American Hotel & Motel Association
1201 New York Avenue, NW
Washington, DC 20005-3917

American Hotel Foundation
610 South Belardo Road, Suite 650
Palm Springs, CA 92264

American Institute of Wine & Food
1550 Bryant Street
San Francisco, CA 94103

American School Food Service Association
1600 Duke Street, 7th Floor
Alexandria, VA 22314

American Society for Hospital Food Service Administrators
840 North Lake Shore Drive
Chicago, IL 60611

American Society of Association Executives
1575 Eye Street, NW
Washington, DC 20005

American Society of Travel Agents
1101 King Street
Alexandria, VA 22314

Association for International Practical Training
10400 Little Patuxent Parkway, Suite 250
Columbia, MD 21044-3510

Association of Travel Marketing Executives
P.O. Box 43563
Washington, DC 20010

Club Managers Association of America
1733 King Street
Alexandria, VA 22314

Commercial Food Equipment Service Association
9240 North Meridien Street, Suite 355
Indianapolis, IN 46260

Consortium of Hospitality Research Information Services
317 Day Hall
Cornell University
Ithaca, NY 14853

Convention Liaison Council
1575 Eye Street, NW, Suite 1200
Washington, DC 20005

Council of Engineering and Scientific Society Executives
2000 Florida Avenue, NW
Washington, DC 20009

Council of Hotel and Restaurant Trainers
c/o Rax of Indiana
9025 Coldwater Road, Suite 100
Fort Wayne, IN 46825

Council on Hotel, Restaurant, and Institutional Education
1200 17th Street, NW, 7th Floor
Washington, DC 20036

Dietary Managers Association
400 East 22nd Street
Lombard, IL 60148

Distributive Education Clubs of America, Inc.
1908 Association Drive
Reston, VA 22091

**Educational Foundation of the National
Restaurant Association**
250 South Wacker Drive, Suite 1400
Chicago, IL 60606

**Educational Institute of the American Hotel
& Motel Association**
P.O. Box 1240
East Lansing, MI 48826

Exhibit Designers and Producers Association
611 East Wells
Milwaukee, WI 53202

Exposition Service Contractors Association
400 S. Houston St., Suite 210
Dallas, TX 75202

Foodservice and Lodging Institute
1919 Pennsylvania Avenue, NW
Washington, DC 20006

Foodservice Consultants Society International
12345 30th Avenue, NE, Suite H
Seattle, WA 98125

Hotel Sales and Marketing Association International
1300 L Street, NW, Suite 800
Washington, DC 20005

Inflight Food Service Association
304 West Liberty Street, Suite 301
Louisville, KY 40202

Institute of Association Management Companies
104 Wilmot Road, Suite 201
Deerfield, IL 60015-5195

Insurance Conference Planners Association
2801 Woodbine Drive
North Vancouver, BC, Canada V7R 2R9

**International Association of Amusement Parks
and Attractions**
4230 King Street
Alexandria, VA 22302

International Association of Auditorium Managers
4425 W. Airport Freeway, Suite 590
Irving, TX 75062

International Association of Conference Centers
900 South Highway Drive
Fenton, MO 63026

**International Association of Convention
and Visitors Bureaus**
P.O. Box 758
Champaign, IL 61820

International Association of Cooking Professionals
304 West Liberty Street, Suite 301
Louisville, KY 40202

International Association of Hospitality Accountants
P.O. Box 27649
Austin, TX 78755-1649

International Exhibitors Association
5501 Backlick Road, Suite 200
Springfield, VA 22151

International Food Service Executives Association
1100 South State Road #7, Suite 103
Margate, FL 33068

**International Foodservice Manufacturers
Association**
321 North Clark Street, Suite 2900
Chicago, IL 60610

International Hotel Association
80, rue de la Roquette
75544 Paris, France (Cedex 11)

International Special Events Society
7080 Hollywood Blvd., Suite 410
Los Angeles, CA 90028

Meeting Planners International
1950 Stemmons Highway, Suite 5018
Dallas, TX 75207-3109

**National Association of Black Hospitality
Professionals**
P.O. Box 5443
Plainfield, NJ 07060

National Association of Catering Executives
304 West Liberty Street, Suite 301
Louisville, KY 40202

**National Association of Colleges and University
Food Services**
1405 South Harrison, Suite 303-4
East Lansing, MI 48824

National Association of Exposition Managers
334 East Garfield Road — P.O. Box 377
Aurora, OH 44202-0377

**National Association of Food Equipment
Manufacturers**
111 East Wacker Drive
Chicago, IL 60601

National Club Association
3050 K Street, NW, Suite 330
Washington, DC 20007

National Coalition of Black Meeting Planners
50 F Street, NW, Suite 1040
Washington, DC 20001

National Executive Housekeepers Association
1001 Eastwind Drive, Suite 301
Westerville, OH 43081

National Restaurant Association
1200 17th Street, NW
Washington, DC 20036

National Tour Association
P.O. Box 3071
Lexington, KY 40596

Professional Convention Management Association
100 Vestavia Office Park, Suite 220
Birmingham, AL 35216

Professional Guides Association of America
2416 South Eads Street
Alexandria, VA 22202

Religious Conference Management Association
One Hoosier Dome, Suite 120
Indianapolis, IN 46225

Roundtable for Women in Foodservice, Inc.
425 Central Park West, Suite 2A
New York, NY 10025

Society for Foodservice Management
304 West Liberty Street, Suite 301
Louisville, KY 40202

Society for the Advancement of Foodservice Research
304 West Liberty Street, Suite 301
Louisville, KY 40202

Society of American Travel Writers
1155 Connecticut Avenue NW
Washington, DC 20036

Society of Corporate Meeting Professionals
2600 Garden Road, Suite 208
Monterey, CA 93940

Society of Government Meeting Planners
Frankenberger Place
219 E. Main Street
Mechanicsburg, PA 17055

Society of Incentive Travel Executives
271 Madison Avenue
New York, NY 10016–1001

Society of Travel Agents in Government
6935 Wisconsin Avenue, NW, #200
Washington, DC 20815

Society of Travel & Tourism Educators Inc.
12605 State Fair
Detroit, MI 48205

Travel and Tourism Government Affairs Council
2 Lafayette Centre
1133 21st Street, NW
Washington, DC 20036

Travel and Tourism Research Association
P.O. Box 8066, Foothill Station
Salt Lake City, UT 84108

Travel Industry Association of America
2 Lafayette Centre
1133 21st Street, NW
Washington, DC 20036

Universal Federation of Travel Agents Associations
17 rue Grimaldi
MC 98000 Monaco

U.S. Travel Data Center
2 Lafayette Centre
1133 21st Street, NW
Washington, DC 20036

appendix e

HOSPITALITY TRADE PRESS

The following is a representative (but not all-inclusive) listing of the major hospitality industry publications that are distributed on a national or international basis.

It is highly recommended that students of hotel management, as well as those working in the lodging industry, read publications devoted to allied disciplines such as food service and travel. Many sales, marketing, and merchandising concepts apply to all facets of the industry. For example, a sales or servicing technique successfully employed by a free-standing restaurant or by the airlines could be adapted and tailored for use in the hotel field.

Similarly, articles in customer and consumer publications often focus on topics of interest or issues of concern to both the buyer and the seller of hotel accommodations and services.

The following publications are listed in alphabetical order within four major classifications: Hotel/Restaurant, Tour and Travel, Convention and Corporate Customer, and Leisure Travel Consumer.

HOTEL/RESTAURANT TRADE PRESS

Canadian Hotel & Restaurant
Box 9100, Postal Station A
Toronto, Ontario, Canada M5W 1V5

Catering & Hotel Management
Dingwall Avenue, Croydon
Surrey, England

Catering Today
P.O. Box 222
Santa Claus, IN 47579

The Cornell Quarterly
255 Statler Hall
Cornell University
Ithaca, NY 14853

Food & Wine
1120 Avenue of The Americas
New York, NY 10036

Food-Service East
545 Boylston Street
Boston, MA 02116

Foodservice Hospitality
980 Yonge St., Suite 400
Toronto, Ontario, Canada M4W 9Z9

Hospitality & Convention News
45–50 Porter Street
Prahran, Victoria, 3181 Australia

Hotel & Catering Review
22 Brookfield Avenue
Blackrock, Co. Dublin, Ireland

Hotel & Motel Management
7500 Old Oak Blvd.
Cleveland, OH 44130

Hotel & Resort Industry
488 Madison Avenue
New York, NY 10022

Hotel & Resort Update
8685 West 96th Street
Overland Park, KS 66212

Hotel/Motel Insider
2718 Dryden Drive
Madison, WI 53704–3086

Hotelier
980 Yonge Street, Suite 400
Toronto, Ontario, Canada M4W 2J8

Hotels & Restaurants International
P.O. Box 5080
1350 E. Touhy Avenue
Des Plaines, IL 60017

HSMAI Marketing Review
(Publication of the Hotel Sales &
Marketing Association International)
1300 L Street NW, Suite 800
Washington, DC 20005

Innkeeping World
P.O. Box 84108
Seattle, Washington 98124

International Hotel Management
1 Pont Street
London SW1, England

Lodging
(Publication of the American
Hotel & Motel Association)
1201 New York Avenue NW
Washington, DC 20005

Lodging Hospitality
1100 Superior Avenue
Cleveland, OH 44144

Nation's Restaurant News
425 Park Avenue
New York, NY 10022

Resorts & Incentives
1515 Broadway
New York, NY 10036

Restaurant & Hotel Management
Possmoorweg 5
2000 Hamburg 60, Germany

Restaurant Business
633 Third Avenue
New York, NY 10017

Restaurants & Institutions
1350 East Touhy Avenue
P.O. Box 5080
Des Plaines, IL 60017–5080

Restaurants USA
(Publication of The National
Restaurant Association)
1200 17th Street NW
Washington, DC 20036

TOUR AND TRAVEL PUBLICATIONS

USA and Canada

Agent Canada
1425 W. Pender Street
Vancouver, BC, Canada V6G 2S3

ASTA Agency Management
666 Fifth Avenue
New York, NY 10103

ASU Travel Guide
1325 Columbus Avenue
San Francisco, CA 94133

Cabell Travel Publications
11411 Cumpston
N. Hollywood, CA 91601

Canadian Travel Courier
Maclean Hunter Building
777 Bay Street
Toronto, Ontario, Canada M5W 1A7

Canadian Travel Press
310 Dupont Street
Toronto, Ontario, Canada M5R 1V9

Jax Fax Travel Marketing Magazine
397 Post Road, P.O. Box 4013
Darien, Conn. 06820–1413

News Line
(Publication of Travel Industry Association
of America)
Two Lafayette Centre
1133 21st Street NW
Washington, DC 20036

Tourism Canada
4E–235 Queen Street
Ottawa, Ontario, Canada K1A OH6

Travel Agent Magazine
825 7th Avenue
New York, NY 10019

Travel & Tourism Executive Newsletter
P.O. Box 65337
Washington, DC 20035

Travel Digest
1654 SW 28th Avenue
Ft. Lauderdale, Florida 33312–3949

Travel/ Holiday Magazine
8 W. 23rd Street, 10th Floor
New York, NY 10010

Travel Industry Network
624 Clearn Street
Winter Springs, FL 32708

Travel Management Daily/ Newsletter
888 Seventh Avenue
New York, NY 10106

Travel Marketing
523 E. Putnam Ave.
Greenwich, CT 06830

Travel North America
14 Ronan Avenue
Toronto, Ontario, Canada M4N 2X9

Travel Profits Magazine
6 East 46th Street
New York, NY 10017

Travel Trade Publications
6 E. 46th Street
New York, NY 10017

Travel Weekly
500 Plaza Drive
Secaucus, NJ 07096

Travelage East
888 Seventh Avenue
New York, NY 10106

Travelage Midamerica
320 N. Michigan Avenue, #601
Chicago, IL 60601

Travelage Southeast
555 N. Birch Road
Ft. Lauderdale, FL 33304

Travelage West
100 Grant Avenue
San Francisco, CA 94108

Travelling on Business
310 Dupont Street
Toronto, Ontario, Canada M5R 1V9

USTOA Newsletters
(Publication of US Tour Operators Association)
211 East 51st Street, Suite 12B
New York, NY 10022

Europe

Air Travel
9–15 Neal Street
London WC2H 9PF, England

Business Traveller
388–396 Oxford Street
London W1N 9HE, England

Der Fremdenverkehr
Jaeger-Verlag
Holzhofallee 38
6100 Darmstadt, Germany

Echo Touristique
1 Cite Bergere
75009 Paris, France

PTN Europe
Morgan-Grampian House
30 Calderwood Street
London SE18 6QH, England

Revue Generale de L'Hotellerie de la Gastronomie et du Tourisme
14, Boulevard Montmartre
F-75009 Paris, France

Tourism Management
P.O. Box 63, Westbury House
Bury Street
Guilderford GU2 5HB, England

Tourismo D'Affari
Via S. Simpliciano 4
20121 Milan, Italy

Touristik Aktuell
Jaeger-Verlag
Holzhofallee 38
6100 Darmstadt, Germany

Travel Agency Magazine
Maclean-Hunter House
Chalk Lane, Cockfosters Road
Boonet, England

Travel News
Business Press International Ltd.
Quadrant House, The Quadrant
Sutton, Surrey SM2 5AS, England

Travel Trade Gazette Europa
Travel Trade Gazette UK & Ireland
Morgan-Grampian House
30 Calderwood Street
London SE18 6QH, England

TW Tagungs-Wirtschaft
Wilhelm-Leuschner-Strasse 13
D-6000 Frankfurt/Main 1, Germany

Asia

Asia Travel Trade
190 Middle Rd. #14-08 Fortune Centre
Singapore 0718

Singapore Travel News
c/o Singapore Tourist Promotion Board
250 North Bridge Road, Raffles City Tower #3700
Singapore 0617

Travel Business Analyst
200 Lockhart Road, 14th Floor
Hong Kong

CONVENTION AND CORPORATE CUSTOMER PUBLICATIONS

Association
(Publication of the Canadian Society of
Association Executives)
45 Charles Street E., #603
Toronto, Ontario, Canada M4Y 1S2

Association Management
1575 Eye Street NW
Washington, DC 20005

Association Meetings
63 Great Road
Maynard, MA 01754

Association & Society Manager
1640 5th Street
Santa Monica, CA 90401

Association Trends
4948 St. Elmo Avenue
Bethesda, MD 20814

Best's Insurance Convention Guide
AM Best Company
Ambest Road
Oldwick, NJ 08858

Business Travel News
600 Community Drive
Manhasset, NY 11030

Conferences & Exhibitions International
2, Queensway Redhill
Surrey RHI 1QS, England

The Convention
Rank Publishing Company Pty. Ltd.
P.O. Box 189
St. Leonard's, NSW 2065, Australia

Convention World
600 Summer Street
Stamford, CT 06901-1306

Conventions & Meetings Canada
5762 Highway 7, Suite 207
Markham, Ontario, Canada L3P 1A8

Corporate & Incentive Travel
488 Madison Avenue
New York, NY 10022

Corporate Meetings & Incentives
747 Third Avenue
New York, NY 10017

Corporate Travel
1515 Broadway
New York, NY 10036

Insurance Conference Planner
600 Summer Street
Stamford, CT 06901-1306

Marketing Magazine
777 Bay Street
Toronto, Ontario, Canada M5W 1A7

Medical Meetings
63 Great Road
Maynard, MA 01754

Meeting News
1515 Broadway
New York, NY 10036

Meetings
204 Clarence Street, 3rd Floor
Sydney, NSW 2000, Australia

Meetings & Congressi
Via S. Simpliciano 4
20120 Milan, Italy

Meetings & Conventions
500 Plaza Drive
Secaucus, NJ 07096

Promotions & Incentives
Bofoers House, Bentinck Road
West Drayton, Middlesex UB7 7RQ, England

Sales & Marketing Management
633 Third Avenue
New York, NY 10017

Successful Meetings
633 Third Avenue
New York, NY 10017

Western Association News
1516 S. Pontius Avenue
Los Angeles, CA 90025

LEISURE TRAVEL CONSUMER PUBLICATIONS

Conde Nast Traveler
360 Madison Avenue
New York, NY 10017

European Travel & Life
122 E. 42nd Street
New York, NY 10168

Southern Living
12 Downing Lane
Decatur, GA 30033

Travel & Leisure
1120 Avenue of The Americas
New York, NY 10036

Note: There are many other consumer magazines which focus on travel destinations. Some of them do this on a regular basis, such as *National Geographic*. Others, whose names might not necessarily indicate so, will periodically feature articles on travel. These would include *Food & Wine* and *Gourmet*.

And there's still another category of publications which, while aimed at industry professionals, are widely read by consumers. These include magazines such as *Food Arts* and *The Wine Spectator*, which similarly have special features devoted not only to food and beverage marketing but also to travel and destination promotion.

appendix f
DICTIONARY OF 100 COMMON SALES AND MARKETING TERMS

Virtually all sales and marketing terms used in this text are explained and often illustrated when they first occur. However, the following list contains 100 of the most common terms that are essential to the understanding of contemporary hotel sales operations and practices.

Additionally, they are the words and phrases most likely to show up on college quizzes and exams. Knowledge of them will also be helpful for successfully completing the examination requirements for such industry certification programs such as CHSE, the Certi-fied Hotel Sales Executive designation awarded by the Hotel Sales and Marketing Association International.

Your authors have also compiled a more comprehensive *Glossary of Hospitality Management Terms*, an $8^1/_2 \times 11''$ spiral bound working reference, which focuses on over 1,000 of the most commonly used (and sometimes misused) hotel, restaurant, and travel management words and phrases. Check your school bookstore or with your instructor for purchase information, or write BlackVillage Presentations, 333 N. Gladstone Avenue, Margate, New Jersey 08402 USA.

Account Executive   A modern designation for the entry-level position in the sales and marketing department, replacing the more traditional title of sales representative.

Advertising   Purchased time or space, used to convey nonpersonal messages about a product or service for purposes of informing and persuading.

Advertising Agency   An independent business firm which specializes in creating, planning, and implementing advertising programs.

Amenities   Special features and services, often in the form of little extras or niceties, which are usually related to a specific type of property or to a market segment.

Association Account Executive   A sales department staff member who specializes in booking business from trade associations and professional societies.

Association Market   A group prospect classification composed of trade associations, professional societies, hobby and avocational groups, and similar organizations of people with common professional or personal interests.

Average Daily Rate   A monetary calculation obtained by dividing total daily room revenue by the number of paid rooms occupied.

Average Occupancy   A percentage calculation obtained by dividing the paid rooms occupied by the number of rooms available for sale.

Benefits   Product or service features which have been transformed into "satisfiers" of user needs or wants.

Brochure   A printed collateral item containing pictorial and descriptive information about a product or service, differing from a "folder" in size and layout.

Business Mix   A percentage breakdown, for a specific period, of the number of guests from each key market segment.

Buyers   People who make purchasing decisions for themselves and/or for others; if the latter case, a buyer may not be an actual user.

Campaign   A coordinated program usually built around a specific theme or objective, designed to run for a specified time, and often but not always involving the integrated use of a variety of media.

Collateral Materials   Descriptive and pictorial printed materials generally used to support the main component of a direct mail or advertising campaign.

Commercial Business   Another name for the individual business travel market.

Communications   The act of transmitting an understandable and unaltered message between two or more people.

Compensatory Selling   The practice of providing something extra to make up for a possible or perceived deficiency.

Competitive Analysis   The determination, usually done on a market segment basis, of what your competitors have to offer which you do not—and vice versa.

Convention/ Congress/ Conference   The main meeting, usually on an annual basis, of a trade association or other professional organization. The term "congress" is usually used by European and Asian groups; a "conference" is used by some organizations to indicate that the meeting is primarily business-oriented.

Convention Service Coordinator   A hotel sales & marketing staff executive whose primary responsibility is to coordinate a group's requirements once a booking is made.

Corporate Account Executive   A sales department staff member who specializes in booking both individual and group business from companies and corporations.

Corporate Market   A prospect classification relating to the business potential available from companies and corporations, including both individuals and groups.

Criss-Cross Selling   The promotion, either verbally or through media, of the products and services of one department by another.

Cross-Training   A program of developing employee skills and knowledge so they can work different positions within a department or in different departments.

Decision-Maker   A business contact who, singly or jointly with others, is responsible for deciding when and where business will be placed.

Demographics   A method of analyzing market segments by grouping them according to such physical characteristics as age, sex, marital status, family size, education, and income.

Direct Mail Advertising   The utilization of the postal system to convey sales messages, usually in the form of letters, folders, brochures, and other collateral materials.

Direct Marketing   The process of selling products and services directly from the seller to the user, without using an intermediary.

Exhibit Space   Public space specifically designed or suited for displays of products and services.

Exhibits and Trade Shows   Events specifically organized for the display of products and services; exhibits are often part of an association convention, while trade shows are often independent functions which are not usually open to the public.

Fam Trip   Short for "familiarization trip," a promotional tour organized by various interests within a destination for purposes of promoting the area to major travel and group business decision-makers.

Features   Specific, tangible characteristics of a product or service which are primarily described in physical or quantitative terms such as numbers, size, or dimensions.

Folder   A descriptive or pictorial mailing piece, similar to but usually smaller than a brochure, and sized to fit a display rack and a #10 (4 × 9″) envelope.

Function Space   A generic term for that portion of public space which is specifically used for meetings, exhibits, receptions, and banquets.

Geographic Segmentation   A method of classifying market segments by point of origin.

Government Business Market   A market segment representing individuals and groups composed of government employees or firms holding government contracts.

Group Business Market   A prospect classification representing both associations and corporations who hold either educational or social meetings or both.

Group Leisure Market   A prospect classification commonly referred to as the "tour and travel market,"

where participants travel on an organized and sometimes all-inclusive package basis.

Guest History   A system of recording information on a specific guest's (or group's) usage of the property and its facilities, including type and rate of room, food and beverage outlet patronage, recreational preferences, and selected demographic and psychographic data.

Guest Profile   An overview of the characteristics of those representing a specific market segment, including information relating to who they are, where they come from, when, why and how.

Hospitality Industry   A broad, all-inclusive term for the field of business incorporating lodging, food and beverage, meeting facilities, travel and transportation, and recreation/entertainment.

Hospitality Suites   Accommodations generally used during conventions and trade shows for purposes of entertaining, socializing, and networking—and which often are sponsored or hosted by a group or company.

Incentive Travel Market   A subsegment of the group business market comprised of organizations, usually companies or firms, who use vacations as production or sales quota rewards.

Individual Business Market   A prospect classification (sometimes referred to as "commercial business") composed of individuals traveling on company or organization business.

Individual Leisure Market   A prospect classification (largely made up of but not restricted to vacationers) composed of individuals traveling for personal reasons.

Intangibles   Features or benefits which are more perceived than physical and which ordinarily cannot be sold or used in specific quantities or units.

Internal Promotion   A system of communications directed at guests in the house, for purposes of encouraging use of additional facilities and services, as well as encouraging repeat and referral business. Also termed "in-house merchandising."

International Account Executive   A sales department staff executive whose primary responsibility is to book business originating from outside the country.

Lifestyle Profiling   A segmentation process similar to psychographics, but with more emphasis on the ways people conduct their family, social, and recreational activities.

Lodging Industry   The segment of the hospitality industry composed of such housing facilities as hotels, resorts, condominiums, clubs, and similar "places to stay" establishments.

Market   A group or set of individuals sharing certain defined and recognizable characteristics, and who can usually be readily identified and targeted.

Market Analysis   The study of the composition of current guest market segments, with particular attention placed on patterns, trends, growth projections, and other indicators influencing future activities.

Market Mix   A comparative analysis, usually by percentage of total guests, room nights, or dollar volume, of the different market segments of a specific property, area, or destination.

Market Profile   A detailed analysis of a specific market segment, including demographic, psychographic, attitudes/interests/opinions, preferences, and other lifestyle characteristics.

Market Research   The systematic process of obtaining and analyzing information and data on users, nonusers, and potential users of products and services.

Marketing   An all-encompassing term involving the research, planning, execution, and evaluation of actions taken to bring sellers and buyers together.

Marketing Concept   A somewhat philosophical view of differentiating marketing from selling. In selling, one starts with a product and then seeks potential users; in marketing, one first determines potential user needs and wants and then develops the product or service to meet them.

Marketing Mix   The combination of factors which influence the acceptance and saleability of a product or service, such as name, price, shape, and size.

Marketplace   Originally, the term referred to a rather general area where one could potentially promote products or services. It has taken on a secondary and more specific meaning: An exhibit or trade show area where food and beverage service (particularly luncheons and receptions) runs concurrently with the times the booths are open.

Medium   A communications outlet for the delivery of sales messages from sellers to potential buyers or users. The plural "media" is specifically used when referring to types of advertising, such as print media or broadcast media.

Meetings Market   A broad category of group business potentials from both associations and corporations, which includes conventions, management conferences, sales meetings, product launchings, training sessions, stockholder meetings, and similar educational or business-oriented gatherings.

Operations   One of two main components of *management* (the other is marketing), primarily concerned with the financial aspects of the property—specifically, the conversion of gross revenue into net profit and return on investment.

Overflow   Business which has been booked or confirmed, but which cannot be handled by the property and which must be accommodated elsewhere.

Positioning   The perception of a product or a product segment, as seen by the market. It also defines the relationship of that product to those of other similar competitive lines.

Product Analysis   The determination of the specific features of a property or destination, which under the marketing concept will then be converted into benefits directed at specific users or potentials.

Product Segmentation   The division of a product or service into subclassifications or variable product lines, according to quantitative or qualitative characteristics.

Promotions   Specific programs designed to entice interest and purchase, often on a temporary basis at a special price for a limited time period.

Prospect   A person who has been identified as either a potential customer or a decision-maker for others.

Psychographics   A method of analyzing market segments by grouping them according to behaviors, attitudes, personal interests, and other lifestyle characteristics.

Public Relations   A systematic program, often teamed with advertising, designed to communicate a positive image to present guests, potential customers, the community, suppliers, competitors, and the public at large.

Publicity   A free or noncompensated mention of a product, person, or service in print or over the broadcast media.

Qualifying   A prospecting/screening process, commonly referred to as "converting suspects into prospects."

Rack Rate   The standard or "official" posted price for a specific accommodation.

Reception   A stand-up food & beverage function, social in nature, but used by many conventions and business organizations for attendee interaction and networking.

Referrals   Business which originates from the recommendations of others, such as guests or business contacts, as well as from properties unable to accommodate a specific piece of business at a specified time.

Response Vehicle   A device, such as a coupon or business-reply card, which stimulates or assists a reader or listener to take action in response to a sales message.

Retailers   Persons or agencies (including intermediaries) who sell directly to the customer or user.

Sales   A term with various meanings: sometimes synonymous with revenue; other times relating to the process of soliciting, selling, and securing business; at still other times referring to business booked.

Sales Call   A meeting between a sales executive and a prospect or buyer for purposes of securing a business commitment.

Sales Executives   A generic designation for staff members of the sales department, including account executives, sales managers, and sales directors.

Sales Promotion   Formerly, part of an accounting term (advertising and sales promotion) used to classify expenditures made to secure business. More commonly, it now refers to a varied assortment of marketing activities other than personal selling, advertising, and public relations—such as discount programs, gift certificates, frequent-guest clubs, special-rate packages, contests, exhibits, and display merchandising.

Sales Representative   The traditional designation for the entry-level position in the sales department, now more commonly called *account executive.*

Segmentation   The process of dividing a general grouping into various subdivisions.

Selling   The act of persuading a buyer to make a purchase through a face-to-face presentation.

Site Inspection   An investigative tour of a destination or set of facilities by travel agents, tour operators, meeting planners, or congress organizers.

SMERF   An acronym for the Social, Military, Ethnic, Religious, and Fraternal association market.

Soliciting   The act of contacting business prospects for purposes of effecting a sale.

SWOT   The acronym for Strengths, Weaknesses, Opportunities, and Threats; used as guidelines for organizing certain types of research, such as competition analysis.

Tangibles   Features or benefits which can be described in specific terms, units, or dimensions.

Target Audience   A designated market segment to which specific messages are directly aimed.

Telemarketing   The use of the phone for researching or prospecting, as well as for delivering a sales message or securing an order or booking.

Tour & Travel Account Executive   A sales department staff executive who specializes in calling on travel agents, wholesalers, tour operators, and incentive travel managers.

Tour and Travel Market   Another name for the Group Leisure Market.

Trade Journals   Publications devoted to specific industries or professions. (There is a listing of hotel, restaurant, travel, and customer trade magazines and newspapers elsewhere in this appendix).

Trade Show   A type of exhibit which is open only to the members of a particular industry or organization and not to the general public.

Travel Agent   A commissioned retailer who arranges hotel accommodations, transportation, and other travel elements as a service to the public.

Unique Selling Proposition   A distinctive yet meaningful feature or benefit which is significantly different from that available from or offered by the competition.

Unique Servicing Proposition   A distinctive service not found in competitive operations which offers significant benefits to the guest.

Visibility   A practical marketing philosophy based on the concept that sales success is directly related to how well known (professionally and personally) a sales executive is within the customer marketplace, the community, and the trade.

Wholesaler   A travel specialist who arranges and packages the components of tours, and makes them available to retail travel agents for sale to the public.

INDEX

Employee hobbies and skills inventory, 108
Entry-level position, job description sample, 254–55
Executive Leader Master's Program, 56
Expressives, 134–35, 137
Extended-stay market, 206

F

Family Man classification, 76
Fear of rejection close, 145
Features appraisal checklist, 109
Features into benefits chart, 110
Files, types of, 98–99
Financial analysis, 113
First-timer close, 145
Folders, 167, 170
    examples of, 170–75
Follow-through, service, 200, 218
Follow-up letter, 147
Front sheet, 99

G

Geographic file cards, 104
Government market, profile guide, 85
Group business traveler, 195
Group confirmation form, 102
Group leisure market, 193
    general market profile, 71–72
Guest profiling, 68–72
    basics of, 69
    business traveler, 69–70
    group leisure market, 71–72
    information sources, 68–69
    leisure traveler, 70–71
Guest relations, commandments of, 233
Guests, as information sources, 56–57
Guest survey form, 231–32

H

Hard buyers, 132
Hard sellers, 131
Harvey Awards Checklist for Effective Advertising, 194
"Hitchhiking," 197
Hold (pending) files, 99
Hospitality industry:
    challenges, 3
    competitive evaluation, 21
    constants, 11
    costs, 3
    future challenges, 245
    history of, 6–8
    market area profiles, 21–23
    marketing concept model, 8–9
    product, 5
    property facilities and services, 17–19
    property information, 24
    public's concept of, 2–3
    purpose/goal, 12–13
    situation overview, 23–24
    starter list for success, 237–38
        imagination, 240–41
        incentive, 239–40
        independence, 243
        individuality, 243–44
        infectiousness, 244
        ingenuity, 241–42
        initiative, 239
        inquisitiveness, 244–45
        inspiration, 242
        instinct, 240
        integrity, 242–43
        intelligence, 238–39
        involvement, 238
    starting points, 3–5
    studying, 13
        competition analysis, 19–21
        functional study, 15–17
        information, 13–14
        research objectives, 14–15
    supply and demand, 237
    uniqueness of, 236–37
    walking the property, 24
Hospitality suites/exhibit booths, as meeting points, 153, 155
Hospitality trade associations, 257–59
Hospitality trade press, 260–63
    convention and corporate customer publications, 262–63
    hotel/restaurant trade press, 260–61
    leisure travel consumer publications, 263
    tour and travel publications, 261–62
Hotel:
    product, 5
    responsibilities, 5–6
Hotel and Travel Index, 194
Hotel/restaurant trade press, 260–62
Hotel Sales and Marketing Association International (HSMA), 5
Howard Johnson system, 66–67
HSMA, *See* Hotel Sales and Marketing Association International (HSMA)

I

Incoming calls, handling, 151–52
Indicator signals, closing, 144–45
Individual business traveler, 195
    service checklist, 206
Individual leisure traveler, 195
Information:
    segmentation, 83–86
    types of, 13–14